WITHDRAWN

the nation's tortured body

D1536425

the nation's tortured body

Violence, Representation,

and the Formation of

a Sikh "Diaspora"

Brian Keith Axel

Duke University Press

Durham and London

2001

Julian Blackburn College
Trent University
Peterborough, Ontario
K9J 7B8

DS 432 .S5 A94 2001 JBC

© 2001 Duke University Press

All rights reserved

Printed in the United States of

America on acid-free paper ∞

Typeset in Carter & Cone Galliard

by Keystone Typesetting, Inc.

Library of Congress Cataloging-in-

Publication Data appear on the last

printed page of this book.

contents

list of figures

acknowledgments

Many people have helped me throughout the years that I have been research-ing and writing about the Sikh diaspora. I must express the greatest debt to Arjun Appadurai, Bernard Cohn, Jean Comaroff, Homi Bhabha, Lauren Berlant, and Elizabeth Povinelli at the University of Chicago, who have read through several drafts of my work and provided me with persistent chal-lenges to write and think more creatively and clearly. Others at the University of Chicago have also contributed to this process: Andrew Apter, Carol Breckenridge, John Comaroff, Dipesh Chakrabarty, Ronald Inden, McKim Marriott, Nancy Munn, Moishe Postone, Marshall Sahlins, Saskia Sassen, and Terry Turner. I must also thank the University of Chicago's Anne Chien, who has given me far more help than I deserved. Paul Silverstein — first in Chicago, then in London, Paris, New York, and elsewhere — has been a dear friend, a persistent critic, and an enduring interlocutor.

My first teachers of anthropology at the University of Texas must be acknowledged for the spirit of inquiry that they introduced to me: James Brow, Steven Feld, and Ward Keeler. Their imprint on this text may be recognizable at least by the fact that it has been written and also by its resistance to offering easy answers. Likewise, I wish to mention Christopher Pinney who, beyond the call of duty, offered an institutional home for me at soas in London, read through and encouraged the writing of early drafts of work, and shared the joy of dialogue and debate. Ken Wissoker at Duke University Press has been a persistent and patient source of encouragement, and I thank him for having confidence in this project.

In India, England, and North America, I have met with great friendships and mentorships. There are too many people to mention here, but I should make special note of Nikky Singh (Colby College), who first introduced me to the study of Sikhism; the late Harbans Singh (of Patiala); Virendra Singh (of Varanasi); W. H. McLeod; Thomas Morrione (Colby College); Mohinder Singh (director of the Bhai Vir Singh Sahitya Sadan, New Delhi); Gerald Barrier (University of Missouri–Columbia); Nicholas Dirks (Columbia University); Debbora Battaglia (Mt. Holyoke College); Verne Dusenbery (Hamline University); Arthur Helweg (Western Michigan University); Darshan Singh Tatla (Warwick); Gurharpal Singh (Hull University); Shinder Thandi (Coventry University); Pashaura Singh (University of Michigan); and Harjot Singh Oberoi (University of British Columbia). Cynthia Kepley Mahmood (University of Maine, Orono) has offered a courageous precedent. I also thank the archivists who assisted me, especially in New Delhi (the Parliamentary Library, the National Archives, and Bhai Vir Singh Sahitya Sadan), London (the India Office, the National Portrait Gallery, and the British Museum), and Oxford (the Bodleian Library). And I cannot express my gratitude enough to the many other Sikh women and men who have so willingly shared their lives with me. I owe a special thank you to Gyani Karamjit Singh — wherever he may be — who, as a friend and teacher, guided me through my first study of Sikhs.

Funding for the research was provided by the National Science Foundation, the MacArthur Foundation (Council for Advanced Studies on Peace and International Cooperation), Fulbright-Hays, a University of Texas Meyerson Fellowship, and a University of Chicago William Rainey Harper Fellowship. I have been substantially aided in revising this book while at Emory University as an Andrew W. Mellon Postdoctoral Faculty Fellow in Ethnography and Historiography. My colleagues at Emory — in the Departments of Anthropology, History, and Asian Studies and the Graduate Institute of Liberal Arts — have provided me with invaluable dialogue: Bobby Paul, Peter Brown, Paul Courtright, Angelika Bammer, Edna Bay, Ellen Schattschneider, Kristin Mann, Randy Packard, Don Donham, Debra Spitulnik, Ivan Karp, Bruce Knauft, and Brad Shore. My students have often offered the most forthright critique and challenge: Jennifer Bagley, Whitney Cook, Romi Singh Dhillon, Blake Eno, Jeremy Hendon, Matthew Sultan, and Karla Waller. The greatest support and inspiration for this work was provided by my family and friends: Nathalie Loveless Axel, Kenneth Axel, Mary Mandis (Axel), Donna Kori Axel, Robert Axel, Richard Axel, George McCauley, Candice "Rev" Breitz, Matthew Byram Burke, Filipa, Garreth Burr, Jessica Funk, Lainey Gerber, Tyler Craig Gore, Bill Hamilton, Varinder S. Kalra, Raninder Kaur, M. Whitney Kelting, Marilou Knight, Sadie Korn, Evelyne Lord, Robert Loveless, Stephanie Loveless, Sangeeta Luthra,

Bill Morrow, Adam Picard, David Rosen, Steve Runge, Curtis Russet, Beth Russet, Shamus Russet, Tiff (wherever you are), Melissa Watson, and Becky Williams. Acknowledgments notwithstanding, I take sole responsibility for the contents of this inquiry.

This book is dedicated to two dear people who have lived in and through its writing: my father, Kenneth Axel, who left the world on December 22, 1990, and Nathalie Loveless Axel, my wife, who entered into my life on July 27, 1996.

introduction: promise and threat

introduction: promise and threat

What is found at the historical beginning of things is not the inviolable

identity of their origin; it is the dissension of other things.

—Michel Foucault, "Nietzsche, Genealogy, History"

There is something peculiar and powerful about diasporas today. Perhaps, at least at first glance, this is because it is so difficult to comprehend a site of belonging and identification that is both spectacularly global and preeminently local. Yet who would deny that there is a Jewish diaspora, or a Chinese diaspora, or a Sikh diaspora? One would be hard put to say that, preferring the local to the global, there are no diasporas, rather Chinese *in* New York or, for example, Sikhs *in* London. The "exemplary" quality of these different populations, however, is, precisely, an indication of what makes diasporas peculiar and powerful. What is it about the lifestyle of a certain people that transforms them into an *example* of a diaspora (i.e., one in a series of something more generally encompassing)? Or, to turn this around, why is it that people identified as members of diasporas are so often susceptible to the procedures of nation-states that aim at making an *example* of them (e.g., through immigration legislation, debates over multiculturalism, or cases of deportation)?

These questions offer a challenge, which I take up in this book, to reconceptualize the formation of peoplehood through an inquiry into conditions of diaspora, belonging, and violence from colonialism to postcoloniality. In the specific instance, I examine the histories of displacement, of changing "homelands," and of corporeality that have grounded the formation of a Sikh diaspora. As of this writing, in 1999, there are an estimated 20 million Sikhs living in the world.[1] Although recent reports vary, it is estimated that 17 million Sikhs live in India and that 3 million are living in and moving between North America, South America, Africa, East and Southeast Asia, Australia, New Zealand, and Europe. By far, the majority of Sikhs outside India are located in Britain and the United States, with the largest concentration (approximately 500,000) in England.

The story that I tell of this dispersed population must be distinguished from the well-known stories of other Indian diasporas. These stories usually begin with the colonial system of indenture, which, in a wide variety of cases, is understood to be the primary factor in the mobilization and dispersal of particular groups of people away from India (e.g., Ballard 1994; Chandan 1986; Kelly 1991; Ram 1989; Shankar and Srikanth 1998; Tinker 1976; and van der Veer 1995). This book, however, does not begin with indenture. The different "beginnings" of this book, rather, emerge out of three aspects of the histories of displacement constitutive of the Sikh diaspora: first is the position of Sikhs just prior to colonial rule within a unique territory; second is the specific manner of mobility within and after the colonial period; and third is the emergence of transnational struggle to create a separate, sovereign Sikh state called Khalistan.[2] In the following pages, I summarize these three points of emergence, which are then discussed at length throughout subsequent chapters.

Prior to colonial rule, most Sikhs lived in Punjab, what is often referred to today as the Sikh Empire or Khalsa Raj, a large territory in the northwest of the South Asian subcontinent. Ruled by Ranjit Singh and his progeny between 1799 and 1849, this indeed was one of the East India Company's last great territorial challenges in South Asia. As I discuss in chapter 1, after the company conquered the Sikhs and annexed the territory in 1849, the movement of Sikhs in the nineteenth century *did not,* for the most part, follow the dictates of the system of indentured servitude that, between 1833 and 1920, was responsible for the migration of people from all over the subcontinent to other colonies. The most important exception to this history of movement and mobility is the recruitment of Sikhs from Punjab to work as indentured laborers on the East African railway between 1897 and 1920 (Barrier and Dusenberry 1989; Bhachu 1985). Otherwise, between 1860 and World War II, Sikh men moved with the empire as soldiers and policemen, often settling in the locations where they were stationed (e.g., Burma, Singapore, and Hong Kong). Between the 1890s and the 1930s, some Sikh men also traveled to England and North America as students, scholars, adventurers, and "free" laborers. This history of mobility would take on an extreme importance in the years before Indian Independence (1935–47), when Sikhs drew on, or re-constituted, their position before colonial rule (as inhabiting a sovereign territory of their own) and their role during colonial rule (as protectors of empire) to construct an argument legitimizing their demand for a separate Sikh homeland, known variously as Sikhistan, Azad Punjab, and Khalistan. This demand, however, was not granted. Instead, in 1947, India and Pakistan were created following the dictates of the Radcliffe Award, which divided the "boundaries of the two parts of the Punjab on the basis of ascertaining the contiguous majority areas of Muslims and non-Muslims" (Kirpal Singh 1991, 473–83).

After Indian Independence, Sikhs in Punjab, led by the Akali Dal political party, continued to fight for the establishment of a Sikh homeland, but this was done through the medium of a "linguistic demand" for the formation of a state whose majority population would be Punjabi speaking. Between 1948 and 1966, the government of India officially redrew the map of Punjab three times because of, or in spite of, Akali "agitation." First, in 1948, a division was made between the state of Punjab and the Patiala and East Punjab States Union (PEPSU). Second, on 1 November 1956, a new Punjab was formed by merging PEPSU with a differently configured Punjab. Third, on 1 November 1966, the Punjabi Suba was formed (making up what is known today as Punjab). Thus, by 1966, the state of Punjab was reduced to an area of small proportions. This reconfigured its population, giving a slight majority to those identified as Sikh. Akali leaders, however, were not satisfied with this territorial "award" or with the position of Sikhs within it. And, between 1966 and the early 1980s, they continued to organize agitations against the central government, hoping to create, if not a Khalistan, at least a state within India where the "preservation of Sikh traditions and identity" would be ensured (Khushwant Singh [1989] 1991, 310).

While the Akalis in Punjab were continuing their fight for the institutionalization of a Sikh homeland within India in the late 1940s, Sikh men began traveling in large numbers to different parts of the globe, following the prior colonial trajectories of movement. They traveled to Southeast Asia, Australia, New Zealand, England, and North America. This movement, however, was fundamentally transformed. Sikh men moved, not as protectors of empire, but as a new postwar labor force. In this book, I am concerned, most particularly, with how this transformation affected the emergence of Sikh life in postwar Britain. Between 1947 and the mid-1960s, the movement of these men to England, as well as to other nation-states, established a pattern of labor and leisure that contributed not only to the reconstitution of those nation-states but also to the discursive formation of a global Sikh *panth* (community) that was specifically gendered. Although, from the 1960s on, entire Sikh families began to travel around the world and new generations began to be brought up as citizens of different nation-states, the initial years of this movement would have an indelible effect on the creation of processes of Sikh identification. By means of particular bodily techniques, religious practices, visual representations, and narratives of Sikh "identity"— which, indeed, had a significant colonial genealogy that was to be globalized in the years after— Sikh men became the privileged site for negotiating who could be recognized as a member of the Sikh *panth*.

The story of a conjunction between a gendered "identity" politics and a fight for Khalistan plays an important part in my discussion of the Sikh diaspora's formation. In a way that may seem counterintuitive, however, neither the processes of gendering nor the fight for Khalistan has stemmed unidirectionally from Sikh practices within India. Khalistan and the presumed masculinity of the Sikh subject, in other words, were not simply lifted from Sikh life in Punjab and transported to the diaspora. Far from it.

I will have more to say about the issue of gender later in this introduction and throughout the other chapters of this book. With regard to Khalistan, a few distinctions must be made immediately. The fight for a Sikh homeland, orchestrated by the Akali Party in Punjab, remained within India between 1947 and 1971 and was not a concern for Sikhs living in other parts of the world— even though the increasingly globalized Sikh population had created efficient networks of communication between different localities (e.g., through monetary remittances and the circulation of newspapers). The Akali's call for a homeland during this period was rarely made with reference to a Khalistan. Indeed, all calls for a Khalistan were either veiled or disclaimed (as I have already noted, political activity was oriented toward a "linguistic demand"). And, whether or not a call for Khalistan was made openly, Akalis envisaged the position of a Sikh homeland to be *within* India. After 1971, owing to the efforts, at first, of a few Sikh men outside India, the struggle for Khalistan began to be popularized in North America and Europe. These early diasporic activities conflicted with the premises of the Akalis within Punjab, most particularly because they were organized around the idea of Khalistan as a sovereign polity *separate* from India— a significant point of differentiation (which I elaborate in chap. 2).

The fight for Khalistan, however, remained somewhat obscure until 1984.

After Prime Minister Indira Gandhi's orchestrated siege of the Golden Temple Complex in Amritsar (Punjab) in June 1984, and after the anti-Sikh riots of October and November 1984 in North India in response to Gandhi's assassination by her two Sikh bodyguards, Sikh life was radically changed. In the following years (1984–98), the proliferation of extreme violence in Punjab, leaving between 10,000 and 100,000 people dead, became a central element in the revitalization and transformation of the idea of Khalistan by Sikhs living around the world. Diasporic supporters of Khalistan began to understand the Sikhs to be a nation, or *qaum*. As we shall see in chapters 1 and 2, the discursive production of the Sikhs as a *qaum* has an important genealogy in nineteenth-century colonialism. As many scholars have noted, colonial discourse generated a shifting theory of peoplehood, race, sect, and caste for which the term *nation* was often a synonym.[3] During the struggles for Indian and Pakistani independence in the 1940s, *nation* clearly took on a different significance as a category that encompassed a diversity of "peoples," "races," and "castes" under a single rubric with a territorial designation. The "two-nation" theory that governed the division of the South Asian subcontinent into Pakistan and India envisaged two disparate nations in need of their own territorialized states. Akali politicians, however, continued to use the term *nation*, or *qaum,* in a way that reiterated some, but not all, aspects of colonial discourse, particularly in their demands for the institutionalization of a territorial homeland (i.e., "Sikhs are a nation in our own right"). In such moments, another term that I have already mentioned, *panth,* was also used in reference to Sikhs, but signifying something somewhat different.[4] *Panth* was used more generally, and much more commonly, to signify the Sikh "community" and its "religious path." *Panth* and *qaum* in specific ways (discussed in chap. 2) remained in tension — although, as we shall see, the two were not irreconcilable. After 1984, the term *nation,* or *qaum,* was transformed, referring to the "peoplehood" not only of Sikhs in India but also of Sikhs around the world. On the basis of the claim that Sikhs were already a *qaum* — and sometimes claiming that the *panth* was a "multistate nation" — Khalistanis, proponents of Khalistan, justified their call for the creation of a separate Sikh state where all Sikhs may live free from discrimination. In short, the post-1984 period has been a crucial time of change, not least for the translation and transformation of the globally dispersed Sikh *panth* as a *qaum*.

Today, although certainly not supported by all Sikhs, Khalistan is an idea that, nevertheless, has become a generalized trope of social practice and representation central to the post-1984 (re)constitution of the Sikh diaspora.

Generated on a global scale, Khalistan has formed the basis not only for militancy or "terrorism" but also for debates about terror and identity and for the creation of specialized commodities, diasporic economies, media technologies, and narratives of place and displacement. It has also infused Sikh diasporic practices with a sense of urgency and anxiety, a development that I discuss at length in chapters 3 and 4.

This urgency and anxiety motivated many Sikhs outside India, soon after the violence of 1984, to begin raising funds to sponsor programs in Sikh studies—programs that they hoped would both represent a more salubrious image of Sikhs to the world and educate Sikh students about their "heritage." Sikh studies scholars benefited greatly from this patronage. The persistent output of these scholars, some of whom have been involved in Sikh studies for thirty-five years or more, has increased dramatically, generating a large body of research on Sikhism, Sikh history, and the Sikh diaspora. A consideration of the diverse publications on the Sikh diaspora, of the increasing number of academic conferences and journals, and of the development of chairs in Sikh studies at prominent North American and European universities since 1984 demonstrates how powerful the practices of these scholars have been, despite their marginality within diaspora studies proper. It also demonstrates the wealth and interest of the many Sikhs who have supported their efforts.

The work of Sikh studies specialists—bringing together research on the history of the Sikh religion and politics with research on the Sikh diaspora in Europe, Southeast Asia, North America, and Africa—aims to articulate the radical heterogeneity of both Sikh political and cultural practice and Sikh histories of movement and mobility. The proposition of this heterogeneity is enough for some scholars to argue or intimate that there is not one Sikh "identity" and that, indeed, there is not *one* Sikh diaspora but many or, at times, none (cf. Barrier and Dusenberry 1989; Bhachu 1985; Hawley and Mann 1993; Oberoi 1994; and Singh and Barrier 1996).[5] These arguments, which also tend to turn on a deconstruction of Sikh identity, have been viewed as extremely troublesome by many Sikhs supporting Sikh studies, particularly those who have been involved with the fight for Khalistan. Against the supposedly empirical plurality of Sikh identities and Sikh diasporas, Khalistanis argue for the creation, not only of a sovereign Sikh homeland, but also of a singular Sikh identity.

The debate between Sikh studies scholars and Khalistanis—the topic of chapter 5—conjures an old anthropological problem in a new guise. We find one instance of this problem in the work of Ruth Benedict ([1934] 1989), who wrote about the sensitivity of "primitive peoples" positioned within modernity: "Even very primitive peoples are sometimes far more conscious of the role of cultural traits than we are, and for good reason. They have had intimate experience of different cultures. They have seen their religion, their economic system, their marriage prohibitions, go down before the white man's" (p. 5). Benedict's notion of *intimate experience* mediates a liberal anthropological enterprise that, in her terms, must interrogate and attempt to disrupt what "from the beginning" appears to be the "first and important distinction," an illusory differentiation between "the Chosen People and dangerous aliens." Ventriloquizing primitive discourse, Benedict enunciates succinctly this originary and dangerous, although apparently illusory, distinction: "Outside the closed group there are no human beings" (p. 7). Both Sikh studies scholars and Khalistanis are concerned to illuminate the "intimate experiences" of Sikhs around the world, particularly as they pertain to the "experience of different cultures" and histories of domination. The notions of a *closed group* and a *chosen people* figure critically into these formulations. The investigations of both Sikh studies scholars and Khalistanis into Sikh identity, however, fall starkly on one side or the other of the closed group. For many Sikh studies scholars, the distinction of the closed group is indeed a caprice that must be dismantled (cf. Oberoi 1993, 1994), whereas, for Khalistanis, the proposition of a closed group — a people with a destiny — represents the only possibility for survival (cf. Giani 1994; Mann, Singh, and Gill 1995).

Diaspora and the "Place of Origin"

This book, a historical anthropology of the Sikh diaspora, emerges from this recent history of knowledge production and violence, and it rests, sometimes uneasily, on the fissures, gaps, and continuities of the Sikh diaspora's involvement in the composition and dissemination of that knowledge. Studies of the Sikh diaspora, today, cannot help but become intertwined in political discourses about the Sikh *qaum*. With this understanding, I have tried to develop a historical anthropology that is sensitive to both the highly politicized nature of its intervention and the exceptional reproductive commitments of the Sikh people. I have decided to make the problems of violence and pain, which many Sikhs know too well, part of my inquiry.[6] But I have also hoped to offer an analytic that, itself, does not recuperate the ideologies of that "people," however defined. In writing this book, I have tried to redirect the argument away from claims and forms of questioning concerned with evaluating the validity or status of the closed group. In other words, I am not concerned with deconstructing the boundaries of Sikh identity, with debating whether Sikhs are a closed group, or with determining whether the Sikh people have a destiny. I am concerned, rather, with how those distinctions have become very real for the Sikh diaspora. To put this more precisely, my object of study is the Sikh diaspora *as a diaspora,* one that has been constantly generated and reconstituted through historically specific kinds of regulatory practices and contradictory discourses about who is a Sikh and the future of the Sikh nation.

This object of study, the Sikh *diaspora,* presents a challenge to analysis. It may be helpful to reflect on this challenge more generally. What makes a certain people a "diaspora"? In the past few decades, scholars of diaspora studies have offered answers that return time and again to a singular proposition: the common denominator exemplifying a diaspora is its vital relation to a place of origin that is *elsewhere.* There is, however, something extremely elusive about the locality of the place of origin within a diaspora. According to these studies, the place of origin lives, is replicated, or is transformed within a population that is globally dispersed.[7] It is elsewhere, yet it is right here. This elusiveness notwithstanding, diaspora studies scholars deploy *place of origin* as a basic category to describe, explain, and distinguish the "identity" of a particular diaspora in relation to other diasporas and in relation to the specific spatial and temporal formations that the phrase signifies (i.e., "the homeland" and "origin" or "descent"). But identifying the place of origin also provides the basis for a much stronger argument, which is not always offered explicitly but rather presumed. The argument is that the place of origin or homeland—embodied in formations of language, religion, tradition, race, ethnicity, indications of territoriality, etc.—*constitutes* the diaspora. In other words, according to this argument, because the homeland is originary and constitutive of its people, regardless of birthplace, those people, wherever they are, form a community, a dispersed community, a diaspora. This argument helps discern what most scholars consider an enduring problem: the ambivalence, or even antagonism, with which the nation-state regards the diaspora. The peculiar and powerful relation of a place of origin to its people not only helps identify a group as a diaspora but also effectively makes the nation-state in which the group resides a host country. With this status as a host country, a nation-state then assumes responsibility for making an example of diasporas by either valorizing their "presence" (e.g., multiculturalism) or limiting where and how they may settle (e.g., immigration or deportation), or both.

To look more closely at the complex difficulties of what I will call *the place of origin thesis,* let us consider work on the South Asian diaspora. The South Asian diaspora, as a diaspora, has only recently become an object of study.[8] Three interrelated moments emerging in the past thirty years are of particular significance for understanding these studies as well as the diasporic populations themselves. First, the category *diaspora* was disengaged from an exclusive reference to Jews and people of African descent.[9] *Diaspora* came to refer, more generally, to immigrant, expatriate, refugee, guest-worker, exile, overseas, and ethnic communities.[10] Second, the diaspora became a way of organizing varying kinds of practices spanning academic institutions, government agencies, and wealthy community organizations. Despite often contradictory goals, these communities have joined together to sponsor academic chairs, conferences, and journals, educational literature for children, and state liaisons. Third, the different practices, interests, and university positions of scholars instituted a division within academic programs concerned with studying the new diaspora: specifically, a separation of work into the domains of cultural studies, on the one hand, and area studies, on the other.[11]

Within this institutional division of practices and approaches, the area studies approach to the South Asian diaspora has been dominated, for the most part, by studies of the Indian diaspora — a category most often defined by the Hindu-Muslim binary (Shankar and Srikanth 1998). Studies of the Indian diaspora, however, have tended to focus primarily on the Hindu side of this binary, constituted implicitly or explicitly in relation to the Muslim. The provenance of this exclusive focus has as much to do with the interests of diaspora studies scholars and the practices of their colonialist and orientalist predecessors as it does with the historical involvement of nation-states in the projects of area studies programs. As we shall see (chap. 5), studies of the Sikh diaspora sit awkwardly among studies of the Indian diaspora, not only because of the hegemonic position of the Hindu, but also because of the creation, since the 1980s, of a transnational Sikh identity politics and particularly a diasporic fight for Khalistan.

Place of origin figures prominently in the area studies approach to the South Asian diaspora.[12] One of the major contributions of this scholarship has been to elucidate the ways in which the "host country" often regards the diaspora as a threat. According to these studies, this threat revolves around the temporal aspect of the place of origin thesis. Put simply, studies of South Asian diasporas suggest that the diaspora embodies a particular time that manifests itself not only in terms of a "memory" but also in the physical and visible presence of the body. Together, the diaspora's memory—which, according to this thesis, allows the diaspora to draw on a homeland in the reproduction of culture, religion, or ethnicity—and its presence enact a process in which, by coming back, the past insinuates itself into the nation-state and threatens the established hierarchical order.

What, in this prominent view, is the character of the diaspora's time? How has it come to be the diaspora's definitive property? The answers to these questions can be found in the way in which the many studies construct the category *diaspora* in terms of the significance of colonialism to the movement of Indians from India, on the one hand, and the significance of the relation between diasporic religion or culture to a place of origin, on the other.

For the most part, scholars agree that there would be no South Asian diaspora without the process of colonialism, which, through the institutionalization of a system of indenture, violently and irreversibly separated large populations from their birthplaces in several regions of India.[13] That this history of colonialism constitutes a time that is immanent to the diaspora is apparently clear. Diaspora studies texts continually stress the transparency of this time by way of narratives of diasporic movement *away from* India, enunciating the diaspora through supplementary terms: "Indian communities outside India," people of "South Asian origin," people with "their roots in India," "people of South Asian descent," and "overseas South Asian communities." These enunciations effectively constitute an identification of the diaspora with a generalized diasporic time. Within this discourse, in terms of ethnicity, the time of the diaspora that threatens nation-states is the time that, between 1833 (the British Act of Abolition of Slavery in the Colonies) and the present, designates the successive movement, through several generations, of persons, often as groups, away from India.

But, according to this approach, the constitution of the diaspora's culture or religion is a different matter. This is evident in the way that, in order to construct the category *diaspora,* different scholars return to precolonial India for an explanation of the diaspora's cultural or religious practices and beliefs. This explanatory modality discerns continuities or transformations of Indian culture or religion, but it also attests to another time that is apparently definitive of the diaspora. In these terms, the cultural or religious time that constitutes the diaspora spans an indefinite period *prior to* colonial intervention.[14]

In terms of this approach to diaspora studies, then, the time of the diaspora, the time that gives the diaspora its embodied and collective identity, is a dual temporality. The first, generated by a colonial rupture, is defined by a movement of Indians away from India, the place of origin. The second, seemingly generated by the place of origin itself, is defined by the putatively a priori character of Indian religion and culture — a characteristic apparently independent of colonial intervention. Together, according to this essentialist argument, these times conjoin to constitute the diaspora, tie it to its particular constitutive space (i.e., the homeland or the place of origin), and generate a threat to the space-cum-territory of the host country. Diaspora studies scholars demonstrate the ways in which the Indian diaspora's ethnicity, religion, and culture have variously changed and remained consistent. Yet, while definitions of ethnicity, religion, and culture may change — owing, it is said, to external factors impinging on the diaspora — the (dual) time of the diaspora, itself, remains the same (i.e., there is always the double constitutive time of movement and religion or culture). According to this trajectory of scholarship, the diaspora's (dual) time is a structural property of the diaspora's *form*.

This conceptualization has several difficulties that, in subsequent chapters, I will counter within specific historical analyses of the Sikh diaspora and of the constitution of its particular form of temporality. For the moment, I would like to question the formulation of the diaspora's structural time, particularly its unchanging character generalized to all South Asian diasporas. Here, within diaspora studies, is evident a recuperation of well-known anthropological discourses. Consider the work of Evans-Pritchard, which, like much of diaspora studies, attempts to explain a moving and segmented society's structural continuity and stability. Evans-Pritchard's relation to studies of South Asian diasporas has a significant genealogy in social scientific practice mediated both through the training of British area studies specialists working on "overseas Indians" in the 1950s and 1960s and through the general hegemonic position of Louis Dumont's work in area studies.[15] In this genealogy, the prominent position of Evans-Pritchard's notion of *structural time* is unmistakable.[16]

Evans-Pritchard details his theory of structural time in the essay "Nuer Time Reckoning" (1939) and in two of the volumes of the Nuer trilogy, *The*

Nuer (1940) and *Nuer Religion* (1956). He draws a sharp distinction between time and space. Whereas *structural space* denotes a functional property of an empirical social system — "the distance between social segments, which are groups of people who compose units in a system" — *structural time* refers to an abstraction "belonging to a different order of reality" (1940, 256, 94). Evans-Pritchard says:

> We have remarked that the movement of structural time is, in a sense, an illusion, for the structure remains fairly constant and the perception of time is no more than the movement of persons, often as groups, through the structure. Thus age-sets succeed one another for ever, but there are never more than six in existence and the relative positions occupied by these six sets at any time are fixed structural points through which actual sets of persons pass in endless succession. . . . If we are right in supposing that lineage structure never grows, it follows that the distance between the beginning of the world and the present day remains unalterable. Time is thus not a continuum, but is a constant structural relationship between two points, the first and last persons in a line of agnatic descent. (1940, 107–8)

Structural time, for Evans-Pritchard, is a stable structural entity, never changing, that (with its static, concrete power) manipulates human movement and thought (i.e., humans are mere pegs filling in unchanging peg holes).[17] Scholars concerned with South Asian diasporas run into the same difficulty as Evans-Pritchard did. The problem is that *time* is more like the geography of a land (of political, lineage, and age-set relations) that configures human existence (and a land, itself, that does not transform through erosion). That is, the suggestion of a nonprocessual time is a suggestion not of time at all but, rather, of the quintessential place.[18] Hence, studies of diasporas can refer to the definitive and continual influence of a place of origin. And Evans-Pritchard creates the stark image: "How shallow is Nuer time may be judged from the fact that the tree under which mankind came into being was still standing in Western Nuerland a few years ago" (1940, 108).

This discursive production of temporality and homeland has been reconstituted many times over since the first scholars of overseas Indians went to the field (between 1950 and 1960) in order to examine, document, and translate the lives of Indians who may never have lived in India. Whether in Fiji, Trinidad, or Mauritius, these studies of overseas Indians entextualized commonsense notions of *community, culture,* or *structure* that necessitated the production of India as a quintessential place of origin to which overseas Indians had a definitive, a priori link. Consider the following excerpts from the texts of two social scientists — Adrian Mayer (Fiji, 1950–51), trained in London, and Arthur Niehoff (Trinidad, ca. 1959), trained at Columbia University[19] — who first studied overseas Indians in the 1950s, both published in 1961:

> The first aim of this book is to provide an account of the rural section of the Fiji Indian community, for people either living in Fiji or interested in the Colony. Such an object should need no justification in a country where populations with such varied interests and customs live side by side. The ignorance of people of one community about the ways of life of another can be a hindrance, if not a danger, in the days of rapid social change into which Fiji is now entering. . . . Research on such questions was undertaken for a year during 1950–1, shortly after a stay in India. The difference between the highly stratified and controlled Indian, and the freer Fiji Indian society was striking. In contrast to Indian villages, settlements in Fiji were both officially and socially ill-defined. . . . The reader should therefore bear in mind the author's acquaintance with India as one of the implicit factors in the fieldwork, since it may have led him to stress the "looseness" of the Fiji Indian settlement. (Mayer 1961, xi–xii)

> To discover, assert, and point out the significance of the fact that in a brief fifty years immigrants from across the world, once strangers in the plantations of the island, have reconstituted in modernity their own variant of a rich and ancient civilization, India's, and done so as they rose to full citizenship and influence in a complex and rising young nation of the developing excolonial world, is not simply a provoking reiteration of the phoenix-like tenacity of the human spirit. It is to add, as this book does, to the penetration, the sweep, and the command of social science and cultural anthropology. . . . To find [the circle of villages] reconstituted in East Indian Trinidad, again without name or explicit rationale, is to find unexpected proof of their essential and integral part in Indian civilization. (Arensberg 1961, xi–xii)

These passages are significant for several reasons. Most important, they demonstrate that the production of India as a spatiotemporal place of origin was *necessary* for an explanation of overseas Indians. Let me address this suggestion more closely.

The two passages are apparently very different. Mayer's narrative produces India as a place of origin through its "striking" absence, while Arensberg's does this by arguing for its essential presence. Nevertheless, whether India is absent or present, these texts constitute it as a place with very similar characteristics. Most important, it is a container of tradition that is rich and ancient. It is highly stratified and controlled in officially and socially well-defined units (i.e., it has its own normativity): villages or a "circle of villages." These are familiar characteristics for those who have studied the history of research done in India.[20] While a genealogy of such a discourse on India may find one of several beginnings within nineteenth-century disciplinary strategies of the colonial administration in India, specialists in studies of overseas Indians came up with techniques of making them travel (see Cohn 1977; Appadurai 1986b, 1988). In a sense, the putative displaced character of the object of study sanctified the "displaced" character of the techniques of knowledge production.

And place is logically presupposed in the category *displacement*. These two texts use many of the same techniques to produce India as a place that is both originary and constitutive. Both construct narratives that show the strong or loose connection of Indians to that place by the descriptions of districts in India that produced the Trinidad or Fiji Indians. They argue that overseas settlement patterns (grouping South Indians, Tamils, Madrassis, etc. here and North Indians, Gujeratis, Punjabis, etc. there) replicate "original" Indian divisions. They support their assertions through analyses of economic activities, agriculture, rituals (marriage, funerals, household rites, Hindu and Muslim festivals), political activities, caste, kinship, and culture. Furthermore, these analyses ground an argument about how internal forms of heterogeneity and conflict constitute India as a whole. Together, in a staggering display of detail, these techniques of knowledge production constitute a map of India as a foundational place, project onto it a series of differentially constituted points of origin (i.e., Punjab, Madras), and fill in these points with cultural/structural information that gives them value and assigns them a hierarchy in relation to other cartographies.

The "data" and the techniques used for producing place in these texts were being put to the test in the 1950s and 1960s—as was India. "Days of rapid social change" should not be taken lightly, nor should mention of "rising young nation," "danger," "hindrance," "modernity," "citizenship," freedom, and "discovery." The sayings and stories of these texts, which, to use de Certeau's (1984) phrasing, organized places through the displacements they described, were producing geographies of action in many ways. These stories are about the constitution of new educational practices — or, as Arensberg (1961) says, "the penetration, the sweep, and the command of social science and cultural anthropology" (p. xi). These stories are also as much about India as they are about modernization and the hopes and fears of a new world order. In other words, as Inden (1990, 16) has argued, these studies were integral to emerging forms of education (as a trope for talking about world order and as a set of practices that included development projects and military training systems) that had been concerned, primarily, with producing modernity.

From Threat to Promise to Threat: Genealogy of a Category

The difficulties that the present-day approach to diasporas runs into in theorizing processes of place and displacement mark the necessity to reassess some of the basic tropes of diaspora studies — a project of reassessment that will continue throughout the chapters of this book. Two of these tropes demand particular note. The first is the trope of the diaspora's "threat." The second is the explanatory trope that reduces time to an originary space.

One way to talk about the trope of threat is to see studies of Indian diasporas in terms of a genealogy of the category *overseas Indians*. This genealogy demonstrates the transformation of discourses about the category *overseas Indians* from "threat" to "promise" and to "threat" again. It also demonstrates the prominent position that government agencies have had in determining objects of study.

Overseas Indians was very likely an invention of British colonial administrators in the nineteenth century who were involved in generating records of and policies for the emigration of Indians to plantation colonies.[21] Through the years of colonial rule, the term was used in a variety of ways by colonial administrators and historians: to refer, first, to those "recruited" into indenture and sent over the seas from India after the abolition of slavery in 1833; then to both indentured and "free" laborers living in the plantation colonies; and then, after the abolition of the indenture system in the 1920s, to the aggregate of Indians living in the colonies (many of whose grandparents had been born in those colonies). Throughout these years, the term was, itself, produced as a value: that is, it is during this period that discourses began to position *overseas Indians* as a "threat" and a "danger" and began to formulate *overseas Indians* as a sign of "warning" about "troubles" *in* the colonies. Likewise, *overseas Indians* was often used in a discourse of economic profit, and it was sometimes used in a discourse about the "vulgarity of colour prejudice."[22]

After 1920, *overseas Indians* became an important category in many discourses of Indian nationalists. *Overseas Indians* was used to articulate a critique of colonial rule by evoking the perspective of Indians who were living, or had lived, in various plantation colonies. It was also deployed in appeals to overseas Indians either to return to the "motherland" or, at least, to support the movement for Indian independence. And *overseas Indians* was often constituted in narratives that detailed the predicament of both Indian and Chinese emigrants to varying degrees (see, e.g., Waiz 1927; Aiyer 1938; Gangulee [1946] 1947; Rajkumar 1951; Kondapi 1951). It was during this period that *overseas Indians* began to be transformed into a sign of a particular kind of "promise"—particularly, in Indian nationalist discourse, regarding the potential liberation of a nation that had *membra disjecta* located all over the world.

After 1947, India and its overseas Indians became one of the crucial sites for a new set of educational practices—not least of all because, in addition to India's size, its newly acquired independence, and its "tutelary democracy," the new nation was positioned "between two political worlds": the Soviet Union and China, on the one hand, and the United States and the rest of the free world, on the other (see Indian Council of World Affairs 1957). The U.S. and British governments, along with private enterprises like the Rockefeller and Ford Foundations, initiated a series of projects with the aim of successfully converting India to a modern, democratic nation-state (see Harrison 1961; Rosen 1967; Singer 1957). With this challenge, and through an array of committees, institutes, funding sources, and international "aid"/ "intelligence" organizations,[23] institutions of formal education went through significant transformations that produced and, in many ways, made up the world of possibilities for these specialists studying overseas Indians.

By the time Britain and the United States produced the first group of anthropologists and sociologists specializing in studies of overseas Indians in the 1950s, *overseas Indians* took on a very different significance.[24] It constituted not just the aggregate of Indians living in ex-colonies but, more specifically, a new kind of relation: that between a new nation (or an ex-colony) and "her" dispersed people. This new relation was not only the object of study for social scientists. It became the focus of constitutional and administrative changes in many governments as well as a significant factor in the creation of various organs of the United Nations.[25] These various practices transformed the understanding of the relation between overseas Indians and Indians in India. Scholars considered overseas Indians to be going through the same kinds of experiences that Indians in India were going through (particularly, changes emerging through the clash of "tradition" and "modernity"). It was during this period that, through the discourses of scholars and government agencies, the notion of the "promise" of overseas Indians was reconfigured. Thus, through the study of overseas Indians, scholars were beginning to come up with explanations, not only about how India produced Indians, but also about how to deal with the promise of India as a new nation and potential ally.

The reconstitution of overseas Indians into a category of threat after the 1950s is a story that I elaborate in later chapters. For the moment, a few comments may be useful. First, it may very well be that the emergence of the category *Indian diaspora* as a synonym and sometimes replacement for *overseas Indian* marks the terms of change from *promise* to *threat*. I have already noted how the emergence of the category *diaspora* had much to do with the influence of wealthy diaspora populations. It is also related to a new generation of scholars who identify themselves as diaspora members. These two overlapping groups have, in a short period, developed various discourses of "multiculturalism," "antiracism," "antifundamentalism," and "feminism" that identify the nation-state as a source of discrimination.[26] The increasing eloquence of diaspora populations in the general domains of nation-states, and in the specific domains of academic institutions, conjoined with an increasing awareness within government agencies that, on the one hand, migrants in large numbers are here to stay and, on the other, development projects in new nations like India have had serious problems — all these processes configured the construction of the category *diaspora* in the 1990s in terms of a trope of threat.

Separating Time and Space

The posited separation between time and space has a particularly important relation to discourses of promise and threat in the history of studies of overseas communities. The production of this separation in studies of the Indian diaspora today cannot be seen as distinct from a series of social scientific debates in the 1940s.[27] One way to understand this relation is to consider how these debates had to do, not only with the ascendance of the social sciences and theories of cultural anthropology and structural-functionalism, but also with the (re)constitution of these very disciplines and theories by U.S. and British government projects that were, in a sense, obsessed with monitoring the threats of some nations (e.g., Japan during World War II and China afterward) and the promises of others (particularly India). In this milieu, the techniques of knowledge production, the disciplines informing these techniques, the data that counted as reliable knowledge, and the functions to which various products were being put — all these, in addition to the very categories of analysis (i.e., *overseas Indians*), were redefined and transformed in a number of ways.

These processes were extextualized in Margaret Mead's 1953 edited volume *The Study of Culture at a Distance*. The text represents the first product of the Research in Contemporary Cultures project that was inaugurated at Columbia University by Ruth Benedict in the 1940s and modeled exclusively on her reformulation of Boasian methodology and theory. Benedict herself detailed the basic propositions of the culture-at-a-distance approach in *The Chrysanthemum and the Sword* (1946).[28] Expanding and generalizing Benedict's work, Mead's volume brings together the research of scholars trained by Franz Boas and Ruth Benedict, conducted between 1945 and 1953.

Mead (1953) describes the aim of the text as follows:

> This Manual is concerned with methods that have been developed during the last decade for analyzing the cultural regularities in the characters of individuals who are members of societies which are inaccessible to direct observation. This inaccessibility may be spatial because a state of active warfare exists — as was the case with Japan and Germany — or it may be — as is now the case with the Soviet Union and Communist China — due to barriers to travel and research. Or the inaccessibility may be temporal, since the society we wish to study may no longer exist. It may have been physically destroyed and the survivors scattered, as is the case with the East European Jewish small towns. . . . We then face a situation in which we have access on the one hand to many living and articulate individuals whose character was formed in the inaccessible society and on the other hand to large amounts of other sorts of material. (p. 3)

She is very clear to state that the object of study and methodology have been developed because of "contexts provided by World War II and the post–World War II divided world." Furthermore, she explains that the goal of such a study is to develop a sketch of spatially or temporally distanced people in terms of their "national character":

This focus on national cultures has been dictated by an interest in the role of nationally originating behavior in warfare, policy making, domestic educational and morale-building campaigns, and so on. The method is, however, equally suitable for the study of . . . a group like the East European Jews, whose communities stretched across several national boundaries. With appropriate redefinitions, the same methods can be used to explore . . . the regular behavior of members of a religious order distributed in many countries. The national emphasis in our studies has been the exigent one that they were studies designed to help national governments to deal with members of other nations who were also behaving nationally. . . . So this Manual is primarily a manual on interdisciplinary research practices as they apply particularly to the study of cultural character structure in cultures that are spatially or temporally inaccessible. (p. 4)

Mead had good reason to be concerned about the provenance of her theory and methodology as well as about the significance of her conclusions. Not only did the U.S. government demand and fund the production of theories of culture at a distance and national character, but it also demanded their immediate use in policy making.[29] In this respect, Mead (1953) reflects on the interrelation of interests between social scientists and government agencies with extreme candor: "Because we are working on contemporary cultures, the processes of research and communication are interwoven in a different way. . . . Results in this field have to be made indelible to policy makers, to experts, and to technicians who are laymen to the disciplines used. Such results become automatically available to other laymen and a part of the climate of opinion within which further work has to be done. This means that the use of the research becomes, in a sense, an integral part of the research method itself" (pp. 7–8).

In Mead's discussion, it is clear, the division of space and time is articulated through the notion of *distance.* Yet this division, configured by the exigencies or violences of war and the interests of the U.S. government, defines space and time in terms of particular kinds of threat. The U.S. government was interested in the threat of the Soviet Union and Communist China. These cultures were spatially inaccessible because they could not be studied in person. Since the U.S. government necessitated a sketch of their national character for strategic purposes, Mead needed to develop a theory of a constitutive relation between those places and Soviet or Chinese people living in the United States. Likewise, the U.S. government was interested in the problem of the displacement of Jews who were "behaving nationally" (i.e., who were "un-American"). Since the places of origin of these populations may have ceased to exist, their "national character" was described as "temporally" inaccessible.

In actuality, for Mead, whether the inaccessible national character was spatially or temporally distant was of no consequence — both qualities would be explained by the same "reconstructive imagination" inspired by theories in psychology and linguistics. This is particularly evident in the way in which she includes "members of religious orders distributed in many countries" in the definition of the object of study. As are those of present day-diasporas, these *membra disjecta* may or may not be from destroyed places of origin. Simply put, the inductive theory of a national character, applicable to all cultures, is one achieved "by fitting together separate sets of clues or traces into a reconstructed living whole" (Mead 1953, 11). The only apparent obstacle in theorizing the relation between a place of origin and a national character of either a spatially or a temporally distant culture was the impossibility of visiting the place of origin itself. But, because of the large populations of Japanese, Germans, Chinese, Soviets, Jews, and others living in the United States, Mead and her colleagues did not have to relinquish all "face to face contact." The importance of Mead's study is not only that it made an explicit argument about the relation between a displaced people and a particular nation-state (i.e., those displaced people who were acting according to their own national character somehow impinged on the United States own national character). Most important, it also created an argument about the relation between a place of origin and a (displaced) people. By making assertions about the essence of a people in terms of embodied linguistic and psychological characteristics, Mead argued that a place has an essence that is substantialized in its people. (This, of course, is the move of studies of overseas Indians and of much of diaspora studies.) By observing its displaced people, Mead could therefore make conclusions about what was expected or taken for granted in Japan, China, the Soviet Union, or the extinguished birthplaces of Jews.

The theory of national character and the study of culture at a distance, initially separating time and space, thus facilitates the collapse of time and space. What makes this possible is an element common to both types of national character: threat. The irony of this collapse, however, is that the theory itself was initially produced by Boas in order to make conclusions about, in Mead's terms, "temporally distant" cultures. These disparate Native American populations were also, at one time, defined in terms of their threat to the nation. It is not insignificant, in terms of theory and analytic methodology, that these people whom Boas and his students studied were a fragmented and dispersed group who were apparently becoming "extinct" because of a history of imperial domination. Most significant is the Boasian attempt to reproduce the cultures of entire *dead* populations through the utterances of a few surviving representatives ("memory ethnographies"). Not only did the assumed validity of Boas's theories and methods provide a base for Mead's study of a culture at a distance — it also provided the U.S. government with the convincing proof needed to allocate funds for such studies. Ultimately, the Boasian approach could provide an analogy for social scientists studying overseas populations. An analytic model for societies and cultures that, according to Boas, existed in another time could be redeployed to talk about societies and cultures that existed in another place.

The relation between Mead's work and the development of specialists from the United States researching overseas Indians is quite close.[30] After World War II, the U.S. government provided funds for the development of institutions specifically designed to study the problem of the threat and promise of postwar overseas communities and new nations — for example, the Research of Contemporary Cultures program at Columbia University, MIT's Center for International Studies, the University of Chicago's Committee for the Study of New Nations, and Cornell University's Southeast Asia Program. Of significance in the genealogy of studies of overseas Indians is that the specialists working on India and Indian communities outside India (trained mainly at Columbia and Chicago) disaggregated Mead's collapse of time and space. Yet, while these scholars acknowledged very clearly that they could study the overseas Indians' place of origin, they defined their object of study as somehow *temporally* distant. In their terms, they discovered that this place of origin itself had an inaccessible character that was temporally distant — specifically, India's "rich and ancient civilization," which constituted such phenomena as caste and religion (Inden 1990).

The Local and the Global

I have suggested thinking about diaspora studies in terms of the practices of knowledge production pertinent to the problem of the place-of-origin thesis — in other words, the constitution of a people through specific formations of promise, threat, time, and space. The point of this genealogy has not been to dismiss either the division of space and time or the vicissitude of promise and threat as an illusion or ideological effect. On the contrary, promise and threat, as well as the division of time and space, exist, have had a reality, and have guided the actions of different peoples in various ways. They have also been produced around, on, and within the categories *Indian diaspora* and *overseas Indian* through changing histories of power and knowledge production. There are many fragments of beginnings that form the genealogy of these relations. And I am less interested in portraying a coherent trajectory, a reversible temporal series, than I am in asking how an understanding of these heterogeneous moments may provide a way to reorient the production of knowledge of the diaspora as an object of study.

Promise and threat, with their relations to formations of time and space, form the basis for my analyses in this book. Informed by, but not attempting to follow, the heterogeneous moments of diaspora studies, my reasons for choosing this analytic stem from two contemporary imperatives. First is that, in the 1990s, the category "diaspora" is, for many Sikhs, constituted as a new sign of promise. The production of the diaspora's promise is directly related, on the one hand, to the very possibility that the diaspora may be threatening to the nation-state and, on the other, to the potential that the diaspora community may have for unification in the face of the discriminatory practices of nation-states. Second, and more generally, is that today the place of origin, translated into the homeland, is an extremely important aspect of post–cold war politics. Sikhs are not the only people fighting to attain a homeland that is a separate, sovereign nation-state. Many of today's "civil" wars are generated around this same goal.

My discussion has demonstrated how most studies of diasporas ultimately say very little about the diaspora as a form of belonging and peoplehood but end up offering analyses of the nation-states in which either diasporas reside or their places of origin are located. The challenge, then, is, not to recuperate the older essentialisms of diaspora studies or of work on overseas Indians, but rather to interrogate precisely how colonialism, the nation-state, and the diaspora are related (Axel 1996a, 1996b). It is to interrogate how the homeland has been constituted as a reality for which people are willing to live and die. And it is to generate an understanding of how the diaspora and the homeland are related.

In part, at least, we can see how this challenge follows from, and intends to specify further, recent work on the relation between the production of locality and globalization, a relation that is seen to have as much to do with the structure of the liberal democratic state and the enduring qualities of colonialism as it does with the vicissitudes of changing forms of capitalism (Appadurai 1986a, 1996a, 1996b; Bhabha 1994; Comaroff 1997; Comaroff and Comaroff 1997; Gilroy 1987, 1993; Hall 1990; Hannerz 1992; Harvey 1989; Jameson 1991; King 1997; Massey 1993; Robertson 1992; Sassen 1991, 1997). An important feature in new theories of globalization has been the elaboration of the concept *flow* in a critique of the contemporary world order. As a sign of rupture from "the shackles of highly localized, boundary-oriented, holistic, primordialist images of cultural form and substance" (Appadurai 1996, 46), flow provides a powerful model for understanding the legacy of mobilities left by nineteenth-century histories of capitalism and colonialism—a model that may seem somewhat counterintuitive. Rather than the "rank ordering" of mobile units of "goods, people, and communications" within a quantitatively identifiable structure—what geographers and economists call a *total flow*—this concept of flow, developed in the work of Arjun Appadurai and others, pertains to the "increasingly *nonisomorphic* paths" of people, machinery, money, images, and ideas.[31] Here, globalization theory opens up a fundamental paradox: that, while characterized by "a new condition of *neighborliness,*" the modern world is driven by a "new set of global *disjunctures*" (emphasis added; Appadurai 1996a, 37, 29, 41). This work, then, reconstitutes the notion of the local, underscoring the historically specific ways in which localities tend to indicate a world beyond themselves, an indication around which, indeed, new sentiments of longing and belonging may be generated (Appadurai 1996a). Locality, in other words, must be understood dialectically as *translocality* (Comaroff 1997). An interest in this type of tension directs us to a shared domain of theoretical concern with postcolonial critique that, similarly, finds "holistic forms of social explanation" and "nativistic pedagogies" inadequate for understanding "spatial histories of displacement—now accompanied by the territorial ambitions of 'global' media technologies" (Bhabha 1994, 173, 172). At this point, theories of globalization and postcoloniality return with a renewed vigor to investigate the nation form as a fragile and obscure, although seemingly ubiquitous, locality (Appadurai 1996a, 178–99; Bhabha 1994, 140).

Taking its cue from these compelling works, this book turns from the nation form to the diaspora form. The story of the Sikh diaspora presents a special case. Most immediately, this is due to the particularities of the violence that has erupted in the fight for Khalistan. But it is also due to the way histories of colonial and postcolonial struggle have set the groundwork for the globalization of Khalistan. Through these histories, Sikhs have produced specific kinds of practices and discourses, generated within particular localities, that can, and indeed do, challenge the authority of the modern nation-state. These historical qualities demand a certain rigor, particularly when it comes to reorienting the older analytics of diaspora studies. Not only is it necessary to produce an analysis of the relations between colonialism, the diaspora, the nation-state, and the homeland. In discussing the formation of the Sikh diaspora, it is also important to distinguish between conceptualizations of the homeland and Khalistan — for, indeed, within different Sikh and nation-state discourses, the two are not always equivalent. For instance, some Sikh discourses constitute Punjab or India, rather than Khalistan, as the homeland. Following these guidelines, the argument that the chapters of this book develop has three parts: (1) emerging out of the enduring legacies of an "age of empire," the diaspora and the modern nation-state have been formed historically through a dialectical relation, a relation, in other words, that is mutually constitutive; (2) the diaspora and, more precisely, historical processes of *displacement* have constituted the different places of origin referred to as *homeland;* and (3) Khalistan, as we know it today, is a historical effect of the formation of this specific kind of relation between Sikh diaspora and the modern nation-state.

The Diaspora and Historical Anthropology

From the standpoint of this argument, I must reiterate a basic point. This book is not a study of Sikhs in England, or in India, or in the United States. Nor is it a comparative study of Sikhs in England and India. My object of study is the historical constitution of the Sikh diaspora *as a diaspora*. Tracking the diaspora, this historical anthropology moves back and forth between "individuals" and "abstractions," just as it does between formations of colonialism and the nation-state, specifying, not only how different figures of the homeland or violence, for example, have different meanings for different people in different places, but also how those differences have emerged and how they have become integral to the constitution of more general, mobile forms. This historical anthropology pauses within different localities to portray their detail. But, no matter how long it resides in the details of local difference, those very details invariably thrust analysis back into the domain of the diasporic global that, itself, with its susceptibility to abstract wholism, threatens to obscure the minutiae of locality. This vicissitude of the *translocal* is stubborn and relentless.

In order to track these kinds of movements, I have developed a historical anthropology that differs from other approaches in anthropology and history. The research, both ethnographic and archival, was conducted during two full years (January 1995–January 1997) and three separate summers (1992, 1993, 1994) — and more intermittently during my years at the University of Chicago and Emory University (1992–99) — in several places in England, India, and the United States: particularly, Southall (London), Smethwick (Birmingham), Coventry, Leicester, Oxford, and Thetford in England; New Delhi, Dehra Dun, Patiala, Banaras, and Amritsar in India; and Ann Arbor, Michigan, and Washington, D.C., in the United States. Both ethnography and historiography are crucial in this text. Indeed, I contend that, as critical and forceful means of locating individual experiences within wider fields of representation and practice, they are inseparable (Comaroff and Comaroff 1991, 1992, 1997). In the most general sense, they provide a method for analyzing the development and transformation of peoples' lives and experiences in a way that is sensitive to the dynamics of disparate cultural contexts. Nevertheless, my approach has necessitated a refinement of these modes of inquiry. This refinement of ethnography and historiography stems, not only from the demands of my object of study and my units of analysis (of which more below), but also from my choice of ethnographic "site," my construction of an archive appropriate to this site, and a desire to specify certain relations between these.

There are many historical precedents for my own work. The integration of ethnography and historiography in anthropology is not new.[32] For example, the early debates introduced by Maitland (1936), Boas (1940), Malinowski (1948), and Radcliffe-Brown (1952) opened up a series of questions that have a continuing significance today: that is, in their delimitation of objects of study, in the ways in which they deal with the unavailability of "authentic" historical records, and in their implicit — although often explicit — concerns with the irreducible effects of colonialism on "primitive" life.

The significance of these former works to my own has been mediated through the applications and critiques made by subsequent scholars, an engagement that, in itself, attests to the power, if not the limits, of those earlier formulations (cf. McDonald 1996). Within anthropology, several different approaches to the relation between ethnography and historiography have emerged that are relevant to my own work: these have been expressed, variously, through concerns with structural change (Evans-Pritchard 1963; Leach 1954), unconscious forms (Lévi-Strauss 1963), structure and event (Sahlins 1981, 1985), colonial encounters (Appadurai 1996a; Asad 1973; Cohn 1957, 1967, 1987, 1996; Comaroff and Comaroff 1991, 1992, 1997; Dirks 1987, 1992), and global capital (Wolf 1982). Joined with research done in and on history (e.g., de Certeau 1988; Foucault 1977; Guha and Spivak 1988; Hobsbawm and Ranger 1983), my research builds on the insights of these works and attempts to introduce new points of interrogation. For example, although many scholars have demonstrated that ethnography and historiography are themselves culturally configured practices, made possible by the colonial encounter with the "unknown other," only a few have begun to extend this inquiry to a fundamental methodological premise: specifically, that the basic unit of study has been defined as a particular cultural order that exists *in* time and space. One of my goals in this text is to make the *production* of time and space an object of analysis (Appadurai 1996b; Bhabha 1994; Cohn 1987; de Certeau 1984; Fabian 1983; Harvey 1989; Kuper 1972; Lefebvre 1984; Levinas [1947] 1987).

A central methodological challenge is that my research has been situated within, and has moved between, several localities in different countries. Facing this challenge, I use ethnography and historiography in a specific way to write about the intimate concerns of people who have not only lived far apart but also remained largely anonymous to each other. The demands of doing a translocal historical anthropology are several. Conducting interviews and "doing" participant observation are extremely important, but they can yield only a certain kind of information, information that must be related to the narratives of people in different places. Within the chapters of this book, however, this methodological procedure of relating the stories generated by people within different localities is not translated into lengthy quoted passages—a technique of entextualization explored by Lisa Malkki (1995). Malkki's very important work offers "panels" or "extended narrative passages" oriented toward exemplifying the "standardized historical narrative that centrally characterized" the ethnographic context. Malkki explains this technique: "Sometimes the panels present a record of one person's words; at other times composites of several persons' accounts on the same theme or topic will form one panel" (p. 56). Although, as is Malkki, I too am concerned to expand ethnography's range in the analysis of sustained human emergencies, my approach, in contrast, does not privilege narrative or intend to exemplify standards. This text, rather, performs a variety of ethnographic knowledges—from "personal stories" to the more conventional "focal lengths"—around historically specific and highly contextualized utterances whose subjects are specified. More often than not, these utterances were enunciated within crucial moments of contestation and doubt that the text intends to engage critically. This engagement, moreover, requires that these utterances be positioned within the archive the text is generating.[33]

My understanding of this archive must be made clear. I gathered materials for this archive in extremely different places: from the India Office Archives in London, the National Portrait Gallery Archives outside London, and the Bodleian Library in Oxford, to the Parliamentary Archives in New Delhi; and from the collections of the Bhai Vir Singh Sahitya Sadan in New Delhi to the collections of the Punjab Research Group in Coventry. As I have indicated, what might have been considered ethnographic material, collected between 1992 and 1999, has itself been translated into archival material: magazines, newspapers, posters, cassettes, videos, photographs, recorded narratives, maps, and Internet web sites. When the ethnographic is translated into the archival, its significance is fundamentally transformed. This is not merely because what was ethnography has turned into history. Every archive is built upon silences and elisions, but through this process of creating an archive, in relation to an ethnography, the position and quality of those silences and elisions have changed, sometimes affecting dramatically what story I can tell about the Sikh diaspora. One important instance of this is the argument of images that emerges between what I call *the maharaja's glorious body,* an artifact from 1854, and *the tortured body,* an artifact from the 1980s and 1990s (cf. chaps. 1 and 3). Isolated within the nineteenth century, the maharaja's glorious body stands alone, the sign of a fallen Sikh sovereign. Isolated within the late twentieth century, the tortured body also stands alone, a sign of violent loss. Positioning these two images, and the significance of them for Sikhs around the world, together within an archive of the Sikh body and the Sikh homeland illuminates a dialectical relation that, as I discuss in several chapters, is of singular import for the Sikh diaspora. To put this simply, seeing this relation helps explain why, in the 1990s, the image of the maharaja's body, reconstituted through a relation to images of tortured bodies, has come, for many Sikhs, to signify a glorious past.

This operation that conjoins the ethnographic and the archival is an act of production. Indeed, it is productive of my object of study, the Sikh diaspora. This historical anthropology, in other words, does not pretend, as do other acts of anthropology and history, to be a "realist" representation of a supposedly dialogic encounter with its informants. Feldman (1991) offers a precise analysis of such pretense:

> A good deal of the "new ethnography" discourse is concerned with the recuperation of presence as embodied by the fieldwork encounter (which is a naïve reading of this encounter). This discourse reads the textualization process as an analogue of the Marxist theory of alienation, where the producer (the informant) is alienated from his product (discourse) by the ethnography. Needless to say the realist representation of a dialogical encounter is a simulation as culturally specific and morally ethnocentric as any other narrative mode of forging presence (as is the Western concept of dialogue). Neither Foucault nor Derrida has shied away from translating, representing (objectifying and deobjectifying) systems of representation in other historical epochs of Western culture, epochs that constitute our internal and anterior others. (p. 284)

To put this plainly, through a strategic act of editing, objectification, and deobjectification, this operation constitutes its object as a subject.[34] Needless to say, this historical anthropology is a deeply political act, made more acute because of the current threat of violence to many Sikhs around the world, whether or not they are involved in the fight for Khalistan. Nevertheless, I accept the risk of this operation in order to offer a critique of that violence and discrimination. In what follows, I describe the analytic that I deploy in order to develop this critical engagement — a discussion of which may help further clarify my refinement of historical anthropology.

The Diaspora and the Fetish

This historical anthropology depicts, within the formation of the Sikh diaspora, a quality that, clearly, may be definitive of all diasporas: that is, I illustrate the diaspora as a transnational social formation that simultaneously transcends the territoriality of the nation-state and utilizes its institutions and forms of knowledge. Many scholars have noted a similar feature in other contexts of transnationalization (Appadurai 1996a, 1996b; Comaroff 1997; Glick Schiller et al. 1992, 1993; Hannerz 1996; Lavie and Swedenburg 1996; Robertson 1992; Rouse 1991, 1995; Sassen 1991, 1997).[35] Let me consider this quality — what might be called, albeit awkwardly, a *transcendent* quality — of the diaspora more closely.

In order for scholars to propose that there is any relation between a diaspora and the modern nation-state, the diaspora must be considered as something that may actually interact with a nation-state; that is, it must be considered at a certain level of abstraction, as a historically specific and logical category on the level of the nation-state. This is a basic issue in diaspora studies. I have referred to this kind of interaction already as one in which both individuals are transformed into examples of diaspora and the nation-state makes an example of diasporic peoples. With the place-of-origin thesis, diaspora studies provides one answer to this problem. I agree that the issue is significant, but, as I have demonstrated, I find the logic of the categories of analysis inadequate to the task. Another way to understand this inadequacy is to consider the relation between the individual and the abstraction (i.e., the diaspora).

The analysis of a diaspora often attempts to show the manifestation of a totality (*the* diaspora) in particular and dispersed points of action (whether referring to groups like Hindu, Sikh, or Gujarati or to different diaspora individuals). Scholars demonstrate that these particular points of action are heterogeneous and often contradictory in the ways they relate to a place of origin, different nation-states, and each other. They posit, however, that the incommensurability of these individual elements is negated or diminished in relation to the totality of the diaspora itself. In this sense, scholars have argued that the abstraction *diaspora* is a totality with a particular kind of aesthetic force that inspires the unification of particular segmented groups (cf. Axel 1996a, 1996b). With the constitution of the diaspora as a totality, these studies also reveal something of how the nation-state is understood. As is the diaspora, the nation-state is conceived of as a totality.

The necessity of explaining the relation between the individual and the abstraction must be spelled out clearly. To put this simply, individuals cannot challenge a nation-state, no matter how charismatic they are. Individuals come to be related to nation-states only to the extent that they are constituted as either representations or representatives of collectivities. It is necessary to understand, with ethnographic and historical specificity, how very complexly localized are these processes — or, from the other side of the dialectic, it is necessary to understand how very complexly localized practices make possible the formation of generalized social formations. The notion, however, that this relation of the local and the global, or of individual and abstraction, may be understood in terms of the formation of a totality is troubling. This problem has nowhere been discussed with more insight than in Marx's *Capital*. Marx poses the question of this relation in terms of the problem of the *disjecta membra poetae* — the scattered members of the poet (Marx 1976, 462, 485, 600). Like diaspora studies specialists, Marx (1976, 163–77, 414, 437–54; 1978a, 128ff.) analyzes the problem of *membra disjecta* in terms of time and space — and with particular attention to questions of simultaneity, cooperation, memory, embodiment, religion, and histories of slavery.[36] Of concern to Marx is the *form of relation* between such an abstraction and particulars. Where his work may be relevant to the study of the diaspora is his point that this form of relation is, itself, highly problematic. Not only is the relation, but so also are the categories deployed for the analysis of such a relation, products of a historically specific process of domination — particularly, the social formation of capital. Marx's insight situates another point of critique for diaspora studies. In diaspora studies of the sort that I have been considering, the totality and its manifestations continue to be understood through commonsense terms or transhistorical assumptions that fail to consider *totality* as a point of inquiry and critique.[37] Marx suggests, in short, that the totality offers itself only as an impossibility.[38]

The dynamic quality of the translocal calls out for an analytic that can speak critically not only to this play of difference and "totality" — or the local and the global — but also, in the particular case of the Sikhs, to the desire of the diaspora for a pure origin or a Khalistan, the "land of the pure." To answer this demand, I deploy the notion of the fetish throughout the book. Bhabha (1994) indicates the critical significance of the term *fetish* for the analysis of colonial discourse: "For fetishism is always a 'play' or vacillation between the archaic affirmation of wholeness/similarity . . . and the anxiety associated with lack and difference. . . . For the scene of fetishism is also the scene of the reactivation and repetition of primal fantasy — the subject's desire for a pure origin that is always threatened by its division" (pp. 74, 75). To extend Bhabha's discussion from colonialism to postcoloniality, this notion of the fetish must be supplemented. The fetish must facilitate an articulation of the global circulation of people and signs with the quality of that circulation to generate sentiments of longing and belonging.

Marx's story of the fetish immediately offers a way to conceptualize this quality of circulation, particularly as it pertains to the formation of relations between commodities and people. He explores several different kinds of fetishism throughout the entirety of *Capital:* for example, the fetishism of the commodity (vol. 1), the fetishism of circulation (vol. 2), and the fetishism of the "accumulation" of realized value through capital investments that set in motion further cycles of valorization, realization, and accumulation (vol. 3) (cf. Pietz 1985, 1987, 1988). Together, these different forms of fetishism elucidate a historically specific form of domination and compulsion. And, while they may be organized around the idea of certain "illusions" generated by capital, they tell of the very real character of those illusions (thus wiping out the spurious distinction between illusion and reality). In other words, fetishism grounds a series of constitutive transformations: the specific forms expressed by such categories as *the commodity* and *value* do not simply disguise the real social relations of capitalism; rather, the abstract structures expressed by those categories are those real social relations (Postone 1993).

For Marx, the figure of the substitute comes into play in fetishism. The classic formulation of this is found in vol. 1 of *Capital* (1990): "[The commodity] reflects the social relation of the producers to the sum total of labour as a social relation between objects, a relation which exists apart from and outside the producers. Through this substitution, the products of labour become commodities, sensuous things which are *at the same time* suprasensible or social" (emphasis added; p. 165). But Marx also sees substitution working in the constitution of *man,* which, in his terms, must be understood as a historically specific category produced within the social formation of capital. Within this social formation, "the process of production has mastery of man" (p. 175), and *man in particular* is located only within "the religious cult of man *in the abstract*" (emphasis added; p. 172). Marx poignantly draws a correlation between this fetishistic process of substitution and the effects of certain forms of identification made possible through the circulation of commodities: "In a certain sense, a man is in the same situation as a commodity. As he neither enters the world in possession of a mirror, nor as a Fichtean philosopher who can say 'I am I', a man first sees and recognizes himself in another man, Peter only relates to himself as a man through his relation to another man, Paul, in whom he recognizes his likeness. With this, however, Paul also becomes from head to toe, in his physical form as Paul, the form of appearance of the species man for Peter" (p. 144).

Marx's story of the fetish opens several ways in which to understand how historically specific processes of recognition and mirroring become integral to processes of identification within the social formation of capital.[39] In common Marxian discourse, the fetish has a tendency to be associated with a *negative* critique of identification, put in terms of "false consciousness" or loss. Within such a view, the fetish pertains to the way specific social characteristics of human relations, along with histories of domination, are elided or veiled and objects of labor take on an abstract power, an autonomous agency.

But there is another way in which to understand the basis of Marx's notion of fetishization as productive — particularly in constituting both commodities and man as "sensuous things which are *at the same time* suprasensible or social" (1976, 165). Another way to put this is to say that fetishism facilitates the transformation of individuals into representations or representatives of a people. In this process, the relations of recognition and identification have the character of being alienated. This alienation, however, does not correspond to a loss, distinguishing the illusion of a present from the real of the precapitalist past. Nor does it refer to a simple reversal of subject and object. Alienation may be understood as *formative* of processes of identification, making possible the discernment of self and other, or, indeed, as psychoanalytic theory would have it, the disturbing recognition of the other within oneself. In more Marxian terms, as Postone (1993) has suggested, alienation is a "historically specific mode of social constitution whereby determinate social forms — characterized by the opposition of an abstract universal, objective, lawlike dimension and a 'thingly', particular dimension — are constituted by structured forms of practice and, in turn, shape practice and thought in their image" (pp. 223–24). The fetish does not veil real relations between individuals but constitutes them.

The Freudian notion of the fetish provides a productive tension with Marxian discourse. This tension offers a basis for the supplementation of Bhabha's work that I am seeking. Between these two analytics, a scenario of constitution and translation emerges, one that, most generally, depicts the conflicting relations of particular and abstract, of difference and sameness, and of movements between the local and the global.

Freud's story of the fetish may be summarized thus: the child makes the disturbing discovery that the mother has no penis. More precisely, the mother has been castrated. The fetish "crystallizes" — indeed, specifically localizes — this discovery and veils it: "The foot or shoe owes its preference as a fetish — or part of it — to the circumstance that the inquisitive boy peered at the woman's genitals from below, from her legs up. . . . Pieces of underclothing, which are so often chosen as a fetish, crystallize the moment of undressing, the last moment in which the woman could still be regarded as phallic" (Freud [1928] 1977, 354–55). By its very presence, the fetish indicates not only a difference or a lack but also a *knowledge* of that difference. That difference, however, is disavowed — it is there, but it is not. This problem of knowledge is joined with one of desire — particularly a desire repeatedly to look, a repetition, indeed, that reconstitutes the "original" moment of discovery. In the retroactive constitution of the discovery scenario, however, the look is arrested, focusing on the "last impression" before the traumatic sight, and the fetish becomes the object of an insistently repeated investigation.

For Freud ([1928] 1977), however, the child's investigation—his inquisitiveness, his desire to see and know—is itself a transgression. It is an effect of the father's prohibition (against desiring the mother) enforced through the threat of castration. The sight of the mother suggests that this threat is very real. Indeed, in the fetish "the horror of castration has set up a memorial to itself. . . . It remains a token of triumph over the threat of castration and a protection against it" (p. 353). Hence, the fetish becomes a substitute for the mother's castrated penis as well as the object of the child's feelings of affection and hostility (ambivalence). As such a substitute, the fetish facilitates a form of multiple and contradictory belief: "the woman has still got a penis," and "my father has castrated the woman" (p. 357).

We can see how these different notions of fetish offer an important analytic to the vicissitudes of the local and the global (or the individual and the people) immanent to the structure of diasporic formation. The Freudian and Marxian notions cannot be collapsed, but they can be used to illuminate disparate, although related, processes. In different ways, they depict the movements between locality and a more general space that, it is presumed, encompasses that locality or disavows that difference, albeit not without difficulty, ambivalence, and negotiation. The fetish stops momentarily within different irresistible localities—the fantasy sites of incommensurable difference such as *use value* or *castrated mother*—and immediately translates them into comfortable globalities. In simple terms, within such a process of substitution and displacement, the Marxian fetish illuminates the dazzling effects of commodification. And the Freudian fetish offers a critique of sexuality, corporeality, visual representation, transgression, and knowledge production.

Body and Homeland

Throughout this book, I utilize the notion of the fetish in order critically to examine certain aspects of the more general process to which I have referred as *the transformation and translation of individuals into representations or representatives. Subjectification* is another way of naming this process. This term designates what I take to be the appropriate unit of analysis for a historical anthropology of the diaspora—in other words, the subject and subject formation rather than the individual. Early on, Marx (1976, 92) identified the individual as a phantasm of bourgeois society imbued with putative agency, intentionality, consciousness, and freedom. The notion of the subject—a sensuous thing that is *at the same time* suprasensible or social—has multiple references that displace this phantasm of self-determination. In linguistics, the subject appears as a grammatical element in a statement. Theorists distinguish the splitting of the subject of the statement (i.e., the "I" of the sentence) from the subject of enunciation (i.e., the "speaking being") (Benveniste [1958] 1971, 223–30; Bakhtin 1986, 90–100; Bhabha 1994, 34–36). In psychoanalytic theory, these linguistic distinctions are related to the philosophical notion of the subject as *self-consciousness* (generated through an other) and the juridical notion of the subject as an entity constituted by the law (e.g., *subject to* the sovereign) (Evans 1996, 196). Lacan's work deploys these disparate conceptualizations of the subject in a variety of ways. For instance, he reconstitutes the juridical notion of the subject, stating that the "world is a universe *subjected to* language" (emphasis added; Lacan [1975] 1991a, 206). Language, in turn, has a specific effect on the subject through its symbolic function: "The world of the symbol . . . is alienating for the subject, or more exactly it causes the subject to always realise himself elsewhere" (Lacan [1978] 1991b, 210). In short, for Lacan, "the subject is a subject only by virtue of his subjection to the field of the Other" (Lacan quoted in Evans 1996, 196). This psychoanalytic understanding of the subject is transformed in the work of Foucault (1978). In his classic statement in *Discipline and Punish,* Foucault plays upon the term *assujetissment* to underscore how the process of becoming a subject is also, simultaneously, the process of subjection, one that takes place through, and indeed constitutes, the body. Butler has noted the paradox written into Foucault's formulation: "One inhabits the figure of *autonomy* only by becoming subjected to a power, a subjection which implies a radical *dependency*" (emphasis added; 1997b, 83).[40]

My understanding of the subject as a unit of analysis owes much to these kinds of formulations, particularly in the way they demonstrate the continuities and ruptures between discourse, alienation, regulatory procedures, and the figure of autonomy—each of which, in highlighting the processual and interruptive quality of subjectification, is helpful for an understanding of the Sikh diaspora. I will have more to say about the details and historical specificity of subject formation in the following chapters, but what is important to clarify immediately is that I am not concerned with a singular Sikh subject. Indeed, there has been a proliferation of Sikh subjects since the nineteenth century. In this book, I am concerned with four kinds of Sikh subjects or, more precisely, four sites of Sikh subjectification. These four, however, cannot be neatly separated, and I do not attempt to do so; they indicate the complex historical interrelations of the Sikh diaspora to formations of empire and nation. They may be referred to as (1) the colonial Sikh subject, (2) the Sikh subject constituted by the nation-state, (3) the Khalistani Sikh subject, and (4) the Sikh subject constituted by Sikh studies. The first of these subjects is constituted through a subjection to the sovereignty of the British Crown, the second through subjection to the juridical and extrajudicial procedures of the modern nation-state, the third through Khalistani militant practice and discourse on Sikh autonomy, and the fourth through procedures of knowledge production institutionalized under the rubric *Sikh studies*. Each of the chapters of this book illuminates these sites of subject formation, and their overlap, in different ways.

But precisely how does the process of subject formation take place? And what does it look like in local qua translocal life? What may now be referred to as Sikh subjectification has historically been grounded in a complex process that relies on, and reconstitutes, the formation of a relation between the homeland and the body. Between 1849 and the present, the Sikh homeland and the Sikh body *seem* to have remained continuous elements in disparate formations of the Sikh subject—so much so that most scholars of Sikh studies presume their position within Sikh life. Yet, throughout this history, Sikhs have valorized several homelands and bodies, as have different colonial regimes and nation-states. I have already noted the changing formations of homeland, from Ranjit Singh's empire in the early nineteenth century to the Azad Punjab and Sikhistan of the 1930s, and from the many Punjabs of post-Partition India to the transnationally generated Khalistan of the past sixteen years. Within the cultural practices of the Sikhs, these different homelands have been related to changing notions of the Sikh body. The most important of bodies, which I discuss at length in this book, is the masculinized body of the *amritdhari*. A man who is an *amritdhari* signifies his membership in the orthodox order of the Sikhs called *the Khalsa* through specific corporeal adornments known as *the Five Ks*. The *amritdhari*, however, is most commonly recognized through the image of the Sikh man with a beard and turban. Yet, more than just the beard and turban, membership in the Khalsa requires that Sikhs revere the teachings of the ten Gurus of Sikhism, whose line of living successors ended with Guru Gobind Singh in 1708, and demands that they adhere to a rigorous set of religious principles (cf. chaps. 1 and 2).

The masculinization of the *amritdhari* body has been a predominant factor in processes of Sikh subjectification — of which one of the most apparent effects concerns the image of Sikh women. Nikky Singh (1993) has reflected on these processes in terms of the ways in which they have been intersected by formations of gender and sexuality. As she demonstrates, from the sixteenth through the early twentieth centuries, Sikh literature valorized "the feminine principle." The Guru Granth Sahib (the holy book of the Sikhs), the writings of Guru Gobind Singh (the tenth Sikh guru), and the novels and poetry of Bhai Vir Singh used either feminized categories (e.g., *raktu* [menstrual blood], *agni* [heat], *than dudhi* [breast milk]) or the images of women (e.g., Durga, Sundari, Rani Raj Kaur) to communicate their "vision of the transcendent" in Sikh life. Nevertheless, as Nikky Singh (1993) argues, a historical process has taken place by which "female symbolism and imagery [has been excised and replaced] with a male one" (p. 253). While Nikky Singh's work focuses on the formation of, to use her terminology, the Sikh Woman as subject, in this book I focus on the figure of the Sikh man, and, particularly, the *amritdhari,* within processes of subject formation. I discuss how, within the context of the formation of the diaspora, Sikh subjectification, through masculinized symbolism and imagery, has been intimately related to the takeover of Punjab by the British, nation-state formation, and the development of a fight for a Sikh homeland.[41]

Another effect of these processes of subjectification is that the *amritdhari* body has attained a hegemonic quality so extensive that all other ways of being a Sikh are constituted in relation to it — particularly, to put it crudely, through a relation of being not *amritdhari*. In a very specific way, the *amritdhari* Sikh has become the measure of all Sikhs. Indeed, according to the discourses of many *amritdharis* today, people who are not *amritdhari* cannot be considered Sikhs even though they claim to be Sikh. This includes, for instance, people known as *namdhari* and *nirankari* Sikhs. *Namdharis* and *nirankaris* may follow an interpretation of the teachings of Sikhism and may maintain the practice of leaving their hair uncut. Nevertheless, within Khalsa discourse, they are considered heretics because they revere a line of living gurus extending beyond Guru Gobind Singh. The hegemonic position of the *amritdhari* also constitutes a relation to what are called *sahajdhari* and *mona* Sikhs. *Sahajdhari* indicates someone who, while maintaining uncut hair, defers becoming a member of the Khalsa or is working toward becoming a Khalsa Sikh in slow stages — this whether or not the person actually ever does become an *amritdhari* (*sahaj* may be translated as "easy" or "simple"). *Mona* is a term used to refer, sometimes in a derogatory way, to the practices of some people who may revere the teachings of Sikhism but who cut their hair (*mona* may be translated as "shaved") (McLeod 1968, 1976, 1984, 1989a and b).

The disparate productions of the Sikh body and the Sikh homeland situate a point of mediation between various populations of Sikhs around the world — commodified as images circulating in media and on Internet web pages, within bodily techniques, and within discourses of who is a Sikh. They have a quality of measure and mobility that exceeds the movement of people. Simultaneously, this kind of circulation has facilitated the emergence of an imperative, a *discourse of necessity,* configuring their place in Khalistani politics (i.e., Khalistan, the land of the pure, is a place created by the Khalsa, the pure ones, the membership of which is signified by the *amritdhari* body). This aspect of Sikh diasporic life may be understood as one outcome of historical processes of power and knowledge within the domains of both empire and nation. This is not to say that the interwoven histories of colonialism, capitalism, and nation-state formation *created* the Sikh body and the Sikh homeland ex nihilo, but rather that they have effectively revalued their appearance and significance: through diverse practices and engagements with regulatory procedures, by means of commodity circulation, and through emerging technologies of visual representation, communication, media, and transportation. These have provided the groundwork for the body and the homeland to become, in the postwar era, transnational representational strategies and sites of violent activity.

Considering these histories of struggle and identification, the relation between the Sikh body and the Sikh homeland must be specified further. The *amritdhari* body has become iconic of the homeland. This relation of iconicity generates a specific form of temporality that locates the Sikh homeland and one particular image of the *amritdhari* Sikh body (what, in chap. 1, I call the *total body*) as an anterior point from which the Sikh diaspora is understood to have emerged. In different ways, as will become clear throughout the rest of this book, these elements of temporality, spatiality, and corporeality indelibly inflect Sikh subjectification. This anteriority, this "time before," is a central concern, particularly for Khalistanis today. Identified with this time before, formulations of the homeland and the body facilitate the creation of a Sikh people with a specific future, indeed, a destiny. Both the Sikh homeland and the Sikh body have become signs of promise for Khalistanis around the world, a promise of liberation from present violence. At the same time, however, these signs of promise also constitute a threat: not only because they make it possible for enemies to identify and target

Sikhs for violent attacks, but also because of the contradictions and ambivalences that emerge *within* a Sikh subject generated through relations with an image — an image, moreover, that has been commodified and crosscut by specific histories of violence, race, gender, and sexuality. Today, while these historically specific processes of identification may trouble any assertion of a singular Sikh identity, they also ground the desire for that assertion — a vicissitude that a historical anthropology of the Sikh diaspora must take very seriously.[42]

Through this historical anthropology, I have tried to illuminate the order, polyvalency, and indeterminacy of the lives of a globally dispersed Sikh population, constituted as a diaspora. My approach has much to do with the character of my object of study and its own history of movement, but it also reflects my commitment to developing a project of historical anthropology that may elucidate the strangenesses and banalities of the contemporary world order — an "order" that, for many Sikhs, is made up of a sense of displacement and disarray and of experiences and representations of violence.

1 : the maharaja's glorious body

We wish to remember a period of history common to us both [Sikhs and British]
which saw a sovereign, independent Sikh Nation signing a treaty of friendship
with the British Government, and to highlight the significant contributions of the
Maharajah [Duleep Singh] and his family to Suffolk and Norfolk.

— Nanaksar That Isher Darbar, Maharaja Duleep Singh Century Festival, 1993

How can we break that wish and vow to our beloved Maharaja? Having expressed
his resolve before his grave to achieve and fight to the last, no Sikh can turn back.
[We] will keep this vow. "We go into the fight, come what may to achieve our
beloved Sikh Homeland KHALISTAN." The lesson we learn from our history is that
disunity, jealousy and greed ruin a brave and respectable community, and illustrates
the old proverb: "United we stand, divided we fall."

— Khalistani Commando Force, 1993

Of Surrender and Visibility

Maharaja Duleep Singh (1838–93) is remembered by Sikhs all over the
world as the last Sikh ruler of Punjab. He was the youngest of the seven sons
of Maharaja Ranjit Singh, whom Sikhs memorialized even more than Duleep
Singh. Maharaja Ranjit Singh was the "Lion of Punjab" and the great leader
who, for the only time in Sikh history, established the Khalsa Raj, a Sikh
empire. Between 1799 and 1839, Maharaja Runjeet Singh consolidated a
territory that, before him, had been a "cockpit for foreign armies contending
for the sovereignty of Hindustan" (Khushwant Singh [1989] 1991, 3). On

one side of his territory, he fought off the Afghans, and, on the other side, he signed treaties of friendship with the British. After Maharaja Ranjit Singh's death in 1839, however, there followed a series of disputes in which one contender after another emerged claiming the throne. The seriously weakened polity was made more so by the threat of invasion from the formerly friendly British. In 1843, an extremely anxious time for the Sikh polity, Duleep Singh ascended to the throne at the age of five: several different Sikh armies, aligned with other claimants to the throne, were already at war, and the British had already begun their plans to invade.

Sikh men had come to be known as extremely courageous soldiers and the strongest challenge to the British.[1] On 24 March 1849, when the East India Company, taking advantage of the weakened Sikh Empire, finally conquered Punjab — the last of the great territories to resist colonial rule — the battle was hailed as one of the empire's greatest triumphs.[2] By this time, colonial acts of appropriation had taken on a unique character; indeed, they were often orchestrated as grand spectacles. The ensuing scene of surrender, on 24 March 1849 in Ferozpore, was perhaps the most spectacular the British had witnessed in India. Governor-General Dalhousie, the director of the spectacle, wrote to Queen Victoria, describing the event in order to include the absent monarch in the "experience" of taking possession:

> All the prisoners were brought safe into our camp. Forty-one pieces of artillery were given up. Chuttur Singh and Shere Singh, with all the Sirdars, delivered their swords to General Gilbert in the presence of his officers and the remains of the Sikh army, 16,000 strong, were marched into camp, by 1000 at a time, and laid down their arms as they passed between the lines of the British troops. Your majesty may well imagine the pride with which the British Officers looked on such a scene, and witnessed this *absolute subjection and humiliation* of so powerful an enemy. . . . Many of [the Sikhs] . . . exclaimed as they threw their arms down upon the heap: "This day Runjeet Singh has died!" (emphasis added; Benson and Esher 1907, 257–58)

The colonial scene of surrender contains certain elements of "the examination," about which Foucault (1977) has written. Foucault directs us to the military review of Louis XIV, on 15 March 1666, a ceremony of discipline in which the examination reaches its ultimate expression. Fifteen thousand men are held at attention, presenting arms, for one hour — a crucial moment, Foucault claims, in the history of disciplinary power. The ostentatious and compulsory visibility of the subjects, now presented as objects, is met with the all too palpable power of a sovereignty that is exercised through its *invisibility:* "They did not receive directly the image of the sovereign power; they only felt its effects — in replica, as it were — on their bodies, which had become precisely legible and docile" (p. 188). This ritual of objectification is accompanied by other rituals that capture and fix those bodies and relate them to new formations of knowledge. Situated within a network of visual representation, writing, registration, and archival documentation, these "legible and docile" bodies, for Foucault, give birth to that celebrated sign of modernity, the individual.

The colonial scene of surrender, however, contains certain elements that the Foucauldian examination lacks. Comaroff and Comaroff (1991) argue that "colonialism has been as much a matter of the politics of perception and experience as it has been an exercise in formal governance" (p. 5). In this meeting of perception, experience, and governance, colonial domination enlists and transforms both visibility and recognition in the dialectical production of an "us" and "them." Constituted between the invisibility of the sovereign, the visibility of British troops, and the distinctive visibility of the bodies of the conquered, the surrender, this celebration of colonial discipline, turns upon what I will call an enchantment of *absolute humiliation*. In this case, brought into the relations of surrender, Sikhs are at once transformed into prisoners and liberated as new colonial subjects. The enchantment of humiliation, with the liberal project of enlightenment, opens the way, one might argue, for the "generosity" and "respect" accorded the ideal colonial subject: "a class of persons," in Macaulay's famous words, "Indian in blood and colour, but English in tastes, in opinions, in morals and intellect" (Macaulay quoted in de Bary 1958, 49). And, around this humiliation, the old interest in bodies, documentary techniques, and visual representation is renewed, or perhaps reconstituted, in a new form of governmentality. As a historically specific act of domination, the colonial scene of surrender outlines new demands of both seeing and being seen.

Surrender offers one beginning for a historical anthropology of the Sikh diaspora. This is not because Sikhs have a "persecution complex," as some commentators ineloquently muse (I. J. Singh 1994; Khushwant Singh [1989] 1991). Nor is it because the Sikh community is unified in the momentousness of the surrender's mass trauma. And, with the analytic of surrender, I certainly do not intend to counter, or "correct," present-day Khalistani claims that Sikhs have *never* surrendered (see chaps. 2 and 5). Through the enchantment of absolute humiliation, in its innumerable repetitions, and in its obsessive procedures of knowledge production, the colonial scene of surrender inaugurates a new relation of identification productive of a Sikh "people" (Balibar 1991) — one that has been reconstituted over and again in the vicissitudes of multicultural England, in the changing formations of the Indian nation-state, in practices and representations of torture, and in the discourses of 1990s Khalistanis. The surrender is a historically specific transformative relation that, through violent processes of appropriation, elevates the "individual" into the domain of representation. For my purposes, the colonial surrender points to a complex of processes that figures into the formation of the colonial Sikh subject, the effects of which may now seem a commonplace: the identification of a Sikh subject by the "distinctive," and "distinctively" gendered, image of the male Sikh body.[3] Today, the postcolonial Sikh diaspora is marked with this indelible imprint of coloniality.

This is not to say that the colonial encounter either created a specific way of visualizing Sikh "identity" ex nihilo or invented visuality itself. When the East India Company finally took possession of Punjab in 1849, a series of practices had already been emerging around the visual recognition of the male Sikh body, although this body was in no way a monolithic site of signification, as Oberoi (1994) has clearly demonstrated. One historical precedent, the ceremony of initiation into the "order of the Khalsa," tells of the production of what is known as the *amritdhari* body. *Amritdhari* means "one who has taken *amrit*" (i.e., one who has been initiated into the Khalsa). The founding of this initiation is attributed to the tenth Sikh Guru, Guru Gobind Singh, in 1699.

Two aspects of the Khalsa initiation ceremony are extremely important for my discussion in this and subsequent chapters: first, the initiation introduces a moment of rupture that, in order to constitute a new Sikh subject, abolishes the relevance of all prior forms of identity or affiliation; second, the ceremony moves through a series of techniques and enunciations that explicitly emphasize "the importance of a *visible* identity, one which makes it impossible for any Sikh to remain anonymous or concealed" (emphasis added; McLeod 1984, 73). The ceremony accomplishes this, on the one hand, by constituting a body as a Sikh body that is *whole* (devoid of piercings or scarification) and displays certain adornments *and,* on the other, by immediately connecting that body to a new kinship and lineage structure originating at a specific location in Punjab. In other words, the Khalsa initiation refers to a specific process that transforms the individual into a representative — and the body into a representation — of a Sikh collectivity. One of the most important sources of knowledge production for this initiation ceremony is the Sikh *Rahit Maryada*, which intends to portray the original initiation created by Guru Gobind Singh in 1699. Composed between 1931 and 1951, the *Rahit Maryada* continues to be used today and is regarded as the definitive rendition of the Khalsa initiation. Let me quote W. H. McLeod's (1984) translation at length:[4]

> Any man or woman who affirms belief in the Sikh faith and vows to live according to its principles may receive initiation, regardless of nationality, *previous* creed, or caste. . . . They should bathe and wash their hair, and should present themselves wearing all five Khalsa symbols [see below]. . . . No symbols associated with other faiths may be worn. The head must be covered, but not with a hat or cap. Ear-rings and nose ornaments must not be worn. . . . One of the five officiants should then address those who are seeking initiation . . . : "The Sikh faith requires you to *abandon* the worship of man-made objects. . . . [Other requirements are mentioned as well.] . . . Do you gladly accept this faith?" [After drinking the sacred water (*amrit*) and repeating the basic credal statement (*mul mantra*),] one of the five officiants should then expound the Rahit as follows: "*As from today* you are 'born to the Guru and freed from rebirth.' You are now a member of the Khalsa. *Guru Gobind Singh is your spiritual father and Sahib Kaur your spiritual mother. Your birthplace is Keshgarh Sahib and your home is Anandpur Sahib*. Because you are *all children of the same father you are spiritual brothers*. . . . You must *renounce your former lineage, occupation, and religious affiliation*. This means you should put aside all concern for caste, status, birth, country and religion, for you are now exclusively a member of the sublime Khalsa." (emphasis added; pp. 83–84)

The evidence par excellence that one has undergone initiation into the Khalsa is provided by specific signs that are displayed on the male Sikh body (this despite the possibility that women may also display these signs [cf. Jakobsh 1996; Mahmood 1996; McLeod 1996; Nikky Singh 1993]). These signs (or "symbols") are called *the Five Ks* (*panj kakke* or *panj kakar*), and, conjoining to designate the gendered figure, they delimit the total body of what is called the *amritdhari* Sikh. In one of many books on Sikh history, W. H. McLeod (1989a) describes these bodily adornments succinctly: "The Five Ks are the five items, each beginning with the letter 'k,' which every initiated member of the Khalsa must wear. Most prominent of the five is the *kes* or uncut hair. The other four are the comb which is worn in the topknot of the uncut hair (*kangha*), the steel bangle (*kara*), the sword or dagger (*kirpan*), and the distinctive shorts (*kacch*)" (p. 45).

We may note immediately that the turban—one of the most important signs today constituting the identification of the gendered Sikh body as "distinctive"—is not included among the Five Ks of the *amritdhari*. For the provenance of this image, we must look to another precolonial historical precedent, one provided by artists from the Kangra and Guler regions who, between the late eighteenth century and the 1830s, were patronized by Sikh *sardars* (or, as Dalhousie referred to them, "Sirdars") (Archer 1966; Aryan 1977).[5] Their compositions depicted Sikh *sardars* in a variety of situations: on horseback on the hunt or in the battlefield, sitting surrounded by henchmen in *darbar*, and carousing with Guler or Kangra women. These *sardars* invariably bore the signs of their status: highly ornamented turbans, jewels on armbands, hunting birds. They also sat with relaxed posture and gesture on elevated thrones or cushions with people around them sitting on the floor (Archer 1966, pls. 1–99). In the early 1800s, Punjabi artists began to portray Sikh *sardars* with British administrators (one example is the Jodhpuri artist Jeevan Ram's 1832 piece depicting Ranjit Singh and Governor-General Bentinck) (Aryan 1977, 16).

Since these portraits were displayed in royal courts, the only people who could possibly have viewed them were individuals with access to particular positions of power. It is likely that these visual representations became necessary for the constitution of a certain kind of Sikh subject—the *sardar*—that had specific characteristics. These representations did not celebrate any notion of a Sikh religion or valorize the Five Ks. Rather, they celebrated the status and political power of different Sikh *sardars* who bore the iconographic signs of their status: most important, the highly ornamented turban, but also the relaxed posture and gesture, the jewels on armbands, and jeweled swords.

Within Sikh studies, the historical, religious, and symbolic features of the Five Ks, as well as the use of the turban to cover the hair, have been debated continually. Many scholars have argued that the widespread practice of the Khalsa initiation, and the knowledge of its details, is an effect of either the practices of colonial military recruitment (which required that all Sikh soldiers undergo the ceremony) or the Singh Sabha movement (which introduced an attempt to codify the tenets of Sikhism), or both (cf. Barrier 1970, 1979, 1986, 1989; Cohn 1996; Fox 1985; Kerr 1988; McLeod 1989a, 1989b; Oberoi 1994). According to such widely differing discussions, which are cogently argued, these two late-nineteenth-century trajectories provided a model for present-day religious and military practices in India (e.g., the Indian army has had its own Sikh-only regiments, which are themselves subdivided by caste affiliation [cf. Ali 1988; Cohen 1971; Farwell 1989]).

It is not my intention to detail these very important formulations, which have set a precedent for the present study.[6] They have demonstrated how extremely necessary it is to specify, not only what effects colonialism may have had on the production of a visible form of recognition of the Sikh subject, but also what historical moments affected those productions differently. What these studies have not addressed, however, is telling. Here we may follow the lead of Nikky Singh (1993), who observes: "The male principle has dominated Sikh studies" (p. 243). With only a few very important exceptions (Jakobsh 1996; Mahmood 1996; McLeod 1996; Nikky Singh 1993), scholars of Sikh history deploy the generic terms *Sikh* and *Sikhs* to indicate their object of study when, for the most part, their discussions center on the constitutive practices of Sikh men. Conversely, and regardless of any critique of the colonial construction of the Sikh body, they use images of the *amritdhari* Sikh man, with beard and turban—positioned on book covers, as frontispieces, and within texts—to stand in for all Sikhs. Within a peculiar, yet seemingly quite banal, logic of signification, "Sikh" and "Sikhs" have come to signify "Sikh men" (a form of signification that is itself veiled), and the visual image of the (ideal) Sikh man has come to signify all Sikhs. Here is a powerful practice whereby, in the constitution of the Sikh subject by Sikh studies specialists, the parameters of the analytic procedure simultaneously explode and diminish the parameters of the object of study. This, perhaps it is needless to say, is an act of signification that reiterates what, during the latter part of the twentieth century, have come to be the referential strategies and reproductive commitments of the object of study, the Sikh people.

We may call this signifying act *performative* to the extent that "it conceals or dissimulates the conventions of which it is a repetition" (Butler 1993, 12; see also Butler 1997, 9).[7] To put this plainly, to say *Sikh* or *Sikhs* but mean "Sikh men," and to offer a visual representation of the *amritdhari* Sikh man as a stand-in for all Sikhs, is to reiterate a norm or a set of norms. These types of enunciation and representation would not succeed if, to use Derrida's words, they were not "identifiable as conforming with an iterable model, if [they] were not then identifiable in some way as a 'citation'" (Derrida 1988, 18). What is missing, or concealed, in the analytic procedure of Sikh studies, strangely, is an interrogation of that model or that citation: namely, the convention that makes *Sikh man* a placeholder for all Sikhs. This convention posits a specific body and gender, the male *amritdhari,* as unquestionable *and* unquestionably prior to signification. In chapter 3, I invert the formula found within Sikh studies. I argue that, through performative processes of signification, the body and gender are constituted as *prior* entities, that is, not susceptible to history or "social construction." In the present chapter, I investigate, within colonial processes of subjectification, the beginnings of that specific practice of repetition and the contours of that model (namely, the masculinized *amritdhari* body) that performative acts cite and conceal.

The colonial scene of surrender opens the possibility for this investigation. That scene, also, draws our attention away from the period to which most of Sikhs studies scholarship on colonialism has given attention: that is, the late nineteenth century and the early twentieth, when, within colonial and Singh Sabha discourses alike, the masculinized *amritdhari* body was already posited as a model of Sikh "identity." Here, we turn to the mid-nineteenth century. This historical period is vital for understanding today's Sikh diaspora for at least two reasons: first, because colonial historiography dates the surrender of the Sikh Empire on 24 March 1849 as chronologically prior to, and as the condition for, subsequent colonial strategies of subjectification (e.g., military recruitment) and, second, because through *the negation of surrender* Khalistani discourse has constituted the integrity of the Sikh subject and Sikh sovereignty (indicated by the Sikh body and the Sikh homeland) as existing prior to the institutionalization of recruitment practices and prior to the Singh Sabha reformist movement in the late nineteenth century. Surrender, in other words, offers a critical point within the genealogy of the Sikh diaspora where questions of the authoritative claims of Khalistan and colonialism converge.

However, the surrender of the Sikh Empire in 1849 was not the only Sikh surrender valorized by the British. I will approach the question of the Sikh surrender, and with it the ways in which the Sikh body was reconstituted and gendered by colonial violence, from a position that highlights the way surrender became, in the nineteenth century, eminently repeatable (and thus negotiable): the production and consumption of visual representations of the last ruler of the Sikh Empire, Maharaja Duleep Singh. John Berger reminds us of how European art, from Van Eyck to Ingres (i.e., from the fifteenth century to the nineteenth), came to be known as "the experience of taking possession"; painting itself became the "metaphorical act of appropriation"

(Berger 1972, 215). Within the colonial context, I argue, the painting of dethroned Indian royalty constituted an acute act of appropriation — reiterating, renegotiating, and revaluing the surrender of former foes. More specifically, the production of portraits of Maharaja Duleep Singh became part of an emerging system of global capital that followed the lines of colonialist expansion, transforming one corporeal image into both a new commodity for consumption and an iterable model for citation. Conversely, portraits of Maharaja Duleep Singh simultaneously reconstituted the masculinized Sikh body and transformed it into an icon of the Sikh "nation," itself subject to the Crown. In later chapters, I call this specific model *the total body* — a body that, in the late twentieth century, collapses the eighteenth- and nineteenth-century distinctions between the *sardar* and the *amritdhari*. As we shall see, until 1984, the total body maintained a preeminent position in the constitution of the Sikh diaspora. Thereafter, owing to the proliferation of violence in Punjab, it was joined by, and its significance fundamentally transformed in relation to, another iterable model, what I call *the tortured body*. These two bodies, and the specific quality of relations between them, would situate new kinds of negotiations about who was a Sikh. This chapter, then, establishes a basic aspect of more complicated historical developments.

Portraits of Maharaja Duleep Singh

When the East India Company annexed Punjab in 1849, Governor-General Dalhousie ordered the young maharaja's dethronement and exile from Punjab to Futteghar, Uttar Pradesh, where he was isolated from any connection to his former life. What followed reads like a classic story of colonial irony. Duleep Singh converted to Christianity in 1852, and in June 1854 he left for London, where Dalhousie and Queen Victoria wanted him to marry Princess Gouramma, daughter of the rajah of Coorg, who was a guest of the queen and had also recently converted to Christianity. Although Duleep Singh did not marry Princess Gouramma, he was required to settle in England, where, sustained on a small pension, he lived as an English gentleman until 1870. Thereafter, fueled by letters from relatives in Punjab, he became convinced of a prophecy: that the Maharaja Duleep Singh would return to Punjab to be the eleventh guru of the Sikhs and the ruler of the Sikh nation. For several years, he attempted to conspire with Punjabi revolutionaries and Russian spies to overthrow the colonial state. Rumors about the maharaja's activities abounded in Punjab, where they were closely monitored by British authorities. In April 1886, he left England to sail to India, but he was arrested in Aden by British police and not allowed to travel onward. It was while he was held at Aden that Duleep Singh reconverted to Sikhism (i.e., he underwent the initiation into the Khalsa). He eventually "escaped" and sailed to Europe, where, followed by British intelligence agents, he traveled to Russia and tried, unsuccessfully, to convince the czar to attack the British and liberate the Sikhs (Thapar 1977). He died in 1893 in Paris, and his body was brought back to be buried in a Thetford graveyard near his former home (Elvedon Hall).

The life of Duleep Singh was chronicled by a series of portraits. Perhaps the earliest portrait of Duleep was composed by Schoefft in 1841: the short-haired three-year-old boy, pulling a sword out of a jeweled scabbard, sits on a tree trunk in a grove before Lahore Fort (Aijazuddin 1979, pl. 3). Later, in 1843 and 1845, Punjabi artist Hasan-al-din produced two portraits much in the older Guler and Kangra style of portraying the *sardar:* in the first, Duleep, in *darbar,* is seated on cushions holding his pet dog, surrounded by his attendants sitting on the ground; in the second, Duleep, again in *darbar,* is leaning back in a chair holding a rifle casually in his lap (Archer 1966, pls. 61, 62). Other portraits by Europeans in Punjab, which were published in the nineteenth century, follow the growing boy through his dethronement and his move to Futteghar in 1849: those by Hardinge (1846), MacKenzie (1846), George Beechey (1852), and P. C. Trench (1853) are examples (see Aijazuddin 1979; Archer 1979; Archer 1966; Chakrabarty 1986; Eden 1866; Kapur 1995; Login 1890; Darshan Singh 1987; Gur Rattan Pal Singh 1980; and Srivastava 1953).

After Duleep Singh arrived in England in July 1854, artists began to produce portraits of him almost immediately. Franz Winterhalter and Queen Victoria were the first to portray the dethroned maharaja (July 1854). In 1863, 1866, and 1871, Duleep sat for individual portraits that were placed in the larger wedding paintings of the Prince of Wales (William Frith, 1863), Princess Helena (Christian Magnussen, 1866), and Princess Louise (Sydney Hall, 1871) (see Millar 1992), and in 1875 Captain Goldingham composed a portrait as well. Finally, Clarke composed a portrait of Duleep in the early 1880s that was widely published in 1893 on the announcement of the maharaja's death. Except for Queen Victoria's sketches, all these portraits were exhibited internationally and reproduced in periodicals and books in the nineteenth century in both Europe and India.[8]

The production of the Winterhalter portrait of 1854 offers a unique opportunity to explore the problem of surrender that I have outlined. This is a portrait that attained wide popularity in the nineteenth century, and of all the portraits of Maharaja Duleep Singh, it has had the most enduring significance in the twentieth century. At the time, in 1854, the composition of the portrait itself was heavily documented by almost everyone involved, making the portrait, and Maharaja Duleep Singh, the object of a specific process of knowledge production about the Sikh "nation" and Sikh bodies.

In the following pages, I offer a historical ethnography of the painting of, or, as John Berger might say, the "taking possession" of, Maharaja Duleep Singh. The locality is Buckingham Palace, London, which in this context is intimately connected to parts of India and Europe. The people involved are Maharaja Duleep Singh, Lady Login (his caretaker), Queen Victoria, Prince Albert, Lord Dalhousie (governor-general of India), and Franz Winterhalter (the artist), among others. The processes that I discuss concern both the colonial strategies for producing and gendering the visual image of the Sikh and the techniques by which the colonial project engaged in an ongoing process of conjuring the image of surrendered "oriental royalty."[9] These processes, perhaps first witnessed in the constructions of Tipu Sultan (the "Tiger of Mysore"), followed in the wake of the confiscation of the territory of an oriental kingdom and the collection and display of the artifacts (i.e., treasures) of an oriental monarch's rule.[10] The detail of this discussion is intended to articulate the minutiae through which the male Sikh body was constituted, not just as the bearer of a Sikh subjectivity, but as the figure of a subjection to the Crown.

The Winterhalter Week

Queen Victoria met Maharaja Duleep Singh on 1 July 1854. She had, no doubt, known about him at least since 1849, when the East India Company forced him to "resign for himself, his heirs, and his successors, all right, title, and claim to sovereignty of the Punjab, or to any sovereign power whatever" (Ganda Singh 1977, 674). Maharaja Duleep Singh took on a peculiar position within Queen Victoria's entourage, a position that was institutionalized in three of the terms of the 1849 treaty that Maharaja Duleep Singh signed with the East India Company: "Term #2) All property of the State, of whatever description and wheresoever found, shall be confiscated to the Honorable East India Company. . . . Term #3) The Gem called the Koh-i-noor . . .

shall be surrendered by the Maharajah of Lahore [i.e., Duleep Singh] to the Queen of England. . . . Term #5) His Highness shall retain the title of Maharajah Dulleep Sing [*sic*] Bahardoor, and shall continue [to receive a pension], provided he shall remain obedient to the British Government, and shall reside at such a place as the Governor-General of India may select" (Ganda Singh 1977, 674–75). Queen Victoria was well aware of the humiliation of the maharaja, or at least she imputed humiliation to the maharaja, who in some ways appeared in London as, so to speak, a trophy of war: "As we are in complete possession since 1849 of the Maharajah's enormous and splendid Kingdom, the Queen thinks we ought to do *everything* (which does not interfere with the safety of her Indian dominions) to render the position of this interesting and peculiarly good and amiable Prince as agreeable as possible, and not to let him have the feeling that he is a *prisoner*" (emphasis added; Aijazuddin 1979, 83).

On their meeting, Queen Victoria commented on the "graceful and dignified manner" of fifteen-year-old Duleep, who had converted to Christianity the year before: "I always feel so much for these deposed Indian Princes" (Alexander and Anand 1980, 43–44). She was taken by his "extremely handsome" (Alexander and Anand 1980, 43–44) appearance, and his "Sikh costume," "his very peculiar dress" (Millar 1992, 318), intrigued her. Compelled by the bodily spectacle of her new exotic subject, Queen Victoria decided to have Franz Winterhalter compose a portrait. The German-born Winterhalter, long since a resident of Paris, spent several months out of each year living in London and the Isle of Wight, where he painted for Queen Victoria. Victoria commented that he "was in ecstasies at the beauty and nobility of the young Maharajah" (Alexander and Anand 1980, 45).

Sittings, two hours at a time, began on 10 July, and the portrait was finished on 17 July. Winterhalter was paid three hundred pounds on 15 July 1854 (Millar 1992, 318). Victoria, who had been present at most of the sittings, composing her own sketches of the maharaja, expressed her satisfaction at the finished product: "Winterhalter has got the whole figure beautifully & the likeness is so grand" (Alexander and Anand 1980, 49). She had the six-and-a-half-foot figure placed in Princesses Corridor in Buckingham Palace and ordered the court lithographer, R. J. Lane, to publish a chromolithographic reproduction of the portrait (Blackett-Ord 1987, 196; Graves 1906, 377; Lister 1984, 252).[11] Likewise, she ordered the Italian sculptor Marochetti to do a bust, "which she had tinted by Millais just as Gibson in Rome had done to his 'Venus'" (Alexander and Anand 1980, 49).[12] The portrait remained in Buckingham Palace until 1912, when it was moved to Osborne House on the Isle of Wight.

During the Winterhalter week, a "most interesting episode"—as Lady Login called it—took place by the side of the dais where Winterhalter had Duleep Singh posing for the portrait (Login 1970, 122).[13] Duleep Singh considered this episode one of the most significant and, later, infamous of his life (D. Singh 1884). This concerned the famous Koh-i-noor (mountain of light) diamond, which, as part of the terms of the 1849 dethronement, Duleep, at the age of eleven, was required to give up to Queen Victoria. Before him, Maharaja Ranjit Singh had worn the diamond, which he had taken by force from Shah Shujah of Afghanistan. As Shah Shujah is rumored to have said, the value of the diamond was "good fortune; for whoever possessed it had conquered their enemies" (Ganda Singh 1977, 44). And, as Wufa Begum, the wife of Shah Shujah, said, "If a strong man were to throw four stones, one north, one south, one east, one west, and a fifth stone up in the air, and if the space between them were to be filled with gold, all would not equal the value of the Koh-i-noor" (Ganda Singh 1977, 44). Dalhousie expressed the matter slightly differently: "The *Koh-i-noor* has become in the lapse of ages a sort of historical emblem of conquest in India. It has now found its proper resting place [in Queen Victoria's hands]" (Ganda Singh 1977, 36).

The Koh-i-noor had reached England in July 1850, but, by the time of Duleep's arrival, four years later, it had not yet been presented in public (Singh and Singh 1985, 63). The emblem of conquest had only recently been sent to a diamond cutter in Amsterdam, who had hewn the body of the rough diamond down to half its size and refined its shape and luster. Queen Victoria now wondered if Duleep wanted to see it. As Lady Login recollected: "There was no other subject that so filled the thoughts and conversation of the Maharajah, his relatives and dependents." At Victoria's request, Lady Login asked Duleep if he would like to see the Koh-i-noor "in its new form." Duleep replied: "Yes, indeed I would! I would give a good deal to hold it again in my hand! Why? Because I was but a child, an infant, when forced to surrender it by treaty; but now that I am a man, I should like to have it in my power to place it myself in her [Queen Victoria's] hand!" (Login 1970, 124–27).

The next day, Queen Victoria sent for the Koh-i-noor to be retrieved from the Tower. She called out to the maharaja, who was standing for Winterhalter on the dais. "Turning hastily—for, in the position he was in, his back was towards the actors in this little scene—Duleep Singh stepped hurriedly down to the floor, and, before he knew what was happening, found himself once more with the Koh-i-noor in his grasp, while the Queen was asking him 'if he thought it improved, and if he would have recognised it again?'" After a quarter of an hour, in which time "he walked with it towards the window, to examine it more closely, turning it hither and thither, to let the light upon its facets, and descanting upon its peculiarities and differences, and the skill of the diamond-cutter, [Duleep] moved deliberately to where her Majesty was standing, and, with a deferential reverence, placed in her hand the famous diamond, with the words: 'It is to me, Ma'am, the greatest pleasure thus to have the opportunity, as a loyal subject, of myself tendering to my Sovereign the Koh-i-noor!' Whereupon he quietly resumed his place on the dais, and the artist continued his work" (Login 1970, 127).

"It is to me, Ma'am, the greatest pleasure thus to have the opportunity, as a loyal subject, *of myself* tendering to *my Sovereign* the Koh-i-noor!" What did this gesture signify? Here we encounter a unique moment of intimacy within a familiar enactment of colonial magic: the surrender. But, unlike most surrenders that were enacted and portrayed in the nineteenth century (e.g., the 1849 Sikh surrender described by Dalhousie), this one occurred between two sovereigns in person—a reiteration, however, within a radically different mise-en-scène, producing a different effect of subjectification, regulation, and constraint. This "second" act constituted the "first" as both originary and nonnegotiable.

The performative act of surrender—a moment of subjugation and celebration—involves a complex transformation. Queen Victoria, receiving the Koh-i-noor from an individual, did not receive it as an individual. Duleep Singh, likewise, did not surrender the diamond as an individual. Duleep surrendered it as Sikh sovereign to English sovereign, and the ceremony was elevated to a new relation: between Sikh nation and colonial state. In what follows, I suggest how we might read Winterhalter's portrait as a reflection of this complex transformation and, indeed, as a political text of surrender (see fig. 1).

Entry 916, "The Maharaja Duleep Singh," in the *Catalogue Raisonne of the Queen's Pictures,* describes Winterhalter's portrait: "Full-length, standing in a landscape in Indian dress, resting his right hand on his sword. He wears a number of the jewels which he had retained at the time when his lands were annexed by the British, including, in his turban, his diamond aigrette and star" (in Millar 1992, 317). I would add to this a description of the colors of

Fig. 1 *Maharaja Duleep Singh,* by Franz Winterhalter, 1854
(from Millar 1992, entry 916)

the "Indian dress": a blue- and gold-striped blouse that matches the turban and a red and green tunic, beneath which show gold-clothed legs. The catalog also refers to a "miniature of the Queen" that Duleep wears. This description, however, is inaccurate—there are *two* miniatures of the queen. The first, quite prominent, is suspended from the fifth row of pearls around Duleep's neck; the second, barely visible, is set on a ring on his right hand.

Most striking in this portrait is the composition of space. The space of the portrait is not divided as are most of the royal portraits composed by Winterhalter and other prominent artists of the nineteenth century (e.g., Ingres). It has none of the concrete solidity of the drawing-room scene or the coarse sensuality of the mountaintop or battlefield. There are no columns or portals with curtains pulled back distinguishing the space of the sitter from that of his possessions or property. As John Berger (1972) has commented, such spatial and proprietary distinctions had been central to portraiture's political and economic symbolics in the nineteenth century: individuals portrayed had "the pleasure of seeing themselves depicted as landowners and this pleasure was enhanced by the ability of oil paint to render their land in all its substantiality" (p. 108). This, certainly, was a problem for the artist, Winterhalter, because, although Duleep Singh was a visage of oriental royalty, he had no property, no empire—the ground of Punjab and all its population were the property of the colonial state. Indeed, the "ground" on which the image of the maharaja stands is no ground at all. The catalogue raisonné says: "standing in a landscape." Its texture is more indexical of the homogeneous, nondescript platform of a stage. This stage or plain, on which the figure stands, projects flatly and directly into an almost objectless background, where, in the distance to the right, appear the outlines of two pillars. The effect of this ambiguity (both of the production of space and of an unconventional subject of portraiture) is to put all the expressive weight of the composition on the body itself, which stands out suspended in motion, tall, and highly ornamented—a male body that, now arrested ambiguously in the space of a colonial frontier, has arrived at the westernmost limit of nineteenth-century Punjab and found, not Afghanistan, but London (Buckingham Palace).

Positioned on the frontier, the maharaja's glorious body redoubles the surrender enacted between Duleep Singh and Queen Victoria, a surrender enacted first, in absentia, on the battlefield of Ferozepore on 24 March 1849 and then again in person, in Buckingham Palace in July 1854. How might we read this text? Within the portrait, the representations of the turban and the miniatures of Queen Victoria provide clues.

The Turban and the Sikh Nation

In the life of Maharaja Duleep Singh, the turban became a site for diverse negotiations of both his royalty and his unique oriental masculinity. Queen Victoria, herself, noted the turban on their first meeting: "His young face is indeed beautiful & one *regrets* that his peculiar headdress hides so much of it" (emphasis added; Millar 1992, 318). Against Victoria's regret, Dalhousie saw a necessity. Dalhousie wrote to Couper on 22 October 1854: "It is very good for the Maharajah to have seen the Royal family under such an aspect as you describe. . . . But I am a little afraid that this exceeding distinction will not be for his future comfort. . . . The 'night-cappy' appearance of his turban is his *strongest national feature.* Do away with that and he has no longer any *outward and visible sign of a Sikh* about him" (emphasis added; Baird 1911, 325). In his own memoirs, Duleep Singh did not reflect on the significance of the turban. But Lady Login, who described herself as Duleep Singh's "confidential servant" (Login 1970, 114) and whom Queen Victoria described as "quite like a mother to the Maharajah" (Alexander and Anand 1980, 46), mentioned Duleep's turban in her *Reflections:* "He had long adopted a semi-European style of dress, and wore his complete *national (Sikh) costume* only when he went to Court, or at any great entertainment. He still continued, however, in his *daily attire* to wear the Sikh turban" (emphasis added; Login 1970, 113).

Let us consider more closely why the turban was represented in the portrait and how it might have affected the constitution of Duleep Singh's body as a bodily representative of the Sikh nation. What kind of history of practice facilitated the recognition, through the body, of a Sikh national feature, to which Dalhousie and Login referred?

One possible answer draws attention to the particular objects, the ornaments, that themselves constituted the turban that Duleep wore as he stood on Winterhalter's dais. Most obviously, there were the lengths of cloth, or, actually, two pieces of cloth. The first was the red *paggari,* which was visible as a piece of cloth wrapped at a sidewise angle on the forehead, underlying the more prominently visible cloth of the turban proper. This was probably what gave the turban the "night-cappy" appearance to which Dalhousie alluded. Next was the prominent, and protruding, gold and light-blue cloth, with silver fringes, that covered Duleep's head completely. Possibly of a length of thirty feet when unwrapped, the cloth reached a point above the "night-cappy" *paggari* and flowed back down around the back of the head, covering the ears. Significant pieces of jewelry adorned the peak of this cloth. Most visible was the diamond aigrette and star attached to the peacock feather, the *kalghi*. To the right of the *kalghi* dangled a cluster of jewels, the *jigha*. Less visible was the double line of pearls, the *sirha*, that traced the periphery of the cloth.

This style of turban, with its particular ornaments, was not in 1854, nor had it been in the preceding centuries, exclusively linked to symbols of Sikh identity. Rather, as Cohn (1989) has discussed, the turban, with its *kalghi, jigha,* and *sirha,* was associated with the attire of the Mughal rulers of India: "These ornamental devices were symbols of royalty, popularized in India by the Mughals" (1996, 109). Appropriated for use in the Sikh courts in Punjab, this type of turban was associated with rulership and the image of the Sikh *sardar.*

Returning to the social milieu of the Winterhalter portrait, several tensions now seem to emerge. First, despite Winterhalter's painstaking attention to the depiction of the ornamental objects constituting the turban, neither Queen Victoria nor Dalhousie seemed to draw attention to them at all. They did not consider the different parts of the turban and, in them, that which was significant for Indian rulers: the symbolic bringing "together of all the powers of the earth" (Cohn 1989, 315). Indeed, in 1854, their narratives skipped over the particular qualitative constituents of the turban. What they narrated, instead, was the obscured beauty of the maharaja and the projection of a form of appearance of the Sikh nation: the Sikh national feature. While the physical body of Duleep Singh bore the concrete signs of a certain history (one in the line of Sikh sovereigns, no matter how short-lived), the value of the turban, abstracted from any particularities, left only that which Duleep supposedly had in common with a proposed population of (male) equivalents (i.e., Sikhs).

But this is only one side of the picture. Another way to answer this question of the Sikh national feature is to undress the maharaja. First take off his turban. As Dalhousie said: "Do away with that and he has no longer any outward and visible sign of a Sikh about him." Without his turban, and without the rest of his drapery, what *was absent* is also significant. Underneath his turban there was no unshorn hair (*kes*), no comb in his hair (*kangha*).[14] Underneath the rest of his drapery there were no knee-length breeches (*kach*), no steel bracelet on his right wrist (*kara*), which rested on the sword (*kirpan*). In other words, there was no evidence of the religious symbols (the Five Ks) associated with the *amritdhari* body that Guru Gobind Singh institutionalized in 1699. In colonial discourse, the Sikh national feature did not signify a Sikh religion.[15] Indeed, as I have noted, in 1854 the Sikh, Duleep Singh, was a celebrated Christian.[16]

The Winterhalter portrait offers a view of a particular moment that, later in the nineteenth century, would become transformed and institutionalized. Appropriating the significance of the turban as a kind of oriental crown, colonial discourse would, in subsequent years, project onto Sikhs a hierarchical position: the Sikhs as the most superior, as well as the most loyal and hearty, of the martial races subject to the queen. As Cohn (1996) has argued: "The current *significance* of the distinctive turban of the Sikhs was constructed out of the colonial context, in which British rulers sought to objectify qualities they thought appropriate to roles that various groups in India were to play" (emphasis added; p. 110; cf. Fox 1985, 115, 142; Oberoi 1990, 154). The accomplishment of this objectification was entextualized in Captain R. W. Falcon's 1896 publication *Handbook on Sikhs for Regimental Officers.*[17] But in 1854 a particular strategy had not yet been developed to construct the "discipline and obedience required for [a] unit [of Sikhs] to act on command" (Cohn 1989, 308). The colonial scene of surrender, and with it the production and circulation of visual images of Sikh bodies, would constitute one condition of possibility for the successful proliferation of the strategies of military recruitment. Yet what is significant for this chapter's discussion is that, although it masculinized the body of its bearer, in 1854 the turban did not yet stand alone in giving the Sikh body the power of signifying the Sikh nation.

Victoria's Miniature and the Sikh Subject

Both Queen Victoria and Albert were present at most of the sittings during the Winterhalter week. While Albert talked with Duleep's "convert attendant" Negemiah Goreh about the "Brahmin and Christian religions" (Queen Victoria, journal entry, 13 July 1854, quoted in Alexander and Anand 1980, 46), Queen Victoria was busy making her own sketches of the maharaja. Crude ink drawings, these inscriptions showed two things most clearly: the turban and the portrait around Duleep's neck (Alexander and Anand 1980). It is clear that the miniature portrait of herself was significant for Queen Victoria's identification of the maharaja. In her journal entry of 11 July 1854, after one of the day's sittings, she notes its particular characteristics: "The portrait of me, set in diamonds, which he generally wears, was the gift of Ld [*sic*] Auckland to his father, as well as the ring with my miniature" (quoted in Alexander and Anand 1980, 46).

While in the Winterhalter painting the turban and the Victoria portrait may have suggested opposed poles of the expression of value (one abstracted from the particular, and one highlighted the particular), they were also two inseparable moments that belonged to and mutually conditioned each other. The Sikh national feature could not be ascertained from the position of the turban alone or from the visuality of the Victoria portrait alone. Its character could appear only *in the relation* of the two.

In the painting, the character of Sikh identity as it was expressed in the turban was indissoluble from the character of colonial rule as it was expressed in the Victoria miniature: both derived their value from a particular historical social formation that was inscribed on the body and for which the body was a site of mediation and evidence. Let me clarify these propositions by showing the history and relations immanent to the miniature of Queen Victoria.

On 20 May 1838, Auckland presented to Maharaja Ranjit Singh the gift of Queen Victoria's miniature portrait (along with "a splendid sword in a golden scabbard . . . and two thorough-bred Cape horses") (Osborne 1840, 69–70). Auckland was not in Lahore at the time, so his secretary, William Osborne, acting as Auckland's representative, presented the gifts. The occasion was the signing of the Tripartite Treaty of 1838 between the British government, "Maharajah Runjeet Singh," and "Shah Shooja-ool-Moolk." This was enacted, as Osborne states, "for the purpose of endeavoring to place our alliance with Runjeet Sing on a more secure and decided footing than had hitherto been the base" (Osborne 1840, 69–70).

Consider one of the many terms of this treaty: "ARTICLE 6th. Each party shall address the other on terms of equality" (Khushwant Singh 1991, 381). Ranjit Singh, no doubt, endeavored to make this article of the treaty apparent in his social relations with the British. He himself presented a gift to Osborne, whose friendship he considered "as apparent to the world as the sun at noon day" (Osborne 1840, 228). Osborne wrote of this interchange in a letter: "He [Ranjit] gave me some magnificent presents when I came away; but I am allowed to keep nothing but the decoration of the military order of the 'Runjeet Star of the Punjab,' of which order he made me a knight, and invested me himself. It is a diamond and enameled star, *with his picture in the centre*" (1840, 218).

It is unlikely that Ranjit Singh ever wore the portrait of Queen Victoria. He was described in countless memoirs as always dressed simply. For example, Osborne (1840) describes him thus: "Dressed in simple white, wearing no ornaments but a single string of enormous pearls round the waist, and the celebrated Koh-y-nur, or mountain of light, on his arm" (p. 73). It is most likely that the Victoria portrait stayed in the maharaja's treasury, *toshakhana*, until Duleep Singh retrieved it before being exiled (most of the treasury was confiscated by the British government and auctioned off) (Duleep Singh 1884, 103).[18] Ranjit Singh himself produced no narratives regarding the portrait. Nevertheless, it may be safe to say that his perspective was similar to that of the nizam of Hyderabad, who, as Cohn recounts, had a particular aversion to wearing the portrait of Queen Victoria, which in 1861 was institutionalized as an ornament for the order of knighthood, the Star of India: "The Nizam through his Prime Minister Salar Jang pointed out to the Viceroy that the 'people of this country have a particular antipathy to wearing costumes different from their own.' This, Salar Jang stated, was especially true of Princes, 'who have always been tenacious of the costume of their ancestors'" (Cohn 1989, 319).[19]

There was a significant difference between the gift exchange of Ranjit Singh and that of the nizam of Hyderabad—between the 1838 Star of the Punjab and the 1861 Star of India. The difference marks the transformation from a politically motivated proclamation of friendship and equality to one of hierarchized subjectification and subordination. In 1854, Winterhalter's painting suspended one moment in this historical transformation. In Winterhalter's portrait, the body of Duleep Singh (dethroned and exiled) mediated, and provided evidence for, this transformation. And, as such, the body of Duleep Singh/Sikh became a mirror for the value and power of Queen Victoria and the colonial state. On it, however, the following terms of the Tripartite Treaty of 1838 signed by Maharaja Runjit Singh were nullified and erased: "These countries and places [on either side of the River Indus] are considered to be the property and to form the estate of the Maharajah. . . . They belong to the Maharajah and his posterity from generation to generation" (Khushwant Singh 1991, 380–81). On it, alternatively, were inscribed, not only the subjugation, but also the forced exile of the Sikh sovereign, proclaimed in the "TERMS granted to, and accepted by, MAHARAJAH DULLEEP SING — 1849" (Ganda Singh 1977, 674–75).

From the miniature portraits of Queen Victoria, let us turn back to the turban. Bernard Cohn (1996) writes of the historical enactment of surrender: "In the eighteenth and nineteenth centuries, an Indian would place his turban at the feet of his conqueror as a sign of complete surrender. This was also used in a metaphoric sense to ask a great favor of someone, indicating a willingness to become their slave" (pp. 115–16). In 1854, the turban, which Winterhalter detailed in the portrait of Duleep Singh, took on significance as, not merely a turban, but a turban laid before the sovereign Queen Victoria. The miniatures of Queen Victoria around Duleep's neck and on his finger were not merely portraits of the queen but iconic representations of colonial subjectification that, although the enchantment of absolute humiliation, liberated a new colonial subject.

With the narratives of Queen Victoria, Dalhousie, and Lady Login, the portrait of Maharaja Duleep Singh offers a unique opportunity to begin to interrogate the workings of the stereotype within the constitution of the colonial Sikh subject. The stereotype, according to Bhabha (1994), is an ambivalent discursive strategy, "a form of knowledge and identification that vacillates between what is always 'in place,' already known, and something that must be anxiously repeated" (p. 66). We see the beginnings of this form of knowledge and identification of the Sikh subject in 1854. The turban fixed the attention of Victoria, Dalhousie, and Login, not to mention countless others, and Duleep, needless to say, was careful to wear it daily. Through a complex series of citations to the practices of Mughal rulers and *sardars,* the turban constituted the body of its bearer as both masculine and of royalty. In 1854, however, the masculinized Sikh body was radically different from the bodies of the Mughal rulers, Sikh *sardars* (i.e., as seen in depictions by Kangra and Guler artists), and the *amritdhari* (i.e., the body generated through Khalsa initiation). Likewise, this body traversed several geopolitical categories, and on it merged an ensemble of similarly translocal ornaments, poses, and gestures. But, for European observers, the stereotypical power of the turban was generated through a complex desire: to cast it off in order to discover what it may conceal inside or, indeed, to reiterate the act of surrender, on the one hand, and, on the other, to keep it in place in order to continue to distinguish, visibly and outwardly, the cultural difference of its bearer as what it should be (i.e., the surrendered Sikh). The turban, concurrently, situated a vicissitude of certainty and doubt. What made possible the certainty of the identification of the Sikh as *Sikh* was what made the observer doubt some aspect of the figure's "identity."

Translocal Circulations of the Maharaja's Glorious Body

Not only did the Sikh surrender become the historical condition of possibility for the production of a Sikh "nation" subject to the queen. It also generated the basis for the identification of that nation with the turban — an identification that disavowed the significance of other aspects of a body re-constituted and gendered by the action of colonial violence. The surrender, as well, opened up the possibility of the fight for that nation's liberation. This was a possibility that the colonial state would anxiously consider over and again. Like many other stories of colonialism, the entity that the empire presumed it could bring into existence (whether to liberate it, enlighten it, or put it to work) could not necessarily be contained.

After 1873, some publishers in Punjab began marketing reproductions of portraits of Duleep Singh. For many Sikhs, the maharaja continued to repre-sent both the power of the British Empire and a Sikh nation loyal to the empire. Yet, for others, the maharaja represented a Sikh identity that stood in opposition to the empire.

With regard to this latter, two organizations appropriated the representa-tion of Duleep Singh. One group, led by Thakur Singh Sandhawalia in Amritsar, hoped to reinstate Duleep Singh as maharaja of Punjab and as the eleventh guru of the Sikhs. Thakur Singh was the maharaja's cousin and had been in communication with him since 1870. He sent information to Duleep regarding Maharaja Ranjit Singh's confiscated property, telling him of the prophecy that I have already noted. As Duleep wrote to Lord Churchill, this prophecy had been "foretold by the last Sikh Goroo or teacher (who died about 1725) that I shall suffer in this manner, and that when I shall have been reduced to absolute poverty then my prosperity is to commence" (Ganda Singh 1977, 190). In short, Duleep would return to India, the prophecy narrated, as the eleventh guru of the Sikhs and take over, again, his position as maharaja of the Sikhs. As "Prime Minister of Maharaja Duleep Singh's Gov-ernment," Thakur Singh organized a project to popularize the image of Du-leep Singh as an emancipator (Gurdial Singh 1968).

The second organization that appropriated the representation of Duleep Singh was a religious reform group, emerging in the 1860s, led by Guru Ram Singh: the Kukas. Ram Singh was regarded by his followers as a guru in the line of Guru Gobind Singh. The narratives of the Kukas joined a strict defini-tion of Sikh religious lifestyle with a project to drive out the English and establish a new Sikh dynasty (Khushwant Singh 1991, 130). The Kuka ap-propriation of the representation of Duleep Singh changed over time. Ini-tially, he was not highly revered. In a letter from Rangoon in 1885 (where he had been exiled), Ram Singh "denounced Maharaja Duleep Singh . . . as a beef-eating alien." He urged his followers to "treat him as a foreigner if he returned to the country" (Ganda Singh 1977, 100). As I will discuss in a moment, it seems that later, after Ram Singh's death, the Kukas came to regard Duleep Singh differently.

The distinctions between these two organizations are somewhat ambiguous. Some individuals became involved in activities that supported both organizations. Portraits of Duleep Singh were particularly important in these activities. For example, in 1883, Sardar Sarup Singh, in Fatehgarh, wrote Duleep Singh requesting reproductions of his portrait. Sardar Sarup Singh had supplied Partap Singh, of Amritsar, and Diwan Butah Singh, of Lahore, with portraits of the maharaja to publish (they owned a printing press) (Ganda Singh 1977, 117, 207).[20] Partap Singh had traveled with Thakur Singh to England, and Diwan Singh corresponded with Thakur Singh. Both these men supported the Kukas and had been agitating with them against the colonial state.

A confidential report filed by the Indian government before Duleep Singh had left England for India shows the contrasting narratives ("rumours") concerning the maharaja's return to Punjab:

> The vernacular newspapers in the Punjab have begun to discuss the Maharajah's return to India, and congratulate Sardar Thakur Singh [Sandhanwalia] on his success in prevailing on His Highness to re-embrace the religion of his fore-fathers. The news of the Maharajah's expected return to India has given rise to a number of more or less wild rumours in the Punjab among others: 1) That he will be made Ruler of the Punjab and sent against the Russians (From Ludhiana); 2) That he will be appointed Commander-in-Chief of the Sikh army (From Amritsar); 3) That the Punjab will be restored to him (From Delhi); 4) That he will settle in Kashmir (From Amritsar). *These reports show that His Highness' projected visit to India is engaging a good deal of attention in this province.* (emphasis added; Ganda Singh 1977, 179–80)

By the time Duleep Singh left for India in 1886, much of Punjab knew about his coming—and, when British officers arrested him in Aden, news moved quickly by telegraph to all parts of Punjab. British officials monitored the movements of Thakur Singh's organization and of the Kukas closely and recorded the reactions to Duleep Singh's arrest in several districts of Punjab, from Lahore to Gurdaspur to Delhi. From their notes, we learn how many Kukas may have changed their view of the maharaja: "The Kukas have given out that the reason why the Government has prohibited Maharaja Dhulip Singh from visiting the Punjab is that the spirit of Guru Ram Singh has entered him" (Ganda Singh 1977, 299). The reflections of Bhagat Lakshan Singh (1965) suggest that the representation of Duleep Singh in Punjab at the time was popular in a more general way: "I remember how the Sikh community felt the wrong done them in the forced return from Aden of their beloved Emperor. And the memory of this grave injustice will, I dare say, rankle long in the breasts of all in whose veins runs the Sikh blood" (p. 17).

Even after it was clear that he could not come to India, people in Punjab continued to talk about Maharaja Duleep Singh, and the colonial state continued its surveillance. In 1887, it was discovered that "in every village Duleep Singh's affairs are freely and constantly discussed. The persons who have suffered through the fall of the Sikh dynasty, and who will gain by Duleep Singh's success, are busy in inciting the people to support Duleep Singh's cause. . . . [A list of names is then given.] . . . All of the above are either Duleep Singh's relatives or servants, and during the Sikh rule, they held very high positions. At present they are nothing, and it is natural that they should clamour to see again the bygone days of their being all powerful" (Dufferin, in Simla, to Cross, India Office, London, 14 July 1887, quoted in Chakrabarty 1986, 177; see also Barrier 1969, 33). A year later, in 1888, the fifty-page pamphlet *Qasi-i-aziz ud-din ahmad*, detailing the efforts of Duleep Singh to regain his lost throne, was published in Urdu by a Lahore agent (Barrier 1969, 33). And, in 1893, on hearing of the death of the maharaja, Indian and British newspapers alike printed his obituary, accompanied, of course, by a portrait (Clarke's 1880 composition).

A Mobile Sign and a Mobile People

The story of Maharaja Duleep Singh portrays important transformations in the historical constitution of the colonial Sikh subject, with all its ambivalences, ironies, and unexpected turns, from surrender to exile to surrender again, and to the development of a relation with the Crown characterized by an acute sense of ressentiment. The story also outlines the emergence of the image of the Sikh as a preeminently mobile sign, created over and again through a particular body crosscut by disparate narratives of the past, and infused with often conflicting desires, longings, fears, and hopes of a future.

But the story of Maharaja Duleep Singh also tells of an experience that was, in the late nineteenth century and the early twentieth, becoming more familiar to Sikhs. While the image of the male Sikh body became increasingly translocal, so too did the Sikh *panth* (community). Duleep Singh was probably the most documented of nineteenth-century Sikh travelers, but he was far from being alone. His life, however, marked the beginning of an era of radically changing conditions and opportunities for movements of people configured by colonialism and an increasingly global form of capitalism. By the time of his death in 1893, it was probably not a surprise to Sikhs living around the world that Duleep Singh was born in Punjab, raised in Uttar Pradesh, exiled to England, followed to Russia, resettled in France (where he died), and, after his death, brought back to England (where he was buried). Indeed, the history of mobility of a Sikh "people" that coincided with Duleep Singh's life far exceeded the mobility of the maharaja himself.

In what follows, I elaborate the proposition of this mobility and introduce some of the problems that form the basis for investigations in later chapters. These concern the circulation of the increasingly familiar image of the Sikh body, the movement of Sikh men around the world, and the establishment of transnational networks of communication and knowledge production — processes of movement and mobility that became central to the production of what is now known as *the Sikh diaspora*.

Soon after the annexation of Punjab in 1849, Sikh soldiers began to be actively sought out by British military recruiters (Barrier 1979, 1989; Fox 1985). The colonial army was the first institution to organize the massive movement of Sikh men around the world. Many Sikh soldiers took up residency in the countries where they fought. For example, by 1860, approximately ten thousand Sikh soldiers were living in Burma. From the early 1870s, Sikh soldiers and policemen began working and living in Singapore, Penang, Taiping, and, after 1880, Hong Kong (Barrier 1989; Dusenbery 1989). Although few Sikh men traveled as indentured labor (perhaps because of the opportunities in the military), large groups did travel to Uganda and Kenya to work on the East African railroad, beginning in 1895 (Barrier 1989; Bhachu 1985, 1989; Mangat 1969; Morris 1968). Sikh men began to travel to England more regularly at that time also. Some went to study and others to work in commerce and trade. In 1897, five students coordinated a Singh Sabha organization in London (Barrier 1989). In the early 1900s, London became an important stop on the lecture route of Sikh preachers and intellectuals. It was at this time, also, that rumors started circulating in Punjab and Southeast Asia about opportunities in Australia (*telia*), Canada (*kaneida*), and the United States (*mitkan* or *miriken*) that would soon be closed because of official bans on nonwhite immigrants. Before the 1901 ban on nonwhite immigration, several hundred "free Punjabis" had arrived in Australia; five thousand Sikh men reached

Canada between 1904 and 1907 before Canadian antiimmigration legislation took effect; and approximately five thousand Sikh men arrived in the United States between 1902 and 1910 (Barrier 1989; Dusenbery 1989; Leonard 1989, 1992; McLeod 1989c; Shankar and Srikanth 1998).

These laborers and adventurers utilized the same networks of communication and transportation that were available to Duleep Singh to exchange news and goods between their different localities and Punjab. Created by colonialism and modern industry in ever expanding projects of "enlightenment" and "progress," these networks brought together numerous and dispersed local struggles and furnished colonial subjects with basic weapons for challenging the authority of the colonial state. This is a part of Sikh history that is extremely important for understanding the constitution of what has come to be known as the Sikh diaspora. Wherever Sikh men settled, they almost invariably established a *gurdwara* (Sikh temple), which became a meeting place and a site for religious, political, and cultural debate. Two newspapers, the *Khalsa Advocate* and the *Khalsa Samachar,* both published and distributed in Punjab, became important venues for communicating these experiences and debates to Sikhs around the world. The *Khalsa Advocate* and the *Khalsa Samachar* were also used to raise money for building *gurdwaras* and schools in Punjab and around the world, seek advice on wedding arrangements (i.e., should Sikhs marry Burmese girls), and get access to information on scriptures and theological issues. These practices and forms of communication, however, were often regarded just as dubiously by the British as were the activities of Maharaja Duleep Singh. Gerald Barrier (1989) has written extensively on these conflicts:

> What was transmitted through these contacts and networks? Appeals, information, news and attempts at political support moved back and forth. The amount of interchange depended on events and also the efforts of the British to modify or interfere with communication. After the beginning of this century, the Government of India became increasingly concerned with Sikh political and religious developments. Future recruitment of Sikhs for military service outside India was curbed, both because [of] the drain on the manpower judged necessary for the Indian army as well as in response to radical movements and even mutiny among Sikh troops. . . . The CID banned some newspapers and tracts, interfered with their transmission in the mails, and placed limits on what literature could circulate in government schools. (p. 77)

The anxiety of the British over the activities of Sikh men living around the world may indeed have been justified (Barrier 1974). Several Sikh, or more generally Punjabi, anticolonial organizations emerged during this period — many of which formed out of interactions in *gurdwaras*. In British Columbia between 1907 and 1909, three newspapers were published with the express purpose of advocating self-rule in India: *Free Hindustan, Aryan,* and *Swadesh Sewak* (Juergensmeyer 1979). These papers were associated with the Hindustan Association, which many scholars consider to have been a precursor to the Ghadar movement that was later formed in 1913. This latter San Francisco–based movement, made up of farmers, lumberjacks, and students, printed revolutionary literature in its own newspaper, *Ghadr,* which circulated beyond North America to British Guiana, Trinidad, South and East Africa, Hong Kong, Japan, and the Philippines (Tinker 1976). The Ghadar movement attempted (unsuccessfully) to send arms and guerrilla soldiers to India for a planned 1915 uprising (Barrier 1989; Juergensmeyer 1979; Puri 1983).

In England, some years later, an organization was formed by Punjabi immigrants that was less militant but no less anticolonial: the Hindustani Mazdoor Sabha or the Indian Workers' Association (IWA). The first IWA was founded in Coventry in 1938 by Punjabi peddlers and local factory laborers working in the Midlands. A second IWA was also formed in London. Collaborating with Indian students in London and the India League (a group formed in 1929 dominated by Gujarati doctors and Englishmen interested in India's independence), the IWA raised money for the independence movement and "propagandized among both Indian immigrants and the British" (Dewitt 1969, 45; cf. Barrier 1974; Ramdin 1987).

The archive that I have brought together to tell the story of Maharaja Duleep Singh is infused with gaps between the time of his death and the 1990s, gaps that may or may not correspond to the character of popular memory about Duleep Singh for Sikhs around the world. Did Sikh farmers in North America know about the revolutionary activities of Maharaja Duleep Singh? Did Sikh students in England hang portraits of the maharaja on the walls of their rooms in 1897 or 1938? The answers to such questions as these are unclear. But what *is* clear is that, beginning in the early twentieth century, German firms began to publish and distribute what are known as *bazaar prints* (see fig. 2). These bazaar prints were mainly portraits of Sikh gurus and especially Guru Gobind Singh, creator of the Khalsa. In these popular portraits, which were just as widely dispersed as the Sikh *panth,* Guru Gobind Singh, like Maharaja Duleep Singh, is portrayed with beard, turban, and

Fig. 2 Bazaar print (photograph by Nathalie Loveless
Axel)

sword as well as with other kinds of bodily decoration. As McLeod (1992)
states: "The kingly Guru Gobind Singh . . . frequently appears in resplen-
dent attire. Decked with jewels, richly embroidered, and armed with an
ostentatious sword, he answers an insistent demand for conspicuous display"
(p. 34). McLeod also attributes this motif of "royal splendor" to artists' mod-
eling their work on portraits of Indian princes (p. 46). Specifying McLeod's
important work, this archive suggests that one of the most powerful models,
whose contours these portraits reiterated in minute form, was the glorious
body of Maharaja Duleep Singh.

Resurrecting the Maharaja's Glorious Body

Emerging from the remnants of colonialism, and given new form by the
changing structures of postwar global capitalism, portraits of Maharaja
Duleep Singh returned to circulation in the 1990s. As a visual sign acting in

relations of recognition and identification, the portrayed body of the maharaja seemed to retain some of the magic that it embodied in 1854. The colonial magic of the surrender, however, with its celebration of the subjugated body, with its spectacle of humiliation, and with its grand gesture of forgiveness, was forced to meet the postcolonial conjurings of the nation-state and the diaspora.

Between October 1990 and March 1991, the National Portrait Gallery put on an extraordinary exhibition entitled "The Raj: India and the British, 1600–1947." This event was extraordinary for two reasons. It was the largest historical exhibition that the gallery had ever mounted, and it attempted to reformulate, for an increasingly skeptical public sphere, the *merits* of colonialism. With 1990s England, after forty years of conflicts organized around the figure of "an empire that strikes back" (see chapter 4), one would think that the nation-state might only hesitatingly make claims that valorized colonialism. Against the confusion and convolution of an emerging multicultural era, "The Raj" proffered a simple Kiplingesque slogan: "East is east, west is west." According to the show's catalog (Bayly 1990), the exhibit would examine a "noble theme: the long relationship between the peoples of one of the great ancient civilizations of the East, largely Hindu but part Muslim, and the representatives of a vigorous Western trading nation which, faced with the dissolution of the Mughal Empire, developed in the course of time one of the most remarkable administrations — efficient and evangelizing — since the heyday of the Roman Empire." In the 1990s, when apparently "no one now disputes [that] the nature of British dominion was shaped by Indian as much as British People, and as much by their cooperation as by their resistance," it was time to celebrate Britain's role in the production of "three great nations of today: India, Pakistan, and Bangladesh" (Bayly 1990, 8, 11).

One painting was selected to be the exhibition's commemorative logo: Franz Winterhalter's 1854 portrait of Maharaja Duleep Singh. The portrait was given wide circulation. It was displayed on books and posters and circulated in national advertising campaigns, and a detail of it was placed on the cover of the exhibit's massive catalog. The six-and-a-half-foot painting was "graciously lent . . . by her Majesty The Queen" for the exhibition (Bayly 1990).

Perhaps it was the story of Maharaja Duleep Singh that made the portrait appealing to the exhibition's organizers, a story corroborating the assertion that the exhibit demonstrated how "the nature of British dominion was shaped by Indian as much as British People, and as much by their coopera-

tion as by their resistance." The story of Maharaja Duleep Singh's life, however, may not have been as important as the unambiguous corporeal image
that he presented, one that very few people would have difficulty recognizing: a royal Sikh man, bearing a turban, *from the past*. Within a classic recuperation of orientalist-cum-colonialist longing, and separated from a long
history of conflicts between Sikhs and the British nation-state, this image was
given an immense responsibility by the National Portrait Gallery.[21] The maharaja's glorious body took on the burden of representing England's past
relation to "the great ancient civilizations of the East, largely Hindu but part
Muslim." But that was not all. The image also had to stand in for the curators'
anthropologizing project "to see the British from the Indian point of view"
(Bayly 1990, 8). Acting as such a representational placeholder, and burdened
with significations of England's "noble" past, the maharaja's body was ultimately given the task of imperso-nation (Comaroff 1997): of imaging the
present grandeur of a multicultural nation-state in human form. In other
words, the 1990–91 exhibition at the National Portrait Gallery attempted to
reposition Maharaja Duleep Singh's surrender to the queen as a new surrender to the nation-state. This form of relation between British Sikhs and
the nation-state will play a central part in my discussion in chapter 4, which
looks closely at the postwar formation of London and its Sikh community.
For the moment, what is important is that, in the 1990s, this surrender was
not so easily accepted by British Sikhs.

In March 1993, two years after the exhibit, the visual image of Maharaja
Duleep Singh was reintroduced into England's public sphere, although oriented toward a more select audience. Owing to the vast efforts of the Nanaksar Thath Isher Darbar (NTID), an international Sikh organization based
outside Birmingham, portraits of the maharaja were widely marketed as part
of the Maharaja Duleep Singh centenary festivities, a commemoration of
Duleep Singh's death in 1893. Two reproductions of the portrait were made
available: one, the official replication of the Winterhalter original, was distributed by the National Portrait Gallery ("reproduced by gracious permission of her Majesty The Queen"); the other, marketed by the Punjabi Guardian Press of Birmingham (Smethwick), was commissioned by the Maharaja
Duleep Singh Centenary Trust (NTID) as part of a variety of commemoration activities. These activities included numerous charity events and prayer
meetings in *gurdwaras* all over England, plans for a research chair in Duleep
Singh's name at the University of East Anglia, and an outdoor festival with
performers, musicians, and poets. Some Sikh entrepreneurs even attempted

ਇਹ ਉਹ ਪੰਬੋ ਹੈ
ਜਿਹਦੀ ਪੂਰਬ ਵਿੱਚੋ ਰਹਿ ਗਈ
ਇਹ ਉਹ ਹਰਿਵਾ ਹੈ
ਜਿਹਦੀ ਆਵਾਜ ਵਿੱਚੋ ਰਹਿ ਗਈ

Maharaja Duleep Singh Centenary Trust

Fig. 3 Official cover of the NTID program, 1993 (courtesy Maharaja Duleep Singh Centenary Trust).

to buy both Duleep Singh's former property in Thetford (Elvedon Hall) and the original Winterhalter portrait.[22]

The two reproductions, which were used side by side in the centenary festival, have somewhat different appearances (see figs. 3 and 4). The National Portrait Gallery's version is an exact replica of Winterhalter's 1854 portrait: the young maharaja, wearing an ornate turban and leaning on a jeweled sword, stands ostentatiously in an ambiguous landscape; prominently displayed among his jeweled necklaces — suspended from a pearl necklace — is a detailed portrait of Queen Victoria. The NTID's version, composed in 1993 by a local Sikh artist, introduces a few changes.[23] Like the National Portrait Gallery's version, the portrait shows the maharaja leaning on his sword and wearing a highly ornamented turban. The maharaja, however, does not stand in an ambiguous landscape; rather, he stands in a plain, rather English-looking room on a lionskin carpet in front of a throne that displays *nishan sahib* (the Sikh flag, which shows the two swords *miri* and *piri;* see chap. 2). There is no ceiling; instead, a cluster of ominous dark clouds opens to a blue sky in which shine a golden light and the Gurmukhi Ik On Kar (the

Fig. 4 *Maharaja Duleep Singh* (courtesy Punjabi Guardian
Press, summer 1993).

Sikh symbol of God). And the effigy that hangs from the pearls around the maharaja's neck depicts Maharaja Ranjit Singh, not Queen Victoria.

Of the two, the National Portrait Gallery's version was used much more extensively in the commemorative activities (a close copy of this "official" image was also painted by a Sikh artist and printed in Birmingham). The portrait commissioned by the NTID had a limited circulation. It was sold mostly as an individual poster, and it was also placed on the cover of a cassette called *Prana Ton Pyari Sikhi,* a musical recording, in the Punjabi genre *dhadi,* celebrating the heroic deeds of the remembered maharaja. The "official" Winterhalter image, in contrast, was featured on the cover of the NTID program for the Maharaja Duleep Singh Centenary Festival and on the covers of several Gurmukhi/Punjabi periodicals, including the newspaper *Des Prades* (produced in Southall) and the magazine *Qaumi Ekta* ("National Unity," produced in Smethwick), both of which have a large international market. It was sold as a poster available at the National Portrait Gallery in London and in Indian-owned shops throughout the United Kingdom. This portrait was also exhibited publicly. In Southall, West London, the proprietors of the newly opened (August 1993) Glassy Junction Pub commissioned a seven-foot reproduction of the Winterhalter portrait from a local poster shop (the shop usually dealt in posters of Hindu gods and goddesses, but, as the owner said, "we can do anything you like"). The reproduction, half a foot larger than the original, hung in the pub's main lounge, positioned centrally above the fireplace and between paintings of Nasrat Fateh Ali Khan and Gurdas Singh (two popular musicians).

On 1 August 1993, the appointed day for the Maharaja Duleep Singh Centenary Festival, an estimated fifteen thousand Sikhs from all over England came to the maharaja's grave in Thetford. This was a unique mobilization built on an infrastructure of transportation and communication networks that had already been in place for several decades. A Sikh bus service had been running daily between Southall and different parts of the Midlands (for the low price of five pounds one-way). This bus service was put to use to move people to Thetford in the northeast. Along with the NTID, over a hundred Sikh *gurdwaras* located all over England provided funding for travelers, who, on this occasion, went to Thetford for free.

In 1993, two years after the National Portrait Gallery's monumental exhibition, the image of Maharaja Duleep Singh thus shifted into new hands, hands that were well equipped to stir up a grand patronage. In what seems like a classic postcolonial struggle over the means of signification (Comaroff and Comaroff 1991, 4), Sikhs transformed the image of Duleep Singh into a mobile sign, at once mediating the diverse relations and cultural practices of British Sikhs and constituting a distinctly Sikh geography within the British nation-state. What emerged, however, was not a singular Sikh subject whose surrender to the state was inscribed on a Victorian icon's singular body.

What kind of identifications convened on the image of the maharaja, and for whom? There were at least three answers. One defined the predicament of many second- and third-generation Sikhs in England, themselves struggling with the self-identification *Sikh*. For these young people in their twenties, Duleep Singh represented the struggle, as they would say, to "cross the border" between Asians and English so that they could enter the "mainstream." A second answer came from the organizers of the festival, for whom the maharaja was a sign "bringing histories and cultures together." Duleep Singh represented the way "the Sikhs of Britain can strengthen their bonds with the host community." Most important, it was said, the image of the maharaja could provide *a link* with "our homeland, the Punjab," which should be developed and sustained with vigor. The third answer came from one of the many organizations struggling to establish a sovereign Sikh state, the Khalistani Commando Force. For these activists, who hoisted a Khalistani flag over the maharaja's grave, Duleep Singh was the last king of Khalsa Raj (Khalistan). According to the Khalistani narrative, the maharaja's "last wish and vow was to free our Sikh State (Khalistan or Khalsa Raj) from the aggressor, which he could not achieve in his lifetime. That wish and vow of Khalistan is still alive and was not buried in his grave." We might add to these three answers a fourth, which came from the Shiromani Gurdwara Parbhandak Committee (SGPC) in Punjab. In December 1993, the SGPC organized its own celebration at Guru Nanak Khalsa College, Ludhiana. This "national-level seminar" produced a small commemorative volume that included contributions from several prominent Punjabi Sikh scholars and politicians, all of whom saw Maharaja Duleep Singh as a nineteenth-century hero of both Sikhism and Indian nationalism. Duleep Singh was someone who "after becoming aware of his glorious heritage lived and suffered to uphold the pride of his people and noble values that Sikhism stands for." Maharaja Duleep Singh was "a relentless crusader against British imperialism and [one who] internationalized the issue of Indian independence" (editor's preface, Kapur 1995).

The resurrection of the maharaja's body by the NTID now takes on a new significance. In the 1990s, the sight of portraits of Maharaja Duleep Singh reminded most Sikhs of other well-known portraits, particularly those of Guru Gobind Singh. Through a correlation with the extremely popular and widely distributed portraits of Guru Gobind Singh, the image of Maharaja Duleep Singh was subject to an interesting historical twist. The body of the maharaja was transformed into an image that Sikhs saw as reiterating the model of Guru Gobind Singh (and some artists accentuated this relation by giving a full beard to the face of the maharaja). Now seen as an *amritdhari*, Maharaja Duleep Singh represented not just a past and last Sikh sovereign. More important, through the display of the male body, he related a point of anteriority to a possible future destiny (e.g., of crossing the border, of Khalistan, of strengthening bonds with the host community). But the portrait also signified a spatial movement — particularly, a history of movement and mobility of people and signs — that increased dramatically after 1947. In some ways, the project of the NTID — even in its conflict with the discourses of British Sikh youths and Khalistanis — may be seen as an attempt to inscribe a history of Sikh mobility onto the maharaja's glorious body, indeed, making Winterhalter's 1854 portrait a frontispiece to the story of the Sikh diaspora.

Such a position is apparent in the proliferation of discourses that accompanied the Maharaja Duleep Singh Centenary Festival. The NTID, which formed "part of an international network with representations in the USA, Canada, Europe, Australia and New Zealand," described Maharaja Duleep Singh as "the earliest Sikh to settle in Britain." And, while the circulation of Maharaja Duleep Singh's body may have been prompted by struggles to resituate the Sikh diaspora *within* England, it also provided the opportunity to reconstitute relations to a Sikh world *panth*. In this, the relation of Sikhs to India and Punjab was extremely important. Consider the following excerpt, entitled "The Sikhs and the British: The Royal Connection," which was included in the official festival pamphlet (*Maharaja Duleep Singh Centenary Trust* 1993) that the NTID produced:

> In the 1984 period, when many Sikhs have become a sore eye to the Indian government, the protection afforded by a civilised state and its administration must find acknowledgment within the British Sikh population. . . . However, like Duleep Singh, our relationship with Britain should remain loyal but also due care should be taken to preserve our distinct cultural roots, religious inheritance and identity. Links with our homeland, the Punjab, must be developed and sustained with vigour —

these are needed as never before. We cannot afford to let our next generation of Sikhs born and bred in Britain become rootless. (p. 14)

The eighty-three pages of the festival pamphlet contain an array of historical essays, textual references, letters from dignitaries, advertisements, and
photographs that accentuate the reach of Sikh relations within England and
around the world. The pamphlet entextualizes a complex space of diasporic
practice. For example, there is a "Guide to Places of Sikh Interest in Britain,"
which, through brief entries, plots out a Sikh space within England along
the following points: Elvedon, Thetford, Norton Blow, Felixtowe, Windsor
Castle, London (where Duleep Singh's mother lived for a year), Cambridge,
Lichfield Cathedral, and Brighton. The thirty pages of business advertisements at the end of the book expand this survey to Southall, Hayes, Letch-
worth, Coventry, Luton, Walsall, Hurley, Wolverhampton, and Smethwick.
But these are not limited to England: for example, there are advertisements
for Hong Kong, New Zealand, and Japan (particularly Akasaka, Roppongi,
Tamagawa, and Kichijoji).

In relation to this globally dispersed population, the NTID's discourse
substantially evaluates the wealth of British Sikhs, their "manpower," the
state of their health, and their regularized activities. Consider the following
quotes: "The [Nanaksar Thath Isher] Darbar operates from a newly constructed 1.5 million pound complex in Wolverhampton." "As a community
Sikhs have performed quite well in their new homes. Educational and economic opportunities provided by Britain remain unparalleled." "The second generation of Sikh youth are now passing through British higher education." "Sikhs are now a very large community of Britain, with about 160
gurdwaras, several cultural centers and political and literary associations."
"Every year, in London, one can see a small contingent of Sikhs at the Re-
membrance Day as the British monarch pays tributes to the memory of
dead during the two World Wars." In addition to these direct statements
of population data, the text also constitutes the image of a population that
is economically self-sufficient. And many of the thirty pages of business advertisements exhibit photographs of the smiling and waving owners, who
announce, "Special Rates of Private Hire," and, "Please pay us a visit and
save $$$$."

At the same time as the festival pamphlet reconstitutes the Sikh diaspora's
relations to England, or to India, or to Punjab, it also repositions the locality
of the Sikh diaspora. Rather than in terms of the constraints of national

boundaries or the location of state capitals, this text produces England as one of the many places through which a collectivity moves—a collectivity that transcends, yet is complexly related to, the boundaries of nation-states. But, not merely moving through, the Sikh diaspora utilizes such movement in a process of identification and reconstitution.

This latter process offers us one more way of looking at the portrait of Maharaja Duleep Singh. The story of the 1993 Maharaja Duleep Singh Centenary Festival demonstrates a fundamental historical change, indicating the historical specificity of the colonial magic of surrender. The colonial magic of surrender has been supplanted by another form of enchantment, what I call *the magic of the postcolonial fetish*—a magic that changes the imperatives of visuality and the dynamics of identification within an emerging domain of commodity production and consumption. The male body and the turban remain basic elements, but their seeming continuity belies a transformation. Their reiteration does not hail their return as the same. They have been reconstituted in specific historical contexts and, as we shall see in following chapters, more often than not, violently so. In the latter part of the twentieth century, for instance, the turban signified, not the *sardar*, but the *amritdhari*. More specifically, through a process of substitution, the turban stood in for the signs of the *amritdhari* body that were not outwardly visible. In J. P. S. Uberoi's (1996) words, the "meaning and effect [of the Five Ks] are made even clearer by the custom of the Sikh turban" (p. 12).

Here, picking up my discussion of the preceding chapter, we may begin to distinguish the specificity of the fetish. As I hope to demonstrate in several discussions in the following chapters, the concept *fetish* cannot be generalized or used as a cover term for every problem of representation. It is important to make this distinction because processes of identification and the (fetishized) power that one object embodies—as well as the relations that constitute that power—may be different in many ways from those that another embodies. For example, the abstract power of the Sikh body is different—in its historical production and in its effects—from that of the Guru Granth Sahib. In the context of this discussion, the fetish of the *amritdhari* and the turban, made possible by the global circulation commodities (themselves signs of a "people"), mediates between specific sites (also signs of a "people") and makes possible the proliferation of a discourse on who is a Sikh. Conversely, the commodification of the image of the *amritdhari* man and the turban, transvalued through that circulation, generates the globalization of sentiments of longing and belonging. Through these complex processes, the *amritdhari* man and the turban dynamically vacillate between and embody, as Marx (1976) would say, "sensuous things which are *at the same time* suprasensible or social" (emphasis added; p. 165).

I have already mentioned that the maharaja's glorious body is not the only Sikh body that is significant in Sikh practices today and that it does not stand alone in its relation to the Sikh diaspora. Indeed, by the time of the Maharaja Duleep Singh Centenary Festival, it had already been drawn into a new relation with another body, the tortured body. This relation will be the object of inquiry in chapters 3–5. Yet, as I noted in my introduction, it is crucial to understand the significance of the total body, and its relation to the colonial magic of surrender, at the outset. For the moment, we may understand that, in its relation to the Sikh diaspora, the circulation and fetishistic investment in the body of Maharaja Duleep Singh contribute to, as I have noted, the formation of temporality produced in the present and oriented, not only toward a past, but also toward a future. This temporality is a key element in my understanding of the fetish as part of Khalistani political practices, which I will explore in different ways in chapters 2–4. Benjamin (1968) has a phrase that suggests the importance of this temporal dynamic, particularly in its relation to visual representation: "One of the foremost tasks of art has always been the creation of a demand which could be fully satisfied only later" (p. 237). The urgency of the demand, and the continual deferral of its full satisfaction, is integral to the retroactive production of a Sikh past and to the projection of a future. We may witness this dynamic of demand and deferral in the circulation of portraits commemorating the life of Maharaja Duleep Singh. Consider two of the narratives of history produced in 1993, the first from the NTID, the second from the Khalistani Commando Force:

> We wish to remember a period of history common to us (Sikhs and British) both of which saw a sovereign, independent Sikh Nation signing a treaty of friendship with the British Government, and to highlight the significant contributions of the Maharajah and his family to Suffolk and Norfolk. (*Maharaja Duleep Singh Centenary Festival* 1993)

> How can we break that wish and vow to our beloved Maharaja? Having expressed his resolve before his grave to achieve and fight to the last, no Sikh can turn back. [We] will keep this vow. "We go into the fight, come what may to achieve our beloved Sikh Homeland KHALISTAN." The lesson we learn from our history is that disunity, jealousy and greed

ruin a brave and respectable community, and illustrates the old proverb: "United we stand, divided we fall." (*Prince Duleep Singh* 1993)

On the historical ground of colonial surrender, a postcolonial demand is harvested. The Sikh diaspora is, in effect, re-created, looking back in order to look ahead. As a visual sign, the image of Duleep Singh facilitates a new process of subjectification, constituting at once an anterior point—a time that preceded the emergence of a diaspora—and possible futures. Through this temporal movement, a desire emerges, a longing for a new space of habitation, whether of an England uncomplicated by racism, a peaceful Punjab, or a Khalistan—diasporic spaces that lack territory and precedent.

2 : the restricted zone

This is not the time to involve ourselves in needless disputes, nor can we ever afford to follow the mirage of many "stans" like Khalistans and Sikhistans.
— Sardar Vallabhai Patel, Patiala, 22 October 1947

Following is the text of the news briefing:

(begin transcript)

THE WHITE HOUSE

Office of the Press Secretary

March 5, 1997

PRESS BRIEFING BY MIKE MCCURRY

The Briefing Room

1:38 P.M. EST

Q: — [interruption] — letter written by the Vice President — [interruption] — Khalistan President in Washington — [interruption] — still is part of the Indian Parliament. What they are saying, some members of the Parliament in India, is that the Vice President doesn't know how many countries are on this Earth because he's calling the conflict in Khalistan that — [interruption] — is it time to recognize or endorse Khalistan which is a part of Punjab?

A: No, of course not. And we have already made clear through the State Department and I would make clear here that the United States does not and never supported the establishment of an independent state of Khalistan. That's been the goal of some, including a group that wrote to him. It was an inadvertent error by the Vice President's staff that led to that letter. But the United States' position on this is well-known. We continue to view Punjab as an integral part of India, and the Vice President firmly supports that policy.

The Threat of Khalistan

When, in the summer of 1992, I was beginning fieldwork in India, I had the opportunity to speak with the director of a prominent funding institution about my proposed research on the Sikh diaspora. He did not try to hide his antagonism. Sarcastically urging me to pursue funding elsewhere, he declared: "Why don't you wait until the Sikhs get their Khalistan, and then apply to them!" At the time, I had little interest in writing about Khalistan, and I was taken aback both by his presumption and by his unrestrained reproach. Frankly, in my naïveté, I had thought that, if not greeted warmly, my proposal would at least have been given a critical evaluation.

The director's hostility—an aggressive performativity that I have elsewhere and since met innumerable times—turned upon an equation of the Sikh diaspora with the fight for Khalistan. This equation must be examined further. There is, certainly, an important relation between the Sikh diaspora and Khalistan, and this book intends to illuminate the question of that relation. Here, however, I should distinguish my own argument from what we see in the director's hostility. I spelled this out in the introduction: (1) Emerging out of the enduring legacies of an "age of empire," the diaspora and the nation-state have been formed historically through a dialectical relation, a relation, in other words, that is mutually constitutive. (2) Khalistan, as we know it today, is a historical effect of the formation of this specific kind of relation between Sikh diaspora and the modern nation-state. (3) The diaspora and, more precisely, historical processes of *displacement* have constituted the "place of origin" referred to as the "homeland." As we have already seen in chapter 1—and this is a complexity that will find more elaboration in chapters 4 and 5—the homeland takes on different meanings, and different political significations, for Khalistanis and for those who do not support Khalistan. For some Sikhs the homeland is Punjab, for others India, and for others Khalistan. To return, then, to the problematic equation of the Sikh diaspora and the fight for Khalistan: simply put, not all Sikhs support Khalistan, nor is Khalistan an immediate consequence, or the singular creation, of the diaspora, as would be suggested by the director's hostility toward my proposed project on the Sikh diaspora.

It may be helpful, and more critically precise, to see the discourse that equates the Sikh diaspora with the fight for Khalistan as a nationalist discourse.[1] Consider how this sense of enmity toward the Sikh diaspora and Khalistan figures more generally into the Indian nation-state's procedures that generate notions of sovereignty and national integration. Just a few months before my interaction with the funding institution's director, the Lok Sabha ended its 11 March session of Parliament with a debate concerning the Bush administration's supposed support for Khalistanis.[2] More particularly, several parties denounced the U.S. government for "aiding and abetting" Khalistani activists in the United States. Such anxiety had been inspired by a letter that C. Gregg Petersmeyer, assistant to the president, sent on 12 February to Dr. Gurmit Singh Aulakh, president of the Council of Khalistan. It read: "Thank you for your letter regarding the plight of the Sikh people. It was a pleasure to meet you briefly on December 9, 1991. . . . As you may know, the Bush Administration continues to be very concerned about the international issue of Human Rights and urges all nations to recognize the Universal Declaration of Human Rights. I hope you will find the strength and courage to continue as an advocate of international human rights." Although Petersmeyer's letter made no mention of a separate Sikh state, Basudev Acharya, Communist Party of India-Marxist (CPI-M) found evidence of "direct U.S. intervention" in the internal affairs of India. Four days later, the *Times of India* ran an article, "The Cry for Khalistan" (1992), that reiterated Parliament's sense of threat and listed over ten Khalistani organizations located in five countries. The proliferation of these organizations unnerved the *Times*'s reporter, not least because dispersed Khalistanis seemed to be uniting under a single banner and receiving official support from several national governments: "The [Indian] government has no matching response to the Sikh separatist leaders and organizations galvanising abroad."

The Lok Sabha debate and the subsequent article in the *Times* reveal an important aspect of nationalist discourse on the Sikh diaspora and the fight for Khalistan. Put plainly, the idea of Khalistan, conjoined to that of the diaspora, generates anxiety. We can see this anxiety as a basic feature by which nationalist discourse constitutes the relation between the nation-state and Khalistan as a relation between an entity that is presumed to be real (India) and one presumed to be an illusion (Khalistan). More than anything else, such anxiety over the idea of Khalistan demonstrates how powerful, and indeed real, Khalistan has become, even — or perhaps especially — in the rejection of it as a reality. Like many supposed illusory nations, however, Khalistan confounds many who try to deal with it or its implications. For example, in 1992, after denouncing the U.S. government for "aiding and abetting" Khalistani activists, members of the Lok Sabha faced a quandary. They were divided about whether to issue a warning to the Bush administration. On the one hand, Petersmeyer's letter to the president of the Council of Khalistan was concerned with "the international issue of Human Rights." To oppose the letter would, in effect, position the Indian government awkwardly against international human rights at a time when the government had not yet set up a National Human Rights Commission (see chap. 3). On the other hand, in 1992, India was trying to establish better relations with the U.S. government, with the hope of being granted most-favored-nation status (which it achieved in 1995).

That the president of the council of Khalistan could solicit a letter of support from the assistant to the president of the United States demonstrated how unfamiliar the United States was with Indian politics. Or perhaps it attested to the ease with which a group claiming persecution might procure a perfunctory letter of appeasement. Indeed, five years later, in March 1997, the same incident was repeated (*Hindu,* 5 March 1997, international news briefs). The president of the Council of Khalistan solicited another letter, this time from Vice President Al Gore, this one referring to the "conflict *in* Khalistan" and articulating concern for the struggles of the Sikh people. In 1997, however, the government of India did not hesitate to reprimand the U.S. government: "The state of normality in Punjab, the high level of economic activity, the successful holding of two elections in the State Assembly, and elections to Parliament, clearly indicate that Khalistan exists only in the figment of some misguided imagination. The Government has forcefully conveyed to authorities in the US to desist from providing any encouragement, even though inadvertent, to such elements." The U.S. State Department and the U.S. ambassador to India immediately released an apology: "The US does not and has never supported the establishment of an independent state of Khalistan. . . . The US continues to view Punjab as an integral part of India. . . . The Vice-President firmly supports this policy."

This incident in 1997, and the ensuing interaction between the Indian and U.S. governments, tells us something else about the nationalist discourse on the Sikh diaspora and the fight for Khalistan. Support for Khalistan can jeopardize the relation between two nation-states, and the reason for this, again to put it plainly, is that the Indian nation-state regards the very idea of Khalistan as a threat. The character of this threat, however, is not self-evident.

Why is Khalistan a threat to the Indian nation-state? Three replies have become familiar to specialists in South Asia (Akbar 1996; Brass 1990; Chadda 1997; Das 1996; Jain 1995; Kapur [1986] 1987; Kaur 1992; Pettigrew 1995; Tambiah 1996): (1) A *Sikh* state is antithetical to the ideal of secularism, to which India has been committed since Independence. (2) The creation of a Sikh state would provide the basis for innumerable secessionist claims in the future, leading to further nightmares akin to the 1947 Partition. (3) Bordering on Pakistan, a proposed Sikh state would allow Pakistanis to proliferate its anti-India campaign. It would be simple to illustrate the problematic nature of these replies. How often, for example, have scholars questioned whether India is a secular state (van der Veer 1994)? The character and provenance of the threat of Khalistan remains unclear. To understand this threat, I offer a different set of propositions oriented toward illuminating the mutually constitutive relation of the diaspora and the nation-state. The history of Khalistan's threat, as I see it, with all its ruptures and continuities, has developed in connection with basic formations of space, time, and corporeality. Through these formations, the diaspora and the nation-state have become conditions of possibility for the emergence of each other. Likewise, they have become sites through which are played out and elaborated a multitude of discourses, disciplinary techniques, and regulatory procedures that posit the supposedly isolable nature of each.

One caveat to this latter proposition: although I refer in general terms to *the nation-state,* such generality is not sufficient to account for the complexity and heterogeneity of nation-states. Certainly, not all nation-states operate or are structured in the same way. The historical specificity of the relation between the Sikh diaspora and India must be distinguished from, for instance, the relation between the Sikh diaspora and Britain—a distinction that is made plain in the work of chapters 1, 4, and 5. This chapter, organized around the story of Khalistan between the 1930s and the 1990s, focuses on the dialectics of the diaspora and the Indian nation-state, considering most closely formations of space and temporality. In chapter 3, I discuss problems of temporality in more detail and demonstrate how a vicissitude of threat and promise has been configured and transformed by recent histories of violence that themselves reconstitute and gender the Sikh body. Chapter 4 returns to the British context.

The formation of a mutually constitutive relation between the Indian

nation-state and the Sikh diaspora emerges out of a different colonial genealogy than that discussed in the previous chapter, this time beginning within
debates over the division of the South Asian subcontinent after the departure
of the British.[3] The call for a Sikh homeland was first made in the 1930s,
addressed to the quickly dissolving empire. In the 1940s, as the possibility of
the creation of Pakistan and India loomed over South Asia, the call was
addressed more and more toward the leaders of the Muslim League and
Congress. Since those years, however, neither Khalistan's geographic designation nor its relation to the Indian nation-state has remained the same. Each
of these aspects of the genealogy must be related to the quality of threat that
Khalistan has taken on at the end of the twentieth century. I argue that this
threat must be understood in terms of three interrelated processes.[4] First,
since the 1970s, the fight for Khalistan has increasingly taken place on a
diasporic landscape. Second, equated in Indian nationalist discourse with the
diaspora, that is, a social formation that signifies a power that transcends the
nation-state, Khalistan represents to the Indian nation-state the very fragile
grounds of its, the nation-state's, own form. Third, in the creation of a relation between the Sikh diaspora and the Indian nation-state over the struggles
for a territory, two forms of *temporality* are brought into conflict. As I will
discuss, the time of the Indian nation comes into tension with, and is inter-
rupted by, what is called, in Punjabi, the *desh-kaal,* literally, the "nation/
country time," of the Sikh *qaum.*

From Azad Punjab to Khalistan

In the 1930s, when the San Francisco–based Ghadar movement was forming
a coalition with international communism (Juergensmeyer 1979), and when
the U.K.-based Indian Workers' Association was forming a coalition with the
India League (Dewitt 1969; Ramdin 1987) — both fighting for *Indian* independence — Sikh politicians (Akalis) in India were beginning to fight for
something very different. Against the nationalist ideology of a united India,
which called for all groups to set aside "communal" differences, the Shiromani Akali Dal Party of the 1930s rallied around the proposition of a Sikh
panth (community) that was separate from Hindus and Muslims. As the
possibility for Indian independence emerged in the 1930s, Akalis hoped to be
granted constitutional and territorial safeguards for the Punjabi language and
Sikh culture, history, and religion, as envisaged in the Guru Granth Sahib.
    The years between 1930 and 1947 were tumultuous. Heavily involved in

both world wars, yet taking a stand against British imperialism, many Sikhs found themselves in a difficult position, at once fighting for and against empire. Moreover, the initial 1930 and 1932 negotiations (the First and Second Round Table Conferences in London) outlining a scheme for a federal India in which Sikh Akalis, Muslims, and Congress leaders were participants, introduced separate electorates for Muslims, Sikhs, Indian Christians, Anglo-Indians, and untouchables. The effect of this was further to confound the position of the Akalis, who, in subsequent years, found themselves variously supporting the Congress Party of Nehru and Gandhi and pitted against it, vying and collaborating with the Muslim League for control over Punjab, and machinating strategies for attaining a "territorial readjustment" that might secure greater political leverage for a Sikh community in a new Punjab (Kaur 1992; Nayar 1966; Gopal Singh 1994; Harbans Singh [1983] 1985; Khushwant Singh [1989] 1991).

In 1940, the Muslim League passed its Lahore Resolution, demanding an independent state for Muslims, Pakistan, that would incorporate the whole of Punjab. In 1942, the British government accepted the principle of Pakistan, in what was called the Cripps Mission (after a formula presented by Sir Stafford Cripps) (Nayar 1966, 82). The Akalis viewed the Lahore Resolution and the Cripps Mission as a betrayal of the Sikhs and an attempt to usurp what, since the time of Maharaja Ranjit Singh, was historically Sikh territory. Drawing on both a well-known colonialist historiography of Sikh rule in Punjab and the results of colonial cartography and census practices, the Akalis sent a representation to Sir Stafford Cripps, arguing against the formation of Pakistan and refusing to surrender, once again, the land of the Sikhs:

> We are sure you know that the Punjab proper extended to the banks of the Jhelum, excluding the Jhelum and Multan districts, and the trans-Jhelum area was added by the conquests of Maharaja Ranjit Singh and retained by the British for administrative convenience. It would be altogether unjust to allow extraneous trans-Jhelum population which only accidentally came into the province to dominate the future of the Punjab proper. We give below the figures which abundantly prove our contention. . . . From the boundary of Delhi to the banks of the Ravi river the population is divided as follows: Muslims, 4,505,000; Sikhs and other non-Muslims, 7,064,600. To this may be added the population of the Sikh states of Patiala, Nabha, Jind, Kapurthala, and Faridkot, which is about 2,600,000. Of this the Muslims constitute barely 20 per cent and this reduces the

ratio of Muslim population still further. We do not wish to labour the point any further. We have lost all hope of receiving any consideration. We shall resist, however, by all possible means, separation of the Punjab from the all-India union. We shall never permit our motherland to be at the mercy of those who disown it. (Harbans Singh [1983] 1985, 299–300)

At the time of the Cripps Mission, the Congress Working Committee resolved that it "cannot think in terms of compelling the people of any territorial unit to remain in an Indian Union against their declared and established will" (Nayar 1966, 83). When it looked like the Congress Party would, indeed, support the principle involved in the formation of Pakistan, Akali leaders changed their tactics and began formulating what was known alternatively as the Azad Punjab (Free Punjab), Taqsim-i-Punjab (Division of the Punjab), Greater East Punjab, and Sikhistan. With this, they were hoping to find a way of gaining political leverage for the Sikh *panth,* a hope that was first introduced in 1932 at the Second Round Table Discussion in terms of a "territorial readjustment" of Punjab that would constitute the Sikhs as a reasonable voting power (Harbans Singh [1983] 1985; Khushwant Singh [1989] 1991). British leaders noted both the sensitivity of this debate and its seemingly reactionary base. But they were also concerned with disengaging themselves from responsibility for any conflicts that might result in further dividing the South Asian subcontinent along "communal" lines — as is demonstrated by the following exchange between Mr. Amery and the marquess of Linlithgow in letters of 20 August and 5 September 1942 (Mansergh 1977, 766–71, 910–13; see also Gurmit Singh 1989, 243, 248):

> Amery: Clearly however the more Pakistan is pressed the more the Sikhs are likely in their turn to press for a degree of autonomy sufficient to protect them from Muslim domination. Advocacy of an independent "Sikhdom" is I imagine bound sooner or later to give us trouble.

> Linlithgow: My judgement is . . . that the Sikhs though a nuisance well worth placating, are a relatively small nuisance. But there are not circumstances I can think of in which it would be practical politics to consider any sort of "Sikhistan." . . . The Hindus have made the mistake of taking Jinnah seriously about Pakistan, and as a result they have given substance to a shadow. For I am certain that if we did show the very slightest sign of taking "Sikhistan" seriously . . . not only should we aggravate communal

tension gravely in the Punjab, but we should never hear the end of it; and the Sikhs . . . find themselves occasionally in a position to wreck a scheme which would have gone down perfectly well with the major communities.

The British were not alone in regarding dubiously the proposal of a "Sikhdom" or a "Sikhistan." Sikh nationalists in India and abroad likewise condemned the idea, as did Congress leaders and the reporters in several Hindu daily newspapers (cf. Kaur 1992; Nayar 1966; Harbans Singh [1983] 1985; and Khushwant Singh [1989] 1991). Nevertheless, in June 1943, the Akali Dal issued a statement: "The Shiromani Akali Dal hereby declares that in the Azad Punjab the boundaries shall be fixed after taking into consideration the population, property, land revenue and historical traditions of each of the communities. . . . If the new demarcations are effected on the above-mentioned principles then the Azad Punjab shall comprise of Ambala, Jullundur, Lahore Divisions and out of the Multan Division Lyallpur district, some portion of Montgomery and Multan Districts. The Shiromani Akali Dal shall *make its demand* of these demarcations and shall fight for the same" (emphasis added; Nayar 1966, 84).

By 1946, three books were published that extended the idea of Azad Punjab further still, calling for the creation of a separate sovereign Sikh state, Khalistan: *Sikh Homeland* (Adhikari 1945), *The Idea of Sikh State* (Singh and Singh Gyani 1946), and *The Sikhs Demand Their Homeland* (Sadhu Swarup Singh 1946). Yet the Akali Dal still seemed torn. On the one hand, they argued in favor of a united India, although under specific conditions that granted Sikhs political leverage. On the other hand, despite their opposition to Pakistan, they insisted on the creation of a separate Sikh state in case Pakistan was conceded (Nayar 1966, 88; cf. Kaur 1992; Gopal Singh 1994; Harbans Singh [1983] 1985; Khushwant Singh [1989] 1991). The difficulty of maintaining this policy translated into a confusion in public statements. For example, in 1946, in a memorandum to the Cabinet Mission, the Akali Dal stated that it preferred a united India "because any partition of India would either bring the Sikh community under Muslim rule or split it into two halves" (Nayar 1966, 89).[5] Yet, on 22 March 1946, the Akali Dal passed an official resolution calling for the construction of a Sikh homeland: "The Sikh Panth demands the splitting up of the existing Province of Punjab . . . so as to constitute a separate Sikh state in those areas . . . in which the overwhelming part of the Sikh population is concentrated, and which, . . . its general character being distinctly Sikh, is also 'de facto' Sikh Homeland. . . . The above demand is the unconditional, *absolute and minimum demand* and political objective of the Sikh Panth as a whole. The Panth visualizes that this proposed state will be democratic in constitution and will have socialistic economic structure, with full protection of the culture and rights of minorities" (Gopal Singh 1994, 64).

That the demands of the Akalis changed should not be taken as a sign of capriciousness. Rather, it reflects the kinds of difficulties that characterized the negotiations for independence. During these years, despite the skepticism of the British, the demand for a Sikh homeland did not always seem unreasonable. Indeed, until at least April 1946, the British continued to ask the three main Akali leaders — Master Tara Singh, Sardar Gyani Kartar Singh, and Sardar Harnam Singh — whether they wanted a Khalistan, what the territorial demarcation of a Khalistan would be, and how a Khalistan would be related to a Pakistan and a Hindustan (see Mansergh 1977, 138–41). Likewise, the leaders of Congress had not developed a firm opposition to Khalistan. For example, Nehru's response to the Akali's pronouncement of its "minimum demand" suggests that, in 1946 at least, the idea of a Sikh homeland did not yet constitute a threat to the proposed Indian nation-state. This response has been resurrected many times over by present-day Khalistanis: "The brave Sikhs of Punjab are entitled to special consideration [and] I see nothing wrong in an area and a set up in the north wherein the Sikhs can also experience the glow of freedom" (Khushwant Singh [1989] 1991, 291; cf. Harbans Singh [1983] 1984).

Khalistan, however, or a Sikh homeland by any name, is a territory that was never created. This unrealized territory may be understood as a locality that a history of colonial rule made possible to imagine, and even measure, but impossible to institute. Akali leaders eventually agreed, in June 1947, to the Mountbatten Plan for the partition of the South Asian subcontinent into two dominions, India and Pakistan. Partition, which would divide the former Punjab in half, would also signify a new Sikh surrender. This surrender, however, was distinct from the colonial surrender of the nineteenth century — for the partition of Punjab, which became the condition of possibility for the formation of the Indian nation-state as well as Pakistan, generated a tremendous displacement, dispersing millions of Sikhs, most of whom left their homes in West Punjab for refugee camps both in what was then the Indian Punjab and in and around Delhi.

This pre-Partition genealogy of the Sikh homeland outlines the formation of a new political subject, the Sikh subject, characterized by a definitive quality, the demand. Through subjection to the juridical and extrajudicial procedures of the Indian nation-state since Partition, the Sikh subject has been repeatedly produced around the category *demand,* specifically, a demand articulated through an antagonistic relation to the Indian nation-state's repeated "answer" of *rashtriya ekta* (national integration). Demand, furthermore, has become a generalized trope within processes constitutive of knowledge of Sikh displacements, although today this may often be dissociated from its provenance in the pre-Partition fight for a homeland. This pre-Partition genealogy, however, does figure greatly into the reconstitution of a movement for Khalistan organized by Sikhs living *outside* India — but it would be at least twenty years before this crucial inversion occurred, an inversion by which the Akali narratives initially proposed in Punjab would be redeployed by diaspora Sikhs *against the Akalis* and by which the demand of the Sikh subject would come to constitute a form of performativity organized by diaspora Sikhs around the image of an independent and sovereign Sikh homeland.

Reconstituting Demand

Despite their formal acceptance of the terms for the partition of India, the Akalis continued to make demands for a Khalistan. Within the new Indian nation-state, however, that demand would not be entertained in the same way it had been under colonial rule. Sardar Vallabhai Patel, the "father of national integration," made the nation-state's position explicit in his address to a predominantly Sikh crowd in Patiala on 22 October 1947: "This is not the time to involve ourselves in needless disputes, *nor can we ever* afford to follow the mirage of many 'stans' like Khalistans and Sikhistans" (emphasis added; Patel 1949).

From 1947 on, the different productions of the "Sikh demand" took place within a new frame, within and against, that is, the process of national integration (*rashtriya ekta*). National integration, as formulated between 1947 and 1956, set a major precedent, not only for productions of the Sikh homeland and the Sikh subject, but also for productions of Indian sovereignty and territoriality. During these years, the category *national integration,* defined primarily by the Patel Scheme (after Sardar Vallabhai Patel), was constituted in terms of the emerging relation between particular territorial units and the production of a total territorial unit, the Indian nation-state.

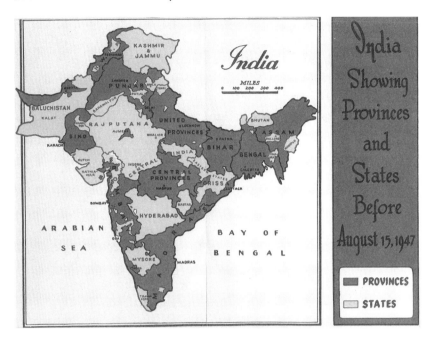

Fig. 5 The territory of India prior to 15 August 1947 (courtesy Bhai Vir Singh Sahitya Sadan Archives).

Specifically, the procedure of the Patel Scheme was (1) to shape and merge the Indian states into viable administrative units, (2) to position these units into what would become the constitutional structure, and (3) to constitute for India "a place in the world polity" (Patel 1949, 51).[6] In 1947, with the "lapse of British suzerainty," 552 Indian states regained their position prior to suzerainty (see figs. 5 and 6). Except for Hyderabad, Kashmir, Bahawalpur, Junagadh, and the North-Western Frontier States, all states acceded to the Dominion of India by 15 August 1947. Under the Patel Scheme, between 1948 and 1950, 216 former Indian states merged into contiguous Indian provinces (forming Part B in the First Schedule of the Constitution in relation to the other Indian provinces, referred to as Part A). Sixty-one states were converted into centrally administrative areas for administrative or strategic reasons (forming Part C in the First Schedule of the Constitution). Another 275 states merged into new viable units known as the Union of States (also under Part B). By 1956, with the Constitution (Seventh Amendment) Act and the States Reorganization Act, the number of states was reduced from twenty-seven to fourteen, and the process of national integra-

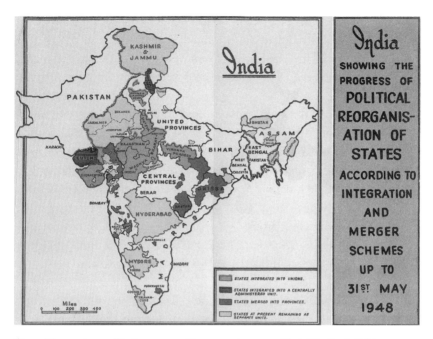

Fig. 6 The territory of India up to 31 May 1948 (courtesy Bhair Vir Singh Sahitya Sadan Archives).

tion was considered "culminated": with this act, the Indian states lost their former "identity," and, since the Part A, B, and C states were constituted as equivalents and placed under a single category, India supposedly became one integral, uniform, and "federal" entity.[7]

The integration of India under the Patel Scheme followed guidelines that were to be embodied in the Indian Constitution in 1949. This is an important point that must be spelled out. India was not created by states "agreeing" to give up their sovereignty to the one sovereignty of the Indian nation — rather, the creation of an independent Indian nation generated the problem of creating a constituency of states. The Indian Constitution and its amendments stipulate that (1) the Constitution does not offer any guarantee to the states against effecting their territorial integrity without their consent (i.e., the central government can redraw the map of its territory at any time by forming new states or by altering the boundaries of the states as they exist); (2) no state may change its own boundaries; (3) the central government may consider the pleas of an existing state or a group of people to change its boundaries or become a new state only under certain conditions of "consensus" and especially only in terms of a secular demand; and (4) advocacy of secession will not have the protection of the freedom of expression.

The histories of the Patel Scheme and of the discourses of the Indian Constitution have been indissolubly related to the creation of the Sikh demand; conversely, demand has emerged as a form of performativity constituting the Sikh subject through a subjection to Indian sovereignty and integrity. After Partition, the Akali Dal, the frequently changing and fragmenting "Sikh" political party of Punjab, continued to take on the authority of articulating demand—deeming itself "the very embodiment of the hopes and aspirations of the Sikh nation (*qaum*) and as such . . . fully entitled to its representation" (Gopal Singh 1994, 137). In the history of practices organized by the various Akali groups, the character of demand, and its negotiations with the Indian nation-state, has changed as different forms of protest emerged in other parts of India (e.g., Potti Sriramulu's "fast unto death" for the formation of Andhra Pradesh in 1952) and as the nation-state experienced international crises (e.g., the "Chinese incursion" in 1962, the "twenty-two-day war" with Pakistan in 1965). In the 1950s, the Akalis reintroduced the slogan *Azad Punjab,* which the central government had made illegal. This led to a confrontation in which, in May 1955, the police entered the Golden Temple, letting off tear gas and making arrests. In the 1960s, the Akalis organized several *morchas,* nonviolent protests volunteering imprisonment. Between 1960 and 1961, over fifty-seven thousand volunteers were arrested, and Fateh Singh went on a "fast unto death," which was halted when, on 9 January 1961, the government released the prisoners and said that it would look into Sikh demands.

During these years, up until 1966, the Akalis were led by Master Tara Singh, the politician who, with Gyani Kartar Singh, Sardar Harnam Singh, and others, was responsible for the pre-Partition call for Azad Punjab and Khalistan. The Akalis officially formulated the Sikh demand in terms of a desire for a Punjabi-speaking state, rather than a Sikh state, because the Constitution would recognize only a secular demand. Sardar Hukam Singh enunciated this position in the presidential address to the Sikh National Convention in 1950: "The cry of establishing Khalistan [is unwise]. . . . The demand for a Punjabi-speaking state is quite a legitimate demand; it is covered by the national policy and the national constitution" (*Presidential Address of the Sikh National Convention* 1950, 3). Nevertheless, Akali leaders, like Master Tara Singh, "made no secret of the fact that they had used the linguistic argument to gain a State in which the Sikhs would be in a majority and so be able to ensure the preservation of Sikh traditions and identity" (Khushwant Singh [1989] 1991, 310). As Master Tara Singh said in a 1948 interview: "I want the right of self-determination for the Panth in matters religious, social, and political. If to ask for the existence of the Panth is communalism, then I am a communalist" (Nayar 1966, 98). Claims to a Punjabi-speaking majority, clearly, were mobilized in an attempt to constitute a Sikh authority.

The quality of this authority revolved around a term that, before 1956, was central to the Akali constitution. The party's constitution stated: "Shiromani Akali Dal stands for the creation of an environment in which the Sikh national expression finds its full satisfaction" (Nayar 1966, 40). This notion of *Sikh national expression* was not the exact correlate of the *Sikh national feature* that I discussed in chapter 1. It was not, as Dalhousie presumed in 1854, a political feature separable from religious practice. In his book *Minority Politics in the Punjab* (written during the culmination of the struggles for a Punjabi Suba in 1966), Baldev Raj Nayar provides a clue in a segment of the Akali constitution that he leaves untranslated from the Punjabi. In the Akali constitution, the phrase *Sikh national expression* is associated with the Punjabi term *desh-kaal,* which literally means "country/nation time." According to Nayar, the linguistic argument for a Punjabi Suba was "considered to be merely a camouflage" for the goal of instituting a Sikh *desh-kaal* (pp. 323–24).

What was this *desh-kaal? Desh-kaal* is a category constituted in relation to a Khalsa discourse about the *inseparability* of religion and politics. Sikh historiography traces this combination of religion and politics to Guru Hargobind, the sixth Sikh guru (1606–44). In response to Mughal oppression, Guru Hargobind instituted a new Sikh symbolics around two swords that he bore, one called *miri,* the other *piri.* This was an important moment in the emergence of Sikh life and religious practice, signifying both a reaffirmation and an extension of the teachings of the first five gurus. McLeod (1989b) explains the significance of these two swords: "One sword designated a newly-assumed temporal role (*miri*) while the other represented the spiritual authority which he had inherited from his five successors" (p. 51). Nikky Singh (1993) explains the political significance of this moment: "Guru Hargobind's overt act of combining *miri* and *piri* marked an important development in the evolution of the Sikh community. . . . Since peaceful resistance to oppression had proved abortive, the Guru recognized recourse to the sword as a lawful alternative" (p. 118). Many Sikh scholars have argued that this doctrine reached its full expression during the time of Guru Gobind Singh, who re-created the *panth* in the form of the Khalsa by introducing the initiation ceremony of the *amritdhari*. I have already discussed in chapter 1 how the Khalsa initiation ceremony gives the *amritdhari* Sikh a new place of origin, abolishes the relevance of all prior forms of identity, and constitutes the masculinized body as a Sikh body. To this, I would add that the Khalsa initiation also inaugurates a new temporality, or *kaal,* that which is signified by the sword of *miri*. In relation to *Akal* (Timeless) or *Akal Purakh* (Timeless Being) — expressions for God — this *kaal* designates, not only the lived time of the *amritdhari,* but also its new origin and, with it, the Sikh *panth's* destiny or fate.

This formulation of the origin of the Sikh nation was rearticulated in 1946 by Sadhu Swarup Singh in his *The Sikhs Demand Their Homeland.* The form of rupture associated with this birth of a nation will play an important part in my subsequent discussion of the Indian nation-state's fantasy: "Historically this is not the first time that the [Sikh] nation has asked for a State. The demand was first sponsored by Guru Gobind Singh when he baptised the Sikhs and turned them into 'Singhs.' In fact the whole process of slow growth of full national consciousness was gone through in a shortened form by the spiritual contact with the great spiritual Alchemist. The slow transformation was replaced by a miraculously sudden metamorphosis, at such an amazing acceleration that seconds represented centuries. The Master uttered the magic formula, 'Henceforth you are a new man, forget your past race, caste and creed; forget your past self, you are reborn a member of a new nation.' Borrowing from biological nomenclature there was sudden creation as contrasted with evolution in the spiritual or national creation. A new species of nationality came into being" (50–51).

Master Tara Singh repeatedly argued that, for all true Sikhs, religion and politics were inseparable. By *true* Sikhs, he meant *amritdhari* Sikhs. *Desh-kaal* did not simply mean a Sikh territory or homeland. It reconstituted a historical discourse attributed to Guru Hargobind Singh and Guru Gobind Singh that revolved around the figure of the sword drawn in the face of an oppressive foe. And it redescribed a Sikh *panth* (community) as a Sikh *qaum* (nation/people). The *kaal* of *desh-kaal* was a temporality that not only was constituted as prior to the Indian nation-state's temporality, inaugurated on 15 August 1947, but also moved separately from the progressive movement of the nation-state's own destiny and teleology (of which more below).

The significance of this *desh-kaal* will play a major role in understanding the violent practices of torture, the representations of torture, and the diasporic reconstitutions of the homeland that have emerged through the transnational fight for Khalistan, which I discuss in chapters 3 and 5. In those chapters, I will draw out the problem of temporality and its relation to the body. For the moment, it is necessary only to indicate how this *desh-kaal* was elided because of the Indian nation-state's procedures involved in forming the Punjabi Suba. By enunciating a demand for a separate Sikh state, or even a Punjabi Suba, in terms of a *desh-kaal,* the Akali Dal required, on the one hand, that the Sikh *panth* identify with "its own" time and destiny and, on the other hand, that the nation-state recognize the distinct authority and sovereignty of the Sikh *panth* that was now *qaum.* This latter was something that the Indian nation-state could not do. Perhaps this is why the Akali Dal dropped the phrase *desh-kaal* from its constitution in 1956. After that, the party redoubled its efforts in a campaign demanding the Punjabi Suba, a demand that was constitutionally sanctioned and to which, when articulated strategically, the nation-state would, indeed, respond.

After the Radcliffe Award in 1947 — which demarcated "the boundaries of the two parts of the Punjab on the basis of ascertaining the contiguous majority areas of Muslims and non-Muslims" — between 1948 and 1966 the government of India officially redrew the map of Punjab three times because of, or in spite of, Akali "agitation" (Kirpal Singh 1991, 473–83). First, in 1948, a division was made between the state of Punjab and the Patiala and East Punjab States Union (PEPSU) — formed out of Patiala, Nabha, Jind, Faridkot, Kaparthala, Kalsia, Malerkotla, and Nalagarh. Second, on 1 November 1956, a new Punjab was formed by merging PEPSU with the rest of Punjab (Gursharan Singh 1991, 240).

On 1 November 1966, after ten years of conflicts with Sikhs over the creation of a Punjab Suba, Indira Gandhi made a grand proclamation: "Punjab takes new shape on 1st November as a predominantly Punjabi-speaking State. With the fulfillment of this aspiration, I trust the dynamic people of Punjab will apply themselves with renewed energy to the task of agricultural and industrial development. Their record since independence in building up a new economy has been a proud one" (Sharma 1995, 161). Thus, the map of Punjab would be redrawn once again, forming the Punjabi Suba — comprising Jullundur, Hoshiarpur, Ludhiana, Ferozepur, Amritsar, Patiala, Bhatinda, Kapurthala, and parts of Gurdaspur, Ambala, and Sangrur. Chandigarh, declared a union territory, was made the capital of *both* Punjab and the newly formed state of Haryana (fig. 7) (see Khushwant Singh [1989] 1991; see also Sharma 1995). With this territorial reorganization, the state of Pun-

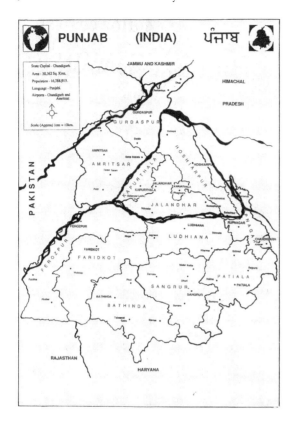

Fig. 7 Punjabi Suba
(courtesy Jas Kalra,
Punjabi Language
Development Board).

jab was reduced to an area of small proportions, compared to the post-Partition territory, which had extended from Lahul and Spiti, in the north, to Palwal, south of Delhi. The reduced territory, however, gave the Sikh population a bare majority, a little more than 50 percent, and this, in itself, seemed a triumph for Akalis. After the formation of the Punjabi Suba, what is the present-day Punjab, the Akali leader Sant Fateh Singh proclaimed what many Sikhs believed: "The Punjabi Suba is our last demand" (Kirpal Singh 1991, 308).

Khalistan in the Diaspora

Sant Fateh Singh's celebratory statement today sounds premature, to say the least. Indeed, with the production of the Punjabi Suba, there ensued a proliferation of new Sikh demands. These were of two sorts.

The first set of demands that issued forth after the formation of the Punjabi

Suba was still positioned within Indian domestic politics.[8] Responding to the failures of the Indian nation-state to comply fully with the terms for the setup of the new state as formulated in 1966, the Akali Party demanded the following: (1) Chandigarh was to be the capital of Punjab. (2) Punjabi-speaking areas contiguous to Punjab were to be brought into Punjab. (3) Control of the waters of the Sutlej, Ravi, and Beas Rivers was to be given to Punjab. None of these demands were fulfilled by the nation-state in 1966, nor have they been since (e.g., Chandigarh is still the shared capital of Punjab and Haryana).

A second set of demands was articulated by Jagjit Singh Chauhan, in England and America, and constituted in relation to Sikhs living around the world. This set of demands, however, was not concerned with redressing the failures of the Indian nation-state to fulfill the terms for the Punjab Suba. This was a call for the creation of Khalistan. Here, in other words, is the point that marks the entrance of the Sikh diaspora into the fight for Khalistan.

J. S. Chauhan had been an active member of the Akali Dal since 1955, when he was elected to the Legislative Assembly. He was reelected three times, and then also became deputy speaker and finance minister. In 1970, he was nominated by the Akali Dal to visit Canada, the United States, and the United Kingdom to procure support for the Akalis in India. He had already been familiar with the Sikh community in England, where he had lived briefly in the early 1950s. In England and North America in 1970 and 1971, he managed to organized a few campaigns to raise awareness of the Sikh cause.

The most important of these early campaigns resulted in a half-page advertisement in the international section of the *New York Times* on 12 October 1971 (see fig. 8). On the page, the text of the advertisement is separated from an article entitled "U.N. Reports a Cartographic Controversy" (which concerned a border dispute between Brunel and Sarawak) by a column in which is repeated:

ADVERTISEMENT   ADVERTISEMENT   ADVERTISEMENT

Chauhan's advertisement displays in boldface type:

Sat Sri Akal.
The Sikhs demand an independent state in India . . . the only guarantee for peace on the sub-continent.

The text begins:

Fig. 8 "The Sikhs Demand an Independent State" (from *New York Times*, 12 October 1971).

The world has been oblivious to the fate of 12 million Sikhs living under political domination in India and in constant fear of genocide. Another 6 million of us live abroad in alienation and exile waiting for the day of deliverance. But all of us, wherever we are, have struggled hard and in silence all these years for our political and cultural redemption. We are going to wait no more. Today we are launching the final crusade till victory is achieved. . . . Who are the Sikhs? We are a religious, ethnic, and cultural entity, distinct from the Hindus who rule India. We are a nation in our own right. We are a people with a sense of history. A people with a dream who have endured persecution and endless suffering at the hands of an intolerant, mercenary majority that rules India — the Hindus. We shall suffer no more.

What would this crusade for victory be? Although the headline states *"in India,"* the five sections of text make it clear that the demand is for "the establishment of a sovereign Sikh state." The advertisement proceeds through a narrative that is in some ways reminiscent of the call for Azad Punjab of 1942, at least initially. In telling of the British annexation of Punjab, it negates the official surrender of the Sikh Empire: "The British Government became caretaker of the independent Sikh state and gave an undertaking to the Sikhs for eventual self-determination." During colonial rule, the advertisement continues, "the Sikh people supported the British on the express understanding that when a final dispensation of power was made on the sub-continent, they would be treated as a nation in their own right." It then discusses Partition, claiming that, although an agreement was made that "the Sikhs shall have an area in which they will have complete freedom to shape their lives according to their beliefs" (this, clearly, referring to Nehru's 1946 statement), Sikhs were "denied self-determination." The advertisement then addresses the United Nations: "An independent Sikh State in Punjab is the only guarantee for peace in the sub-continent. This is a fact which the United Nations must recognise. An independent Sikh state will act as a buffer between India and Pakistan. It will be a restraining influence on the two countries. It is the only solution which can prevent a holocaust." It ends with a threat: "No power on earth can suppress the Sikhs. They are a people with a destiny. There will always be a Sikh nation. There always has been. Let the Hindu rulers in Delhi understand this because if they persist in their treachery and deceit, the sub-continent will be engulfed in a war the like of which the world has never seen."

Sikh historians for the most part regard the 1971 *New York Times* advertisement with disdain, dismissing Chauhan as a quack and an equivocator. They also point out that the advertisement had no effect and that, moreover, it was hardly noticed. Chauhan certainly did take it upon himself to invent or revise a Sikh history — filling its gaps with certainties, and simplifying its contradictions. And the article did fail to inspire world outrage. What I think is most important about the advertisement, however, is not its supposed inaccuracies or its rhetoric. Rather, this was the first time that the demand for a Sikh homeland was made to an audience other than the empire, the Indian nation-state, or Sikhs living in Punjab. The advertisement, moreover, did not circulate in a medium akin to the *Ghadr,* the *Khalsa Samachar,* or the *Khalsa Advocate* — the newspapers used in the late nineteenth century and the early twentieth to communicate debates about Sikh identity and Indian nationalism. Chauhan deployed what was at the time one of the most efficient global media to attempt to reach, no matter how unsuccessfully, a much broader audience. The *New York Times* advertisement signaled a moment of struggle — a new kind of struggle — in which Sikhs, no matter how few, sought to come into representation as a world community, a dispersed nation barred from its state. Diaspora Sikhs would return over and over again to this advertisement in years to come, repeating and supplementing it, constituting it as an originary text for the Khalistani movement (see chap. 5).

In 1971, however, the Akalis in India were fighting to secure the Punjabi Suba through forms of relations with the nation-state set down in the Constitution. They were demanding the fulfillment of the terms associated with the 1966 territorial adjustment of Punjab. In short, no matter how many Akalis may have wished for it, they could not be affiliated with a call for Khalistan. On his return to India, J. S. Chauhan was dismissed from the Akali Party. He eventually traveled back to England, where, in London, he lived in self-imposed exile, occasionally returning to India (although, in the 1990s, the Indian government denied him entrance). While Akalis in Punjab were struggling to procure the Punjabi Suba that they had envisioned in 1966, Chauhan continued to stage campaigns to raise awareness for the fight for Khalistan in India and Europe. He described his activities as revolutionary, inspired by Maharaja Duleep Singh, the Kukas, and the Singh Sabhas of the nineteenth century (Satinder Singh 1982, 153). Chauhan's endeavors, however, at least initially, were not militant or violent, but, if I may make a crude distinction, they were what might be called *symbolic.* This is an important point because, at least until 1984, diaspora Sikhs were not, for the most part, involved in a violent conflict with the Indian nation-state. As I will discuss further in chapter 3, the use of violence began in India in 1979 and was organized by militants *within* India. Chauhan, at least until 1984, tried to distance himself from the violent practices of militants (Satinder Singh 1982).

The symbolic acts staged in protests in India and England were of several sorts. In 1979, Chauhan attempted to install a radio transmitter in the Golden Temple in Amritsar, claiming that it was one of the Sikh demands that the Indian government had neglected: "The *Darbar Sahib* is a central religious place. Leave aside political, economic and social rights, the Sikhs don't even have religious rights! We wanted a powered transmitter to send the message of the *kirtans* to Sikhs all over the world" (Satinder Singh 1982, 80). On 12 April 1980, Chauhan returned again to India, where, in front of the Golden Temple in Amritsar, he announced his election as president of the National Council of Khalistan and appointed cabinet ministers and ambassadors to foreign countries (Khushwant Singh [1989] 1991, 412). In 1981, Chauhan, with others, printed and distributed a five-dollar Khalistani currency, Khalistani postage stamps, and Khalistani passports. The five-dollar note bore the image of the Golden Temple on one side and a portrait of Maharaja Ranjit Singh on the other, with the words *Republic of Khalistan.* The stamp bore only the number *30,* which referred to the *takas* that were in circulation during the reign of Maharaja Ranjit Singh.[9] At the same time, two very different maps of Khalistan were released to the Indian press, one resembling present-day Punjab, distributed in the *Indian Express* (see fig. 9), the other resembling the 1956 Punjab, distributed in the *Hindustan Times* (see fig. 10) (Gopal Singh 1994). A year later, an "All Parties Sikh Conference" held in London released another Khalistan map, displaying a territory that stretched from China in the northeast to the Arabian Sea in the southwest (see fig. 11) (Gopal Singh 1994). The constitution of Khalistan, distributed by Chauhan on 26 January 1984 in front of the Golden Temple in Amritsar, clarified the territory: "The present Punjabi speaking areas left out in Himachal, Haryana and Rajasthan shall be integral and shall constitute indivisible part of Khalistan. (The Khalsa Panth does not accept the present boundaries of Himachal, Haryana and Rajasthan as these were imposed upon it by Hindu imperialism at the time of creation of Punjabi Suba)" (Gopal Singh 1994, 110).

J. S. Chauhan was not alone in staging these symbolic acts of appropria-

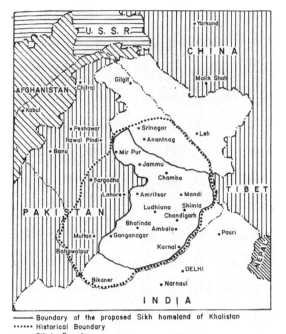

Boundary of the proposed Sikh homeland of Khalistan
••••• Historical Boundary
—·—·— Ethnic Boundary

Fig. 9 Map of Khalistan, *Indian Express*, 1981 (from Gopal Singh 1994, 68a).

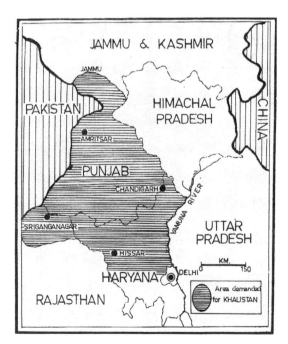

Fig. 10 Map of Khalistan, *Hindustan Times*, 1981 (from Gopal Singh 1994, 110a).

Fig. 11 Map of Khalistan, 1982 (from Gopal Singh 1994, 110b).

tion, some of which mimicked the procedures of the nation-state, some of which obviously played with the nation-state's absurdities. Increasingly, more wealthy Sikh men in North America and England became involved in one way or another. Several people claimed to be Khalistani heads of state or executors of the Khalistani government in exile, each generating his own series of demands. Several constitutions of Khalistan were published and distributed. After 1984, many of these groups became involved in military campaigns against the nation-state and in "terrorist" activities elsewhere. I discuss the effects of these violent practices in the following chapter. What is important for the present discussion is the way in which Khalistani practices of signification and knowledge production, formed in relation both to a Sikh diaspora and to the Indian nation-state, provided a basis for the constitution of the Sikh homeland as a new kind of threat to India and effectively made any representational practice concerned with Punjab and its inhabitants a potential threat. To illustrate this, I now turn to an episode that occurred in the 1990s. Although it was not enacted by Khalistanis, it could not escape being constituted as a threat to the Indian nation-state.

The Restricted Zone

Before the publication of the inaugural issue of the *International Journal of Punjab Studies* in January 1994, the editors of the journal, the world's most distinguished scholars of Sikh studies (cf. chap. 5), found themselves in an unforeseen conflict with certain representatives of the Indian nation-state. The journal was created to bring together scholarship, not just on the Indian and Pakistani Punjabs, but also on a "third Punjab" — defined as the "strong vibrant Punjabi diaspora that covers most of the developed world." The production of knowledge of these three Punjabs, however, was not, apparently, the point of conflict with the Indian government. Rather, the problem was the journal's cover design: a map of a pre-1947 Punjab, undivided. Sage Publications, in New Delhi, notified the journal's editors, in England, that they risked imprisonment for publishing and exporting such a map. The editors, wanting to hasten publication, redesigned the cover, which now displays an abstract series of lines indicating a global projection of the earth. How can it be that maps inspire such passion and become so politically charged?[10]

The conflict between the *International Journal of Punjab Studies* and the Indian nation-state may be understood in precise constitutional terms. On the basis of two constitutional acts directly concerned with the access of a national and international audience to forms of representations of India, the government of India has imposed specific prohibitions on the scale and contents of maps published in India.[11] For the most part, these interdictions concern the cartographic representation of what the Survey of India calls *the Restricted Zone*. The term refers, for the most part, to the entire periphery of the territory of India, including all of Jammu and Kashmir, all the northeast states, all the "outlying islands," and most of Punjab (see fig. 12).

The first prohibition on cartographic representation, drawing authority from the Official Secret Act (Act 19 of 1923), as amended by Act 24 of 1967, is extremely clear-cut.[12] Specifically, the government of India does not allow the publication of maps of the Restricted Zone on scales of 1 : 1 million or larger. Maps on acceptable scales cannot depict contours, trigonometric/spot heights, spherical lines/ticks or their values, mile/kilometer stone ticks, or "Vital Areas and Defence installations." In other words, these guidelines forbid any accurate cartographic representation of the Restricted Zone. According to the Official Secret Act, any transgression of these guidelines is "likely to affect the sovereignty and integrity of India." Thus, "a person guilty

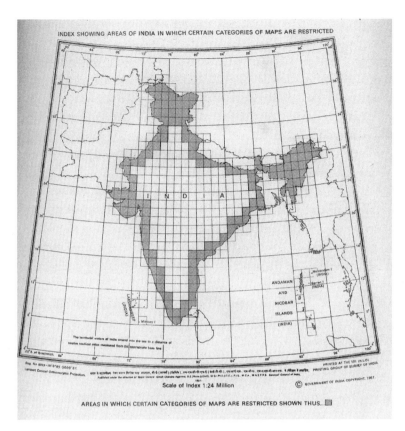

Fig. 12 The Restricted Zone (courtesy Survey of India).

of an offence under this section shall be punishable with imprisonment for a term which may extend to three years, or with fine, or with both."

While the guidelines of the second prohibition are less explicit, they cover a broader domain of possible transgressions. Section 2 of the Criminal Law Amendment Act (Act 23 of 1961) states: "Whoever by words either spoken or written, or by signs, or visible representation or otherwise, questions the territorial integrity or frontiers of India in a manner which is, or is likely to be prejudicial to the interests of the safety or security of India, shall be punishable with imprisonment for a term which may extend to three years, or with fine, or with both." The Survey of India clarifies the relation of this statement to cartography: the publication of any map "depicting *inaccurate* external boundaries and coast-lines of India tantamounts to questioning the territorial integrity of India."

The initial cover design of the *International Journal of Punjab Studies* did not depict the Restricted Zone on a large scale or display specific forms of representation that would be of interest only to cartographers or military institutions. The more likely point of conflict was that the map, which combined East and West Punjab, showed neither international nor interstate boundaries of the present day. In this case, the journal's apparent offense would have fallen under the jurisdiction of the Criminal Law Amendment Act: a problem of questioning the territorial integrity and frontiers of India by depicting, inaccurately, the Restricted Zone.

The interdiction that the *International Journal of Punjab Studies* nearly transgressed is not a small or an isolated matter. Nor is the production of representations of Punjab. Despite the generalizing nature of Indian constitutional law, the opposition of the Indian government to the journal's cover cannot be separated from the significance of a cover displaying an image of pre-1947 Punjab and indications of a "third Punjab." Overdetermined by histories of displacement, violence, and both Akali and Khalistani discourses about a separate Sikh identity, Punjab, being constituted as the Sikh homeland, has become an index not just for the Sikh but for the Sikh diaspora. By directing us, through the procedures of cartographic imagery, to the problem of questioning or affecting the sovereignty and territorial integrity of India, the *International Journal of Punjab Studies* opens up a more general problem about the significance of space and difference to the transformation of the threat of the Sikh homeland. It may now be appropriate to ask again, Why is the idea of a Sikh homeland a threat?

Cartographic technology and representation have become sites for the convergence of a variety of legal and juridical discourses about the sovereignty and integrity of India. The story of the *International Journal of Punjab Studies,* however, does not merely demonstrate how the juridicopolitical procedures of the Indian nation-state are preoccupied with certain minute details of producing and representing the space of the nation. The particular characteristic of the conflict also demonstrates the central importance of an *image* to the nation-state's historically specific processes of recognition and identification (Appadurai 1996a and b; Berlant 1991; Bhabha 1994; Lacan 1977a and b, [1975] 1991a, [1978] 1991b; Lefort [1978] 1986; Metz 1982; Mulvey 1989). As such, the conflict is also suggestive of a certain national anxiety emerging around repeated attempts to maintain the image of the nation-state as a totality.

One way to understand this anxiety is to consider how the Restricted Zone

has become a sign for the limit of Indian sovereignty and territorial integrity —
a limit in the double sense of marking the territorial border of Indian interiority / exteriority and signifying the instability and indeterminacy of the margins
of identity.[13] A limit, in short, represented by an emergent Sikh diaspora.

Punjab — not so much a state adjacent to a border as a "sensitive border
state"[14] — has repeatedly been the site for the constitution of this limit, at least
since Partition and the violent displacement of people between the new India
and Pakistan. The Restricted Zone of Punjab persistently conjures the nightmare of that first — what for many is regarded as an originary — rupture.
Punjab, as such, may be understood as a site for the production of a territorial
boundary susceptible to the "influx and infiltration" of "external forces" that,
according to the nation-state's alarmist discourse on Khalistani activism, "attempt to drive a wedge between communities in Punjab with a view to
bringing about a similar cleavage all over the country" (*Report of the National
Integration Committee* [hereafter *RNIC*], *7th April, 1986*). Within the terms of
this discourse, in the 1980s and 1990s, the external forces that seem to intrude
upon the territory of India have been of several kinds, most of which are
often alleged to be connected with the Khalistani movement: for example,
drug dealers, gunrunners, and spies trained or facilitated by Pakistan's Inter-
Services Intelligence (ISI), an agency that, helping external forces cross the
border, is continually perpetuating "designs to foment communal trouble"
(*RNIC, 7th April 1986*) within India.

Punjab, however, is also susceptible to "designs" that may or may not
necessitate crossing the border between Pakistan and India. These have definitive effects on the constitution of the people of Punjab as marginal, a people
living *within* a sensitive border. These designs come from what the *International Journal of Punjab Studies* calls *the third Punjab,* wherein, according to
LaBrack's (1989) popular formulation, the "Punjabi village remains the psychological 'homebase,' but increasingly 'home' is in England, Canada, or the
United States" (p. 289). The activities, after 1984, of Khalistani militants from
Canada or England, who, supposedly supported by the ISI, move through
Pakistan into Punjab, are only one, although an extremely significant, factor in
this formulation. Also of concern to the Indian nation-state are the "new patrons" living in the third Punjab who, through the medium of "remittances,"
have, most significantly since the mid-1970s, produced an "external economy"
for Indian Punjab (Helweg 1979; LaBrack 1989; Nayyar 1994). The effects of
this external economy mark the landscape of the Restricted Zone: in the form
of new houses and telecommunications technologies (Helweg 1979; LaBrack

1989), but also in the form of *gurdwaras* (Sikh temples), including, for example, an exact, to-scale replica in Matsuana of the Golden Temple.

What also marks the landscape of Punjab is the military presence of the state, which, in 1990, was counted as subject to one of the highest per capita police deployments in the world (see *RNIC, 11th April, 1990*). As we shall see in the following chapter, this military presence, which has marked the landscape of Punjab continually since 1983, redoubles the Sikh population's sense of marginality — even when Punjab is asked to take part in national rituals constitutive of the nation's center. For example, in March 1996, in preparation for the Lok Sabha elections, the Congress government "stepped up" its "surveillance," sending more than two hundred companies of paramilitary forces, seventy thousand policemen, and fifteen thousand Home Guards to the Restricted Zone of Punjab "to ensure free, fair, and peaceful polling" (*Hindu,* 22 March 1996). This "stepping up" of a military presence, this marking of the marginality of Punjab, came at a time when Congress was simultaneously reconstituting the possibility of articulating and "nationalizing" the "heterogeneity" of its population through the valorization of "unity in diversity." Consider the representation displayed and exhibited in Delhi (and in most national newspapers) prior to the 1996 elections during the celebration of the fiftieth anniversary of the United Nations: a map of India superimposed upon an Indian flag. The map, showing no internal boundaries, instead displays the Hindi words

EKTA
(*ekta,* "unity, identity, integration")
rajya -anek
(*rajya,* "state"; *-anek,* "not one, several")
dharam -anek
(*dharam,* "religion")
bhasha -anek
(*bhasha,* "language")
jati -anek
(*jati,* "caste")
granth -anek
(*granth,* "holy book")
PHIR BHI HAM SAB
EK
(*phir bhi ham sab ek,* "even then / still we are all one")[15]

THERE IS ONLY ONE INDIA
IT BELONOS TO ALL OF US

Fig. 13 National integration graffiti on India Gate, New Delhi, 1995 (photograph by Brian Keith Axel).

Identifications of national integration with a cartographic image of India's totality are certainly ubiquitous. For example, the two-rupee coin, perhaps the most widespread of these images, has, since 1982, displayed just such a map with the Hindi and English inscriptions *rashtriya ekta* and *national integration*. The 1982 ten-rupee coin, now out of circulation, displayed the same image; and the 1982 fifty-paise coin (still circulating) has a similar image.[16] (Consider also Congress graffiti, one of which, on the wall of a building adjacent to India Gate, has a map of India made up of human stick figures colored black, white, green, and red, with the words "There is only one India—It belonos [*sic*] to all of us" [see fig. 13].) Nevertheless, the 1996 commemorative logo is somewhat different: "Not one—one, not one—one, not one—one, not one—one." Addressed to the people of India and to the international community of the United Nations, the reiterative utterance of ambivalence refers to a history of practices by which, despite the singularity of the image of the people, the Indian nation-state has been compelled repeatedly to articulate and enforce sovereignty through the elaboration of an originary totality ("*still* we are all one").

The people of Punjab thus have been susceptible to, or constituted by, certain other "designs"—specifically, those of the Indian nation-state that, to use Appadurai's (1996a) words, have been involved in creating "a vast network of formal and informal techniques for the nationalization of all space considered to be under its sovereign authority" (p. 189). Within these techniques, however, the nation-state constitutes the Sikh people in terms of an image of unity in diversity just as the *indeterminacy* of the Sikh diaspora intrudes upon and disrupts the formations of power and knowledge productive of the nation-state's sovereignty and integrity.

Fantasy and Difference

The problem of unity in diversity indicates another way in which Sikh subjectification and the production of the threat of the Sikh homeland have been related to processes of national integration. Since the 1950s, procedures of national integration have changed in several ways. The first important change occurred with the culmination of the Patel Scheme in 1956. After that, despite the fact that the territories of India continued to be renegotiated, *rashtriya ekta* was reconstituted as a problem of citizenship and sovereignty — both of which are called into question by the Khalistani activism of the Sikh diaspora.

The repeated address of *ekta,* or integration/oneness, has been organized and mediated, historically, by the procedures of the National Integration Committee (NIC), the "sentinel of the nation's unity" (*RNIC, 7th April, 1986*). The NIC was initially convened by the Congress Working Committee in 1958, after the 1957 "Jabalpur riot," to address the emerging problem of "fissiparious tendencies in the body-politic of our country" (Aiyer 1961). The NIC has been reconstituted several times since 1958, and discourses on national integration have repeatedly identified the urgent problem of the "contemporary" social situation in India by reference to Nehru's words: "Let us the citizens of the Republic of India . . . bring about this synthesis, the integration of the Indian people . . . so that we might be welded into one, and made into one strong national unit, maintaining at the same time all our wonderful diversity" (Vyas 1993, 245). Nevertheless, since 1958, the category *national integration* has been reconfigured in different ways — referring first to problems of education and raising national consciousness, then, throughout the 1960s, to problems of valorizing unity and diversity. In the 1970s, the NIC turned its efforts to problems of "internal dangers": casteism, communalism, and separatism. Between 1983 and 1992, the activities of the NIC were almost exclusively concerned with the threat of Sikh "terrorists." Between 1992 and 1995, this obsession was tempered by concerns about Kashmir and Hindu fundamentalists.[17] The continual applicability of Nehru's narrative (references to which may be found in every NIC transcript) to these diverse historical processes illuminates how, in the discursive production of a "national unit," the nation is always emerging. The nation's emergence, however, is contingent on the *continual deferral* of national integration, of being "welded into one."

The juridical discourses of the Supreme Court have constituted the repeated problem encountered in producing the oneness of citizens as an unfortunate effect of forgetting: "We tend to forget that India is a one nation [*sic*] and we are all Indians first and Indians least [*sic*]" (Vyas 1993, 2). For Indira Gandhi, who often presided over the NIC between 1960 and 1984 (*RNIC, 1960*), this problem, which marked *citizens* as potential adversaries, emerged despite the fact that "there is a oneness among our people which has held us together" (*RNIC, 11 April, 1990*). That citizens may represent a threat to sovereignty and territorial integrity is, in Indira Gandhi's terms, the natural consequence of this slippage of social cohesion, which must be continually and persistently maintained.

In 1983, responding to more Akali demands and to the increasing threat of Sikh militancy, Indira Gandhi, through the NIC, instituted a fifteen-point program providing comprehensive instructions for the production of the "internal defence of India." In her formulation, which abstracted from the problem of Sikh conflicts to a more general problem of sovereignty and territoriality, the threat from *within* the nation is constituted as analogous to the threat from *without:* "National integration is the internal defence of the country — the domestic and civilian counterpart of the work of the Defence Services to safeguard the territorial integrity of the nation. . . . No country can ignore defence. It cannot assume that just because it is sovereign, its neighbors will not attack it. It has to be vigilant, ever careful not to lag behind technology. Similarly, we should not imagine that merely because we are free and have a Constitution, the social cohesion will remain on its own. It has to be guarded just as the nation's frontiers are guarded. But in one case we have the defence forces and in the other it has to be *all the citizens*" (emphasis added). Thus, the citizens of India take on a double role, constituted as both the subjects and the objects of civilian defense services, as both the forces of "internal defence" and potential/actual violators who cannot maintain "social cohesion" on their own. Not being able to maintain social cohesion, however, the citizen risks being constituted either as a representative of destructive forces deriving from a prior society or as a foreigner, or a combination of both.[18] This depiction of a prior or foreign threat, which I elaborate in a moment, cannot veil its antagonism to what I have referred to as the *deshkaal* of the Sikh *qaum*. Against the threat of internal/external destructive forces, the nation-state poses a scenic view of frontiers, figuring a horizon for the nation to take place, coupled with a progressive, linear temporality — over both of which *"all the citizens"* must be vigilant.

What I am trying to point out here is not so much Foucault's distinction of a juridical system that defines subjects according to universal norms and egalitarian principles yet veils the constitutive disciplinary mechanism (the "counter-law") that institutes "insuperable asymmetries" (Foucault 1977, 222–23). Nor am I indicating the "philosophical poverty and even incoherence" of the nation as an "imagined community" (Anderson 1991, 5). Rather, I cast my argument in terms of the *fantasy* of the nation-state.

Fantasy may be understood as a crucial aspect for the production of a peculiar and powerful *collective* subject, "the people of India" — and in this book I use the term *fantasy* exclusively to refer to this domain, that is, the historical formation of the nation-state.[19] As I have demonstrated in my discussion of national integration, part of the discourse of the nation-state constitutes the nation and the citizen as always emerging. The repetitive productions of the nation-state's emergence are inseparable from the reconstitution of what I am calling *fantasy,* which envisages the oneness of the people as both already constituted and just ahead. The working of fantasy marks the nation-state's sovereignty with a certain ambivalence the moment it emerges *as such* — for it illuminates the fictive, although no less "real," character of the nation-state's totality.

Let me put this somewhat differently. Not a "visual fallacy" or an "involuntary delusion," implying the separation of an internal world of "imagination" and an external world of "reality" (Burgin 1986; Laplanche and Pontalis [1964] 1986; Rose 1996), fantasy, rather, indicates the ambivalent processes that form the basis for identifications with an *image of a totality* (the nation-state). Played out in terms of the production of certain pleasures, desires, prohibitions, displacements, spatial scenes, and disjunctive temporalities, fantasy is central not only to the production of a national affect but also to the means by which, simultaneously, "national culture becomes local" and "local affiliations" are disrupted (Berlant 1991, 5, 49). In other words, national fantasy, at least in part, has much to do with the constitution of relations of identification that transform individuals and bodies into representations and representatives of an abstract entity. Following Lauren Berlant, we may see the fantasy of the nation-state as operating at the level of the "National Symbolic," a register of language and the law concerned at once with generating a national history, transforming individuals into citizens, and "interpellating the citizen within a symbolic nationalist context" (Berlant 1991, 225). Fantasy, indeed, underscores the points at which the register of the symbolic meets the constitution of the images of the people as one and territorial integrity, the "origins" for the people and territory, and the laws regulating practices that must represent their proposed sovereignty.

In the history of productions of the Indian nation-state, there have been several "myths of origin," so to speak, not all of which conjoin with an image of the people as one.[20] What I am interested in now is the way in which the image of the people as one, conflated with a notion of the origin of the nation, has marked out an anterior temporality that forms the precedent for explanations of national territory, sovereignty, and integrity, on the one hand, and regulatory practices, on the other. This, however, is not an instance of what Anderson (1991) has outlined. "The objective modernity of nations to the historian's eye," he argues, is opposed by "their subjective antiquity in the eyes of nationalists" (p. 5). In contrast, in the social and material process of the objectification under discussion here, the Indian nation-state is constituted as essentially *modern* — a process that, as we shall see, has specific implications in its relation to the Khalistani *desh-kaal* and the affiliation of the *amritdhari* Sikh (chaps. 3, 5).

There is an important historical reference for the nation-state's fantasy in the Indian Supreme Court's 1955 proclamation (in *Virendra Singh v. State of U.P.*) that dramatized the moment of emergence of the Indian nation-state (15 August 1947) as the *beginning* of a history marked by *surrender:*

> Every vestige of sovereignty was abandoned by the dominion of India and by the States and surrendered to the peoples of the land who through their representatives in the Constituent Assembly hammered out for themselves a new Constitution in which all are citizens in a new order having but one tie and owing but one allegiance, devotion, loyalty, fidelity to the sovereign, democratic Republic that is India. At one stroke territorial allegiance were wiped out and the past was obliterated except where expressly preserved, at one moment in time the new order was born and its allegiances springing from the same source, all grounded on the same basis, the sovereign will of the people of India with no class, no caste, no race, no creed, no distinction, no reservation. (quoted in Vyas 1993)

In the same way that Dumont ([1966] 1980) describes "structure" as a "form of organization that does not change [but] is replaced by another" (p. 219) or that Lévi-Strauss ([1950] 1987) explains that "language can only have arisen all at once" (p. 59), the fantasy of the new order of Indian sovereignty elaborates a *rupture* constituting identity "at one stroke," "at one moment in time."[21] This fantasy of a classless society with a singular, undifferentiated territory as its base constitutes the foundation of the nation-state's integrated totality, not as something known through "experience," but as an image that "transcends both individual experience and what is imagined" (Laplanche and Pontalis 1986, 16).

According to Dicey and his successors in constitutional law, a certain desire — the "desire for union" — is a prerequisite for the formation of a federal system (Basu 1995; Dicey 1927; Krishnamurti 1939; Sharma 1968).[22] Additionally, such a desire, embodied in the "opinion of the population of the territory" and "freely expressed by informed and democratic processes," is a definitive factor in the UN charter, which determines "whether a territory is or is not a territory whose people have not yet attained a full measure of self-government" (Sharma 1968, 202–3). There is an important connection between this desire and the fantasy of the nation-state. Laplanche and Pontalis (1973, [1964] 1986) have explained that, rather than being the object, fantasy is the setting for desire (Burgin 1986, 1992). In the Indian nation-state's fantasy, the fulfillment of desire — the formation of the sovereign subject — necessitates an annihilation that the fantasy setting elaborates as a series of images collapsed into a simultaneity. Within this setting, the moment of simultaneity (i.e., the founding moment for the nation-state's teleology) conjoins desire and pleasure with a certain violence: "at one moment in time," incommensurable territories, pasts, and social divisions are obliterated, and a new order is put in its place, one characterized by new forms of valorized difference that are commensurable.[23] In short, the moment of emergence of the nation-state portrays "the transformation of the individual from a member of a tribe or village or a caste or a creed or a language group to a citizen of India" (Vyas 1993, 83).

It is important to specify the quality of the space instituted by the new order of the nation-state. In dramatizing a rupture, a moment of separation that creates the land of the people, the fantasy of the nation-state, thus, produces not only the sovereign subject but also prior subjects of difference defined by prior territorial allegiances, all of which the space of the nation-state must contain. In other words, in the new order that the nation-state inaugurates, a spatial separation between a putative interior and exterior necessitates a *temporal* production of a "before," an anteriority, without which the telos of the nation-state cannot progress. The history of cartography has an important relation to this fantasy procedure, *producing time through space,* which I would like to indicate.

Cartography is of central importance to the nation-state's fantasy, not least because it signifies a valorized past that, within the fantasy, has been "expressly preserved" by the nation-state: "The Survey of India is the *national survey and mapping organization* of our country . . . and is *the oldest scientific department* of the Government of India. It was *set up in 1767*" (Survey of India 1995).[24] In other words, as a discipline and a form of knowledge, cartography represents a past, prior to the emergence of the new order, that, unlike the subjects and territories of prior difference, has the sanction of a fantasy that produces and selectively abolishes a past. But, apart from its position *within* the fantasy of the people as one, cartography has an important significance for the historical *constitution and reiteration* of that fantasy.

Cartography may be understood as a product and vehicle of colonial domination that not only transformed *land* into *territory* but also constituted colonial sovereignty (Cohn 1996). I would also argue that cartography seeks to produce and visualize knowledge of India as a whole constituted by innumerable differences. After 1947, as a technique of enumeration and visualization, cartography has been reconstituted as an apparatus of the nation-state's power, which is both "totalizing" and "individualizing" (Appadurai 1996b; Cohn 1996b). "Drawing up maps of zones and sub-zones of selected material traits which appear to have persisted over long historical periods" (Survey quoted in Cohn 1996b, 19), the Survey of India has been involved not only with the production of India's frontiers and boundaries (i.e., the Restricted Zone) but also with the constitution and visualization of the *internal* differentiation of India (i.e., "culture areas") in the most minute fashion: for example, village settlement patterns, types of cottages, staple diet, kinds of fats and oils used, kinds of oil presses, types of plows, types of husking implements, men's dress, foot gear, and bullock carts (Cohn 1996b). By generating and visualizing constitutive relations of people and places, cartography has not merely made possible a certain scopic recognition of the formative moment of the "new order" of territorial allegiance — that is, the sight, both pleasurable and violent, of subjectification. It has also constituted the anterior difference from which, in the fantasy of the people as one, the nation-state *must* emerge. In national cartography, the production of particular places, thus, also facilitates a displacement dramatized in the nation-state's fantasy as an abolition of places in the creation of a general place: the Dominion of India.

Constituted in the interrelated procedures of cartography and fantasy, the ambivalence of the valorized "unity in diversity" of the people of India may be understood to turn upon a complex relation of *diversity* to *difference,* illuminating how *difference* cannot be singularized. Two forms of difference are at stake here. First of all, for *unity in diversity,* the subject of difference appears as an individual transformed into a citizen. This is the subject constituted *at the time of* the advent of the new order of the nation-state. And this is the form of difference addressed, for example, in the 1996 campaign of *rashtriya ekta* that repeated ". . . rajya-anek, dharam-anek, . . . jati-anek, . . . PHIR BHI HAM SAB EK." In distinction, the emergence of the nation-state necessitates the production, and valorization, of the ontological integrity of particular subjects of difference *before* the imposition of the law of the nation (i.e., states, religions, castes). To use Nehru's words, so that the Republic of India "might be welded into one," there must be a prior form of difference to be "surrendered" and "obliterated" — difference typified by formerly incommensurable categories of class, caste, race, creed, and territorial allegiance. In the next chapter, we shall see how the *amritdhari* body has been constituted as a dangerous sign of this form of difference. In other words, the desire for union is based on a prior disunion of difference, insofar as the constitution of the sovereignty and integrity of the nation-state is signified by the absence of incommensurable difference established through surrender, annihilation, and integration.[25] Difference thus has become both a valued sign of democracy and the basic premise legitimizing the use of violence within a given territory. Prior difference, as incommensurable, as that which was there before the nation-state, stands against the egalitarian desires of representational democracy. The return of difference as incommensurable, and particularly as an irruption into the present of an incommensurable past, is always a potential threat that the nation-state must perpetually negotiate. And, with these negotiations, the nation-state repeatedly conjures the fantasy moment of national rupture.

The Questioning Subject

In the light of these processes of fantasy and national integration, the threat of Khalistan takes on a very different quality. The threat is not merely a problem of territoriality. It is the threat of a particular subject: the Sikh subject constituted by national subjectification as both diasporic and demanding, both "within" and "without" the nation-state. It is a threat of a particular kind of difference that works its way through cartographic practice and visual representations of territory (as we shall see in the next chapter, this difference also works its way through the body). This threat, constituted between the nation-state and a Sikh diaspora, now poses a new problem for the nation-state. The image of a Khalistan, and of the demanding Sikh subject, makes reference to a territorial dispute — certainly. But the image of a Khalistan also acts as a mirror in which is reflected the fragile basis of the nation-state's form, a form that revolves not only around the image of territorial integrity but also around the tensions of a national belonging and temporality. One effect of a history of conflicts that has made the fight for Khalistan a diasporic struggle is that Punjab now has become one site for staging this symbolic scene of reflection. What exactly is this reflection? Let me return to the problem of the Restricted Zone to clarify this process.

Recall the prohibitions articulated in the Official Secret Act and the Criminal Law Amendment Act: basically, *anyone* who publishes or circulates a map that is "likely to affect the sovereignty and integrity of India" or that "tantamounts to *questioning* the territorial integrity of India" shall be "punishable with imprisonment for a term which may extend to three years, or with fine, or with both." What is crucial here is that the juridicopolitical procedures of the Indian nation-state produce a specific kind of subject of difference — what I will call *the questioning subject* — characterized by a discursivity and addressivity that may be facilitated by, and embodied in, maps or visual representations in general. These juridicopolitical procedures also constitute a sovereign subject — the people of India — the extent and limit of which are circumscribed by the Indian territoriality. Additionally, these procedures position the questioning subject in a specific antagonistic relation with the sovereignty and territorial integrity of India, a relation that maps mediate.

The anxiety of the Indian nation-state, formed around this antagonistic relation, may be described in functional terms. The questioning subject signifies a lack of knowledge or respect for the sovereignty and integrity of India — thus taking on the quality of an outsider, the enemy of the people, whose appearance calls forth the imperative of the Indian nation-state anxiously to elaborate and enforce its sovereignty and integrity. In turn, the opposition of the questioning subject and the sovereign subject qualifies the space of the Indian nation-state as an interiority that serves as the base from which relations with a threatening exteriority can be managed. The Restricted Zone demands careful surveillance because, being contiguous with an international boundary, the periphery of the nation-state's territory may constitute a conjunction as well as a disjunction between interiority and exteriority. In this sense, the Restricted Zone is like the older cartographic category *the frontier zone,* of which East (1965) has written: "In the frontier zone are usually concentrated a large part of the defensive forces and strongholds of the state, for the purpose of the frontier is to create a strong frame within which the state may exercise its functions and its citizens may live in security" (p. 98). In this functional conceptualization, cartography thus serves to delimit and visualize (or conceal for purposes of defense) the division of a spatial totality into values of interiority and exteriority.

Let me take this formulation a few steps further to show how a functional reading belies an ambivalence in the form of the nation-state. The authority of the government of India, which determines what is "likely to affect the sovereignty and integrity of India" or what "tantamounts to questioning the territorial integrity of India," is based, in part, on the power to produce and evaluate forms of knowledge as "accurate" or "inaccurate." The enactment of this authority, however, is characterized by a certain vicissitude. On the one hand, it is illegal to produce and circulate a detailed map of the Restricted Zone (i.e., an accurate map) yet, on the other hand, it is illegal to produce and circulate a map of the Restricted Zone that inaccurately depicts the boundaries and frontiers of India.

These two mutually incompatible assertions have certain implications that must be spelled out. If the rules were followed, it would be impossible for any institution, other than the Survey of India (for the exclusive use of the government of India), to make a map of India. What makes the questioning subject a threat is not only that it expressed doubt or incomprehension regarding the territorial integrity of India but also that it produces and circulates maps that display this particular lack. What makes the Survey of India a protectorate of sovereignty and integrity is that it *does not* make available any detailed or large-scale maps of the Restricted Zone. This suggests, however, that it is impossible for the people of India, who embody ultimate sovereignty, to "know" or "represent" precisely the constitution and limits of their (India's) sovereignty and integrity. Caught between an inability to know and an inability to represent, the people of India are put in a troubling place. Not having the ability to know or represent their own sovereignty or integrity, the people of India, it would seem, now appear to take on the qualities that define the alterity of the questioning subject.[26] Unable to know what the sovereign subject must know, are the people of India not bound to question the integrity of India? And is the Indian nation-state thus not bound to regard the people of India, simultaneously, with varying degrees of affection and hostility? This ambivalence, by which the part that stands in for the whole paradoxically reintroduces the figure of the Other, is indicative of a definitive split that interrupts any notion of spatial totality, exteriority, or interiority — not *between* "state apparatus" and society, or between (national) self and (external) other (or, for that matter, between the demanding Sikh diaspora and the nation), but *within* the sovereign subject.

We may now begin to understand how the threat of Khalistan stems from, and has become an operative term in, the mutually constitutive relation between the diaspora and the nation-state — a topic that I continue to investigate in the following chapters. Threat here is generated in terms of ambivalence and demand. The ambivalence of the sovereign subject signifies the impossibility of the nation-state's totality. This ambivalence, moreover, is reflected in every enunciation of a diasporic demand for Khalistan. The demanding subject of the Sikh diaspora, in other words, holds up to the nation-state the visage of the citizen as a questioning subject, laying bare the incomplete quality of a process of national integration that is always deferred. In relation to this ambivalence, demand has become a category of repetition (responding to the nation-state's repeated address of national integration), a form of performativity (which resists being encompassed within the sovereignty and integrity of the Indian people), and a means for constructing authority in terms of a temporality (*desh-kaal*) incommensurable with the nation-state.

Anticipating the inquiry of the following chapter, let me draw out the effects of this conjunction of repetition, performativity, and temporality. Demand has also become a means of reproducing Sikh subjectification to the Indian nation-state in terms of a teleology of violence. Most explanations of the emergence of the fight for Khalistan rely on this posited teleology, an example of which is offered by the historical writings of Khushwant Singh ([1989] 1991): "The government's tardiness in resolving these basic issues gave the Akalis grounds to charge it of being anti-Sikh. They [the Akalis] assiduously cultivated a discrimination complex and kept adding to their list of demands. On its part, the central government, instead of conceding what was legitimately asked for, adopted delaying tactics thus forcing the Akalis to launch a succession of passive resistance movements which often escalated into violence. Alongside the peaceful *morchas* grew terrorism which the police countered by brutal repression, often killing innocent people in staged encounters and torturing suspects. Police methods proved counterproductive and brought more recruits to terrorist groups" (p. 342).

Reinserting the demand of this Sikh subject into this teleological formulation is troublesome. Positioned within this teleology, demand facilitates an elision of the indeterminacy of both the Sikh diaspora and the nation-state. The category *demand* is separated from both the productivity of the nation-state and the negotiation of incommensurable difference. In other words, a singular, intentional, and autonomous agency is attributed to the category *demand*. Consequently, *demand* is constituted as a *coherent* category of marginality and irreverence in relation to the putative totality of the nation-state's sovereignty and integrity. Not only does this legitimize and give reason to state violence, a classic problem of modernist ideology elaborated by Weber and others, but it also positions violence as an *effect* of difference that the fantasy of the nation-state qualifies as either prior or foreign.[27] Understood in this way, as a sign of incommensurable *and* totalized difference, demand necessitates violent retaliation and makes violence reasonable. State violence, then, comes to be explained as an inevitable result of demand, rather than a constituent element in the production of difference.

This agonistic movement between diaspora and nation-state, which I characterize as a fantastic struggle between two putatively totalized sovereign subjects anxiously encountering the impossibility of their totality, has had a specific effect in the production of one kind of violent practice that has emerged in India since 1983. I discuss this violent practice, the torture of Sikhs by the Indian police, in the following chapter. One way to address the complexities and grotesqueries of torture is through a careful examination of the vicissitudes of identification around ambivalence. In this chapter, I have demonstrated that this formation of ambivalence is a historically specific precipitate of colonial and postcolonial struggles over both the territoriality and the temporality of sovereignty. Within these struggles, the formation of a Sikh diaspora around the call for Khalistan has added a particular dimension to both Sikh subjectification and the nationhood of India. In short, Khalistan has made the negotiation of ambivalence a matter of life and death.

3 : the tortured body

The physical pain [of torture] is so incontestably real that it seems to confer its quality of "incontestable reality" on that power that has brought it into being. It is, of course, precisely because the reality of that power is so highly contestable, the regime so unstable, that torture is being used.

— Elaine Scarry, *The Body in Pain*

The body accumulates political biographies, a multiplicity of subject positions, as it passes in and out of various political technologies of commensuration.

— Allen Feldman, *Formations of Violence*

A Historical Anthropology of Violence

With the transformation of the fight for Khalistan into a transnational struggle, the historical anthropology of the Sikh diaspora turns into a historical anthropology of violence. My argument may be stated simply: as a lived reality, as a cultural-historical artifact, and as an ever present possibility, violence today is the common thread constantly creating and transforming the relations that make up the Sikh diaspora. It is also the condition of possibility for any study of the Sikh diaspora (see chap. 5). Fostering dreams of a homeland or of emancipation, resettling the ground from which that dream may emerge, violence engenders both a threat to the diaspora and a promise.

Am I suggesting that violence is *the* necessary condition for the production of any diaspora or any homeland? No. Notions of *violence, diaspora,* and *homeland* have taken on a universal appeal and applicability. These are each extremely slippery terms that all too easily have found their way into the narratives of one people or another. The story of the Sikh diaspora may, however, teach us something about the very historicity of those terms and the specific problems of producing a "people" (Balibar 1991). It may also teach us something about the production of knowledge and its limits.

Khalistan provides a general frame for these lessons. It is clear that I do not see Khalistan, or the Sikh demand, as a cause of violence. As my discussion in the previous chapter demonstrates, I understand Khalistan to be a historical effect, emerging out of the dialectics of diaspora and nation-state. As such, however, Khalistan, particularly since 1984, has become a *constitutive* aspect of the Sikh diaspora and a social formation around which categories of violence have come to be organized. The present chapter explores an extreme instance. I look at the relation between one kind of violence, the torture of Sikhs by the police in India, and one kind of cultural representation of that violence, the reproduction and circulation of images of tortured bodies on the Internet. Drawing out my discussions in chapter 1 of the gendered total body into a more complex analysis, and extending the problematic of chapter 2, my purpose is now doubled. I look more closely at the constitution of Khalistan as a threat to the Indian nation-state, pursuing further the contradictory elements of temporality. Additionally, I hope to show that a political artifact of state violence—the tortured body—has become a central element in processes of a diasporic imaginary, designating a fundamental, and historically specific, aspect of not just Sikh subjectification but the formation of diaspora itself.

A genealogy of this violence may be traced variously to nineteenth-century processes of surrender and constructions of the Sikh body or to twentieth-century processes of national integration and constructions of the Sikh homeland. But the history of torture since the 1980s indicates how difficult it may be to argue for a simple continuity between all these phenomena. Torture attests to, and effectively transforms, the specificity of what *can* be known as violence, of what can be understood as the effectivity of violence, and of what conclusions may be drawn about how violence is inflected differently by race, class, gender, and sexuality. In short, the history of torture in the fight for Khalistan demonstrates that violence is not a transhistorical category. What it *does not* show, however, is a singular Sikh community or a unified Sikh subject built upon a singular wound.[1] Rather, a discussion of torture contributes to an understanding of how manifold forms of violence, wounding, and cultural representation have come together, however tenuously, in the transnational production and discursive translation of Sikhs as a *persecuted* people. Let me briefly indicate the history in which these processes have developed.

As I have noted in chapter 2, the Sikh diaspora became involved in struggles for Khalistan only after 1971 and increasingly after 1984. Between 1979 and 1984, violent, militant activity was organized within Punjab around the charismatic figure of Sant Jarnail Singh Bhindranwale and enacted by individuals affiliated with the Damdami Taksal and the Akhand Kirtni Jatha, two Sikh religious institutions in Punjab. What is often identified as the beginning of violence in Punjab, however, apparently had nothing to do with a call for Khalistan but rather with a conflict between a religious group called the Nirankaris and members of the Damdami Taksal and the Akhand Kirtni Jatha. The Akhand Kirtni Jatha and the Nirankaris traced their origins back to revolutionary figures of the nineteenth century. The former was founded by Bhai Randhir Singh (1878–1961), who was a major figure in the Ghadar movement and, indeed, had been imprisoned by the British for his militant activities (cf. chap. 1; Mahmood 1996, 78). In the 1970s, this group was committed to the Khalsa identity, inaugurated by Guru Gobind Singh in 1699, and saw *kirtan* (religious songs of the Guru Granth Sahib) as a path toward spiritual enlightenment. The Nirankaris, a Sikh "sect," was founded by Baba Dayal Das (1783–1855) in the nineteenth century as a reaction to what was considered the corrupt religious practices of both Sikhs and Hindus (McLeod 1984; Oberoi 1994; Khushwant Singh [1989] 1991). Baba Dayal Das condemned the popular practice of idol worship and, from a particular reading of the Sikh Guru Granth Sahib, promulgated a religious teaching based on the notion of God as formless, *nirankar*. His followers regarded him as a guru, and it was because of this, and because of his critique of the religious practices of others, that he met with opposition from both Hindu Brahmins and Khalsa Sikhs (for whom the line of living gurus ended with Guru Gobind). On 13 April 1978, the Akhand Kirtni Jatha, with the Dam Dami Taksal, protested a procession of Nirankaris in Amritsar because of the Nirankari "heresy" (i.e., that they worshiped a living guru, who was indeed in the procession). It is unclear exactly who provoked whom, but, in the ensuing melee, fifteen men were killed, thirteen Khalsa Sikhs and two Nirankaris (Akbar 1996; Mahmood 1996; Khushwant Singh 1992; Tully and Jacob 1985).

Although at the time this conflict may have seemed a marginal dispute, historians and journalists point out that it heralded the emergence of Bhindranwale into the public sphere of Indian political life. Many argue that Bhindranwale was a puppet created by Congress in order to counter the threat of the Akali Dal, which, in 1978, had taken the majority in the Punjab government after several years of Congress Party rule (1971–77). It may very well be true that the Congress Party did support and encourage Bhindranwale initially. But he eventually turned on both Congress and the Akali Dal.

Bhindranwale toured Punjab, Haryana, and Delhi as both a preacher and a political critic. He encouraged Sikhs to undergo the Khalsa initiation at the same time as he decried the Akalis for their seeming impotence and lashed out against the central government's neglect to fulfill its promises to the people of Punjab (i.e., the river waters, Punjabi-speaking territories, and Chandigarh; see chap. 2). However, perhaps Bhindranwale's most significant effect was on the people of the Punjabi countryside: "There used to be baptism ceremonies at least twice a month, later more often as Santji [Bhindranwale] became more popular. Sometimes thousands of people would get baptised in a single day. Santji's impact was so powerful, people would rush forward not only to get baptized but to join him, to give up their homes and their families to stay with him" (Mahmood 1996, 78). In Bhindranwale's view, moreover, and crucially, *amritdharis* should also be *shastridharis* (weapon bearers) to protect themselves from the Hindu hegemony that threatened the livelihood of Sikhs. When asked whether he supported a demand for Khalistan, Bhindranwale would often answer: "I am neither in favour of it nor against it. If they give it to us, we won't reject it" (Tully and Jacob 1985, 92). Despite this public ambivalence, Bhindranwale drew a wide range of people to his side who clearly could provide support for strategic militant action, including two retired major-generals from the Indian army, Jaswant Singh Bhullar and Shabeg Singh (who was a hero of the 1971 Pakistan War).

The period between 1979 and 1984 has been well documented by many scholars, and there is no need to repeat the details of their studies here.[2] What is important is to stress how, within a few short years, Punjab was thrown into extreme turmoil in a way that was unprecedented. This violence transformed the image of the Sikh and its relation to the nation-state. As more and more robberies, murders, and hijackings occurred, and as more and more Indian military troops were moved into Punjab, Sikhs, and particularly *amritdhari* Sikh men, came to be regarded by many as national enemies. This was a difficult problem because, indeed, many Sikh men held powerful positions in the central government and the military. The president of India, Giani Zail Singh, was a Sikh, and some of the most important military units were constituted by exclusively Sikh regiments. The poignancy and convolution of identifying the Sikh as a national enemy was made particularly apparent when, during the 1983 Asian Games in New Delhi, Harayana chief minister Bhajan Lal ordered police to stop all Sikhs coming into New Delhi. Among those who were stopped, searched, and humiliated were retired Indian air force chief marshal Arjun Singh, former foreign minister of India Swaran Singh, and Lieutenant General Jagjit Singh Auroroa (who had accepted the surrender of Pakistan after the 1971 war).

Bhindranwale and his followers took up residence in the Golden Temple complex in Amritsar. In the face of escalating violence between the police and Bhindranwale's followers, in June 1984, as is well known, Indira Gandhi ordered an armed attack, "Operation Bluestar," on the Golden Temple complex. The assault was commanded by Major-General Kuldip Singh Brar, himself a Sikh from the same area of Punjab as Bhindranwale. On 3 June, all rail, bus, and air services were stopped in Punjab, and telephone lines were cut. In addition to the Golden Temple complex, thirty-seven other Sikh temples around Punjab were surrounded. All journalists were forced to leave Amritsar, and a communications blackout was enforced. Between 5 and 6 June, what the Indian army encountered was a well-armed defense by militants who used the Golden Temple complex, and its labyrinthine underground passages, to their own advantage against soldiers who were unfamiliar with the temple's layout. The army was also not prepared to do battle against Chinese rocket-propelled antitank grenade launchers. After incurring many casualties, and after damaging several buildings and destroying a library with extremely valuable relics of Sikh history, the army took control of the temple. The body of Bhindranwale was found with hundreds of others, most of whom had been pilgrims (Tully and Jacob 1985).

When news of the attack on the Golden Temple complex was leaked, Sikhs in India and around the world were outraged and protested loudly. On 7 June, 600 soldiers of the Ninth Battalion of the Sikh regiment in Ganganagar, near the Pakistani border, mutinied, as did 1,461 soldiers in the Sikh Regimental Centre at Ramgarh in Bihar. In the United Kingdom, on 7 June, several Sikh men attempted an attack on the Indian High Commission in London (*The Times,* 11 June 1984, 26A). On 8 June, a protest in Liverpool ended in violent confrontations between Sikh men and the police (*The Times,* 9 June 1984, 32F). And, on 10 June, more than 25,000 Sikhs marched from Hyde Park to India House, where, in the presence of several thousand London police officers, Jagjit Singh Chauhan, the president of Khalistan in London, and other "Sikh leaders" burned an effigy of Indira Gandhi and attempted to give a petition of protest to the Indian High Commission (*The Times*, 11 June 1984, 26A). Similar protests were enacted throughout the summer in North America and other parts of Europe and Asia. Also, Jagjit Singh Chauhan "prophesied" on the BBC that Indira Gandhi would be killed (and some say that he offered a reward for her assassination) (Tully and Jacob 1985, 211).

The months between June and October 1984 witnessed a proliferation of confusion in the relations between the Indian nation-state and the Sikh diaspora. Throughout this period, however, Indira Gandhi maintained that her actions were correct and that they were to be interpreted, not as against Sikhs, but as against terrorists. As a demonstration of this position, she refused, against the advice of many, to dismiss her bodyguards, who were Sikh. For many observers, this seems to have been a perfect example of both her stubbornness and her underestimation of the humiliation inflicted on Sikhs by Operation Bluestar. On 31 October 1984, Indira Gandhi was assassinated by her two Sikh bodyguards. In the days following, thousands of Sikhs were targeted and murdered by "rioters" in Delhi and different parts of North India (it was later "discovered" that these rioters were organized by members of the Congress Party).

Reconsidering the production of the threat of Khalistan, my account of torture in this chapter is most concerned with the period between 1983 and 1998. During this period, Sikh men in Punjab were routinely and indiscriminately rounded up by police, refused access to lawyers, held in unacknowledged detention, tortured, and often killed (Kumar, Muktsar, and Singh 1999). Despite the widespread and enduring practice of these violations, the relations among torture, its documentation by international human rights groups, and its circulation and reproduction on the Internet have been radically disjunct. The disjunction between the practice of torture and the production of knowledge about torture has several complicated facets. Owing to a series of constitutional acts passed since 1983 (see below), very few cases against police officers have been heard in the Indian courts. Most of the cases that have been heard have been either dismissed or stalled in the courts. Likewise, the Indian government has denied international human rights groups wishing to monitor conditions access to prisons in Punjab (nevertheless, a few groups have investigated the problems without permission). It also, until recently, denied that torture was systematically practiced by the police. In 1993, an international campaign forced the Indian government to establish the National Human Rights Commission (NHRC). In its 1995–96 report, the NHRC recorded 444 deaths in detention, many a result of torture. On 17 October 1997, India signed the United Nations Convention against Torture.[3] Nevertheless, Amnesty International, among other human rights groups and independent scholars, attests that the police continue routinely and systematically to use torture as a form of "interrogation." In crude statistical terms, the peak of these violent practices in Punjab occurred between 1992 and 1993. The circulation of images of tortured Sikhs, along with the proliferation of discourses on torture, on the Internet, however, did not begin until, at the earliest, 1996. Most of the web sites are now used by Khalistani activists both to record the continuing practice of torture and to generate a visual and narrative archive of past atrocities against Sikhs.[4]

Doubt and Certainty

The complex relations and gaps between torture and its representation ensure that the production of knowledge about the torture of Sikhs in Punjab is infused with vicissitudes of doubt — doubt about what "really" happened or about what can be known. As we saw in chapter 1, the problem of doubt was intrinsic to colonialist processes of Sikh subjectification. Reconstituted in a historically specific form, doubt, in ways that are abundantly clear, has become repositioned within discourses of both the Indian nation-state and Khalistanis. But it also configures other domains of social practice. I encountered a common example after I gave a presentation on torture in 1997. I was accosted by an anthropologist, herself from India, who told me that she, in her own words, was aware that "there was a problem with the Sikhs." Her family, self-identified Hindus, had regularly worshiped at a Sikh *gurdwara* (temple). However, they stopped going in 1984 because, as she said, Sikhs were "causing trouble." Nevertheless, against her understanding of troublesome Sikhs, she could not believe what I was saying about police brutality. Very emotionally, she asked how the government could commit such atrocities against its own people, no matter how "troubled" they were.[5]

Embodied in the formation of doubt — doubt about what can be known — is, obviously, a *desire* to know. This, too, is very common. One day, a student — a young Sikh man brought up in the United States — came to my class on the Sikh diaspora. Having been only five years old in 1984 when Operation Bluestar occurred, and having been sheltered by his parents from the struggles of Sikhs in Punjab, he now — nineteen years old and in college — wanted desperately to know if I could tell him anything about the Delhi riots or the attack on the Golden Temple, about which he had only ever heard vague allusions. I suggested a series of books in which he might be interested and asked if he had ever used the Internet to search out Sikh-related sites, to which he responded: "Yeah, but aren't all of those Khalistani web sites? How can I trust them?"

My own introduction to Sikhs and Sikhism, when I was nineteen, was itself configured by formations of doubt and desire. This was in 1987, three years after Operation Bluestar — about which I knew nothing when I traveled to India to spend a year studying in Banaras, Uttar Pradesh. In Banaras, I had intended to study languages and music. Serendipitously, I came across a Sikh *gurdwara.* Fascinated by what I saw, and welcomed by the people I met, I decided to conduct research on *sabad kirtan,* the holy music of the Sikhs. I was introduced to a man named Gyani-ji who became my mentor. I spent most days speaking with him and the *ragis* (trained *kirtan* musicians) in the *gurdwara,* where Gyani-ji maintained a peculiar position of authority. He was clearly treated with great respect by all the Sikhs who knew him. He, indeed, was *giani* (a knowledgeable one), and he wore all the signs of a venerable Sikh man: turban, long flowing beard, and a sword. Outside the *gurdwara,* however, my Banarasi friends treated him coldly and regarded him with suspicion. They asked me why I wanted to study the Sikhs, and they warned me to be careful about Gyani-ji.

Gyani-ji was from Amritsar in Punjab, where, apparently, he had left his family. In Banaras, he lived alone, and he appeared to me to be a loner, distracted. He told me very little about his life, and I, whether out of politeness or otherwise, failed to ask. It was clear that Gyani-ji desperately wanted me to know about Sikhism but that he did not want me to know about Punjab. I was aware that, as a *videshi* (foreigner), I was not allowed to travel to Punjab because there was some "trouble." I surmised that Gyani-ji's melancholic character may have had something to do with that "trouble" in Punjab, but I had no idea exactly what the trouble was. I had met many a *videshi* who had "snuck into Punjab," reporting that they had not come across any signs of "trouble." Gyani-ji and Punjab both remained enigmatic to me.

At the time, I had a beard and long hair, which I wore tied up in a bun and sometimes covered with a bandana, especially when I was in the *gurdwara* (see fig. 14). I also spoke Punjabi (although haltingly). Many people assumed that I was Sikh. This led to some interesting situations, some humorous, but some confusing. Although I had a great respect for Sikhism, I

Fig. 14 Gyani-ji and Brian Keith Axel (photograph by Kenneth Axel).

had no desire to "be Sikh." My Hindi teacher used to joke with me by introducing me to people as "Brian Singh." More disturbingly, I noticed that when I was with Gyani-ji in public places we were often watched closely by the police, who passed by or who came and sat near us. I found their stares more than a little intimidating. One night, my last night in Banaras, when Gyani-ji took me to the train station, we were harassed by the police, who refused to let me into the compartment for which I had purchased a ticket. Gyani-ji, a large man with a loud voice, pushed his way through with my bags and sat me down. He hugged me quickly and, saying "Sat Sri Akal" (the name of the Eternal One is true), jumped back onto the platform and into the crowd. I sat in my berth wondering what had caused the conflict. Was it something I had done, or Gyani-ji? Was it merely because I was with Gyani-ji, or he with me?

In the years after 1987, I have returned to Banaras several times, but I have never been able to find Gyani-ji again to speak with him about those troubling episodes or about the specter of violence that haunted my time with him. I can only guess about him from what I have learned since from the stories of other Sikh men like him (i.e., that he, too, was running from the fear and anxiety of a very real threat to his life in Punjab). In retrospect, I see that I was privileged to learn from Gyani-ji, not just about *sabad kirtan* or

Sikhism or the Punjabi language, but about the intimate relations of recognition and objectification that can be inscribed on the body. I did not understand this at the time, but my long hair and beard had allowed me to enter, no matter how ambiguously or briefly, into a coded relation whereby I was acted toward as if I were a Sikh. Thus, I also learned that the social formations of doubt and desire that inflect knowledge of violence against Sikhs are often countered by a *certainty*—a certainty about how to identify Sikh men.

The possibility that a fragment of a body, indeed, merely a profile, may provide the basis for processes of identification is a crucial problem in the history of both torture and the transnational circulation of images of torture. Writing of political violence in Northern Ireland, Allen Feldman (1991) has commented: "The body accumulates political biographies, a multiplicity of subject positions, as it passes in and out of political technologies of commensuration" (p. 9). In the entangled histories of the Khalistani movement and Sikh subjectification, this process of accumulation has been interwoven with a historical politics of gender and a politicization of religion, in effect constituting an iconic relation between images of the Sikh man and the Sikh homeland. But it is not just any male Sikh body that has become the privileged site for this coding of iconicity and violence. It is the *amritdhari* body that bears the burden of these significations. It is the *amritdhari* body that has become the object of doubt, desire, and certainty.

In chapter 1, I discussed several possible historical trajectories for understanding the constitution of the *amritdhari* body and its relation to the royal image of the *sardar:* the founding of Khalsa initiation attributed to Guru Gobind Singh, in 1699; the visual representations of the late eighteenth- and early nineteenth-century *sardars;* and the nineteenth-century surrender of Maharaja Duleep Singh. I also indicated how other scholars have attributed the valorization of the *amritdhari* body to either British military recruitment practices or the Singh Sabha movement of the late nineteenth century.

These various histories of disciplinary and religious practice seem to have ensured that the Five Ks and the turban have been set up as necessary aspects for the identification of the Sikh subject. J. P. S. Uberoi articulates this generalized formation of certainty when (lacking a historical critique of colonialism or the Singh Sabha) he argues, first, that the "meaning and effect [of the Five Ks] are made even clearer by the custom of the Sikh turban" and, second, that "we can establish a definite connection between the five symbols of Sikhism, and its *whole nature as a religion*" (emphasis added; Uberoi 1996, 12, 17). I will have occasion, throughout this chapter and in chapter 5, to return to Uberoi's formulation. Within the historical context of the fight for Khalistan and practices of torture, the distinction that Uberoi draws is not so clear and must be radically transformed to have any significance at all. The history of violence in Punjab provides another basis, and a different set of terms, for Sikh subject formation and the constitution and gendering of the *amritdhari* body. I now turn to this historical problem.

Torture and the Nation-State

At the convoluted intersection of Indian military operations and Sikh insurgency, what has resulted since the early 1980s is the implementation in India of a set of official and unofficial policies that has effectively positioned Punjab and its inhabitants, not just in the Restricted Zone, but within a point of marginality beyond the reach of national and international human rights jurisdiction.[6] Although many scholars might argue that Operation Bluestar inaugurated Punjab into a zone of marginality, I would suggest a different historical moment: 6 October 1983, when Indira Gandhi simultaneously imposed president's rule in Punjab and created a new ordinance declaring parts of the state "disturbed." Since that day, parts of Punjab, and at times Punjab as a whole, have been subject to this ordinance on several occasions (and almost continually between 1984 and 1994). According to the Punjab Disturbed Areas Act, the declaration of Punjab, or any part of Punjab, as a disturbed area "empowers any commissioned officer, warrant officer, non-commissioned officer or any other person of equivalent rank in the armed forces to, after giving such due warning as *he may consider necessary,* fire upon or otherwise use force, *even to the causing of death,* against any person who is acting in contravention of *any law*" (emphasis added).[7] Under this act also, "no Court shall take cognizance of any offense alleged to have been committed by any member of the Armed forces of the Union while acting *or purporting to act* in the discharge of his official duty" (emphasis added; Punjab Disturbed Areas Act cited in Asia Watch 1991, 42).

With such license, police officials in Punjab have developed and institutionalized a system of identification to facilitate the elimination of anyone suspected of insurgency. In July 1984, the signposts of this system were set down in *Batchit,* the official magazine circulated throughout the army to keep soldiers informed of current operations: "Any knowledge of the Amritdharis who are dangerous people and pledged to commit murder, arson and acts of terrorism should immediately be brought to the notice of authorities. These people may appear harmless from outside but they are basically committed to terrorism. In the interest of all of us, their identity and whereabouts must always be disclosed" (Tully and Jacob 1985, 204; see also Citizens for Democracy 1986, 29). By the 1990s, it seems, the identification of *amritdharis* as terrorists had become well established in police discourse. As one police officer stated: "A profile was developed of who was considered to be anti-government and pro-Khalistan. Based on that profile, young Sikh men between the ages of eighteen and forty, who have long beards and wear turbans, are considered to be pro-Khalistan" (HRW/PHR 1994, 20).[8] Positioned within this tautological discourse, men with beards and turbans (i.e., *amritdhari* Sikhs) became the object of obsessive knowledge production and arbitrary violence. As another police officer said: "Police authorities maintain intelligence on all *amritdhari* Sikhs in a given geographical area. They are routinely characterized as supporters of the movement for an independent state known as Khalistan. When the police have no suspect for a case or need to arrest someone in order to fulfill an arrest quota, *amritdhari* Sikhs are often the victims" (HRW/PHR 1994, 20).

Within this system of knowledge production, identification, and disciplinary strategy, what is at stake is not a relation between the nation-state and a *person acting in contravention of any law.* Rather, it is a relation between the nation-state and the body, or, more precisely, a *fragment* of a body reconstituted and gendered by the action of state violence. What is definitive is a profile, the *amritdhari* head and face. This disciplinary practice transforms the significance of the total *amritdhari* body as depicted by Uberoi (1996) and others. From the standpoint of police surveillance, as is clear, it is not necessarily the visual display of the Five Ks so much as it is the male body with a beard and turban that has come to facilitate the identification of the individual with the collectivity. This identification, however, does not draw a correlation between the gendered *amritdhari* body and the whole of the Sikh religion. Rather, the fragment of the gendered body is related to certain isolated aspects of the *Rahit Maryada*'s discourse on the origin of the Khalsa. I discuss how this concerns formations of temporality at the end of this section of the chapter. But, most immediately, we may see how the *Rahit Maryada*'s foundation of the religion in Punjab takes on a particular importance. Extending my analysis in chapter 2, we may see that Punjab—a "disturbed area" *and* a "sensitive border state"—and the fragment of the *amritdhari* body have come to pose a challenge to the putative "incontestable reality" (Scarry 1985, 27) of the Indian nation-state's sovereignty and territoriality.

In other words, this body fragment is reconstituted by nationalist pedagogy as the a priori signifier of an act of contravention characterized by a particular extraterritorial and antinational desire (this, needless to say, despite the many, and often conflicting, "meanings" that Sikhs attribute to the religious practices and political affiliations of the *amritdhari*). Marked by contravention and desire, the *amritdhari* body, moreover, is marked with a price. On 30 August 1989, the director general of police for Punjab issued an order promising rewards of Rs 25,000 and higher for the arrest "or liquidation" of alleged militants. "Such rewards may go as high as Rs. 100,000 for killing 'hard-core' terrorists; unofficially the payoff may be Rs. 2 million" (Asia Watch 1991, 40). The Supreme Court repealed this order on 21 February 1991. Nevertheless, the bounty system continues to be used without official sanction. This intricate bounty system employs not only official police and military troops but also convicts and *amritdhari* Sikhs who, usually through violent coercion, have been "turned" (i.e., into collaborators with the nation-state). The constitution of what might be called *the turned subject* insinuates a division into the gendered system of identification of *amritdhari* Sikhs. The popular yet derogatory term for these people is *billi,* "cat" — itself, in Punjabi, a gendered category that feminizes the turned subject and, feminizing it, both enables and dishonors it. While the *billi* may act under cover, it is also acting as a traitor.

This process of gendering may be related to formations of invisibility and silence that infuse the "Sikh Woman" as subject (Nikky Singh 1993). Many scholars have discussed the long history, characterized by many shifts and determinations, of the valorization of the *amritdhari,* whether being identified as a key instance of the "martial races" or being praised as exemplary postcolonial laborers (Cohn 1996; Fox 1988; Oberoi 1994; Nikky Singh 1993). In chapter 1, I have supplemented these discussions with an analysis of the production and consumption of visual representations of Maharaja Duleep Singh. These works, resonating with the work of Feldman (1991), Malkki (1995), and Appadurai (1998), demonstrate how "earlier colonial efforts to reduce the complex social differences among local ethnic groups to a simple taxonomy of racial-physical signs" (Appadurai 1998, 9) have been reconstituted in the post-Independence period. These various historical formations have formed the condition of possibility for developing a system of identification by which the Indian army has come to target *amritdhari* Sikh men. Such a system recognizes the category of *Sikh woman,* not as an agent of violence and terror, but as the potential bearer of terrorist children, a vessel of sexual reproduction that exists *only* in relation to the *amritdhari* man. Women are the alibi in this discourse, passively bearing forward the reproductive cycle, the schema of genealogy, and the temporal community initiated by the male. This latter, indeed, is the identification of the Sikh woman that many Khalistani and Sikh studies discourses also reiterate (Jakobsh 1996; Mahmood 1996; McLeod 1996; Nikky Singh 1993). Whether as a citizen of India or of Khalistan, the Sikh woman, in these terms, can exist only as a heterosexual *object,* generating a tacit, taken-for-granted form of sexuality. Nevertheless, in Punjab, this system of identification has also made it possible for women covertly to contribute to the militant cause: not only providing shelter to men, but also transferring arms and, at times, taking part in armed attacks (Mahmood 1996). Nikky Singh (1993) has argued that the position of women is "narrowly circumscribed in Sikh society" (p. 254). The history of torture since 1983 provides a specification of this formulation. Within practices of torture, the Sikh woman does not exist only within a functional and static relation to the *amritdhari* man. More precisely, the Sikh woman's susceptibility to narrow circumscription and shifting forms of exclusion and indeterminacy is constituted in relations, both dynamic and ambiguous, to the *amritdhari* and the *billi.*[9]

Through these shifting relations of gender construction and sexual differentiation—and, in part, masking them—the historical development of India's counterinsurgency procedures have facilitated and encouraged the apprehension, torture, and murder of almost any Sikh man with a beard and turban, a routine of violence that has become as banal for the police as it is terrifying for its victims.[10] Against the abstracting or "disincorporating" (Lefort [1978] 1986) procedures of nationalist pedagogy, the practice of this violence, a putative redemption of national life, constitutes the Sikh subject in disruptive moments of radical and horrific embodiment. Consider the testimony of two survivors of torture. The first is from a young man from Punjab apprehended in 1984 while protesting the Indian army's attack on the Golden Temple in Amritsar:

> Many of them [the police] were drunk. . . . When I got inside they caught me by the arms and legs and put me down on the floor. . . . They were joking around. "Just tell us. How do you want to be tortured?" They

thought they were having fun. . . . They caught me on my right leg and my left leg and spread them wide, wide like this. And they were hitting me at the same time. . . . Then they got electric shocks and gave me shocks on the private parts of my body. They shocked me and shocked me. They said, "We will finish you. Now you can't be married, you can't produce any more terrorists. . . ." This continued on and on. I couldn't feel anything on most of my body anymore. But they tried to find out where I still felt pain and then they would hit me there. (Mahmood 1996, 39–40)

The second testimony is from Atinder Pal Singh, arrested in September 1988 in Patiala and released in July 1990 after being elected to Parliament in November 1989:

My both legs were stretched out and on both sides of my sexual organs, on the joints of my thighs, a boiling wax was poured. . . . The police people inserted red chilies inside my rectum . . . [saying,] "This will now give you trouble for the rest of your life. . . ." [Then they] applied petroleum on my anus. This gave me such a bitter pain I was yearning for my death to come. . . . During the course of my torture I was unclothed and kept completely naked. (Asia Watch 1991, 148)

Torture enacted by state representatives in a democratic society, torture enacted on the body of a nation's own citizen: such practices, in their grotesquerie, make explicit the ambivalent structures of citizenship and belonging, disrupting any possible recognition of the individual body within the totalizing image of the nation's body politic. Yet these practices also seemingly literalize the nation-state's fantasy of the inaugural moment of interpellation by which the individual is transformed into a citizen (see chap. 2). Through torture, the nation-state constitutes and comes into deliberate contact with citizens, a contact that is based on a specific knowledge of the body and its manifold zones of sensitivity ("they tried to find out where I still felt pain and then they would hit me there"), forcing an extreme identification with the body in pain (Scarry 1985). Indeed, this process of subject formation and individuation pursues the citizen through pain and affect. Terror becomes a strategy of state effectivity that constitutes the tortured citizen, which is, after all, subject to the nation-state's regulatory procedures, as *evidence* of the very actuality of the nation-state's existence.

When it is the police, however, who submit citizens to this transgression, torture cannot be understood in terms of Foucault's (1978, 50) model of monarchy: that is, a public ceremony displaying the infinite power of the sovereign for all to see.[11] Most often situated out of public sight, detainees, denied access to the outside world, are held in "unacknowledged detention," spaces of secrecy that themselves should be differentiated: police stations, private houses, abandoned fields. This clandestine landscape of torture is inhabited by a multitude of torturers who share the secret, although widely generalized, techniques of "interrogation." There is a repetitive and systematic quality to these techniques that suggests specialist training. One recent study, reiterating the conclusions of several international human rights organizations, detailed seven categories of torture that have been standardized throughout Punjab: (1) leg stretching, by which the legs of the victim are spread out widely in opposite directions from the groin area; (2) use of the "roller," by which a heavy wooden roller is placed on and moved back and forth over the thighs of the victim; (3) suspension, by which the victim is hung from the ceiling by cords; (4) electric shock to the genitals; (5) beating the soles of the feet; (6) burning; and (7) "other" (e.g., water torture, threatened torture, chili peppers shoved in anus).[12]

The possibility that these forms of torture may have as their goal the disclosure of information is, of course, absurd. The practice of torture is antagonistic to notions of cause and effect. It confounds the significance of means and ends (Benjamin 1978). Against the secrecy, standardization, and certainty of torture techniques, there is a proliferation of a diffuse uncertainty made palpable in the repetitive contact between body and body. Will torture eradicate terrorism? Will the tortured victim reveal the skeleton of a Khalistani conspiracy? Will the torture leave scars on the body? Will the victim be turned? Will he produce more terrorists? Torture, then, in the modern nation-state is a private scene of perverse intimacy, seduction, and eroticism, constituting not the power relation of sovereign to law but the state's anxiety and desire.

During torture, as has been demonstrated by many survivor testimonies, the value of the *amritdhari* head is transformed. Often the first act during an arrest is to cast off the detainee's turban, effectively enforcing a *surrender* by deploying the symbolics of Sikh history against the victim. After this surrender, the genitals and anus become the foci of taunts ("this will give you trouble for the rest of your life") and violation ("they shocked me and shocked me"; "the police people inserted red chilies inside my rectum"). This regulatory practice and this transvaluation produce a particular body that is made intelligible, both *as citizen* and *as Sikh,* through sexuality, itself an effect of regulatory force. What I am suggesting is that torture in Punjab is a practice of repeated and violent circumscription that not only produces bodies as sexed but also produces a form of sexual differentiation. This is a form of differentiation, not between putatively prediscursive categories of male and female, but between a national-normative sexuality (which may perpetuate the nation's community) and an antinational perversity (which interrupts that community), both of which the pathologized and criminalized Sikh subject, as citizen, embodies. Torture constitutes national-normative sexuality as a fundamental modality of citizen production in relation to an antinational perversity that postulates sex as a cause, not only of sexual experience, but also of subversive behavior and extraterritorial desire ("now you can't be *married*, you can't *produce* any more terrorists"). The form of punishment corresponds to the putative "source" of transgression: sexual reproduction identified as a property of masculine agency within the male body. The point here is that the subject comes into being not merely through subjection but through a subjection to norms of sex and sexuality and through historically specific forms of disciplinary practice, discursivity, and substitution that reiterate and reconstitute that normativity.[13] Sex and sexuality mediate between both the relations of body and nation, on the one hand, and the relations of kinship and territoriality, on the other.

Torture locates a preeminent site of struggle over, and between, the "reality" of the Indian nation-state's community and the "illusory" peoplehood of Khalistan (cf. chap. 2). Yet the performative moment of torture constitutes its object, the body, as both Sikh and male, as both citizen and monsters, as both something that belongs to the state and something that exceeds the state.[14] Conjoined to the Punjab, the "disturbed area" and the "sensitive border state," the tortured male *amritdhari* body has become a sign of the limit of territoriality. And, in India, it is the tortured male *amritdhari* body that has also become a sexualized sign of sovereignty's limit.

The notion of performativity, introduced in chapter 1, helps specify how, through citation and reiteration, sexuality and gender become integral to the constitution of temporality within torture. Together, the *amritdhari* profile, elaborated through the law's discourse of contravention, and the tortured body invoke "a temporal 'before'" of a Sikh subject against which the nation-state generates the "fictive foundation of its own claim to legitimacy" (Butler 1990, 2–3). Reconstituted within the practice of torture, this is the point at which the *desh-kaal* of Khalistan, which Khalistanis understand to be enunciated during the Khalsa initiation and entextualized by the *Rahit Maryada*, stands against the nation-state's fantasy beginning. Compare these two formations of temporal authority that I have introduced in chapters 1 and 2, first the Rahit Maryada, then the Indian Supreme Court (1955):

> Any man or woman who affirms belief in the Sikh faith and vows to live according to its principles may receive initiation, regardless of nationality, previous creed, or caste. . . . They should bathe and wash their hair, and should present themselves wearing all five Khalsa symbols. . . . No symbols associated with other faiths may be worn. The head must be covered, but not with a hat or cap. Ear-rings and nose ornaments must not be worn. . . . One of the five officiants should then address those who are seeking initiation. . . . "The Sikh faith requires you to abandon the worship of man-made objects. . . . Do you gladly accept this faith?" [After drinking the sacred water (*amrit*) and repeating the basic credal statement (*mul mantra*),] one of the five officiants should then expound the Rahit as follows: As from today you are "born to the Guru and freed from rebirth." You are now a member of the Khalsa. Guru Gobind Singh is your spiritual father and Sahib Kaur your spiritual mother. Your birthplace is Keshgarh Sahib and your home is Anandpur Sahib. Because you are all children of the same father you are spiritual brothers. . . . You must renounce your former lineage, occupation, and religious affiliation. This means you should put aside all concern for caste, status, birth, country and religion, for you are now exclusively a member of the sublime Khalsa.

> Every vestige of sovereignty was abandoned by the dominion of India and by the States and surrendered to the peoples of the land who through their representatives in the Constituent Assembly hammered out for themselves a new Constitution in which all are citizens in a new order having but one tie and owing but one allegiance, devotion, loyalty, fidelity to the sovereign, democratic Republic that is India. At one stroke territorial allegiance were wiped out and the past was obliterated except where expressly preserved, at one moment in time the new order was born and its allegiances springing from the same source, all grounded on the same basis, the sovereign will of the people of India with no class, no caste, no race, no creed, no distinction, no reservation.

The nation-state's fantasy moment of abandonment, surrender, and obliteration not only stands against the rupture introduced by the Khalsa initiation. It is intended to incorporate Sikh "identity" while eliding the significance of one of the Khalsa initiation's requirements (i.e., the *amritdhari*'s putting aside of "all concern . . . for country"). The power of this elision is itself valorized by the nation-state in its own visual forms of representation of Sikh identity and the gendered Sikh body as one part of the "great tradition" of Indian culture. Striking examples of this are the portraits of Guru Nanak (Sikhism's first guru) and Guru Gobind Singh (the tenth guru, who introduced the order of the Khalsa) that hang in the portrait gallery that encircles the halls of Parliament in New Delhi. These portraits of *total* bodies become signifiers of the idealized body politic, particularly in their proximate relations to portraits of Gandhi, on the one side, and the Buddha, on the other. Against these images of total bodies, the body fragments that are objectified in police strategies and the fragmented bodies produced through torture become sites for the startling discovery of the nation-state's ineffectivity and of the *incomplete* obliteration or interpellation of prior forms of allegiance. In other words, the masculinized *amritdhari* embodies a threat to the bearing forth of the nation's extended family — a threat, indeed, that any citizen may offer at any time. The ambivalent character of torture thus reveals a continual slippage of categories, such as sexuality, gender, religious affiliation, territorial paranoia, or cultural difference, in the act of inscribing the nation on its object (Bhabha 1994, 140).

Circulation of the Tortured Body

There is also a slippage between the putatively separate categories *private* and *public*. Torture resists the privacy of its enactment. It leaves traces. Survivors provide testimonies and medical evidence, rumors act as witnesses, disappearances speak through absence, and abandoned corpses display the scars of transgression. Sikhs around the world have formed a specific modality of identification and pedagogy around such remnants of torture and particularly around gendered images of tortured bodies and corpses. And, in doing so, many Sikhs have established a set of practices that remake the private scene of national torture into a transnational spectacle of subjectification.

In other words, in the past fourteen years, pictures of the mutilated corpses of Sikh men have become a well-known, and singularly important, sight for most Sikhs living around the world. My initial decision to write about torture was inspired by the widespread popularity of images of the tortured body and the general import that Sikhs attribute to them. In a Sikh temple in London, for instance, these images are exhibited in a room adjacent to a congregation hall, forming a space of knowledge production and reverence for men known as *shahids,* martyrs who have met a heroic death. Such rooms can be found in many Sikh temples and homes around the world. These pictures also circulate in innumerable books, magazines, newspapers, and Internet web sites. Referring to these pictures as "massacre art," Mahmood (1996) comments insightfully: "In their very gruesomeness, [they] assert themselves in a room; they are impossible to ignore, and intrude in conversation, meditation, and everyday activities. Their potency derives only in part from their blood; it derives also from their unwillingness to be masked, covered, or distorted" (p. 189).[15]

These images have also become interrelated with a variety of practices and institutions organized around historically specific discourses of the *shahid.* For example, the city of Coventry, in the English Midlands, holds an annual sports tournament named after the Shaheed Udham Singh,[16] and Sikhs in the United Kingdom have set up "Shaheedi Funds" through which, as Thandi (1996) comments, "as much as 10 million pounds finds its way by 'dubious' means into Punjab" (p. 232). There are also several "Illustrated Martyrdom Tradition" publications that are used to teach Sikh children around the world about the Sikh *shahids* between the sixteenth and the twentieth centuries through narratives accompanied by drawings and paintings of men with mutilated bodies (see fig. 15). These books find their basis in the words of Guru Nanak, the first Sikh guru (1469–1539): "Shouldst thou wish to play the game of love, come unto my path with thy head on thy palm. And, once you step unto this path, you may well give up thy head, rather than the cause" (S. Singh 1994, 1).[17] In other words, through a breadth of practices that I can only begin to indicate here, conditioned and made possible through authoritative state practices of terror and violence constituting citizenship, Sikhs around the world have generated disparate strategies for the discursive production of Sikh authenticity. Here, we may pinpoint one site for the formation of the Khalistani Sikh subject formed through Khalistani militant practice and discourse on Sikh autonomy.

One of the most important places for these strategic practices is the Internet, a "place" that is regarded as a translocality par excellence and that highlights the inadequacy of the nation-state's discourse of closure. Developed during the 1960s by the Advanced Research Projects Agency, and funded by the U.S. Department of Defense, the Internet seems to have preserved very little of its former cold war character. Over the years, and particularly since the 1980s, the breadth of its capabilities has increased tremendously, ac-

While founding the Sikh Faith, the first foundation stone that Guru Nanak laid was of 'Self-sacrifice', thereby, specifically enjoining that whosoever, wished to enter the path of His Faith, must come with 'his head on his palm'-not to a spirit of seeking any obligation, but out of sheer divine love. Said Guru Nanak Dev Ji.

"Shouldst thou wish to play the game of love, come unto my Path with thy head on thy palm. And, once you step unto this path, You may well give up thy head, rather than the cause.

Similarly, Guru Arjan Dev Ji has also enjoined on the intending Sikhs to accept the ideal of death first.

According to the Guru, 'every true hero must be enthused at the prospects of a righteous fight'. In holy Gurbani, he alone is accepted as a true hero who would prefer to be cut to pieces rather than give up fight for righteousness. The same ideal is enshrined in the commandment of Shri Guru Angad Dev Ji to Bhai Maloo that 'the odds involved in the fight for righteousness should not deter a true Sikh'. In similar strain, Guru Amar Das had ordained that 'Although every Sikh must be basically kind-hearted, yet, when it comes to defending the Truth, he must resolutely face every odd'. The Lord himself comes to the aid of such a person and humbles his adversary according to the Guru. Sri Arjan Dev also said that 'he who is martyred in such a fight, attains to such a divine bliss that even the holiest of holy yogi would envy. Guru Hargobind Ji had also enjoined on every Sikh that while the Sikh should extend warm hospitality to every guest, he must also keep his arms ready for dealing with any misguided adversary.

Fig. 15 *Illustrated Martyrs'* image (from S. Singh 1994).

companied by a series of protocols used to link up different types of systems of communication and information exchange. Perhaps the most basic yet singularly important aspect of the Internet is that it provides dynamic and open connections with many people simultaneously. These types of connections range from emailing (actually an asynchronous form of communication), to mailing lists (subscriber-supported discussion groups), to newsgroups (more like a series of dialogues around a specific topic), to the World Wide Web (a graphic system that combines typography and images on screen and that supports a wide variety of protocols). Over the years, a complex jargon has developed around these different forms of connections, which have been used for different purposes. What is relevant for my discussion is that they have become an important means for interactions among Sikh populations in several different countries. Although the Internet is only one of many places in which one can identify the translocality of the subject of Khalistan, it is on the Internet that the production and circulation of the body of the *shahid* attains a certain generality that must be carefully distinguished.

Today, there may be over six hundred Internet web sites concerned in some way with Sikhs or with Khalistan. I say *may be,* not only because the number is continually increasing, but also because many of the sites are interrelated, providing access both to other Khalistani sites and to sites that may not be devoted to Khalistan but that, nevertheless, contain information of interest (e.g., Amnesty International's reports on human rights violations in Punjab). The multitude of Internet sites, and their popularity, has emerged only recently, most dramatically since 1997. In 1994, for example, there were only two sites concerned with Khalistan or, more generally, "Sikh life." These, however, were basically subscription mailing lists and news groups that facilitated and generated conversations and commentaries on the experiences of Sikhs around the world who were students, engineers, or computer specialists with Internet access. The sites with which I am concerned certainly may have emerged from these earlier forms of practice and technology. They are not, however, still limited to a textual format. Also, they are open to a larger population of users, although certainly limited to those with economic and social resources to use the Internet. It is possible to visit these sites, without subscribing, merely by doing a search for *Sikh* or *Khalistan.* These sites on the World Wide Web, created and maintained by a variety of political, religious, entrepreneurial, and student organizations, use programs that facilitate an interarticulation of graphic, audio, and textual mediums. Many of these sites, moreover, are updated daily so that not only what visitors see and hear but how they see and hear it is constantly changing. These technologies of "change" notwithstanding, what remains consistent is an explicit discourse of history and "purpose" — the Sikh freedom struggle. This discourse, facilitated by Internet technology, forms the basis for the production of a distinctive space of performativity within a peculiar, although common, intimacy of dispersal, repeatedly engaging and negotiating the disparate and often contradictory knowledges of what constitutes a struggle and what it means to be a Sikh.

One such space is ⟨www.khalistan.com⟩, the web page maintained by the Council of Khalistan — the organization responsible for soliciting letters of support from both the Bush and the Clinton governments (see chap. 2). The Council of Khalistan is based in Washington, D.C., and describes itself "as the government *pro tempore* charged with leading international efforts to free Khalistan from Indian Government occupation." Although it may not be the only organization to claim to represent Khalistan — there are several competing groups in North America and England — the Council of Khalistan, which propounds nonviolent militancy, has had a significant effect on the international popularization of the Khalistani struggle (Tatla, 1999). For example, Dr. Gurmit Singh Aulakh, president of the Council, presented the case for Khalistan before the fifty-first session of the United Nations Working Group on Enforced or Involuntary Disappearances in May 1997. Aulakh also lobbied the U.S. Congress to urge an investigation into human rights violations in Punjab, resulting in a letter sent, on 30 January 1998, to the chief minister of Punjab, Parkash Singh Badal. The letter, signed by twenty-three U.S. Representatives, in many ways seems to give legitimacy to the notion of Khalistan — for example, articulating the Sikh struggle in terms of the struggles of other new nations, it declared: "Just as we are witnessing in South Africa's Truth Commission, it is time for the truth to come out in Punjab, for better or for worse."

Click on ⟨www.khalistan.com⟩: "WARNING: This page contains graphic pictures of torture victims which are now loading. If you do not wish to view such photographs, please click." This warning is a common feature of Khalistani web sites. For example, after providing a series of options ("click here to view tortured Sikh"), the Fort Panth Khalsa site warns: "The above pictures are graphic in nature." Likewise, the Bleeding Punjab site states: "In this area, various pictures regarding the human rights abuses against the Sikhs will be presented. . . . Pictures may contain very graphic material. To begin viewing pictures . . . select one of the topics below."

From warning, to selection, to body image: in this movement, there is certainly an element of seduction, an enticement to view and consume, that is fundamental to almost all practices on the Internet, where it is just as easy to view pornography as corpses (see figs. 16 and 17). The potential for porno-troping the image of the *shahid,* indeed, does suggest a tension within the production of Khalistan on the Internet, a tension and a desire to which I will return in a moment. What I would like to address first, however, is the importance, and perhaps what appears to be a necessity, in Sikh dis-courses of framing the Sikh struggle within a domain of visuality. The pro-duction of the image of the tortured body constitutes and legitimizes the Khalistani Sikh subject, through this spectacle, within a relation to a mon-strous, inhuman Other — a historically specific relation that must be speci-fied. The interarticulation of the image of the tortured body with a narrative of genocide and conspiracy positions the Sikh subject in relation, not just to the Indian nation-state, but to Sikhs who represent the nation-state — in this case, Akalis, the political group that introduced the idea of Azad Punjab and Khalistan in the 1930s and 1940s.[18] Consider this note on the Council of Khalistan's home page: "Akalis are coming to a Gurdwara, restaurant or meeting hall near you! Thanks to Indian government sponsorship, their job is to take your money and tell the world that Sikhs have forgotten Golden Temple and the 13 years of genocide since. That Sikhs have ignored over 70 atrocities [in the past year] committed by the Badal government itself! Click in to find out what you should know about the Akalis and what questions and demands they must answer!"

This visual domain also constitutes the viewer as either Sikh or non-Sikh: "Because so many people have written this office requesting information on the movement, we have designed www.khalistan.com as an educational tool for both Sikhs and non-Sikhs. . . . However, we are here primarily to serve the Sikh nation and it is through your moral and financial support that this site exists." The *you* to which this site is primarily addressed, then, has a certain diacritic. It is not just the *you* of the "Sikh nation" but of the *you* of what the Council of Khalistan calls "the sovereign cyberspace of Khalistan." In an-other web site, ⟨khalistan.net⟩, which is linked to ⟨www.khalistan.com⟩, this *you* is pictured on the same page as images of tortured bodies and corpses: a world map, flanked by globes and Khalistani flags, on which is inscribed "KHALISTAN: The New Global Reality." This globally dispersed sovereignty also has a familiar name, *the diaspora,* a category deployed, ultimately, in a specific economic discourse: "As our work in furtherance of the Sikh freedom

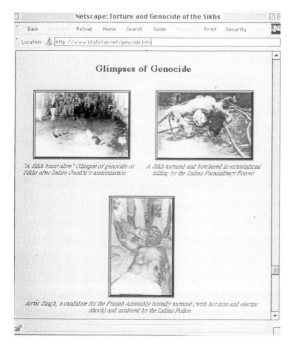

Fig. 16 Khalistan on the Internet (from www.khalistan.net).

Fig. 17 "Click to view tortured body" (from www.community.net).

struggle relies solely on the good works of the Sikh Diaspora, we urge you to contribute to this office regularly. Please click here for more information."

The Body and the Fetish

There is a danger of interpreting the relation between the production of Khalistan and the Internet in terms of what Žižek (1997) calls "an ambiguity in the impact of cyberspace on community life." Žižek claims that, while cyberspace lends itself to the "dream of the new populism, in which de-centralized networks will allow individuals to band together and build a participatory grass-roots political system, . . . the use of computers and [virtual reality] as a tool to rebuild community results in the building of a community *inside* the machine, reducing individuals to isolated monads, each of them alone, facing a computer" (pp. 138–39). The body has a specific position in this "ambiguity": "With VR [virtual reality] and technobiology, we are dealing with the loss of the surface which separates inside from outside. This loss jeopardizes our most elementary perception of 'our own body' as it is related to its environs; it cripples our standard phenomenological attitude towards the body of another person" (p. 134).

Strangely constituting the computer interface as an analogy of the work-ings of the Lacanian symbolic order, Žižek (1997, 142, 143, 151, 158) posits a universalized and surprisingly antihistorical phenomenology of the Internet. In terms of the production of Khalistan and images of the tortured bodies of *shahids,* the appropriation of the Internet cannot be separated from a history of violence and sexuality that constitutes not only bodies as Sikh but also an imperative of the Sikh subject: the incitement to visuality, the incitement to build specific relations of proximity between different kinds of bodies, and the incitement to build a community with not only a *territory* but also a *temporality.* Not only does Žižek's argument miss these historically specific processes; it elides a series of contradictions that emerge with the process of dreaming a community within an era of globalization.[19] Entering the domain of computer technology and commodity circulation, the image of the muti-lated and gendered body of the Sikh *shahid,* separated from its site of produc-tion, makes possible a process of mediation—constituting forms of relations between bodies and populations of Sikhs living in North America, Europe, and Southeast Asia and those in India.

The Sikh *shahid,* it must be pointed out, is not the only instance of images of torture and martyrdom mediating the relations of a dispersed population.

Such images have made appearances in several societies and historical moments. Distinguishing these may prove helpful. Dumezil (1970), for example, discusses the Celtic myths in which the hero, Cuchulainn, is envisaged and celebrated in "monstrous forms." The purpose of Cuchulainn's violation is not to "rob the society" of a hero but "to bring him to such a state of exaltation that he even places his own society . . . in danger. . . . The exploit has its good effect . . . only after a bad phase in which the power acquired by the hero appears in disordered form, either a diminution analogous to an annihilation, or an intolerable excess" (p. 134). In a similar line of inquiry, Bruce Lincoln (1991) has written extensively of the "cosmogonic accounts of the various peoples who spoke Indo-European languages in which it is . . . described how the physical universe was created from the dismembered body of a primordial victim" (p. 180). There is also the *Kidush Hashem* of Judaism, which celebrates one as a martyr when (a) a Jew sacrifices his life when others attempt to make him abandon the Jewish faith, (b) a Jew gives his life to save a fellow Jew, or (c) a Jew dies while fighting to defend other Jews. (According to one discourse of the *Kidush Hashem,* every "Jew who is killed by a Gentile, for whatever cause, even in the case of a robbery or murder, is considered a martyr" [Huberband 1987, 247].)

One of the most well known of these cultural forms is, of course, Christianity. On this, Stephen Moore (1996) has written simply: "The central symbol of Christianity is the figure of the tortured man. . . . God's forgiveness is extended to the sinner over the mutilated body of his Son" (pp. 4, 31). This powerful image of the tortured body of Christ has a complex history into which I cannot enter here. However, let me briefly indicate one aspect of this history in medieval Europe. The tortured body of Christ formed the basis, not only for a specific religious system that prevailed between the twelfth and the seventeenth centuries (the Cult of the Five Wounds), but also for the production of poetry and artistic representations that obsessively detail the points of puncturing and the amount of blood spilled during crucifixion (Beckwith 1993; Gray 1963; Moore 1996). Perhaps the best known of visual representations revered by this cult were the paintings (found in cathedral walls, roof bosses, bench ends, and books) that displayed the mutilated Christ, whose wounds pour blood into chalices held by sinners or angels.[20] Sarah Beckwith (1993) has written insightfully of this "loving contemplation of the tortured Christ" and the "centrality of Christ's body to the political construction of a [medieval] Christian culture imagined as a unity" (pp. 53, 3). Following Gray (1963), one of Beckwith's main concerns is with the texts and visual representations that itemize "everything that pierces or touches the surface of Christ's skin" (p. 62). Through the spectacle of this itemization, Beckwith argues, the worshiper would be brought into a crucial relation to the Passion: the worshiper was "besought to be present at the crucifixion" (p. 63). Yet, as she clearly demonstrates, while "Christ's body is used as a very medium of identification . . . the formation of identity becomes an arena of social control" (p. 41). Beckwith indicates the highly contested quality of this process of imagining and social control: "If Christ's body . . . was where the integrity of an entire culture was most celebrated and consequently protested, if belief in transubstantiation could literally define your bona fide membership of that 'imaginary community,' then Christ's body as it was violated, eaten, transgressed and otherwise played with, was also the symbol which suffered from the most extreme degree of inner contestation and self-difference" (p. 3).

My interest in drawing attention to these disparate practices of visualization and reverence of tortured bodies of martyrs is not to imply a parallel or homology but rather to help clarify the historical specificity of the Khalistani practices that I have been discussing. Indeed, there are certain radical differences that must be immediately noted. For example, Sikhism is not based on a discourse of sin and atonement, nor does it valorize a single martyr or moment of martyrdom. Different historical formations of the Sikh subject, moreover, have privileged different corporeal images that were totalized rather than mutilated. Not least of these are the intertwined histories of nineteenth-century portraiture, colonial military practice, and religious practice that transformed and mapped what could be known as a Sikh through identifications with a total body. Just as important are the historical shifts and paradoxes by which a national discourse of secularism emerging after Indian Independence came to be built upon, and perhaps motivated by, the politicization of religion. As I discussed in chapter 2, this latter became a significant factor in the introduction of the notion of a *desh-kaal,* which was related to the image of the *amritdhari* body. All these historical formations of the total body must be understood as indissolubly related to the globalization of the Sikh *panth* as *qaum,* a formation itself made possible by the expansions of colonialism and the disparate modes of production and circulation of global capitalism.

The transformation, since 1984, of the global Sikh *panth* into a global Sikh *qaum* has utilized this production and circulation in a new way—at first through technologies of print media and transportation, and then, more recently, through Internet technologies. As a result, the total body, which has had such an enduring significance since the mid-nineteenth century, has been met with another corporeal image. This transformation suggests one way in which to return to the question of fetishism. This fetishism is difficult to navigate, not least because what is at stake is the production of knowledge of violence and the ambivalent constitution of the Khalistani Sikh subject—an ambivalence characterized by a repulsion at the sight of the tortured body and a desire to visualize and return to both that scene of violation and the mise-en-scène of the Khalsa initiation that inaugurates the Sikh subject into history. Allen Feldman's (1991) analysis of the "staging and commodification of the body by political violence" is instructive. In his discussion of the circulation of bodies as political texts, Feldman notes the way in which economic fetishism and the economic logic of political fetishism infuse each other, making explicit how "political power increasingly becomes a matter of regimenting the circulation of bodies in time and space in a manner analogous to the circulation of things" (p. 8). The fetishism of the image of the Sikh's tortured body by Khalistanis may be understood as an effect of the Indian nation-state's political violence and of the circulation of that image as a commodity. The fetishism of the image of the tortured body generates generalized and abstract notions of similitude and difference that then become embedded within procedures that mediate violence and terror both between Sikhs and nation-states and between different Sikh Khalistani organizations. This fetishism, a basic feature of Sikh liberatory politics, forces us to think closely, not only about "the rights of the corpse," as Benjamin argues (1978, 153), but about the relations of recognition and identification between the organic and the inorganic, the living body and the body in bits and pieces.

Within Khalistani processes of subject formation, the tortured body directly inverts the significance of the total body of the Five Ks. Recall the image of the total body constituted by the *Rahit Maryada*'s narrative of the Khalsa initiation: a body devoid of piercings, ordered with hair unshorn but cleanly kept, etc. J. P. S. Uberoi (1996) has argued that what is most important in this image is its relation of antagonism to the spiritual order of certain medieval forms of Hinduism in which the initiate "gives away whatever he possesses, severing all connection with the social world . . . [and performs] the *atma-shraddha* or his own death" (p. 6). In the valorization of the modern Sikh *shahid*, however—contra Uberoi's analysis—it is the *violation* of the body displaying the Five Ks and the *death* of the *amritdhari* that makes possible the division of social worlds into disparate intimate domains of affiliation. The significance of the tortured body of the *shahid* is constituted in relation to not one or another of the Five Ks but specific wounds, piercings, and defilements — the widespread identification of which is itself an effect of the standardization of training in torture techniques. These systematized wounds generate a relation, not only between members of a Sikh community, but also between Sikhs and the monstrous practices of the Indian nation-state. Indeed, Khalistani discourses on trauma and suffering define the authenticity and authority of the modern Sikh subject in a relation of ressentiment to the nation-state (Brown 1995). Consider the captions that accompany two photos of *shahids* on the Internet (⟨www.khalistan.net⟩):

1) This photo was taken secretly at a torture center in Punjab. Words can not describe what ordeal this GurSikh went through. Thousands of Gur-Sikhs have been murdered in such torture centers throughout Hindu dominated "Democratic" India.

2) Another example of the barbaric behavior of Hindoostani forces. This is the treatment Sikhs get in the so-called "largest democracy in the world." Bhai Avatar Singh Ji, pictured above had received the following barbaric treatment for being a Sikh:
    * His abdomen was burnt by using a hot ironing-press.
    * His right fore-arm was cut open. (Click here to see close-up)
    * All the major bones in both of his arms were broken. (Click here to see another view)
    * Hot pincers were used on his wrists to burn his skin. (Click here to see another view)
    * Hot Steel rods were used to burn the soles of his feet (not shown).

The affectivity of these images is created through a process of substitution and displacement. It is also enacted through a process of discovery, investigation, and obsessive detailing, directed at, or constituting, an incitement to look. Here, the social relations of a globally dispersed population are both mediated through and envisioned within a "virtual complex" of images and not merely a relation between "objects" (Marx 1976, 165).[21] The process of substitution is not so much one of an image of a corpse for the "thing itself" as it is a substitution of a specular image for a *history* of concealed violence. This is a process of substitution, also, by which a body marked as male stands in for all Sikhs, male and female.

The constitution of the Sikh subject as gendered, along with the invisibility and silence of women, is indissoluble from the production and circulation of the tortured body. Through global circulation, no doubt, the tortured body accumulates a new form of value. But this process also has a supplementary effect, whereby the tortured body becomes entextualized, making it possible for the body to be both seen and read. In contrast to the way in which the Five Ks have been used to read the *amritdhari* body's relation to its "whole nature as a religion" (Uberoi 1996, 17), the specific detail of scars, for example, can tell the story of the contradictions of Indian democracy. Furthermore, the very position of this fetishized image itself, in the temple or on the Internet, is inseparable from a diverse history of displacements that has made possible the presence of Sikhs, *as Sikhs,* in England, America, and elsewhere.

The Tortured Body and the Total Body

The gendered image of a total body — with beard, turban, etc. — has not in any way been banished from the specialized circuits of Khalistani production and consumption. Indeed, it has an important place. Valorizing a precolonial past, representations of Sikh gurus and royalty are commonly found in homes, *gurdwaras,* and books (see chap. 1). These representations also have entire web sites devoted to them.

Here, then, we may see how the fetishistic investment in the *amritdhari* body turns on what Jean Comaroff (1997), after Fernandez (1982), has called an "argument of images" or two conflicting modes of imaging a people. This argument of images, made possible by the transnational practices of Khalistanis, must be distinguished from the relation invoked by the nation-state's constitution of the Sikh subject. Within procedures of torture, what takes on significance is the relation of the profile of the *amritdhari* to the tortured body. In Khalistani practice, however, the tortured body stands against the *total* body: that is, a rupturous system of wounds and piercings stands against a holistic religious system of bodily adornments (the Five Ks).

An important instance of this argument of images is provided by the many Khalistani militants who have portrait photographs taken of themselves so that, if, and when, they die, their images may be circulated, exhibited, or posted on the web. And, in fact, many such photographs of men who have become martyrs do circulate on the Internet. It should be made

MARTYR
Jathedar Talwinder Singh Babbar
FOUNDER:
Babbar Khalsa International
(1944-1992)

Precious Quotations from the discourses of
MARTYR
Jathedar Talwinder Singh Babbar

* High ethical standards make a Hindu proper Hindu, a Muslim a proper Muslim and a Sikh a proper Sikh.
* The Sikhs had to choose between life of degrace and freedom; the Sikhs have opted for freedom.
* A warrior should first become a saint and a soldier later.
* When tyranny crosses all limits, a Sikh should forsake life of leisure and join the battle field.
* Those who loose moral are defeated, a Sikh can never be defeated.
* Convant of a Sikh meditation, his ambition is the Sovereignty of Sikh Nation and his thought is *Chardi Kala* (Sikh Euphoria).
* A Sikh can be a *Sewadar* (administrator) but not an authoritarian.
* One who surrenders in the battlefield can not be a genuine Sikh; a Sikh fights for justice till his death.

Fig. 18 Pre-fecto martyr image (original circulated in private collection).

clear: these men are not represented in a wounded or dismembered state. They are, rather, dressed cleanly, sometimes holding guns, displaying what can be displayed of the Five Ks (see fig. 18).

These representations, which may or may not be circulated after the fact of martyrdom, may be related to the model offered by portraits of Maharaja Duleep Singh. In some ways, there is a reiterative dialogic set up between the pre-facto martyr image and these by-now classic portraits. The classic portraits, with their history of production and circulation based in the nineteenth century, set a precedent, not only for kinds of fashion that indicate nobility and reverence, but also for particular postures. Whether represented in three-quarters view, full-face view, or a particular way of tying the turban, these kinds of codings find their way into the pictures of the martyrs.[22]

There is a specific sense of anticipation configuring the production of the pre-facto martyr images that is historically specific. The ongoing struggles in Punjab, the struggles of many to create a Khalistan, and the very real possibility of torture and death take away the surreal quality of even posing for these photographs. The history of violence in Punjab is the condition of possibility for this representational practice that itself appropriates and transforms the significance of all prior forms of portraiture. Yet the translocal character of Khalistani activities also provides the possibility that there will be an audience — a globally dispersed "Sovereign Cyberspace of Khalistan" — that will consume these photographs and, perhaps, be inspired by them. How then might we understand the relation of these images of total bodies to the images of tortured bodies? What might the interplay of these images, and their constitutive histories and practices, tell us about the formation of a Sikh diaspora?

In the previous chapter, I introduced *fantasy* as a category of analysis oriented toward a similar set of questions about the formation of the nation-state and the citizen-subject. As I argue there, the processes constitutive of the nation-state and the citizen-subject must not be confused with those concerned with the diaspora, no matter how intertwined those processes may be. To flag this distinction, I propose the analytic of the *diasporic imaginary* to address the historically specific procedures constitutive of the diasporic subject and the preeminent position of corporeal images within those procedures.

Immediately, the reader should note that *imaginary* here is *not* an adjective that describes or qualifies the diaspora, its people, or community as illusory or as a mere figment of some misguided imagination. The latter — for example, *imaginary nation* — is the way in which Indian nationalist discourse qualifies Khalistan (see chap. 2), but many scholars of diaspora studies also deploy the term *imaginary* in much the same way when referring, variously, to the diaspora "community" or the "homeland." I provide a detailed critique of such a use of *imaginary* in chapter 5. In contrast, the *diasporic imaginary* — here a noun — indicates a precise and powerful kind of identification that is very "real," and specifies processes by which formations of temporality and corporeality have become integral to the relations of recognition and alienation forming the Sikh subject and the Sikh homeland. Hence, I am not drawing from a commonsense notion of illusions and mirages, and I am not recuperating the notion *imagination* developed by Benedict Anderson. Rather, I use the notion *imaginary* in this context to bring to mind Balibar's (1991) Althusserian proposal that "only imaginary communities are real" (p. 93). With this nod toward Balibar and Althusser, I also want to position my discussion within a productive critique of psychoanalytic theory, a discipline that includes a somewhat different notion of the Imaginary.

Lacanian psychoanalysis, particularly, deploys the notion of the Imaginary to elaborate the structure of the subject and, specifically, the formation of the ego and its splitting, a process in which is imbricated elements of sexuality, aggressivity, and narcissism.[23] Lacan's (1977a, 1–7; [1975] 1991a; [1978] 1991b) *mirror stage* may be the most important articulation of this. According to Lacan, "The mirror stage is an identification — the transformation that takes place in the subject when he assumes an image" (1977a, 2). The mirror stage describes the formation and splitting of the ego in relation to the image of a total body. As Lacan ([1975] 1991a) says, following Freud's ([1923] 1960) lead, "The image of the body gives the subject the first form which allows him to locate what pertains to the ego and what does not" (p. 79).[24] As a *structural* rather than a developmental model (Lacan [1975] 1991a, 137), the mirror stage depicts how "the subject becomes aware of his body as a totality *prior* to this particular moment" (emphasis added; p. 79). What is crucial for Lacan (1977a) in this model is what he calls *a temporal dialectic:* the mirror stage generates a successive order of images that "extends from a fragmented body-image to a form of its totality" (p. 2). In other words, from the visual recognition of the total body an anteriority is retroactively generated: a time prior to the total body, that is, the time of the body in bits in pieces, which then becomes a threat and force of anxiety for the subject. This anteriority, moreover, then acts, not according to linear temporality, but as a form of temporality that is interruptive of chronology (Lacan [1975] 1991a, 170; see also Forrester 1990).

Khalistani social practice constitutes a relation between the total body and the tortured body that resonates with many of the Lacanian themes but institutes a different temporality and a different succession of corporeal images. This aspect of the diasporic imaginary, crosscut by historical formations of sexuality, gender, and violence — and formed in relation to the procedures of the Indian nation-state and the struggles in Punjab since the early 1980s — reconstitutes the notion of *desh-kaal*. This *desh-kaal* is not equivalent to the *desh-kaal* entextualized in the pre-1956 Akali Dal constitution. Although it may allude similarly to the Khalsa initiation ceremony, the "nation-time" of Khalistan is now generated as a position of social and cultural knowledge for the Sikh diaspora, constituted through agonistic relations to both the Indian nation-state and the Akali Dal.

Within this Khalistani *desh-kaal,* it is rather the image of the *total* body that corresponds to an anterior point, to a time prior to corporeal and community violation, and to the moment from which the Sikh diaspora *must emerge.* The valorized image of the *shahid,* of the body in bits and pieces, pertains to the *priority of the present,* which, in its extreme violence, contains the contradictory conditions for the repeated retroactive production of a time before. This may lend a certain specificity to Benjamin's (1978) important oeuvre. Modernity, he claims, is characterized by "tendencies [that] direct the visual imagination, which has been *activated by the new,* back to the primeval past" (emphasis added; p. 148). With the performative iterability of the torture scene or the click on the Internet web page, the image of the tortured body reproduces, animates, and makes actual the indication of that anteriority, of "the primeval past" that becomes the starting point for all elaboration of the diasporic imaginary. The pre-facto martyr image sets up a form of identification that anticipates the tortured body, not as a possible future, but as a present that may activate the visual imagination back to the past of the martyr's former total body.

In contrast, the Lacanian scheme may be suggestive of an analogy with the fantasy of the nation-state, characterizing the moment prior to the nation's emergence in terms of a proliferation of incommensurable fragments of affiliation that must be obliterated to form a total body politic. In this national fantasy, the *amritdhari* profile conjures the horrific image of the body politic in bits and pieces (i.e., the nation-state's anteriority), which initiates a form of anxiety and then, within the mise-en-scène of torture, a compulsion to realize that fantasy. Khalistani practices of subject formation counter this national fantasy. The sight of the tortured body provides the opportunity repeatedly to elaborate the proposition of *desh-kaal* within the diasporic imaginary of a time *before* contemporary violence and *before* a history of movement and mobility that scattered the members of a Sikh people — an image of the total body politic that has become iconic of the homeland. And, for some, the sight of the tortured body *presents* the basis for producing an image of the future, of an independent Khalistan, into which that prior totality *will have* reemerged.[25] It is through these historically specific processes that the Khalistani Sikh subject is repeatedly constituted as the object of violent transgression, as persecuted and martyred. And it is through these processes that the idea of the Sikh homeland, in this case, Khalistan, is reconstituted as a threat to the Indian nation-state — and as the Sikh diaspora's promise.

Pursuing further these problems of body, temporality, and territory, I would like to return to the question of violence, wounding, and cultural representation that I introduced in the beginning of this chapter. This is one point at which we may identify something shared between diaspora and the nation-state. Both Sikh diaspora and India are involved in an ongoing investigation into the question, How does a dispersed and segmented population constitute knowledge of, and reproduce itself as, a community? I hope that it has become evident that when this question is answered — whether by the nation-state or by the people of Khalistan — it will be through a discourse of trauma, a founding trauma that, while apparently unifying society, itself sets into motion a desire for, not just order, but a *return to order*. For the Indian nation-state, this is a return that itself dictates the very terms of terror (i.e., the nightmare of disintegration).[26] And, for many Khalistanis, this is a return that legitimizes a militant struggle. The desire for return institutes a process of knowledge production that is necessarily incomplete, a possibility that foils the fetishistic procedures of discovery and investigation that characterize both the grotesque interrogation of torture and the translocalization of Khalistan.

My argument, with which I began this chapter, is perhaps too simply stated: violence is the thread by which the diaspora is constituted as a community. With this, however, I do not mean to imply that all Sikhs experience violence, or, more specifically, torture, or that all Sikhs even know about the practices of torture in Punjab. As I have noted, knowledge of violence against Sikhs is itself a problem, although Khalistanis are generating a standard narrative about torture that corresponds to the standardization of that practice in Punjab. Nevertheless, all Sikhs have at least heard about Operation Bluestar and the Delhi riots — even if they are in doubt about the specific details. And, whether or not younger generations of diaspora Sikhs in the 1990s know about these histories of violence, the education that they may receive about Sikhism in general, whether it be in a *gurdwara* or in a university, has been made possible because of the conflicts in Punjab (I discuss this at length in chap. 5). Likewise, the knowledge that non-Sikhs may have about Sikhs is also invariably related to knowledge, mediated by the press or otherwise, about "terrorism" or about human rights violations. I need not belabor this point. What is crucial, however, is that since the 1980s the fight for Khalistan has transformed the threat that the Sikh homeland poses to the Indian nation-state and that it has effectively transformed what it means to be Sikh. It has also opened up possibilities for new forms of violence to enter into the lives of Sikhs around the world. Conversely, the fight for Khalistan has played a part in transforming the dialectical relation between diaspora and nation-states other than India.

4 : glassy junction

There we are, *inside* the culture, going to their schools, speaking their language, playing their music, walking down their streets, looking like we own part of the turf, looking like we belong. Some third generation Blacks are starting to say "We are the Black British." After all, who are we?

— Stuart Hall, "Ethnicity: Identity and Difference"

Diasporic Landscapes within the Nation

On 17 January 1995, Tarsem Singh Purewal, editor of the Punjabi newspaper *Des Pardes,* was murdered in Southall, West London. The homicide immediately became a national news focus, fueled by rumors that such violence was a result of conflicts between different U.K.-based groups fighting for a Khalistan. Scotland Yard's Anti-Terrorist Branch began an investigation, as did the Greater London Action for Race Equality. Translators went to work on back issues of *Des Pardes.* The national media sent out teams of reporters. Race specialists and public intellectuals offered commentary. Details, however, remained murky. No one was convicted of the crime, nor did any individual or group immediately claim responsibility. Nevertheless, the image of Purewal, envisioned at the moment of death, was made abundantly clear: a man with a dark beard and a yellow turban whose body "practically exploded, spraying blood 2ft into the air" (*Independent,* 9 February 1997, 7).

Throughout 1995, the national media would repeatedly explode Purewal's body, using the bloody scene as a means through which to examine the Sikhs of Southall. On 28 January, the *Guardian* reported the initial findings of Detective Superintendent Colin Hardingham, who said that he was "unable to say how many people were involved in the murder"; but, he added, "whoever shot him would have been very heavily bloodstained" (p. 7). Attempting to consider all possible motives, Hardingham suggested that something "more personal" may have been at stake: "For example, his newspaper takes a particular stance on community issues such as individuals' personal lives or the way people run their businesses." A spokesman from the Indian High Commission challenged this view, saying: "Violence against individuals is not a part of India's ethos." In February, the *Independent* sent reporters to Southall to uncover the particularities of this "ethos" imagined to be embodied in the neighborhood's Indian population of 26,620 (most of whom were Sikh):[1]

> The investigation has uncovered a hidden community that appears happy to police itself rather than attract the spotlight of publicity.
>
> A stroll down the High Street reveals how different the district is. Almost every shop is Asian, windows piled high with brilliantly coloured sweets, rolls of brightly coloured cloth, exotic fruits and Halal meats.
>
> After translating the past three month's editions of weekly tabloid in the search for clues to a motive, the police have discovered the newspaper . . . regularly names adulterers, rapists . . . and child abusers.
>
> Chief Inspector Gordon Cuthburton, community liaison officer for Ealing, said: "The Sikh population sees this as part and parcel of their community. Southall is still seen as a community within a community, a self-contained unit unaffected by the surrounding areas." (*Independent*, 9 February 1995, 7)

The national media would continue investigating this troubling enclave within the nation's capital for months to come, a landscape that, it was presumed, veiled the real activities of its inhabitants — characterized as rapists, disciplinarians, and terrorists. Scotland Yard, in contrast, following a well-worn British Sikh geography (see chap. 1), turned away from Southall's "Little India," or, as some called it, "Amritsar-on-Brent," and traveled northwest to the Midlands.[2] In Smethwick (Birmingham), on 29 March, seven members of the International Sikh Youth Federation were arrested. Of these seven, only one was detained in Winson Green Prison: Raghbir Singh Johal, the general secretary of the federation and the editor of the Punjabi weekly *Awaz-e-Qaum* (Voice of the nation). Johal had lived in the United Kingdom since 1980 and was married to a British national. In 1982, he was granted indefinite leave to remain. He had been involved with the struggle for Khalistan since at least 1984. In his own words: "Being a Sikh I am a staunch supporter of an independent homeland Khalistan which I believe should be achieved in a democratic manner. To date, I have condemned violence regardless of the perpetrator" (Amnesty International: EUR 45/01/96).

On arresting him, the Home Office issued a notice of intention to deport Raghbir Singh Johal under section 3(5)(b) of the 1971 Immigration Act, stating that the home secretary "has decided [he] should be detained" pending his deportation "for reasons of national security and other reasons of a political nature, namely the fight against international terrorism" (Amnesty International: EUR 45/01/96). The police, however, arrested Johal without providing any precise evidence to substantiate the Home Office's claim.

It was at about this time that the press in India began to follow the story. In an article titled "At Pains with Home Sikhness," Dipankar De Sarkar (1995) used the story of Purewal's murder to reflect on the "extra-territorial ramifications of Sikh militancy."[3] According to De Sarkar, "the British government has been worried over the phenomenon [of overseas Sikh militants and the import of Punjab politics in the United Kingdom] for the past decade." He went on to comment on "the militant leader, Jagjit Singh Chauhan, [who in 1984] had publicly announced a reward for the 'head of Indira Gandhi.'" After reflecting on the way in which funds collected in *gurdwaras* all over the United Kingdom were being transferred to militants in Punjab, De Sarkar concluded the article with dismay: "A Scotland Yard spokeswoman said deportations tend to take 'months.' Going by past experience, Raghbir Singh [Johal's] deportation will take some time to materialise, if at all."

In April, Johal began his first month of solitary confinement while deportation remained pending. Indeed, as De Sarkar has surmised, under the terms of the Immigration Act, detention could go on indefinitely.[4] Moreover, rather than having access to a trial and legal representation, Johal would be taken before a three-person "independent advisory panel" appointed by the home secretary — the proceedings and recommendations of which would remain secret. On 19 October 1995, the home secretary reiterated the (unsubstantiated) allegation that Raghbir Singh was "involved in terrorism." He also stated that, because he was a "threat to national security," Raghbir Singh's deportation "would be conducive to the public good" (Amnesty International: EUR 45/01/96).

By December 1995, when Raghbir Singh was entering his ninth month of detention, the national media, continuing their vigilant watch over Southall, had placed Sikhs in a queue with other diasporic populations: Muslims, Libyans, Turks, and Algerians. Here, the threat that the Home Office saw in Raghbir Singh was transferred onto Sikhs in general. English conservatives and liberals alike found evidence in Southall, and in the remnants of Purewal's murder, that the multiculturalism otherwise valorized in post-Thatcherite Britain may indeed pose a threat to the nation: "Britain is becoming a battlefield for the world's wars in exile" (*Guardian,* 19 December 1995, T4). Returning to the murder scene, the *Guardian* depicted the battlefield's hybrid landscape, a landscape that was English, but not quite: "From the roof of Sri Guru Singh sports hall, or the Glassy Junction Pub, there is a good view of the entrance to the *Des Pardes* newspaper office. . . . It was probably from one of these vantage points that the sniper fired the bullet which . . . killed the paper's editor" (19 December 1995, T4).[5]

Purewal's murder and the case of Raghbir Singh Johal's detention demonstrate a crucial problem for the historical anthropology of the Sikh diaspora. With the transnationalization of the fight for Khalistan, violence has indeed entered the lives of Sikhs around the world in new ways. But the forms that this violence takes, and the kinds of cultural and material practices that accompany that violence, are not necessarily the same within the contexts of different nation-states. Likewise, differently constituted nation-states may generate relations with the Sikh diaspora that are radically heterogeneous. For example, around the image of the mutilated body of a Sikh man, and through the projection of a fight for Khalistan onto that body, the Sikh subject in England is constituted by the national media, Scotland Yard, and the Home Office as a threat to the nation-state. This threat, however, cannot be equated with the threat that the Indian nation-state sees in the idea of Khalistan, even though the Indian national press may translate the murder of Purewal into the problem of a diasporic Sikh militancy. The threat that the British Sikh subject represents to England in the 1990s is generated through a very different history of conflicts, concerned not with national integration but with immigration and multiculturalism.

My concern in this chapter is this history of conflict and the creation of a specific kind of dialectic between the Sikh diaspora and the British nation-state. Some of the themes in this history carry over from my discussion in the previous chapters, particularly the way in which I have characterized the formation of the Sikh subject and citizenship at the intersection of formations of time, space, and corporeality. Similarly, throughout these formations we see the interplay of anxiety and threat within state disciplinary procedures and the fetishization of a specifically gendered Sikh body. These themes, however, take on different qualities and values, partly because, within British Sikh history, the fight for Khalistan is a latecomer. In the fantasy of the British nation-state, Khalistan builds on national fears and anxieties over the transformation of former colonial subjects into citizens and former English landscapes into Little Indias. Chapter 1 introduces one set of historical and ethnographic parameters for understanding these kinds of issues. This chapter complicates that story, which now must be rearticulated from a position concerned with the constitution of the British Sikh citizen in relation to a transnational fight for Khalistan. For British Sikhs, the fight for Khalistan arrived on the scene after years of other kinds of struggles against the nation-state's attempt to reconstitute and revitalize a Sikh surrender: struggles by Sikh laborers in the 1950s and 1960s to gain access to equal rights as producers and struggles by Sikh youths in the 1970s and 1980s to gain equal rights as consumers. During these years, the constitution of the British Sikh subject engendered different kinds of threats that, themselves, lay the groundwork for the emergence of the homeland, after 1984, as a new promise.

The Permanent Way

How did Southall become a Little India or an Amritsar-on-Brent? One way to answer this question is first to look at the emergence of Southall as a particular kind of locality, a valorized site of British industrialization and progress. The production of this locality was determined in many ways by the transportation industry and particularly the railway industry, which made the arrival of other kinds of industry in Southall possible. In technical discourse, the railway structure is referred to as the Permanent Way, an apt term for something that came to symbolize the dynamic mobility of capitalism, a privileged mode of national circulation, and the fantasy of a nation-state's durability. Running from Paddington to Bristol,[6] the Permanent Way formed the basis around which Southall has developed since the mid-nineteenth century.[7] Within Permanent Way historiography, the measurement of this development has been a point of obsessive knowledge production. Let me give a sense of this detail, which demonstrates, at least, how closely the nation-state has been concerned with this section of West London.

Initially, Southall formed a junction for the Brentford Branch of the Great Western Railway Company (GWR). On 15 July 1859, the GWR opened a four-mile broad-gauge track (measuring seven feet, five inches) between Southall and Brentford Dock for the transportation of goods and to provide a water outlet on the Thames. The speed of transport on this service made it possible to move fifty-eight thousand tons of goods and minerals in its first year. Clocked at twenty to thirty miles an hour, the Permanent Way moved these goods three times the speed of any other mode of transportation (Schivelbusch 1978, 31). On 1 May 1860, the branch was opened for passenger traffic, a service that ran infrequently and that Permanent Way historiography considers inconsequential. In 1861, the track was changed from broad to narrow gauge (measuring four feet, eight and a half inches). While goods transport continues to run this route today, passenger transport was withdrawn on 4 May 1942.[8]

In the nineteenth century, Southall also became a junction for trains to central London: on 1 April 1863, the GWR opened a branch running trains from Southall, via Kensington and the West London Extension Railway, to Victoria on both broad and narrow gauge (by October 1866, these were solely narrow gauge). This passenger service eventually closed on 22 March 1915, after which services to Paddington, in central London, and Slough, west of London, became the major routes for passenger transport (Course 1962, 97; Davies and Grant 1983, 66; White 1963, 127). In 1885, the GWR opened a locomotive depot and servicing point, making Southall a junction for a variety of uses necessary to the efficient maintenance of Britain's Permanent Way system (Davies and Grant 1983, 177). This site was taken over by British Rail on 1 January 1948, thus constituting Southall as the sign of a fourth junction: the joining of the entirety of Britain's independent railway industry under the British government in the nationalization of railways inaugurated by the Transport Act of 1947.

In the 1990s, Southall continues to be a point of departure and arrival for passenger and goods traffic as well as a depot and servicing point for specialist freight. It is also the site of a museum, the Southall Railway Center, which memorializes the history of the British Permanent Way and a specific era of displacement. The center, opened in 1994 by the GWR Preservation Group, has the largest collection of preserved steam and diesel locomotives in London. Along with an expansive railway historiography, this museum valorizes Southall as the site of many junctions. It depicts the Permanent Way as a structure of national mobility and mediation, but it also measures the historical transformation of Southall from a site of production, central to the nation-state, to a site of marginality.

Southall then is not merely a junction. The history of the Permanent Way—a history of gauge sizes, distances, durations, speeds, and goods quantities—has constituted Southall as a precisely and repeatedly measured junction of industry and the nation-state. As such, the Permanent Way provides one condition of possibility for generalized and repeated practices of those living in Southall. This measured junction defines the everyday itineraries of many Southall residents through forms of knowledge, bodily technique, and desire: residents who daily see the Permanent Way running through and dividing the neighborhood must cross over it to get from the Broadway to the "older part" of the neighborhood, must take it to travel to central London or to points west, and hear it as trains move through Southall with measured periodicity. In other words, the story of the Permanent Way is a story of localization, of creating Southall as a particular place with a certain social life within London.[9]

The Arrival of Producers

The Permanent Way also made possible a story of an emergent "globalization," creating relations between India and Britain. After World War II, the preexisting structure of the Permanent Way set the basis for the establishment of new industry in Southall (see below) and the increasing mobility of people within the United Kingdom. It also became a basic factor for other kinds of circulation that emerged from changes in the empire: specifically, the system of indentured servitude, which was made illegal in the 1920s, and the standardization of Sikh recruitment into military service, which ended with Indian Independence in 1947 (see chap. 1; cf. Aiyer 1938; Gangulee [1946] 1947; Gillion 1962; Kale 1995; Kondapi 1951; Waiz 1927). Previous institutions that mobilized people, organized by the British Empire around disparate forms of labor, were altered and embodied in the formation of the nation. After World War II, the movement of men from Punjab, and particularly Hoshiarpur and Jallandhar (sites for military and indentured recruitment since the 1850s), proceeded along new lines. Along with the movement of "Asian" men from Punjab to Southall came the transformation of those men from "immigrant" to "settler," or, more precisely, "coloured worker."

In chapter 1, I note how Sikh men began arriving in England in the nineteenth century. Maharaja Duleep Singh was, of course, a unique figure. But so too were the first students and merchants who, in relatively small numbers, arrived between the 1890s and the 1930s. Southall has been the site for practices constituting different forms of immigration since at least the

1930s. At first, however, it was not a place where Sikhs settled. Immigration histories detail the neighborhood's early arrivals, configured by demands for labor, in terms of a variety of categories of color, gender, and places of origin. In the 1930s, "poor whites" from South Wales, Durham, and Ireland came to work at Woolf's Rubber Company—a site for the production of rubber accessories that would, in turn, be provided to pram manufacturers and motor industries; a production site, moreover, facilitated by the processes of circulation made possible by Southall's position as a railway junction. Directly after World War II, "Poles" and "ex-servicemen" also came to the area to find work at Woolf's (Institute of Race Relations and Southall Rights 1982, 6, 14).

After 1948, and concurrent with the British government's attempts to resolve the labor shortage that plagued the British economy,[10] different categories of "colored" men began increasingly to travel to Southall from the Commonwealth, notably from the West Indies and India, and to find work at Woolf's Rubber Company. Heathrow Airport also became an important site for labor. Around this time, many other industries were established in and around Southall in which immigrants found work, including Nestlés, Batchelors Canning Factory, Rockware Glass, Lyons Maid, Dura Tube Wire, Injection Moulding, Wynum Corset, Combined Optical, Perivale Gutterman, Artid Plastics, Crown Cork, Booth's Gin, Mother's Pride, Chix, and Investacast and Meaden Plastics (Institute of Race Relations and Southall Rights 1981). That the English government facilitated the early movement of colored workers to England is indicated by "the fact that as Commonwealth citizens they [could] enter and leave the United Kingdom at will without any official registration [and were not forced to] report at set intervals to their local police station" (Griffith et al. 1960, 4).[11]

From 1948 through the 1950s, the majority of colored workers—young men from Jallandhar and Hoshiarpur—were willing to work longer hours (often up to seventy-five hours a week) for lower wages, and they quickly began to usurp the positions of the regular employees. These men, however, had a difficult time finding places to live, not only because most could not speak English well, but also because whites refused to let rooms or flats to "coloureds." The difficulties of working and living in Southall as well as the fact that many of these men came from the same areas of Punjab became points around which informal and formal organizations emerged, not only to provide support, but also to reconstitute their forms of relation to the British nation-state. Thus, during this period, particular kinds of labor and lifestyle came to be marked by a discourse of race, itself inflected by a new production of knowledge of "places of origin."

The first formal organization created in the 1950s was the Indo-Pakistan Cultural Society (IPCS), the second, in March 1957, was the Indian Workers' Association (IWA), and the third was a Sikh temple (*gurdwara*) in 1959 (built into a structure that had formerly been a milk depot).[12] Indian workers' associations had also been established in the Midlands, for example, in Coventry in 1953. The IWA and the *gurdwara* took on a double purpose of organizing Sikh men working in Southall and providing housing and information for new arrivals from Punjab (Institute of Race Relations and Southall Rights 1982, 9–10).

The IWA is of particular importance for understanding the production of the British Sikh subject in the 1950s and 1960s.[13] As I have noted in chapter 1, the first IWA, or Hindustani Mazdoor Sabha, was founded in Coventry in 1938 by Punjabi peddlers and local factory workers living and traveling in the Midlands. Another IWA was also formed in London. In conjunction with different Indian Leagues, formed by middle-class Indians and Englishmen interested in India's independence, the IWA's main orientation was the fight for India's independence. The IWA and the leagues raised money for the independence movement and "propagandized" among both Indian immigrants and the British (Dewitt 1969, 45). After Independence, however, these organizations broke up.

In the 1950s, the IWAs were reorganized by Sikhs newly arrived from Punjab. The goals of the IWA–Great Britain, as stated in its constitution, were different from those of the pre-1947 IWA, highlighting the importance of fighting discrimination and improving working conditions, creating cooperative relations with India through the Indian High Commission, creating relations with the British government by working through the trade union and labor movement, and educating the British public about India. According to its constitution, the IWA was a voluntary organization that any Indian laborer in Britain could join. Nevertheless, non-Punjabi Indians had little to do with the IWA (John 1969, 46). The IWA, whose leaders were often prominent men in *gurdwaras,* frequently held meetings in the Sikh *gurdwara.* Yet perhaps one of the IWA's most important sites for organizing Sikh men working in England was the pub. One IWA leader, Chanan Singh, "at election time, and occasionally between elections, went from pub to pub standing drinks for all Indians." Another IWA activist described the significance of pubs for organizing: "We rented a hall or a room in a pub and people would come and drink and sing. For the first half hour or so, the committee members would have to stand up and sing, but after that the other people would join and everyone would be singing. It was a very good time and everyone enjoyed it. We held three or four of these socials and after a while there would be two hundred people there, everyone enjoying themselves. Then we started a membership campaign for the IWA and everyone joined" (Dewitt 1969, 54, 52). In Southall, the IWA — with the IPCS — also hired halls every Sunday where they showed Indian films and raised money for English classes and Indian newspapers that were put in the IWA center (Institute of Race Relations and Southall Rights 1981, 10). Through these events situated in *gurdwaras,* hired halls, and pubs, the IWA provided a means for Sikh men in Southall to congregate, organize around the labor struggles, maintain ties to India, and make connections with Sikhs living in other parts of England (including Leeds, Manchester, Huddersfield, Nottingham, Leicester, Wolverhampton, Birmingham, Coventry, Leamington Spa, Slough, and Gravesend).

The relations between Sikhs in Southall and the nation-state were characterized by a specific dialectic in the 1950s. The history of the Permanent Way in Southall suggests one way to understand the mutually constitutive character of these relations, around which processes constituting the category *immigration* emerged in the twentieth century. I have discussed how the history of the Permanent Way constituted Southall as a particular kind of place, a measured junction, and facilitated the development of industries in Southall. The Permanent Way, too, was an *industry.* Specifically, what did the railway industry produce?

Marx (1978a) provides one way to understand the product of railways:

The result in each case, whether it is people or commodities that are transported, is a change in their spatial location, e.g., that the yarn finds itself in India instead of in England, where it was produced. But *what the transport industry sells is the actual change of place itself.* The useful effect produced is inseparably connected with the transport, i.e. the production process specific to the transport industry. People and commodities travel together with the means of transport, and this journeying, the spatial movement of the means of transport, is precisely the production process accomplished by the transport industry.

The change of place [is] necessarily consumed the moment [it is] produced. (p. 135)

Marx suggests two important points that indicate a dialectic immanent to the railway industry: first, the product of the railway industry is the "actual change of place itself"; second, the railway industry has a specific character in that its product and the production process are constituted in a simultaneous moment of consumption. This conjunction facilitates the constitution of a simultaneity of two forms of time, circulation time and production time, that, although embodied in the value of the commodity, in other cases are mutually exclusive.[14] The railway industry, and more generally the transportation industry, also constitutes the possibility for two forms of circulation: of commodities and of people. As Marx specifies in volume 2 of *Capital,* circulation generates a form of valorization that, in turn, adds value to the commodity. In the case of the circulation of commodities made possible by transport, this valorization dialectically reconstitutes the possibility of and necessity for an industry (e.g., Woolf's factory) to continually engage in the production process. In the case of the commodity that the transport industry produces, the actual change of place itself, circulation valorizes the *consumption of the exchange of place.* The transport industry produces a specific form of *desire,* configured by specific constitutive categories of space and time, *to exchange place.* In this process, to use de Certeau's (1984) words, "consumers are transformed into immigrants" (p. 40).

Together, these various processes constituted specific forms of relations between the practices of colored laborers in Southall, the production of Punjab (as a place exchanged for Southall), the procedures of the British nation-state, and the dynamic of postwar global capital. If these relations grounded the transformation of consumers into immigrants, Southall's factories, as did Woolf's, facilitated the *transformation of immigrants into producers of both capital and the nation-state.* Laborers from Punjab constituted the possibility for Woolf's continual production of rubber accessories and the reproduction of themselves as producers. Conversely, Southall, formerly a junction measuring the development of one kind of Permanent Way, became a junction of another putatively Permanent Way: the British nation-state's postwar progress. Yet, as the movement of laborers from Punjab increased, these forms of relations also generated a series of contradictions.

The Pub and the Pint

Despite the undeniable presence of these new male residents in Southall (i.e., in factories) in the late 1950s, the British government found it difficult to enumerate them. Reflecting on this period, one of the first documents produced by the Institute of Race Relations stated: "Little was known about the numbers or manner of life of the immigrants. . . . It proved impossible to get a general picture of the coloured workers who live in London. They lose themselves in its cosmopolitan population of 8,000,000 people" (Griffith et al. 1960, 3, 4). In other words, immigration was *not* constituted by the government as an object of regulation. Although potentially identifiable through racialized signs of presence (i.e., as producers) and visibility (i.e., color), colored workers nevertheless moved within a zone of diffuse invisibility (i.e., "impossible to get a general picture"): they did not have to register with the police on arrival, and they had their own meeting places in pubs and *gurdwaras*. Here, we may note the emergence of a certain vicissitude that characterized the relation of the nation-state to its new labor force: the postwar nation-state desired the presence of colored workers ("they play a valued part in our prosperity, particularly in filling the less attractive jobs"), yet that desired presence was simultaneously a point of anxiety ("they move from the area of one local authority to another almost daily . . . these movements are not easy to observe" [Griffith et al. 1960, 3]).

In August 1958, however, the government began to reformulate the presence of colored workers in England. Hiro pinpoints one of the moments significant for the unveiling of this presence. This violent confrontation followed a "scuffle" in a "mixed" Nottingham pub (North England):

Next evening, a Saturday [23 August], a group of West Indians returned to the pub bearing knives and razors. At closing time they attacked, injuring six whites. The word spread quickly. A mob of 1500 whites launched a counter-attack with razors, knives, palings and bottles. Eight people, including policemen, were hospitalized. . . . This flare-up made national radio and newspaper headlines, and had an immediate effect on the Notting Hill area of London, where trouble had been brewing for several weeks. Within hours of the news of the Nottingham riot, a gang . . . went "nigger-hunting" . . . and left at least five blacks unconscious on the pavement. . . . The following Saturday, 30 August, more violence erupted in Nottingham [where a crowd of 3,000–4,000 whites congregated] and Notting Hill [where 200 whites attacked blacks' houses near Bramley Road] . . . and [on Sunday] in Latimer Road, Harrow Road and Kensal Rise. Violent activity, albeit in a low key, went on for another fortnight. (Hiro 1991, 39–40)

In 1960, Philip Mason wrote about the significance of these conflicts for the British government:

> In the late summer of 1958 there were outbreaks of violence in Nottingham and Notting Hill. They received in the world's press an attention hardly justified by the incidents themselves; no lives were lost and in both areas the disturbances *occurred only on Saturday nights;* during the week, *when people were at work,* the pressure of hostility was not sufficient to bring them into the streets. None the less, these incidents were *harmful to Britain's name abroad.* . . . To many people in the United States and South Africa it was gratifying that Britain . . . had herself proved to be no better than she should be. . . . The affair was damaging. (emphasis added; Griffith et al. 1960, vii)

During the late 1950s and early 1960s, when immigrants could still be explicitly distinguished from the *we* of the nation — that is, before the apotheosis of multiculturalism — within the fantasy of the nation-state such violence was supposed to happen elsewhere, constituting a difference between *home* and *away.* Almost immediately, the government set up procedures to police a hidden community wherein it might locate, identify, and confine the colored worker. In other words, the anxiety regarding colored workers transformed into a desire to make "immigrants" *visible* and controllable, in specifically defined ways and settings.[15]

The 1958 riot startled Britain into a new awareness of its postcoloniality determined by issues of race and labor. There has been much work on the history of race in Britain, and I do not intend to reiterate it here (e.g., Asad 1993; Bhabha 1994; Brah 1996; Centre for Contemporary Cultural Studies 1982; Gilroy 1987; Hall 1981, 1988, 1989a and b, 1990, 1997; Hall and Jefferson 1976; Mercer 1994). What I would like to do instead is draw attention to the setting around which the 1958 "race riot" began: the pub. In my view, it is not insignificant that Philip Mason, concerned with "Britain's name abroad," seemed relieved that the "disturbances occurred only on Saturday nights" rather than "during the week, when people were at work." This discourse of leisure and labor outlined what, at the time, was a crucial distinction between whites and blacks. Put simply, no matter what economic class, whites could have access to leisure time, as a specific modality constituting their Englishness, and blacks were acceptable within the nation so long as they retained their exclusive role as laborers who did not enter into the national leisure force. Blacks — and in Britain *black* referred to both Afro-

Caribbeans and South Asians—certainly did have their own practices of leisure, which I have already noted in terms of Southall Sikhs. These practices may even have been set within pubs, but these pubs were black pubs, and they remained, in the 1950s, outside the purview of the white English settings of leisure activity. Until 1958, the pub, within the mise-en-scène of national fantasy, was a place where the English negotiated the *invisible generality* of English equivalence. The conflict in the Nottingham pub inaugurated a new form of relation in which the white invisibility of the English would meet the differently valued invisibility of the colored worker. The Nottingham pub, moreover, as a pub, or "public house," could suggest a relation to, and the possibility of conflicts between whites and blacks within, other similar settings all over Britain. In order to specify this leisure setting as a site for negotiating Englishness, let me consider the pub at a more abstract level.

In Britain, these sites of mass consumption—pubs—are called *locals* by their regular customers. Its name notwithstanding, the local tends to indicate both a locale and a displacement, a movement between the intimate boundaries of a neighborhood and a generalized public domain. At lunchtime, on the way home from work, or in the evening after dinner, Londoners, or, for example, Liverpudlians, might stop at their local—a spatializing category that at once discerns one kind of difference (the Hamborough Tavern on the Broadway, Glassy Junction on South Road) in a domain of public equivalence (to the extent that, in England, "a pub is a pub"). This localization of social relations of consumption (Appadurai 1996b) and of pleasure and leisure has been given a certain definition by proliferating strategies of the alcohol industry (i.e., a pub is a "tied house" or a "free house"). Conversely, tourist agencies and international pub aficionados have valorized the architecture of the English pub as a monument in which one can recognize and experience the peculiarity of what is typically English (Girouard 1984; Jackson 1976; McGill 1969). In the 1950s, the local drew together very different orders of cultural capital, national culture, and legal process (i.e., zoning, licensing). It imposed a specific temporal structure on consumption ("time gentlemen," "last call"). And it facilitated a slippage of normal procedure into normative transgression (i.e., the "lock-in," underage drinking).

In postwar Britain, nationality began to be produced increasingly through common consumption. Individuals participated easily in this meeting of consumption and nationality by pausing at the local for a pint. By merely pausing, however, they would be moving through and inhabiting a disjunct series of translocal relations that conjoined in the local and in local acts of consumption. The local illuminated one locality in terms of diverse relations of equivalence to other English localities: spaces and temporalities defined by leisure and labor, industrial sponsorship, architectural tradition, and juridicolegal procedures. In turn, the pint, the local object of consumption par excellence, indicated a history of practices whereby specific kinds of consumption formed the basis for the constitution of certain forms of English equality and difference in the most minute fashion.

The pint is first of all a standardized measure indicating an abstract spatial quality. This abstraction has, historically, been made known, in all English pubs, through the glass container that takes the same name as the measure and through the liquid — whether lager, bitter, stout, or ale — that fills the container. As a standard measure, however, the pint is itself the product of a juridicolegal procedure. In 1826, the pint, or, more precisely, the "imperial pint," was made the legal measure in Britain — defined in a relation of equivalence to two other forms of measure: 34.66 cubic inches or 0.57 liter (*OED,* 1991 ed., 1347). The necessity of this measure emerged out of complications and confusions concerned specifically with the exchange of liquids, corn, and other powdery or dry substances as commodities (*OED,* 1991 ed., 1347), the values of which were determined by specific quantities of socially necessary labor time (Marx 1976, 129, 303). In other words, the pint signifies capital's historical imperative of commensurability configured by historically specific productions of space (i.e., the container) and time (i.e., the Marxian notion of the substance of value), productions that make possible the translation of disparate kinds of contents into a relation of abstract forms.

After World War II, the historical formation of the pint also became an aspect of the production of a particular difference (something with which Philip Mason was extremely concerned). In a general sense, the very measurement of the imperial pint signifies this difference, an *English* difference, in relation to what is decidedly *not English:* a difference, for example, from the United States, where the standard pint is equal to 28⅞ cubic inches or 0.47 liter. And, to the extent that all pubs in England might serve beer as pints, the pint became part of a visual regime of recognition of that valorized difference: by legal imperative, a white line marks the measure on the glass, and, indeed, Britons "know a good pint when they see one." In the locality of mass consumption, the generalized epistemology of the pint, as a measure of English equivalence and difference, becomes conflated with a "technique of the body" (i.e., the feel of the glass in the hands and the drinking of the pint, the knowledge of the amount of liquid in the stomach) (see Appadurai 1996a;

Mauss [1935] 1973), specific desires (i.e., to "have" a pint or to find out how much one can "take"), certain pleasures (i.e., having just enough), and obvious displeasures (i.e., having one pint too many or too few).

In the 1950s, the local was one of several intimate settings for a specific dialectical process. With this we might recognize the classic workings of the fetishism of the commodity form that Marx discusses briefly in the first chapter of the first volume of *Capital*. Summarizing the preceding discussion, the pint may be described in terms of three qualities that Marx (1976, 163–67) discerns in the commodity as fetish: (1) the equality of human labor takes on a physical form in the equal objectivity of the products of labor as values; (2) the measure of the expenditure of human laborpower by its duration takes on the form of the magnitude of the value of the products of labor; (3) the relation between producers take on the form of a social relation between the products of labor. But perhaps just as important are the forms of relations, and productions of knowledge and desire, that the pint as fetish made possible *in* the local. It is not merely that the fetish constituted a relation within the commodity itself (i.e., use value and value) or between producers and their products (i.e., alienation). Rather, the fetish facilitated a relation between *consumers* and the production of a racist discourse of equality and freedom, by which whites were allowed access to the rights of leisure time and blacks were not. In the local, the equality of English citizens took on a physical form in the reflection of a pint: "The pub, reduced to its lowest terms, is a house where during certain hours everyone is free to buy and drink a glass of beer" (Harrison 1961, 17).[16] Or, as Jackson (1976), reflecting on the history of the pub, has mused, the local "is even more English than *Punch* magazine. . . . The pub is exclusively English" (p. 5). We might understand the pub and the pint in slightly different terms—terms that indicate the emergence of techniques for negotiating Englishness. In this setting, characterized by an unparalleled impulse, repetition, and regularity, consumption mediated a particular production—of the nation-state. In 1958, however, this practice of consumption, which created for England the subjects for whom the specific determinations of space and time were products, began to be challenged.

Delinquents in Our Midst

Soon after the 1958 riots, during the same year as India's Congress Working Committee convened the first National Integration Committee, the Institute of Race Relations was founded. The institute commissioned a pamphlet, *Colour in Britain,* published in London in October 1958. In the House of Commons on 5 December 1958, David Renton, joint undersecretary of state for the Home Office, enumerated the "estimated coloured population from the Commonwealth" in England: West Indians, 115,000; West Africans, 25,000; Indians and Pakistanis, 55,000; other "coloured" Commonwealth citizens, 15,000 (Griffith et al. 1960, 3). But these were estimates based on disparate authorities that varied widely. Colored workers continued to be elusive: for example, in Banton's 1959 *White and Coloured,* the total number of "coloured persons" is set at 167,500 but, a year earlier, the official estimate had been 190,000, and the official estimate the year of Banton's publication was 210,000 (Banton 1959; Griffith et al. 1960). The disparity of these enumerative processes notwithstanding, the violence of the riots was soon translated into a discourse of commensurability and pathology that transcended and bridged white and colored communities in troubling ways. This relation of equivalence, however, was not located in the pub. The outbreak of violence was attributed to "the presence of a number of *coloured delinquents* . . . known to be . . . responsible for organizing white prostitution in a previously respectable neighborhood" (Griffith et al. 1960, 89). The cause of the violence thus was located within a domain of desire and transgression: not of consumption, but of prostitution. Colored workers who attempted to enter the locality of national leisure were transformed into colored delinquents, and, to remedy a national pathology (i.e., prostitution), it would then be necessary to discipline the delinquency, if not eliminate the delinquents.[17]

In 1959, Conservatives, who had gained a majority in Parliament, began lobbying against immigration, with the goal of controlling and drastically restricting the movement of colored people to Britain. This is a well-known story. Between 1959 and 1961, movements of people from the Commonwealth to Britain accelerated. Then legislation began to be instituted that limited these movements: the 1961 Commonwealth Immigrants Act, which required prospective immigrants to obtain vouchers; the acts of 1963–65, which shifted the emphasis of limitations from unskilled to skilled labor; the Government White Paper of 1965, which restricted the number of vouchers to eighty-five hundred and limited dependents coming to Britain to wives, children under the age of sixteen, and dependent parents over sixty-five (Agnihotri 1987; Chandan 1986; Ram 1989).

During this period, Southall became a site for whites to articulate their anxieties about the presence of colored workers. For example, in 1963, "hundreds of angry white residents, calling for 'peace and quiet, not Indians,' mobbed the Council, . . . demanding that it 'stop the silent invasion.'" In October of that year, white residents formed the Southall Residents' Association to pressure the council to "take more action about the problems arising from the undesirable elements in our midst" (Institute of Race Relations and Southall Rights 1982, 25, 26).

In January 1965, at a time when almost 90 percent of the Sikh men living in Southall worked as unskilled laborers at Woolf's Rubber Company (Institute of Race Relations and Southall Rights 1982, 13), a journalist who covered race relations for the *Observer* reflected on a particular characteristic of "Asians" in Southall, suggesting another moment of translation and assimilation: "Southall's paternalistic Indian Workers' Association has spent nine years lecturing, cajoling and bullying its members into trying to be *more British than the locals*. . . . Southall's problems don't stem from insular Asians refusing to change their habits and traditions. . . . The real trouble is that it takes two to integrate and one side hasn't yet started trying. Fortunately, the newcomers are prepared to wait" (emphasis added; Dewitt 1969, 1).

Being "more British than the locals," colored workers maintained relations with the British nation-state in precisely the terms of visibility that the nation-state privileged: a visibility configured by discourses of labor integration. This was a visibility, in other words, that necessitated a virtual invisibility, an erasure of signs productive of difference. Between the 1950s and the 1960s, "Southall problems" emerged within confrontations that persistently reiterated these terms. With few exceptions, these confrontations were organized by Sikh men of the IWA who had been born in specific districts of Punjab (mostly Jallandhar and Hoshiarpur). Two points: first, these confrontations were based around factories and other places of employment. Second, and most important, rather than deploying violence, these men organized their protests around peaceful negotiation through official liaisons with representatives of the nation-state (see Ballard 1989, 1994; Ballard and Ballard 1977; Dummett 1980; Helweg 1979; Hiro 1991; Institute of Race Relations and Southall Rights 1982; Ramdin 1987; Tatla 1993; Thandi 1996). In other words, protests were about *production,* admission to sites of production, and access to "equality" (i.e., fair wages, the length of the workday) *as producers.* Could Sikh men contribute to the production of the nation and still not be a part of it, still not be translated into a domain of national commensurability? As producers, at least, Sikh men could avoid the stigma of delinquency.

From Producer to Consumer

In the historical structuring of the working day, there is a dialectic immanent to surplus value that constitutes the production of leisure time as a necessity — specifically, in order to perpetuate the production of socially necessary labor time (the "substance of value"), it is necessary to provide for the means of subsistence that allows for the reproduction of the laborers (Marx 1978b, 303). Laborers must have time to consume. In other words, *leisure time* must be understood as a category constituted historically in relation to the processes of capital. Leisure time, as such, embodies a compulsion of capital — "*enforced* idleness" — in a temporal measure (Marx 1978a, 403).

Between 1961 and 1971, Britain's South Asian population increased more than threefold, from 106,300 to 413,155. And, between 1971 and 1981, the number almost tripled again, from 413,155 to 1,215,048 (Ballard 1994, 7). With an increased population, and with generations growing up in Britain as British citizens, the cultural practices of Indians in England began to change as well. In the 1970s and 1980s, younger generations of Sikh men began to reorient the use of leisure time in relation to both cultural capital and national culture (see Hall and Jefferson 1976). During these years, emerging out of a history of conflicts over immigration and race relations, and facilitated by the changing welfare system, the demand for leisure time made possible a new form of practice and a new form of visibility producing the Sikh citizen in England. At this point, the earlier significance of pubs as meeting points for the Southall IWA to stir up support among colored workers was transformed. Pubs came to be marked as points of congregation for more general categories of the younger generation: Asians, blacks, whites. Conversely, in Southall between 1972 (a year after the Immigration Act of 1971) and 1981, pubs, as points of congregation and consumption, often became the sites for and objects of violent confrontations between the British nation-state and Southall "youth." But these confrontations had a different quality than the 1958 "scuffle" that preceded the race riots in Nottingham and elsewhere. Pubs became preeminent sites for generating the threat of Southall's changing Sikh population.

The Institute of Race Relations and Southall Rights provides one history of confrontations in Southall pubs that appears in many immigration studies as an inevitable telos mapped out along an essential grid of "good black subject" and "bad white subject": in 1972, the police raided the George Pub and beat up several "West Indian youths"; also in 1972, "white thugs" beat up "Asians" in the Swan Pub "on a number of occasions" (the police would watch the fights and then arrest the Asians); in 1978, the Southall youth movement picketed the Hamborough Tavern because it refused to serve "blacks" (i.e., "Asians," "Afro-Caribbeans"); in November 1979, a gang of "skinheads" threw bottles, bricks, and knives into "a pub full of Asians"; in July 1980, two Asian men were chased out of a "white pub" and attacked; and, on 3 July 1981,

> three coachloads of young skinheads from the East End came into South-all for a concert at the notorious Hamborough Tavern. On the way to the pub the skinheads terrorised Asian shopkeepers and shoppers, smashed shop windows, shouted racial abuse and attacked one Asian woman. . . . Within an hour several hundred local youths — mostly Asian, but with a fair number of West Indians and some white youths — gathered at the Hamborough to do battle with the skinheads and send them packing. Police arrived to protect the skinheads from the anger of the town's youth. The evening ended with the Hamborough Tavern burnt out, many police injured — and the skinheads gone. The following day, the youths justified their action to the national media. "If the police will not protect our community, we have to defend ourselves." (Institute of Race Relations and Southall Rights 1982, 50, 54, 62, 63)

This 3 July riot, conjuring the memory of the August 1958 crisis, marked off the beginning of ten days of violence between blacks and police in inner-city areas all over England: Toxteth (Liverpool), Moss Side (Manchester), Brixton (London), and Handsworth (Birmingham), among other places (Hiro 1991).[18] Generating a circuit of national violence, these riots cost the nation-state an estimated £45 billion (Hiro 1991, 90). Yet Southall's position in relation to the other outbreaks of violence was, in the terms of the nation-state's etiology of race riots, a source of confoundment and incongruity: "Southall was not an inner city area in decline. Its 30,000 Asian residents formed a cohesive, hardworking community; and the unemployment and crime rates were lower than those of other riot-torn areas" (Hiro 1991, 174). In other words, as an exemplary site of *national production,* Southall did not warrant such rebellion.

The emergence of these struggles, conjoined with changing uses of leisure time, indicates an important moment of transformation in the 1970s and 1980s. In contrast to a prior labor history concerned with negotiations within factories, the violent confrontations in Southall between "Asian youths," "white thugs"/"skinheads," and representatives of the nation-state ("police") were specifically about *consumption*. Whites were attacking blacks and Asians who wanted admission to sites of consumption and who wanted to experience the typically English pleasure of leisure time. They were fighting for, among other things, the right to a pint. While former labor negotiations in Southall had been about maintaining a certain *invisibility* acceding to a regime of national normativity and mimicry ("trying to be more British than the locals"), the struggles of Asian youths were about the visibility of consumption, about being visibly British, and about being visibly black. As sites of both consumption and leisure time, pubs became localities around which to organize that visibility and embodiment. They also became sites around which blacks would constitute their citizenship or their own antinational normativity. Consumption of leisure time in Southall became a threatening practice pitted against the nation-state's project to, in Appadurai's (1996a) words, "incubate and reproduce compliant national citizens" (p. 190).

Khalistan in England

Since 1984, the fight for Khalistan has added a new element to this history of national violence and struggle. Although certainly not supported by all Sikhs, the idea of Khalistan has nevertheless become intimately linked to the transformation of British Sikh life. Generated on a global scale, Khalistan has formed the basis not only for militancy or "terrorism," and debates about terrorism, but also for the creation of specialized commodities, diasporic economies, media technologies, and narratives of place and displacement.

After Indira Gandhi's attack on the Golden Temple complex in Amritsar in June 1984, Sikhs began to differentiate themselves from other generalizing categories of identification, such as *black* and *Asian* (for a fuller account, see Tatla 1993, 1999). Formerly constructed networks of Sikhs around Britain were used to mobilize protests, under the rubric of the Sikh *qaum* rather than a black or an Asian people. I have noted some of the effects of these mobilizations in chapter 2. Sikhs attempted an attack on the Indian High Commission in London and organized protests all over England culminating, on 10 June, with a march on India House, with more than twenty-five thousand

Sikhs led by Jagjit Singh Chauhan, in the presence of several thousand London police officers (*The Times,* 11 June 1984, 26A). In Southall, on 1 November, after the assassination of Indira Gandhi, thousands of militant Sikhs celebrated in Havelock Road outside the Sikh *gurdwara.* Thus, within a brief period, the processes of identification of the Sikh subject changed, forming around a new domain of contestation. Questioning the procedures of the Indian nation-state rather than the British nation-state, these practices began to reorient the production of the locality of the British Sikh subject in terms of emerging discourses about the sanctity of the homeland.

Southall became one of many places for organizing the fight for Khalistan (Tatla 1999). Jagjit Singh Chauhan, the president of Khalistan (see chaps. 2 and 3), lived in Bayswater on the western edge of central London. Gurmej Singh Gill, the prime minister of the Khalistan government in exile, was based in Smethwick (Birmingham). Jaswant Singh Thekedar, the defense minister of Khalistan, was based in Southall, along with other leaders of competing Khalistani governments. The confusion, and perhaps humor, of so many different Khalistani governments should not distract from the ways in which their very "presence" and activity reconstituted the English landscape. Situated within Southall, the presence of Khalistan introduced into the nation's capital a particular and perhaps troubling "sense of place which is extraverted, which integrates . . . the global and the local" (Massey 1993, 66).

Becoming one center for the organization of Khalistani struggles, Southall also became a site for new forms of violent confrontation and subject formation: not between Sikhs and the British or Indian nation-state, but among Khalistanis interested in further disaggregating Sikh subjectivity from the generalizing categories *Asian* or *Indian* subject. For example, on 24 January 1986, while working in his off-license (liquor store) on the Broadway, Tarsem Singh Toor, the general secretary of the Indian Overseas Congress, was shot and killed by a "swarthy man [who] came in and ordered a bottle of whiskey" (*The Times,* 25 January 1986, 2A). And, on 11 November 1987, two male Khalistani militants killed Guru Darsham Das, the leader of the Sachkhand Nanak Dham International, an Indian spiritual organization, during a religious meeting in Southall's Dormers Wells High School.[19]

Within these moments of violence, a powerful series of practices emerged, in conjunction with discourses generated by the international news media and the procedures of antiterrorist agencies in Scotland Yard. Khalistani activism in Southall since 1984 has illuminated and played upon historically specific relations between Southall and Punjab, producing and transforming

Punjab from place of departure or birth to homeland and to future Sikh polity — an elsewhere of compromised citizens. Khalistani violence has also translated and transformed the commodification of colored male bodies as sites for the inscription of national productivity. Visible *amritdhari* bodies have become the site for the inscription of a diasporic Sikh *qaum*'s embodied subjectivity signified by the spectacle of the beard and turban. Through the medium of *amritdhari* bodies, these disparate acts and discourses reconstituted the Sikh subject, not just in terms of troubles in Punjab, but also in terms of relations to both a diaspora and a Khalistan. With varying degrees of support, hostility, and indifference, the production of the Sikh diaspora and Khalistan became a fundamental part of the everyday fabrication and experience of locality for Sikhs in Southall. Concurrently, these practices transformed the significance of already-standing buildings and offices in Southall that had been settings in and through which Sikh social life was produced (Appadurai 1996a, 182).

These buildings and offices would come to embody the new threat of the British Sikh to the nation-state, just as they would reconfigure the social lives of British Sikhs in Southall in relation to a Sikh diaspora. One particular kind of setting, the pub, offers one site to interrogate these transformations effected by the fight for Khalistan. I have already discussed how the pub had been a site for Sikhs to congregate in since the IWAs of the 1950s and for confrontations between "immigrant" populations and the nation-state between the 1950s and the 1980s. And I have already noted how, in the fantasy of the British nation-state, the pub holds a preeminent position signifying *Englishness*, an "institution unique to England" (Jackson 1976, 5), and "something solidly, enduringly, uniquely British" (McGill 1969, 1). In other words, the pub has achieved an iconicity equivalent to the Permanent Way. This icon of English durability, however, embodies a new series of contradictions in post-1984 Southall.

Glassy Junction

One Southall pub in particular — Glassy Junction, the pub that the national media implicated in the murder scene of Tarsem Singh Purewal in 1995 — demonstrates these contradictions: "From the roof of Sri Guru Singh sports hall, or the Glassy Junction Pub, there is a good view of the entrance to the *Des Pardes* newspaper office. . . . It was probably from one of these vantage points that the sniper fired the bullet which . . . killed the paper's editor." In

Glassy Junction, British Sikh citizens draw unevenly from, just as they constitute, both England, the location of citizenship, and Punjab, a Sikh homeland. Here, in this local, in the 1990s, consumption orients the locals toward the production of different localities, different histories (occurring elsewhere), and different forms of belonging.

I first visited Glassy Junction in the summer of 1993, just after it had its grand opening. At the time, more than the pub itself, I was interested in the Maharaja Duleep Singh Centenary Festival and the spectacular reproduction of the 1854 Winterhalter portrait that hung in the pub's lounge. I spent more time speaking to the owners of the poster shop around the corner that had made the reproduction of the portrait and traveling back and forth between Southall and Smethwick on the private Sikh bus service. When I returned to Glassy Junction at the end of January 1995, after spending time in Sikh pubs in Smethwick and Leicester, I saw the pub differently. This was not an easy time for Glassy Junction or for Southall. With Purewal's murder on 15 January, many people were shocked and outraged. The doors of the pub were guarded by locally hired security men. Why were they there? "The neighborhood's a bit dodgey, mate." As an unknown, I was treated cordially but obviously with suspicion. The owner of the pub, a dentist and businessman with offices in a neighboring building, graciously sat with me for an interview. But, when he realized I wanted to talk about the pub and the history of conflicts in Southall, he directed me to his manager.

Reflecting on the idea for the pub and on the name itself, the manager referred to both a history of Southall and a history of Sikh mobility. Consider *glassy*. The word has multiple significances and is a pun. As the manager put it: "Many, many years ago when lots of Asians came to England . . . they all wanted to go to drink, and they would say to their mates: Let's go for a *gilassy*." In British English, *glassy* is an adjective used to refer, for instance, to a kind of look, *glassy eyed,* that implies drunkenness or childlike incredulity. Additionally, in colloquial British English discourses, in attributing to something a quality of or a likeness to glass, *glassy* carries the trace of *glass. Glass* may indicate an object that facilitates seeing, reflecting, and recognizing (i.e., spectacles, a window, a mirror). *Glass* also refers to a quantity of beer and the beer's container, particularly a half pint. I have already noted the significance of the local as a medium for processes of recognition and identification configured by practices of consumption. If, however, I may extrapolate from the manager's narrative, *glassy* has a further significance. In colloquial Punjabi, the word *gilassy,* an English loanword, signifies a specific history of translation and transfiguration, transposing categories of Sikh and English practices of consumption.

Consider, now, *junction*. In addition to a colloquial significance that indicates a point of congregation, *junction* has a historical significance particular to Southall and its residents. In the manager's words: "Junction came . . . this pub was called the Railway Tavern, so to maintain that . . . thing . . . we called it Glassy Junction." As I have already noted, Southall is the site for a railway junction, which is located across the street, south of the pub. *Glassy Junction* appropriates and transforms the building and name of the former site, the Railway Tavern, which, in its relation to a history of the Permanent Way in England, indicates a history of changes in the emergence of Southall as a site of production and consumption. Making reference to the Permanent Way, *Glassy Junction* may be seen to interrogate, not just the English institution of the pub, but also that icon of England's privileged mode of national circulation.

On the corner of South Road and Park Avenue, and within a few minutes' walk of the Broadway, Glassy Junction is situated diagonally across the road from the offices of *Des Pardes,* where Tarsem S. Purewal was murdered. Directly to the south of *Des Pardes* is the Sri Guru Gobind Singh Sports Center, named after the tenth guru of the Sikhs, who lived from 1666 to 1708. Glassy Junction stands in stark contrast to the other buildings in the neighborhood, which maintain a drabness characteristic of postwar London architecture (see fig. 19). Although built into the similarly drab building that formerly housed the Railway Tavern, Glassy Junction plays on and transforms the stereotyped architecture of the typically English pub. Indeed, Glassy Junction projects out into the landscape in a way that explicitly redefines the significance of the neighborhood. The building is a three-story structure. On the two sides of the pub that face South Road and Park Avenue, five figures of male *bhangra* musicians have been affixed, spanning one story, dressed in colorful *bhangra* costumes, holding *kirpans* (a *kirpan* is a long sword, one of the Five Ks indicating membership in the Sikh Khalsa), and wearing turbans and full beards (two of these figures are on the South Road side, three on the Park Avenue side). In other words, these figures are grand representations of the *amritdhari* Sikh. *Glassy Junction* is written in both English and Gurmukhi script in large letters on both sides as well, with signs saying "Live Music Every Thu, Fri, and Sat" and "Fully Licensed." Attached to the entrances, on both the South Road and the Park Avenue sides, are pint glasses that have been styled into lanterns inscribed with the Glassy Junc-

Fig. 19 Glassy Junction. *a*, Interior. *b*, Exterior. (Courtesy ITV, *Big City*.)

tion logo below the visage of a male *bhangra* musician (a miniature of the *amritdhari* images on the sides of the building).

Glassy Junction appropriates and transforms familiar and powerful signs of Englishness: the pub and the pint. This local literally inscribes the body of the old colonial other, the iconic figure of the Sikh (i.e., the man with beard and turban), on the pint that, placed at the entranceway, offers a welcome to consume and lights the way. That same figure looms large over the building, stating clearly: WE ARE HERE. Playfully visualizing a series of displacements, Glassy Junction might be taken as an exemplification of Geertz's (1986) well-known reflections on the "irremovable strangeness" of postmodern diversity "scrambled together in ill-defined expanses, social spaces whose edges are unfixed, irregular, and difficult to locate": no need to travel to Punjab; just go to west London to see that the "world is coming at each of its local points to look more like a . . . bazaar than like an English gentlemen's club" (p. 121). Indeed, what customers may consume in Glassy Junction lends some credence to Geertz's celebration: English and European beers on tap and in bottles (i.e., Heineken, Holstein Export) are sold along with Indian lagers (Lal Toofan, Kingfisher) and Punjabi whiskey (Kacch Nai); a large kitchen prepares both English and Punjabi cuisine, the menus for which are displayed by the side of the bar in both Gurmukhi and English script. Geertz's formulation, however, sets up a juxtaposition (bazaar–English club) in order hastily to herald its conflation. Yet the story of Glassy Junction and Southall suggests a more unsettled relation. Against Geertz's liberal celebration of multiculturalism, the relation between the bazaar and the club may be, as Bhabha argues (in response to Geertz), "more agonistic and ambivalent"; between them we may see an "overlap without equivalence" (Bhabha 1998, 36; see also Derrida 1987) that speaks to the complexity of the constitution of the British Sikh citizen in the 1990s.

This overlap without equivalence is made into a spectacle through Glassy Junction's interior design, about which the manager commented: "We thought: we'll bring the original India to London in a pub. . . . The whole theme running through the pub is a village scene from Punjab." Although the design of the pub creates not so much a scene from Punjab as it does a privileged setting of consumption in which to view a series of stereotyped images of Punjab, the very desire to position India (or Punjab) within the national capital indicates how Glassy Junction's overlap must be understood as an effect of histories of colonialism and industrialization.

In 1995, the portrait of Maharaja Duleep Singh no longer hangs in the pub's lounge. Rather, a series of large photographs and several agricultural tools are exhibited on two of the walls, and above the bar, in the main room. These tools and photographs — men with long beards and red turbans performing *bhangra* in traditional costumes, women working with grain — play upon and visualize a nostalgic discourse, historically produced by immigrants, not to mention orientalist and area studies scholars, fascinated with the trope of the village (Appadurai 1986, 1988b; Inden 1990).

The centerpiece of the pub is a map of Punjab that hangs on the wall opposite the bar in the main room (see fig. 19 above). The map stands five feet tall and projects out from the wall, being made of cardboard, rather than paper, approximately two inches thick. This projection is exaggerated by the bright solid colors (orange, green, yellow, and red) that fill in and designate, variously, thirteen of the fourteen districts of the post-1966 Punjab state of India: Bathinda, Sangrur, Patiala, Faridkot, Ferozpur, Ludhiana, Rupnagar, Hoshiarpur, Jallandhar, Kapurthala, Gurdaspur, Phagwara, and Chandigarh. The district of Amritsar, where the Golden Temple is situated, is given a subdued color, gray, accentuating its position on the map. Each of the districts is, additionally, labeled in English, and, at the top, so too is Punjab. This map envisages the territory to which all the pictures and tools in the pub, as Punjabi, refer — and the map assigns them, perhaps, their "proper" place (de Certeau 1984). Indeed, it is this map that qualifies the originary theme of Glassy Junction as "from Punjab."

On one of the walls, above a few agricultural tools, are two clocks: one displays "Southall" time, the other "Punjab" time. These clocks indicate the uneven relation that the pub embodies: between Punjab and Southall rather than between India and England. The knowledge of this relation relies on a standardized temporal measure that pertains to both leisure time and labor time. While this temporality may indicate a measure of duration, it also measures a putative simultaneity of Southall and Punjab (10:45 P.M. Southall time equals 9:45 A.M. Punjab time). The measure of simultaneity, furthermore, facilitates the possibility of prediction (of what friends or relatives will be doing "just now" in Jallandhar) and the implantation of memory (of what "we used to do" in Hoshiarpur at this time) into discourse. Conversely, while these indications of time may delimit when customers can productively consume (times of opening or closing), they also permit the identification of disparate spaces in a single moment of consumption. These clocks, then, refer not only to two different localities and identities. Pointing out a specific relation between Southall and Punjab and the impossibility of being in two places at once, they literally make visible the generative conditions of the Sikh diaspora, its relations to colonial histories of mobility, postwar histories of immigration, and the changing processes of global capitalism. These histories have made possible the central tension that this local embodies: Glassy Junction provides the context for the production of generalized forms of identity that, positioned *within* a national frame, *project onto* a transnational domain. Glassy Junction organizes points of conjuncture for the particular forms of difference and equivalence productive of the nation, but it also produces the different desires and pleasures constitutive of a transnational Sikh *qaum*.

Consuming Southall

In a gesture that contradicted most of Britain's 1995 national media coverage of Southall, on 22 July 1995 Channel 4's *Big City* sent its film crew to Glassy Junction to shoot a special for its show on London's fun hot spots. Airing every Friday, *Big City* was a program that took on the form of a weekly advertisement. As such, the show produced knowledge of London of a specific kind: what to do with leisure time. Drawing a relation to the other master signs of national signification that I have discussed (the pub, the pint, the Permanent Way), *Big City* located sites and practices of consumption that, while still undiscovered and somewhat strange, were considered fashionable and, most important, "typically English." Conjoining practices of consumption with signs of Englishness, *Big City* relied on a certain strangeness of sites and practices as an organizing principle for the show's commentary and humorous segues (recall Geertz's "irremovable strangeness"). The character of this valorized strangeness is significant for it mediated the visual pleasure of watching *Big City* and the generalized pleasure and desire of consumption. For *Big City,* the strangeness of a particular practice of consumption was what made it desirable, but there was a certain limit to the difference that this strangeness discerned: it must also be familiar and thus not threatening.

Being covered on *Big City* can bring customers and profits. Glassy Junction indeed was privileged to have a four-minute feature on the show, and the owners and many of the customers were eager to have this opportunity. For this event, Glassy Junction organized a concert for Alaap, one of the oldest and most popular *bhangra* groups in England, and Kacch Nai representatives came to the pub to hang banners and give out free shots of whiskey.

The segment eventually aired on 14 August.[20] It begins with the presenter being drawn down South Avenue in a horse and buggy in front of the pub, led by a young man in a beard and turban (see figs. 20 and 21).[21] The presenter introduces the segment, saying: "I've always wanted to go to India, you know, and it would seem as I've arrived because here in Southall you can take a trip to the *Poonjab* for the price of a pint." While a soundtrack of dance music dubbed with a sitar plays, the frame moves quickly through a series of images: the outside of the pub with the *bhangra* figures, the lantern outside the pub door, a young man sitting beneath the map of Punjab smiling while reaching for a pint, the barmaid pulling a pint, a photograph of a *bhangra* musician, the Southall clock, the Punjab clock, an old man with a beard and turban toasting with a shot glass (of Kacch Nai), a scene from behind the bar showing the rushing of customers, and then another shot from outside the pub of the sign "Live Music Every Thur Fri Sat." Over the last set of clips, the presenter's voice says: "The Glassy Junction is London's first Indian pub, and it's celebrating its second birthday. . . . It's a magnet for locals and those recently arriving from the subcontinent."

Then follow a few short interviews. In one, a young woman says: "I just came from India three days back, and my friends said we have to take you to this place. It's called *Classy* Junction. I said, Ooh, is it really that *classy*? They said, No, not *classy* . . . *Glassy!*" Then a young man: "It's just the atmosphere. . . . Like Punjab, it's the friendliest place in the world." Then the presenter says: "Here there's a fabulous selection of imported beers [image of the Heineken handle on the bar] . . . there's also a draft Indian lager [image of the Lal Toofan handle] . . . and there's a lethal version of scotch [image of a bottle of Kacch Nai]. . . . What's more, you could pay for the whole lot with rupees [image of presenter paying in rupees]."

Having established Glassy Junction's (safe) difference, *Big City* then returns to the recognizable. The presenter explains: "But, despite the exotic ambience, *it's still a local*" (i.e., it's still a pub). She then interviews the white barmaid, Donna, who mediates Glassy Junction's familiarity: "Not a lot different really. The atmosphere. What they've created is different, obviously, but, at the same time, a pub is a pub." The presenter then says: "Glassy Junction is the perfect place for a potpourri of pints." Grounding Glassy Junction's familiarity in the pub and the pint, the presenter moves on to what accentuates the pub's postcolonial familiarity and appeal: Indian food.[22] "When it comes to eating curry. . . ." Then there is a quick shot of a young man with a beard and turban who says: "The food's nice . . . kabobs, tandoori

Fig. 20 *a*, The introductory sequence of the *Big City* feature on Glassy Junction. *b*, The view of Glassy Junction's exterior shown on *Big City*. (Courtesy ITV, *Big City*.)

Fig. 21 The filming of *Big City* (photograph by Brian Keith Axel).

chicken . . . luv it. . . . Tell you something, it's better than some Indian
restaurants."

The final part of the segment highlights the music of Alaap and a crowd of
young men dancing. The presenter says: "And here it's less a case of 'roll
out the barrel,' more like 'bring on the *bhangra*'!" After a shot of a young
man dancing with his cellular phone and a woman — surrounded by men —
wearing a "Just Do It" T-shirt, there is a short clip of Channi, Alaap's lead
singer, talking about *bhangra:* "It's a very old form of farmer's dance which
comes from Punjab." After another clip of a crowd of men dancing, the frame
shifts back to the pub's main room, where the presenter sits with Glassy
Junction's manager: "D'ya know . . . I don't notice many women here." The
manager laughs and says: "Because all the men like a good drink on their
own . . . they don't want the women yapping them. . . . If my wife watches
this, I'm in trouble." The segment on Glassy Junction then concludes with a
freeze-frame of an old man with a beard and turban drinking a shot of whiskey, overlaid with the words *Glassy Junction, 97 South Road*. A stark contrast to
the image of the exploded body of Tarsem Singh Purewal, whose murder
occurred across the street six months earlier.

The perpetuation of certain stereotypes and an implicit reliance upon
nostalgia for the age of empire are certainly noteworthy in this production.

But, in terms of the issues of this chapter, what is most significant is the way in which, by constructing Glassy Junction as a tourist site, *Big City* admits Southall into the domain of national consumption. This admission rests upon the discourse of a "good" multiculturalism that elides Glassy Junction's troubling "difference" on several levels: for example, Southall's history of violent conflict in and around pubs, Khalistani militancy, Glassy Junction as a Sikh pub. The sight of Glassy Junction's exotic ambience is averted by means of discerning camera work (focusing on the familiar aspects of a pub), implications of commonality (to Indian restaurants in general), and articulations of commensurability ("it's still a local"). Ultimately, *Big City* harkens to a 1970s discourse of the "Asian," returning the Sikh subject to a generalizing category that may then be returned to the nation. Sikhs in Southall may now demonstrate the intimate signs of multicultural citizenship.

Only the barmaid enunciates the tension of a difference within similitude: Glassy Junction is "not a lot different really. . . . What they've created is different, obviously, . . . *at the same time,* a pub is a pub." And the presenter offers a potential liberal critique: "I don't notice many women here." What *Big City* produces and valorizes, then, is London's apparent ability to encompass diversity and conflate distance — appealing to popular discourses about multiculturalism, globalization, and the collapse of space (i.e., India can be here in London); making these procedures accessible, equally, to all citizens through relations mediated by commodities; and reproducing the pint as a passport to commensurability (i.e., "because here in Southall you can take a trip to the Poonjab for the price of a pint"). In short, through a banal representational strategy, *Big City* meets a national desire to constitute the Sikh as citizen. Yet it accomplishes this by displacing and disavowing the Khalistani Sikh subject as a political subject and by transforming Southall into an admissible and consumable Little India.

Between Consumption and the Scenario of Representation

What, then, is the threat of the Sikh subject to the British nation-state? I have argued that, in the 1950s and 1990s, this threat has had much to do with the shifting of minority groups from the status of producers to that of consumers. Considering the effect of post-1984 struggles for Khalistan, there is another way in which to view these tensions. Glassy Junction demonstrates how the cultural and material practices of consumption are met with a politics of representation. The threat of the British Sikh emerges, not only when

Sikhs take the position of consumers, but also when, through the act of consumption, and within the setting of consumption, they take control of their own self-representation. In simple terms, the ITV special on Glassy Junction may be seen as a strategy of wrenching apart consumption and Sikh self-representation. As a tourist site, Southall, and its residents, is easier for the nation-state to digest.

The complexity of this process, however, should not be passed over. In 1997, the British government, through the Ealing Borough Council, began providing Southall with funds to boost its image by making it into a national, and indeed international, tourist site. In order to attain these funds, however, Southall organizers had to make use of the very trope around which the neighborhood has been built: threat. A report commissioned by the Ealing Council, titled "Community Solutions," was put forward to the government to determine how money should be spent to improve the area. According to the report, "The rapidly changing and diverse population of Southall presents as big a threat to its future as it does an opportunity." Southall is described as a "stressful environment, where elements can react together to create undesirable results." Of this "stressful environment," the report comments that "the threat to the Asian population of white racism in the 1970s has been replaced in the 1990s by inter-racial tension between different religious communities, especially among young men." This split between different groups correlates with a split in the landscape of Southall itself: "The location of the over-ground railway station at the centre of town divides north from south [and] the lack of an underground station contributes to Southall's sense of isolation from Ealing and the rest of London." Praising the police "for developing strong community links and preventing tensions developing into confrontation," the report suggests introducing security cameras into the town center to "help reduce crime and the fear of it." Already, the funds have been used in a variety of ways, organizing advertising campaigns for businesses, marking buildings as historic landmarks, and scheduling historic walks (another valorized English pastime). Not least, the money has been used to organize a Southall Internet web site, launched in September 1998. According to the creators of the web site, WebInc, Southall is deploying the Internet "in order to promote Southall town as a tourist attraction . . . as well as promoting its culturally rich communities. Raising Southall's profile will help in attracting more visitors to the town, some purely to experience the magic of its buzzing Broadway shops and restaurants and others for commercial reasons which will help boost the local business community."[23]

The potentiality of Southall Sikhs to come into a new form of self-representation in the 1990s has been configured by the promise of a new social status in Britain, a promise itself made possible by the struggles for Khalistan that brought together the British Sikh population in new ways. This promise was evident to many Sikhs in 1993, the year in which Glassy Junction opened and the Maharaja Duleep Singh Centenary Festival was held. But the success of such moments of celebration was fleeting. In 1995, with the murder of Purewal, this promise was not necessarily shattered, but it was certainly challenged. With the ITV Glassy Junction special, and with the subsequent aid provided by the government, Southall and its Sikh population seem to be entering into a new era of promise. Although that promise may not be what Khalistanis have hoped for, the specter of the homeland cannot be missed amid the bustle of new possibilities.

Following Stuart Hall (1989b), I would note the uneven and unsettled historical shift for Sikhs in Britain since the 1980s from the "relations of representation to a politics of representation." The transformations of the Sikh threat to the nation-state may be situated within this shifting domain. Hall correctly comments that "scenarios of representation"—emerging out of regulated, governed, and normalized "representational and discursive spaces of English society"—are not so much *expressive* of an already-formed identity as they are "*formative* . . . in the constitution of social and political life" (pp. 442–43). Glassy Junction has made several appearances within scenarios of particular sorts. And Glassy Junction, which is now described as a "must-see" for any visitor to Southall, offers the possibility of refining the understanding of the threat and promise of British Sikhs.

Recall the visage of the Glassy Junction Pub. Offering an exterior and interior designed with ostentatious visibility, no other structures in Southall inscribe their difference in the way in which Glassy Junction does, creating a certain incitement *to look*. A certain incitement, yes, but so too an insistence: to arrest one's look, to pause before proceeding to witness the rest of Southall and its historical signs of a population struggling to participate fully in either being British or being Sikh, or both. Glassy Junction embodies a certain fullness, overflowing with signs that repeatedly return to disparate "origins": significations of the enduring legacy of colonialism, of the emergence of global capitalism, of conflicts over colored labor and English exclusivity, *and* of a Sikh "homeland." Although this structure was certainly built with a sense of pride and, perhaps, triumph, I would hasten to point out that there is an earnestness, if not anxiety, that surrounds it.

What I am suggesting with these remarks — highlighting the incitement to look and to pause, the insistent repetition, the pride, the anxiety — is that Glassy Junction may be understood as another kind of "scenario of representation" (to use Hall's phrase). Organized around the figure of the Sikh man with beard and turban — repeated multiply in different magnitudes, from one story tall to pint size — Glassy Junction's scenario of representation is transformed into a fetishistic scenario of identification constitutive of the diasporic imaginary. In this context, however, the fetish of the Sikh body in Southall must be distinguished from the fetish of the tortured body discussed in the preceding chapter. Putting this in somewhat programmatic terms, in that chapter I argue that, produced within histories of torture, the Indian nation-state's claims to legitimacy come into conflict with Khalistani claims over two disparate temporal formations and through the medium of the body circulated as a political text. Constituting a relation between the *amritdhari* profile and the tortured body, the nation-state evokes a fantasy of a temporal before — that which preceded the nation-state's apotheosis — that is imputed to the Sikh and that the Sikh subject is said to brandish before the nation. As a threat to national integration — a threat from abroad and from a discontinuous past — the Sikh is a danger to the common good. The nation-state thus finds legitimacy for developing special procedures (sometimes called *extrajudicial*) that closely govern and monitor the Sikh population of Punjab.[24] Against these procedures, Khalistani discourse has been formed around the relation of the tortured body to the *total* body of the *amritdhari*, conjuring an anteriority that, in Khalistani terms, is not threatening but promising: this anteriority is the before from which the Sikh *qaum* must emerge and into which it will have reemerged in the utopian vision of a Khalistani state. This analysis offers a framework for a much broader argument about the diasporic imaginary: that it has not been an already-constituted subject, the Sikh, that has *undergone or moved through* a history of struggle, violence, and discrimination, but rather that disparate Sikh subjects have been formed *having gone through* historically specific regulatory practices.

In 1995, the total body displayed on and within the structure of Glassy Junction indeed stood in relation to the image of a body in bits and pieces. Across the street from the pub, Purewal's body has been "practically exploded, spraying blood 2ft into the air." Spatially, the total body and the exploded body stand side by side. Historically, the exploded body of 15 January 1995 stood between the maharaja's glorious body of 1993 and the anonymous Sikh body appearing in the summer 1995 *Big City* special. These images emerged out of histories of conflict very different from the context of Indian practices of internal security and the representational practices of Khalistanis on the Internet, although they certainly may be positioned within that context. I am more concerned with the way in which Glassy Junction's images of total Sikh bodies, looming over the offices of *Des Pardes,* signify the ambiguities and ambivalences configuring the British Sikh subject — ambiguities and ambivalences affected not only by Khalistani struggles but also by histories of immigration and race violence. What is operative here is the vicissitude of citizenship in postcolonial England during the 1990s — that is, the ambivalence of the Sikh subject that is both citizen and the racialized other, both promise and threat. Glassy Junction speaks amply to this ambivalence, and — in its very visuality, its exhibition of commodities, and its invitation to consume — it draws out further the correspondence between postcolonial histories, global capitalism, and national identification.

Both an *object* and an *aspect* of knowledge production, the fetish emerges within, just as it constitutes, a particular kind of scenario that must be specified. The scenario of fetishism, illuminated brilliantly in Freud's ([1928] 1977) work, is one of inquisitiveness, investigation, and discovery. These themes provide one way in which to reconsider Glassy Junction and the fetish of the Sikh body, which have been given a specific quality through histories of racist violence and race riots. In the 1990s especially, the discovery of a horrifying lack of a sovereign totality seems to demand constant rechecking — to see "whether there was any black in the Union Jack" (Hall 1989b, 448).

The repeated attempts to identify the black in the Union Jack come from all directions. In this sense, the image of the total body of the Sikh cannot be separated from the structure of Glassy Junction. Glassy Junction may form one site for the nation's investigations into the status of Southall's Sikh community. But this pub also provides a scenario in which the formation of the British Sikh subject coincides with an investigation — both the Sikh community's and the nation-state's — of citizenship and Englishness. In both cases, the gigantic images of Sikh men haling customers into Glassy Junction also offer the opportunity to pause and divert one's gaze. Glassy Junction's locals stop for a pint, taking part in the preeminent English pastime; *Big City* turns Southall into a Little India. What are the results of these investigations? Whatever the answer, these investigations themselves repeatedly constitute their objects in different ways, making the psychic and social struggle to come into representation meet the unsettling terrain of the politics of representation. Historically, within this conjuncture, the discovery of a lack has more often than not been met with the reprise of disavowal: Yes, the nation is one, "in spite of everything," but the one is "no longer as it was before" (Freud [1928] 1977, 353).

One must regard the attempt of Glassy Junction to "bring the original India to London in a pub" as both courageous and tenuous. Not only does this local incorporation of the "original India" within London play upon the vicissitudes of England's form of citizenship. It also opens up the indeterminacy of identifications with both *a here* (i.e., the nation-state) and *an elsewhere* (i.e., Punjab or Khalistan). This indeterminacy complicates my characterization of the diasporic imaginary. But within this indeterminacy lies the vicissitude of the Sikh diaspora's promise and threat.

Consider Glassy Junction's map (see fig. 19 above). The map of Punjab may refer to an original India. But, in relation to the image of the Sikh body, and overdetermined by a history of Khalistani activism in Southall, the map is also metonymic of the Sikh homeland, a place that, in the terms of Khalistani discourses about the Sikh nation, is originary and constitutive of the Sikh subject. In this sense, one way in which to understand Glassy Junction's scenario of representation for Sikhs is in terms of a certain longing for *Sikh* commensurability met with a longing for the rights of inclusion in the British polity. Within the intimate domain of a marginal locality, Glassy Junction provides a public space in which, by identifying with an image, Sikhs *may, or may not,* recognize and construct themselves in relations of equivalence with other Sikhs. (It also constitutes the possibility for non-Sikhs to recognize, or not, Sikhs as other.)

The effectivity of this fetishistic scenario proceeds by way of a complex play of substitutions. For example, in the manager's narrative, a generalized abstraction, *the original India,* takes the place of *Punjab,* which is specifically valorized and visualized in the pub. The image of India, however, maintains a pronounced absence in the pub (except for the Indian beers and the fact that, if they wish, customers can pay in rupees). Indeed, a definitive feature of the pub's map of Punjab, as a map of the Sikh homeland, is precisely that it *does not* represent India. Unlike more conventional cartographic representations of Punjab, the map shows no territories other than the territory of Punjab. It indicates no interstate or international boundaries: specifically, of Indian states and interstate borders, there are no indications of Haryana, Himachal Pradesh, Janmu and Kashmir, or Rajasthan; and, of international territories and boundaries, there is no Pakistan. Likewise, the map does not represent Chandigarh as the capital of both Punjab and Haryana.

The visuality of the map relates, again, to the visuality of the Sikh body, indicating another form of substitution. What is at work is the substitution of a thing that is pictorial for a history of movement (i.e., the Permanent Way, immigration), the content of which could never be a singular object of actual perception (cf. Freud [1922] 1991, 454). In other words, while Glassy Junction builds up a scenario of representation around images of Sikh bodies and Punjab, that scenario is yet inseparable from a diverse history of displacements that has made possible the presence of British Sikhs, *as* citizens and *as* Sikhs, *in* Southall in the 1990s — Sikhs who know very well that, while they may be British, they also "are from" Punjab, or Hoshiarpur, or Jallandhar (whether or not they have ever been to India). Here, we see the vicissitudes of the diasporic imaginary most plainly. Glassy Junction signifies, combines into equivalence, and stands in for multiple histories of placement and displacement that, dialectically, have determined both the local's logic of abbreviation and the logic of promise and threat. As a junction for several distinct *displacements,* Glassy Junction produces a distance (of Southall from Punjab) and a difference (Sikh) that comes into tension with a fantastic desire for proximity and equivalence — for England, for Punjab, for the homeland.

5 : the homeland

While India (Hindustan) is celebrating the 50th anniversary of its independence
from the British, for the Sikh nation and other minorities it is a day of mourning
and beginning of a genocide. The Sikhs actively participated in India's
independence movement and their share of sacrifices far exceeded their small
number. . . . During the partition fiasco of 1947 . . . the Sikhs (who ruled sovereign
Punjab and many neighboring states until the British annexation in 1849) put their
trust in the Hindu majority to share a common destiny in free India. . . . However,
within a few years of independence the Sikhs discovered to their dismay that the
promise of an autonomous homeland was a political hoax. . . . In a series of
protests, during the 1970s and 1980s, thousands of Sikhs were arrested and
confined to jails. This non-violent movement for a genuine autonomy in Punjab
has been repeatedly subjected to India's barbaric state terrorism, which generated
counter-violence. The police atrocities during the ASIAD games (1982) were
followed by the Indian Army's bloody assault on the Golden Temple Complex
(The Sikh Vatican) and around forty other Sikh Shrines in June 1984. . . . The
savage wave of mass murder of the Sikhs, which followed the assassination of Mrs.
Gandhi in November 1984 further alienated the Sikhs from India's imperial
system. These traumatic events were followed by continuous genocide in the Sikh
homeland (Khalistan).
— "Independence Day for India Dooms Day for the Sikhs," advertisement, *New
York Times,* 13 August 1997, sponsored by the Council for Khalistan, the Khalistan
Affairs Center, and other Khalistani organizations

Since Jagjit Singh Chauhan's 1971 advertisement (see chap. 2), readers of the *New York Times* have been reminded of the fight for Khalistan on many occasions. More often than not, this reminder has been provided by journalists covering "terrorism" in Punjab. Sometimes, journalists have reported on Sikh "terrorism" or terrorist training camps in other parts of the world (i.e., the United States, Canada, and Europe). On one other occasion, the story of Khalistan has been narrated by Khalistanis themselves. This was a paid advertisement placed in the *Times*'s Op-Ed section on 13 August 1997, two days prior to the commemoration of India's fifty years of independence. The advertisement, excerpted in the epigraph to this chapter, tells the story of Khalistan in what has, for some, become an easily identifiable narrative style (Das 1995; Jeffrey 1987; Juergensmeyer 1988; Oberoi 1987). Having mentioned the precolonial sovereign Punjab and the struggles for Indian independence, the story proceeds through a list of events detailing the violent discrimination practiced against the Sikh people and culminates with a call for the creation of Khalistan.[1] In the case of my epigraph — an entextualized countermemory posed at the fiftieth anniversary of Indian independence — the narrative moves through the threat of a Sikh people's continual persecution and ends with the image of promise. Redeploying Chauhan's phrasing from the 1971 advertisement, this narrative claims that the creation of Khalistan "would provide a neutral buffer between Pakistan and India" and cause a peaceful transformation of South Asia as a whole: "In this new geopolitical landscape, the existing arbitrary frontiers, guarded by lethal military machines, nuclear arsenals and electronic booby-traps, would be replaced by administrative lines of jurisdiction between one another resembling the European Union. This insane armament race between India and Pakistan would become redundant. The industrial countries would be saved from subsidizing the production of weapons of mass destruction and genocide in South Asia."[2]

There is a certain equivocation in this story of Khalistan that a historical anthropology must attempt to avoid but that nevertheless has a tendency to emerge with the "projection of individual existence into the weft of a collective narrative" (Balibar 1991, 93) or within the historiography of a "people" who have moved through and been caught between apparatuses of domination and the almost palpable promise of liberation. This is an equivocation over the *nature* of the homeland and its relation to a people. I raise this point not out of disrespect for the atrocities to which many Sikhs have been subjected or out of any desire to evade a critical engagement with the contradictions of the modern nation-state. Rather, I hope to specify further the character of these problems. Etienne Balibar (1991) indicates the parameters of this equivocation when he writes of the position of a *schema of genealogy* within fictive ethnicity: "The filiation of individuals [putatively] transmits from generation to generation a substance both biological and spiritual and thereby inscribes them in a *temporal community* known as 'kinship'" (emphasis added; p. 100). In a critique of politicojuridical procedures, Judith Butler (1990) questions how "the invocation of a temporal 'before' [may be] *constituted by the law* as the fictive foundation of its own claim to legitimacy" (emphasis added; pp. 2–3). And, in a similarly incisive fashion, Homi Bhabha (1994), attempting to displace the linear temporality of historicism, asks: "How are we to understand this *anteriority* of signification as a position of social and cultural knowledge, this time of the 'before' of signification, which will not issue harmoniously into the present like the continuity of tradition — invented or otherwise" (p. 159)?

These articulations of the destinies of historic peoples and individuals within the symbolic scene of the nation call for a return to, and a reassessment of, my analyses of the Sikh homeland, the homeland that travels with the mobile imaginary of the Sikh diaspora. One of the central arguments of this book is that it is this mobility, within specific histories of displacement, that has been a central element in the very constitution of the homeland. Inverting the common place-of-origin thesis (cf. the introduction), I argue that the *diaspora* has produced the homeland. Diasporic claims to a definitive form of relation between a globally dispersed Sikh people fall into place — and the relations of that people, "in the diaspora," are traced back to the homeland itself. I argue this inversion, not to "denaturalize" the homeland, but to try to come to terms with its very nature. But this simple inversion is itself complicated by the very different contexts of struggle and violence that have prompted such a production: the surrender of Maharaja Duleep Singh, the Maharaja Duleep Singh Centenary Festival, pre-Partition struggles for a Sikh state, post-Partition struggles for Punjabi Suba, the torture of Sikhs and representations of torture, diasporic calls for Khalistan, and British histories of immigration and multiculturalism. The character of these historical contexts suggests, not only that the homeland means different things to different people, but also that the homeland, now a necessary part of diasporic processes of identification, proliferates a specificity that comes into tension with its own formalized generality. This tension itself locates a flash point of conflict.

In this chapter, I address one more critical flash point of conflict over the production of the Sikh homeland: between Khalistanis and Sikh studies scholars. The import and sensitivity of this site of struggle should not be underestimated. The ascendance of Sikh studies, and its establishment as an internationally respected discipline, has coincided with the emergence of the Sikh diaspora itself, particularly since the 1970s. I have noted the significance of this relationship in the introduction. In some respects, the project of Sikh studies in the past thirty-five years has always been defined by a study of the diaspora, or at least prompted by the diaspora. After 1984 and Operation Bluestar, when the notion of Sikhs as a persecuted community was radically reconstituted, Sikhs in North America and England began to be more and more interested in supporting the work of Sikh studies, as a means of both popularizing Sikh problems and creating a more salubrious image of Sikhs around the world. It was at this point that Sikh studies became a political project in a way that it had never been before, despite the intentions of many Sikh studies scholars.

The transnationalization of Sikh studies has met the transnationalization of the Khalistani struggles. When the various Khalistani organizations, which may have formerly supported Sikh studies programs, started to evaluate the work of Sikh studies, conflicts quickly emerged. Deploying the latest academic modes of analysis, Sikh studies scholars were not easily enlisted in the Khalistani cause — not least because they spent much of their effort deconstructing hegemonic forms of Sikh identity and history. Against such deconstructive, or, as some Khalistanis would have it, *destructive,* analyses, Khalistanis have posed essentialist notions of a Sikh homeland and its relation to a people. This conflict, however, may not be simply characterized as one between deconstruction and essentialization. Sikh studies scholars have often maintained originary notions of a Sikh homeland and a Sikh people, but these were not the notions that Khalistanis have adopted. And Khalistanis have generated their own deconstructive analyses — not of Sikh identity, however, but of the nation-state and of Sikh studies scholars.

This conflict has become a vital site for the production of knowledge of the homeland and the reconstitution of the Sikh diaspora. The recent history of work in Sikh studies has formed the basis, not only for a prominent trajectory of academic inquiry, but also for a series of pedagogical practices that inform primary educational structures, international media representations, politicojuridical procedures in various nation-states, and the activities of human rights organizations. Countering the proliferation of these Sikh studies projects, Khalistanis, often backed by the Sikh leaders of the Akal Takht in Amritsar (of which more below), have developed their own pedagogical procedures, which, in many ways, have begun to challenge those established by Sikh studies academics, affecting greatly the manner in which the world has come to recognize Sikh identity politics. In addition to an expansive deployment of the Internet, they have funded, and controlled, their own academic programs, conferences, periodicals, and state liaisons. And they have launched global campaigns to defame some of the most important Sikh studies scholars, who have often been personally threatened.

My own work emerges out of these conflicts. I am well aware of the political nature of my narratives, but neither can I agree fully with the pedagogical procedures of much of Sikh studies (even though I am indebted to the field), nor can I accept those of Khalistanis (no matter how much I appreciate their struggle). I offer alternative formulations to what, for many involved in these conflicts, are familiar problems. The conflicts between Sikh studies and Khalistanis present a challenge to historical anthropology to generate a sensitivity to its own political intervention. And they present a challenge to historical anthropology also to develop an analytic that may understand the exceptional reproductive commitments of a "people" without reproducing that ideology.

In previous chapters, I have considered the historical emergence and transformation of the Sikh homeland in various guises, from the Sikh Empire to Azad Punjab, and from the Punjabi Suba to Khalistan. The conflicts between Sikh studies and Khalistanis suggest another history of formation of the homeland, situated within a diasporic landscape, moving within and between North America, Europe, and South Asia. In the following discussion, I trace out one genealogy of these conflicts, demonstrating their relation to procedures of the postwar U.S. nation-state and their implications for the production of knowledge of the Sikh diaspora.

Sikh Studies and Place

In February 1994, I attended a conference entitled "Transmission of Sikh/ Punjabi Heritage to the Diaspora" held at the University of Michigan for scholars from North America, Britain, and India. Funded by both the university's International Institute and New Delhi's National Institute of Punjab Studies, this was the first major event organized by the university's Center for South and Southeast Asian Studies in conjunction with the new Program in

Sikh Studies, a program itself developed through the Sikh diaspora community's substantial financial support. The cosponsorship of the conference by both an American institution and an Indian institution is noteworthy, as is the conjuncture of efforts of the Center for South Asian Studies and the Program in Sikh Studies. Just as significant is the positioning of a conference on the diaspora within the milieu of area studies. These institutional, pedagogical, and community relationships are suggestive of one critical point of intersection between Sikh studies and Khalistani activism. These relations and their conflicts, however, are not self-evident — nor is their position in a controversial era of proliferating minority studies programs (Kaplan and Levine 1997; Shankar and Srikanth 1998).

This conference represented an important moment for many of those who attended, a moment attesting not only to the validity of the topic, Sikh studies, but also to the strength, indeed the "community," of the object of study — the Sikh diaspora. After fifteen years of occasional Sikh studies conferences (Berkeley in 1979, Michigan in 1986, Columbia in 1989), this one inaugurated the first Sikh studies program in a U.S. university, effectively transforming the significance of *Ann Arbor, Michigan,* for Sikhs around the world. In the light of the struggles of many Sikhs in the United States who began funding university programs in Sikh studies after the escalation of violence in Punjab in the 1980s — a fund-raising process that, at Michigan, took over ten years — this conference was a major triumph. To paraphrase de Certeau, the conference seemed to hail a moment when geographies of diasporic action began to drift into the commonplaces of an order (de Certeau 1984, 116). Yet, while the conference represented itself through an inaugural discourse signifying the institutionalization of a "proper place" (de Certeau 1984) from which Sikh studies, and perhaps the Sikh diaspora, would enunciate its "identity," that place itself was constituted through a series of seemingly irresolvable tensions (tensions, indeed, of which many conference participants were aware and by which they were troubled). These tensions indicate the meeting points, and the points of friction, between the Sikh diaspora and the nation-state, particularly where productions of knowledge of the homeland come into play. They also outline the shadow of Khalistan seeking to come into representation.

The "Sikh Studies at Michigan" bulletin distributed at the conference provides one way to talk about these intersections, which, in many ways, demonstrate the effects of the conflicts between area studies and diaspora studies: "The University of Michigan has initiated one of the most ambitious programs in Sikh Studies in North America, and indeed, outside of India. Our goal is twofold. We seek to provide Sikh Americans with university-level instruction in their religious and cultural tradition, and we aim to make that tradition accessible to the wider non-Sikh community." Perhaps the key words from this passage are *university, provide, instruction, tradition,* and *make . . . accessible.* These provide one way in which to explain the relation between area studies and diaspora studies as well as the mission of the Sikh Studies Program. They suggest a recent postwar history of the production of area studies specialists in American universities. This is a history of knowledge production that has generated a particular theory of place, of the homeland as originary and constitutive of identity (Appadurai 1986, 1988), coupled with a pragmatic philosophy of education (Inden 1990). As I have noted in the introduction, this theory of place emerged within the projects of area studies specialists, who, after World War II, were recruited by the U.S. government to travel between different "areas" (i.e., ex-colonies) to examine, document, and translate the changing traditions of new nations (e.g., India) in order to convert the old colonial "others" into modern, democratic "selves." In terms of the discourse of Sikh studies at Michigan, the project may not have been so much to convert as to attest to a conversion that had apparently already taken place. During his welcoming speech at the conference, David William Cohen, the director of the International Institute, whose interests were specifically defined by area studies, indicated the extent to which an understanding of the power of this conversion may have become a part of the project of area studies: "In these communities important programs of critique, discussion, interpretation, cultural production, political activity take place that *are of equal intellectual* and scholarly importance to those that are taking place *in the home and source regions*" (emphasis added; Singh and Barrier 1996, 4).

Related to this latter trajectory of area studies is a history of the production, in the social sciences, of specialists in *migration studies* (or, in the case of India, the term for many years was *overseas Indians studies*) and what later came to be known as *diaspora studies* (see the introduction). It is important to note that, although the object of study of these specialists has been the failures, and sometimes successes, of people who have *left* their place of origin — that is, *displacement* — most of the work of these specialists has amounted to examinations of the *originary place,* of the homeland, from the standpoint of *its* manifestation in the diaspora's stable or changing traditions. These studies have often been based on a theory of place similar to that of area studies, with the added complexity that an empirical location such as India is said to generate and contain not only a tradition but also a diaspora. And, similar to that of area studies, the mission of these studies — articulated in prefaces and epilogues — has been to suggest steps that either the displaced peoples might take to adjust (i.e., modernize) their lives in the host nation or the host nations might take to accommodate their new citizens (or short-term migrant laborers).[3] Within this historical trajectory, the aim of the Sikh Studies Program, and of the diaspora conference, might be understood to continue that nationalist project of facilitation and documentation of a specific transformation: of prior subjects of difference into proper citizens.

These possible versions of history, however, meet a complication presented by the conference itself. Many of the speakers, moderators, discussants, institutional representatives, and organizing committee members were themselves "diaspora" Sikh men. This feature of the conference certainly pertains to the gendering of Sikh studies. But it also disrupts the old stereotypical distinction between specialists and objects of study, making it difficult to know what is distinguished by the terms *our* and *we* in the excerpt offered above from the Michigan bulletin.

Perhaps, then, the key words in the "Sikh Studies at Michigan" passage are *Sikh Americans, their,* and *wider non-Sikh community.* These suggest a history of the practices of Sikhs "abroad," not of area and diaspora studies specialists.[4] This can be read as a history of the movement of various people between South Asia/Punjab and the United States, a history of the production of new citizens, and a history of these new citizens infiltrating the hierarchical order of an uncomprehending community of individuals who, like the American Sikhs, were citizens but, unlike them, were non-Sikh.[5] These various histories propose a theory of community that includes a concept of place very similar to the one that I described above. One distinguishing feature — the one that defines the American as Sikh, the one that fragments the totality of American citizens — is the *hierarchical* law of place, of proper and distinct location (de Certeau 1984, 117). In other words, insofar as it has an order by which its different populations are distributed in relations of coexistence, the United States is a place that supposedly produces an exclusive community: Americans. Yet there is a tension immanent to this order because of the disjuncture between the Sikh Americans and their (putatively real) defining location, the homeland. Thus, the mission of Sikh studies and the diaspora conference might also be understood in terms of an attempt, simultaneously, to ameliorate the effects of this disjuncture caused by the initial displacement and to reestablish an American order of place.[6]

These tensions, however, were not the only ones to make the foundation of the Program in Sikh Studies fragile. On one day of the conference, a team of protesters arrived holding placards and giving out pamphlets to passersby. These protesters were themselves diaspora Sikh men whose activism was organized by several Sikh professors from various institutions in the United States and Canada, most of whom were avowed Khalistanis, representing a different group of scholars than those invited to the conference.[7] They were asking some basic questions: "Who is funding this conference? And what is the hidden agenda? Closed door conference . . . Why?" According to the protesters, the "dominant viewpoint" in Sikh studies promotes research "without requisite *analytical, rational or academic* effort or approach," research that has been conducted "in clear contradiction [to] academically known and authentic facts."[8]

Several of the scholars who represented this dominant viewpoint, including W. H. McLeod and two of his students, Pashaura Singh (who held the University of Michigan's chair in Sikh studies) and Harjot S. Oberoi (who held the recently created chair in Sikh studies at the University of British Columbia), were under attack. Indeed, many of the people who sponsored the protesters at the conference had also been involved with the publication of *Invasion of Religious Boundaries* (Mann, Singh, and Gill 1995), which constituted a four-hundred-page critique of Oberoi's otherwise highly praised *The Construction of Religious Boundaries* (1994). This critique is worth noting because it spells out the precise terms of the conflict between Khalistanis and Sikh studies specialists.[9] This conflict differs significantly from the tensions that, as I have noted, are embedded within the historical intersections of nation formation and area or migration studies programs.

Oberoi's book is a thorough analysis of the "culture, identity, and diversity in Sikh tradition." It consists of a reevaluation of the essentializing strategies of the Singh Sabha, a nineteenth-century religiopolitical organization that, reconstituted many times over, continues to influence Sikh politics today. Oberoi (1994) argues that there is nothing natural about such categories as *Sikh* or *Hindu* but rather that "they are specific constructions rooted in particular historical epochs" (p. 418).

Yet, at a moment when many Khalistanis are fighting to establish a homeland for a bounded identity, Oberoi's critique of "reification" may appear, to many diaspora Sikhs, somewhat troublesome. Generating a narrative about the history of struggle that spurred Sikhs to fund Sikh studies programs in North America, Mann, Singh, and Gill (1995), the critics of Oberoi, argue:

> As the Sikhs have no political independent power to promote their own identity, the Punjab crisis in the early 1980s forced the western Sikh community to take the responsibility on themselves to project the *authentic image* of Sikhism in the West (which was being eroded politically by anti-Sikh forces). . . .
>
> The Sikh community gave all their trust, understanding, commitment and respect to the western university tradition of freedom of academic inquiry. . . . They also hoped that the evidence and critical analysis would not mean hostility or insensitivity. But all the dreams of the perspective donors [to programs in Sikh studies] were shattered. (emphasis added; p. 2)

The "critique" is also concerned with the position from which Oberoi, as a self-identified Sikh, writes his history: "Oberoi has produced a disjointed, cynical, conscienceless and unscrupulous book . . . to attack the independent Sikh identity. His parasitic personality has caused embarrassment, *humiliation* and disgrace to the independently emerging Sikh community of Canada. In writing this book, he has shown his *pathological identification* with Eurocentric paradigms, and has attempted to bring nihilistic depersonalization by biting the hands that fed him. A strong reaction formation to his childhood socialization gets verbalized in this book, which could be easily called an incoherent Eurocentric autoecholalia or anthropological word salad" (emphasis added; pp. 1–2). Supplementing an elaboration of Oberoi's apparent identification with Eurocentric paradigms, and the supposedly pathological structure of that identification, with another psychoanalytic process, that of the masquerade (Riviere 1986), the critique continues: "Dr. Oberoi, *masquerading* as a Sikh historian, will identify with the aggressor due to his repression, projection oriented personality and would become a turn-coated Sikh scholar, thereby inflicting subjective pain to 16 million Sikhs" (emphasis added; Mann, Singh, and Gill 1995, 3).

This narrative — and this way of conceiving of a wounding of a people — demonstrates another facet of the formations of surrender and trauma that I have introduced in chapters 1 and 3. Positioned within an "analysis" and ad hominem critique of Oberoi's personality structure, the narrative conjures the image of the prisoner who, having been confined within the secret space of police torture, has been turned. According to this account, Oberoi has surrendered to the violent institutional structures of Western academe — he has been transformed into a *billi*. Moreover, he is accused of becoming a traitor to all the Sikhs of the world. He uses his privileged position, not to promulgate the singularity of a Sikh identity and its homeland, but to take those two entities, and what is considered their indissoluble relation, apart. Hence, within these precise terms of antagonism, the protesters at the Michigan conference saw Western academic practice as a danger to identity politics.

The Michigan conference protesters, as did the critics of Oberoi, questioned one aspect of the notions of place to which I have alluded above, the *separation* of the place of representation (i.e., the university) from the authoritative place of a diasporic identity's putative origination (i.e., Punjab): "It is therefore time that we in the academic world at least come out of the grooves of an old mentality, and of making distinctions and claims of superiority on the basis of a particular locale [i.e., the Western university]." Instead of the place of the university, which they also termed a *pulpit,* the protesters argued that the place of representation should be the Akal Takhat in Amritsar, which is also the "temporal seat of authority" of Sikh religious and cultural tradition: "Akal Takhat is supreme for the Sikhs. Sikhism is a way of life. Way of life covers all aspects of life — religious, social and political. For this we need the direction and guidance of the Akal Takhat. . . . In the life of a Sikh any directive from the chief of Akal Takhat is equivalent to an order from our Guru."

In the light of this form of contestation, another term in the excerpt from the "Sikh Studies at Michigan" bulletin takes on particular significance: "outside of India." Here, then, is another history and purpose of Sikh studies or the humanities and social sciences more generally: a history of the democratization and secularization of both the practice of knowledge production and the practice of authority. In this view, while diaspora studies specialists, and particularly Sikh studies specialists, may often attest to originary and foundational aspects of a place of origin (i.e., a temporally *prior* place that generates, contains, and transmits tradition, religion, custom, etc.; see the introduction), their analyses *must* demonstrate that the mode of transmission of that heritage is ultimately modern. That is, according to Sikh studies, the university may well be the place for authoritative statements, debates, and dialogues about the definitive qualities of Sikh identity.

The series of tensions surrounding Sikh studies that I have highlighted tell much about the nuances and problems that come with setting up area, minority, or ethnic studies programs with community support — something with which I have become much more familiar since the 1994 diaspora conference. Area studies and other similar programs inevitably run into conflicts when it comes to deciding how to represent the community that partly supports them. These conflicts, of course, are also crosscut by the tensions that inhere between area studies programs and other departments, between those departments and the administration, and between different factions within the donor community. The general features of this problem take on a certain specificity with Sikh studies programs that, despite a relatively small population of donors, have been established in several universities in North America and England. The programs at Vancouver and Michigan have been joined in the past few years by, for example, programs at East Anglia (England), the University of California, Santa Barbara, and the University of Wisconsin, Milwaukee. Additionally, Columbia and Berkeley have received community support for developing Sikh-related curricula and conferences. Many of the people who support these programs also provide funding to other, more specifically Sikh enterprises. For example, the Sikh Youth Federation (in North America, Europe, India, and New Zealand) publishes a newspaper and organizes educational programs in secondary schools; the Nanaksar Thath Isher Darbar (in England and New Zealand) has coordinated festivals and publications to educate diaspora Sikhs about their history, heroes, and martyrs; the Guru Gobind Singh Khalsa College and the Guru Nanak Sikh College, located outside London in Middlesex and Essex, provide accredited secondary education to Sikhs who would prefer to be taught, or whose parents would prefer that they be taught, in a context that is more sensitive to Sikh interests.

The most important Sikh studies scholars, however, have failed to satisfy some of the most wealthy and influential groups who fund, or would like to fund, these programs. McLeod, Oberoi, and Pashaura Singh have been repeatedly harassed in public, on the Internet, and in such Sikh periodicals as *World Sikh News* by Khalistanis and by some who are only marginally connected with the Khalistani movement (cf. Helweg 1996; McLeod 2000; Oberoi 1995; O'Connel 1996). They, with other Sikh studies scholars, have also received a barrage of threats by post, a problem that makes it difficult to maintain the distinction between their public lives as academics and their private lives as family men.[10]

These public and private batterings have made the names of W. H. Mc-Leod, Harjot Oberoi, and Pashaura Singh commonly known to Sikhs all over the world. In fact, I have often been questioned about them, and more often plainly *told* about their supposedly malicious practices, by Sikhs in India and Europe. Very often, I have been told about them by people who nevertheless refuse to read their work. The generation and circulation of these kinds of anti-Sikh studies opinions on a transnational scale represent only one effect that the violence surrounding the fight for Khalistan has had on practices of knowledge production since the 1980s. Another effect of the ever-present specter of violence against Sikhs and its widespread cultural representation is that any interrogation of a Sikh people and their homeland cannot now help but be appropriated, translated, and reconstituted in Khalistani discourse as an inquiry into Khalistan. This is the case regardless of the presence or absence of Khalistan as an officially recognized state, whether or not one dismisses its possibility, and certainly whether or not Khalistan is named by scholars as the object of inquiry. The story of Michigan's Sikh diaspora conference may now be understood to be about something crucial to the formation of the Sikh diaspora: it is about where the Sikh people may or may not be going, and it is about where they may or may not have come from. In other words, the story of the Michigan conference is about the character and quality of the Sikh homeland.

Place and Displacement

My discussion of the Sikh diaspora conference may help supplement de Certeau's (1984) notion of place as a "calculation of power relationships that becomes possible as soon as a subject with will and power can be isolated." In this case, however, place does not merely correspond, as de Certeau suggests, to the delimitation of a "base from which relations with an *exteriority* composed of targets or threats . . . can be managed" (pp. 35–36). Place, created in this context of diasporic struggle, has been installed in social practice as a definitive place of origin. Moreover, the production of knowledge of *displacement,* which apparently defines the diaspora *as* diaspora, effectively collapses that place into the temporality to which I have been referring as an anteriority, positioning the homeland within a time prior to the diaspora's emergence.

The basic conflict that was articulated at the Sikh diaspora conference follows from techniques of knowledge production concerned with the effects of two different notions of displacement: on the one hand, the dispersal of a Sikh people from its homeland and, on the other hand, the separation of that people's place of representation from the authoritative place of the subject's origination. These techniques, however, do not put Sikh studies and the nation-state on one side of the fence and Khalistanis on the other. Indeed, both Khalistanis and Sikh studies constitute the homeland as a place of origin that locates the Sikh subject's anteriority. The invocation of this "temporal before" comes into tension with the "fictive foundation" (Butler 1990, 3) of the nation-state as a place of origin for national citizenship (i.e., American), a secular and democratic proposition to which Sikh studies is also devoted. The positioning of the Michigan conference within the national landscape of the United States complicates this further: the construction of U.S. citizenship valorizes the homelands of America's minority communities as part of a discourse of multiculturalism that conceptualizes America as a country of immigrants. Let me try to specify the lines of conflict that are operative here.

In terms of American politicojuridical procedure, the homeland of the Sikhs has never been a matter to be specified, as it has been by either Sikh studies or Khalistani discourse. This is a phenomenon that the Asian American studies literature often refers to as *lumping:* disparate categories of people are brought together under one rubric. Between the late nineteenth century and the early twentieth, the U.S. government went back and forth between categorizing "the Aryans of India" as either *White* or *Hindu* (Shankar 1998, 49–50). In the censuses of 1930 and 1940, these "people" were categorized as *Hindu.* Afterward, as Lee (1993), Espiritu (1992), Shankar (1998), and others have discussed, "the 1950 census returned South Asians to their earlier designations as 'Whites,' converted them to 'Other' in 1960 and 1970, 'Asian Indian' in 1980, and 'Asian and Pacific Islander' in 1990" (Shankar 1998, 50). The specificity of a homeland for Sikhs, as for other people who fall under these generalizing categories, has been less important than indications of race, ethnicity, or broadly defined area of origin (this regardless of place of birth). Some scholars have argued convincingly that what is most important in these politics of immigration and citizenship is whether an individual may be identified as white and male (cf. Berlant 1993, 1997; Shankar and Srikanth 1998). Ultimately, U.S. citizenship demands that the significance of the homeland be reduced to factors of culture, language, and race that do not threaten the congeries of alliances that make up the fantasy telos of American community.

Against this formulation, Khalistani discourse constitutes the homeland, Khalistan, as a unique place that was given to the Sikhs by God, that was later given by the Sikhs to the British, and that, as Punjab, is presently occupied by an alien polity, the Indian nation-state. This is a discourse that effectively counters my formulation of surrender (chap. 1) in a very specific way: "God gave the Sikhs their land, a rich and fertile land blessed with much sun and irrigation, the 'land of five rivers,' the *Punjab*. . . . Maharaja Ranjit Singh gave the Sikhs their state, later handed in trust, first to the British then to the Hindu Raj — but *the Sikhs never surrendered their ultimate sovereignty* to any power other than their own. Today, after forty years abuse of their trust, the Sikhs are ready to create again their independent, sovereign state" (emphasis added; Sihra 1985, cited in Oberoi 1987, 39).

Khalistan is a place that, moreover, is irreducibly tied, in historiography and hagiography, to a discourse of the Sikh religion that designates specific places within Punjab both as sacred and as embodying ultimate authority over all Sikhs wherever they may be in the world. Three of these places are noteworthy: Keshgarh Sahib, Anandpur Sahib, and Amritsar. As the *Rahit Maryada* states: "Your birthplace is Keshgarh Sahib and your home is Anandpur Sahib" (McLeod 1984, 84). Built in the time of Guru Ram Das, the fourth Sikh guru (1574–81), the Golden Temple, or Harimandir (what Khalistanis call the *Sikh Vatican*), is located in Amritsar. Harimandir is the place where the first Guru Granth Sahib (the *Sikh Bible,* as some say) was installed by Guru Arjun, the fifth Sikh guru (1581–1606), on 16 August 1604. In front of Harimandir, Guru Hargobind, the sixth Sikh guru (1606–44), at the time confronted by the active hostility of the Mughal authorities, instituted the doctrine of *miri-piri* and built the Akal Takht (the Throne of the Timeless One) in order to establish a central seat (also called a *temporal seat*) of ecclesiastical authority. Today, Akal Takht is highly revered. Special decisions are made by the religious leaders of the Sikh *panth* at the Akal Takht, whose *granthi* (priest) has been given access to a high level of power. In the words of the protesters at the Michigan conference: "Akal Takhat is supreme for the Sikhs. Sikhism is a way of life. Way of life covers all aspects of life — religious, social and political. For this we need the direction and guidance of the Akal Takhat. . . . In the life of a Sikh any directive from the chief of Akal Takhat is equivalent to an order from our Guru."

The figure of the homeland is central to the formation of the Sikh subject within Sikhs studies. As the title of the Michigan conference — "Transmission of *Sikh/Punjabi* Heritage to the Diaspora" — might indicate, Sikh studies scholars conceive of the Sikh homeland as Punjab. They have produced studies showing the circumstances of colonialism under which people first left their homeland and the histories of movements around the globe (Barrier 1989, 1993; Bachu 1985). They have shown how various homeland organizations have tried to control the lives of their temporarily or permanently dispersed relations (Helweg 1979, 1993), and they have told the tale of diaspora communities attempting to control their homeland from afar (Helweg 1979; LaBrack 1988, 1989). These relations have been articulated in a variety of contexts: for example, in terms of religion (Dusenbery 1989), education and racism (Gibson 1989; Hall 1993), gender differentiation (Bachu 1985, Leonard 1992), political activism (Mann 1993; Tatla 1993), and capitalism (LaBrack 1989). Together, these studies have constituted the homeland by examining the heterogeneity of practices and the variety of experiences of individuals that make the complexity of forms of long-distance diaspora-homeland relations.

Some of the most powerful of these studies show the disorienting effects of the changing diaspora-homeland relations that have accompanied the political and economic transformations of late twentieth-century capitalism. LaBrack analyzes these effects in a study of what he calls the *new patrons* — that is, Sikh businessmen living around the world whose remittances produce Punjab's external economy. For LaBrack (1989), what is of interest is how several of the established Sikh communities, "mini-Punjabs," in various nations, have become the key economic and social centers of the Sikh world: "As a group, [these mini-Punjabs] have monetary clout. They make decisions abroad which affect financial and familial affairs in half a dozen countries around the world as well as within India itself" (pp. 289, 297). LaBrack argues that the significance of Punjab as a homeland has changed radically over the past twenty years, creating a significant disjuncture between putatively essential practices that mediate Sikh identity (i.e., tradition and religion) and the dynamic practices that constitute a global Sikh community (i.e., political and economic activity).

As a corollary to LaBrack's work, Helweg (1979) has analyzed the effects that have accompanied the political and economic transformations of the late twentieth century from a different angle. He discusses Jandiali, a Punjabi village, which has an external economy supported by money sent from relations in England: "[The Jandialians] have just completed a new gurdwara costing Rs 1.3 lacks (to fulfill an emigrant's dream of having a gurdwara tower so high that Phagwara could be seen from its top). . . . About five new houses were built recently which cost about a lakh of rupees each. Jandialians are modernizing, with eight homes boasting flush toilets. In 1978 there was a television set and a telephone in the village — all of which were unheard of in 1971" (p. 142). These kinds of transformations have had a severe effect on village life: "Returning to Jandiali produces a shock — it is a ghost village. . . . The villagers claim that a family a week goes abroad. Silence reigns in lane after lane where noises of children once echoed. Only locked doors greet the observer as he walks through the alleys" (p. 141).

The conflicting procedures of producing knowledge of the homeland that move back and forth between the nation-state, Sikh studies, and Khalistanis now take on a more specific form. The conflict is not merely about displacing the representational authority of the Sikh subject from the homeland or, more specifically, from the privileged site of Akal Takht. It is about constituting the homeland as a particular kind of place with a specific relation to a people. Where is the homeland? According to a recent history of U.S. politicojuridical procedures, it is, since 1990, Asia. For Khalistanis: Khalistan. And for Sikh studies: Punjab, but not quite. Sikh studies describes the production of a disjuncture *between* "home" and the homeland that has been effected by the changing structures of global capitalism in the late twentieth century. In LaBrack's words: the "Punjabi village remains the psychological 'homebase,' but increasingly 'home' is in England, Canada, or the United States" (LaBrack 1989, 289).

The where of the homeland corresponds to a when. Within Khalistani discourse, this is not merely the when of origin but the when from which the telos of the Sikh subject must emerge in order to be made intelligible within processes of signification that ground claims to a people's legitimacy and authority *as a people* (this is, in effect, a rearticulation of the Khalistani *deshkaal*). The contexts for these claims have become interrelated in specific ways. The nation-state's promises of democracy and freedom provide the frame for the continuing growth of Sikh studies and its enterprise of producing knowledge about an underrepresented minority population. Those promises also inspire, enable, and sometimes corroborate the projects of Khalistani organizations that set up shop on U.S. soil (see chaps. 2 and 3). Yet, in order to gain access to the rights of citizenship and the institutions of democracy, the United States demands that the Sikh people trade their place and time of origin, whether Khalistan or Punjab, for another. As a result, while the three different homelands and three different structures of temporality are mutually constitutive, they may not necessarily be mutually intelligible.

Let me stress how this view of the homeland, as a problem of a subject's anteriority, differs from others that are prevalent today. Ghosh (1989), Rushdie (1991), and Karamcheti (1992), discussing Indian diasporas in general, provide an example. Enlisting Anderson's (1991) idea of imagined communities and Baudrillard's (1983) idea of the simulacrum, these writers celebrate a new quality of the homeland for the diaspora community. They argue that "diasporic communities are imaginary" (Karamcheti 1992, 268; Ghosh 1989, 76),[11] that normative discourses configuring diaspora life rely on "a simulacrum of 'India'" (Karamcheti 1992, 270), and that homelands are "not actual cities or villages, but invisible ones" (Rushdie 1991, 10). By formulating their arguments in this way, these works provide an important challenge to the many studies of diasporas that have given primacy to the "empirical" (i.e., Skinner 1982; Connor 1986; Safran 1991).

These writers argue that the imaginary homeland is definitive in the Indian diaspora experience of community (itself imaginary). This proposition has had importance because, inverting the many analyses of the homeland as an empirical place—that is, the origin or destination of diaspora mobilizations—it explores the extent to which the homeland is a discursive formation, an imaginary point, that exists for the diaspora in powerful ways. However, the notion *imaginary* here does not correspond to my discussion of the diasporic imaginary in chapter 3 (i.e., I do not argue that either the homeland or the diaspora is imaginary). It corresponds more closely to the notion *ideological fantasy* popularized by Žižek (1989; cf. Axel 1998). Let me distinguish this use of *imaginary*. In this perspective, the tools used to gain access to the homeland are memory and nostalgia. Thus Karamcheti (1992): "And 'home' is no longer a geographical place, but the two-dimensionality of memory and nostalgia" (p. 261). And Rushdie (1991): "The past is home, albeit a lost home in a lost city in the mists of a lost time" (p. 9). The homeland is a bricolage of fragments of the past—fragments that, in their resurrected and reconstructed union, are distorted, sacrilized, or trivialized. Karamcheti (1992) points out that, just as these "distortive powers of memory and of nostalgia" empower the Indian diaspora to "create itself as subject" and "speak its own erased narrative," so also do they provide it with "policing mechanisms" that enforce "fixity and rigidity of cultural actions and beliefs" (pp. 274, 270).[12] Thus, according to these writers, the Indian diaspora's imagined community constitutes itself, as *imagined*, in relation to a homeland that exists, not within a present, but within the past.

The concept of the imaginary homeland as a social construction contains more than a hint of primordialism. Both the social constructivist and the primordialist sides of the imaginary homeland argument must be reconsidered. Arjun Appadurai has discussed the problem of primordialism: an affective and political discourse that constitutes "we-ness" through "shared claims to blood, soil, or language" given definition by "historical roots [located] in some distant past" (Appadurai 1996a, 140, 141). The homeland, obviously, is an important aspect of diasporic experience, however it is conceptualized. Yet the argument that the homeland of the diaspora is imaginary because it only supposedly existed in the past as a real place and because that real place of the past cannot persist in its original form in the present naturalizes the real and attributes to diasporic consciousness a disturbing disability. This is the sentiment of many diaspora movements, including the Khalistani movement, that aim to cure that disability and return to the homeland. For Khalistanis in the 1990s, of course, this formulation is amended: the real homeland continues to exist but, occupied by a foreign polity, is not allowed to manifest its original and full potentiality as a dispersed nation's territorial state.

Recourse to social constructivism to arrive at an understanding of the homeland as imaginary is not much more helpful. Although this technique of analysis is deployed brilliantly by the authors discussed, it does not adequately account for the homeland as a *relational* phenomenon inflected by prevailing historical, social, and material conditions (cf. Comaroff 1997, 133). These conditions, which are given a certain urgency by the conflicts that inhere between different nation-states and a Sikh transnational social formation and between Sikh studies specialists and Khalistanis, have made a situation in which claims to the authority of the homeland are *necessary* to identity politics. My argument is that the homeland indeed exists *in the present*. Confronting the past must be understood, not as a problem of locating the "real" place of the homeland, but as a problem of the anteriority of the subject. Through specific conflicts over the nature of the Sikh, the temporalization of that subject has been retroactively constituted by the very systems, structures, and practices of knowledge production that presume to represent it.

By asserting the retroactive construction of temporality, I am not attempting to invert the formulation of the imaginary homeland (for which the past is real and the present illusory). I am, rather, highlighting the imperatives of the present in formulating the "real."[13] An understanding of these imperatives helps demonstrate how the competing demands of the university and Khalistanis for scholars to develop or dismantle programs in Sikh studies have become interrelated with other demands. Most prominently, these include the demands of the nation-state for its citizens to relinquish prior forms of difference to multicultural society or national integration. And, as I have discussed in chapter 3, these intersect with the demands of Khalistanis, addressed to all Sikhs, to identify with the victims of torture and inscribe those prior forms of difference on their bodies. This is the point at which the politics of place once again meets the politics of the body.

The Total Body in Solitude

In 1996, Manohar Publishers of New Delhi issued the volume (edited by Pashaura Singh and Gerald Barrier) resulting from the Michigan diaspora conference. The cover announces a slightly different title, *The Transmission of Sikh Heritage in the Diaspora,* and exhibits an image, noble and peaceful, yet somewhat rugged, of an *amritdhari* Sikh man sitting in meditation (see fig. 22). Beneath the folds of his jacket lies a small dagger (*kirpan*). A sleeve falls down toward the elbow, revealing the outline of a steel bangle (*kara*) on the wrist. One hand holds a staff upright, and the other lightly grasps a sword, the features of which fade into the foreground.

This is a familiar portrait, an instance of what in chapter 1 I have called an *iterable model.* The convention reiterated here, which has one genealogy in the portraits of Maharaja Duleep Singh, makes the identifiable Sikh man a placeholder for all Sikhs "in the diaspora." Images such as this may be found in many academic texts and popular media presentations on the Sikhs. The cover also resonates with one side of the "argument of images" that I discussed in chapter 3. The only difference, and the difference that is at stake here, is that the image of the total body of the male *amritdhari* is not coupled with the tortured body. It stands alone. And its solitude tells something about the virtual absence of, not just an interrogation of that iterable model of the Sikh, but discussions of violence within Sikh studies.[14] Instead, as the title of the text suggests, Sikh studies is concerned with "transmission." The total body in isolation sets up a model of center and periphery for a global Sikh kinship structure, the relations of which are mediated by circuits of heritage and heterosexual reproduction. What concerns Sikh studies is the way in which a Sikh "identity" from the past is changed, modified, or maintained at a distance *in* the diaspora. The titles of several contributors indicate this: "'Flawed Transmission'? Punjabi Pioneers in California"; "Socializing Sikhs in Singapore"; "Observing the Khalsa Rahit in North America."[15]

What happens when the image of the *amritdhari* man's total body stands alone, outside a relation to the tortured body? What is the effect of this

Fig. 22 The cover of *The Transmission of Sikh Heritage in the Diaspora* (from Singh and Barrier 1996).

representational strategy on the formation of the Sikh subject within Sikh studies? To answer these questions, let me explore the logic of the total body in solitude.

Louis Marin (1989) offers a way in which to illuminate this question with his felicitous construction of an autoerotic scene in which the monarch contemplates a portrait of himself, uttering, "That is the King," "I am the King," "We are the King" — to which must be added, "This is my body" (pp. 192–94). In this scene, the subject *must* recognize himself in the representation. In this scene, the portrait of the king is a presence in the same way that the Eucharist is the presence of Jesus. This redoubling of the royal presence, however, forms an unresolvable tension. Specifically, the necessary presence of the "individual [the King] . . . renders the adequation unequal to itself." The "disappearance of the individual" is the condition of possibility by which the Monarch, inhabiting an eternal instance (of the portrait) and an infinite duration (of lineage and kinship), acquires "for himself a title that begins with a capital letter — the King" (p. 190).

My interest in invoking Marin is not to draw an equation between the scopic regimes of medieval European monarchy and modern Sikh subjectivity but to suggest another historical point of departure for understanding the production of the image of the *amritdhari* body. It may be that Marin's "The Portrait of the King's Glorious Body" illuminates a structure of displacement and a form of relation that, constituted as prior to the apotheosis of capitalism, continue to be at work within the discursive productions of Sikh studies.[16] Or perhaps it is that the visual and discursive productions of the Sikh subject within Sikh studies turn upon a desire for an understanding of the "transmission" of what is presumed to have been already, a desire, that is, for an *anteriority* of signification as an authoritative position of social and cultural knowledge (Bhabha 1994).

Marin (1989, 189, 207) suggests that, when the king contemplates his own portrait, the mystery of royal power is constituted through a specific kind of displacement: not only of the "real referent," the referential body, but also of "real history" (a notion that undermines the eternal instance and infinite duration of monarchy). Yet, emerging with a desire to see oneself as the absolute, this displacement is transformed when another spectator takes the position in front of the king's portrait — and herein lies a displacement and a form of relation between representation and subject that is pertinent to the constitution of the Sikh subject within Sikh studies. Echoing Foucault's formulation of the "parade" in which " 'subjects' were presented as 'objects' to the observation of a power that was manifested only by its gaze" (Foucault 1977, 188), Marin (1989) writes: "The spectator does anything but look at the King's portrait and is anything but a subject caught staring at the King. Instead, the spectator is the object of the Monarch's gaze, he or she is constituted by and subjected to this gaze, and thereby transformed into a political subject. . . . The portrait of the King is the theory of the King, it is the theologico-political theory of the royal body" (pp. 199–200). In other words, the form of relation that concerns me is one in which the regime of representation constitutes the *viewing* subject rather than its "real" referent (the king?). Conversely, the structure of displacement is one in which the subject is dialectically constituted by relinquishing the possibility of any self-governing property to the sovereign and the social. It is this vicissitude of representation and displacement that forms a fundamental mechanism in the constitution of the Sikh subject within Sikh studies. This is a subject whose whole and masculinized body stands alone, a subject that, inaugurated in the past, continues to unfold in the present through the site and sight of the Five Ks.

This kind of relation between temporality and corporeality sets up a tension with other aspects of the discursive production of the Sikh subject within Sikh studies, particularly with the aspect that valorizes Sikh identity as ultimately *modern*. Embodying the problem of transmission, the portrait on the cover of the *Transmission* text reduplicates the visual power of the Five Ks. It brings to the significatory power of the Five Ks and the *amritdhari*'s total body, not only the sense, indeed the imperative, of visuality, but also the sight of an anterior *presence* that reiterates (i.e., is retroactively constituted by) the discursive production of the Five Ks' *premodern* legitimacy and authority (and particularly the *kirpan* and the *kangha*). In other words, this portrait visualizes a prior sovereignty that, through the figure of a total body, metonymically relates to the source of the Sikh subject and Sikhism's "whole nature as a religion" (Uberoi 1996, 17; see chap. 1).

This tension figures somewhat differently in the work of Harjot Oberoi (1993). Reflecting on "Sikh fundamentalism" (by which he means Khalistani, Singh Sabha, *and* Akali discourses), he argues that Sikh *politics* is essentially premodern: "Whether dealing with the oppression of the Mughal state in the eighteenth century or the economic exploitation of British colonial rule, the Sikhs have *always* responded with social movements mediated through religion" (emphasis added; p. 278). Oberoi explains: "There is a *fundamental chasm* between the worldview of Sikh fundamentalists and what Habermas has described as the 'project of modernity.' A key element in the 'project of modernity' has been its separation of the domain of politics from the sphere of religion. It was this differentiation across 'cultural value spheres' that Max Weber convincingly used to distinguish modern and *premodern* politics. This distinction between the political and religious domains is anathema to Sikh fundamentalists. For them religion and politics are inseparable" (emphasis added; p. 277). These reflections thus open up a point of ambivalence immanent to the Sikh subject constituted by Sikh studies.[17] This Sikh subject, identified by the solitary figure of the *amritdhari* body, is generated through an ambivalent desire for an anteriority that, lending a certain priority to a premodern world, must nevertheless provide a source that issues forth in modernity, generating a modern subjectivity. Needless to say, this *amritdhari* body fetishized by Sikh studies stands awkwardly beside the tortured body of the Khalistani *shahid*.

Together, however, with the disparate formations of homeland, these conflicting ways of constituting relations between corporeality and temporality provide the basis for another crucial project that both Sikh studies and Khalistanis, indeed, share: a project to prove the humanity of the Sikh project.

Proving Humanity

One way to understand the project of Sikh studies is in terms of its intervention into the procedures of nation formation. Sikh studies begins by valorizing the diaspora's challenge to the nation-state, defining the Sikh subject as the postcolonial other that, coming to the metropole, is caught within the racist and patriarchal logic of Western nation-states. The basic categories of analysis correspond, accordingly, to what are considered fundamental aspects of the diasporic experience: displacement, loss, maintenance of heritage, etc. Within a liberal discourse of national integration or multiculturalism, these studies articulate a project: to ameliorate the effects of original displacement, loss, and discrimination and to help Sikhs celebrate their particularity by translating and explaining their presence and difference to an uncomprehending "host country," and by arguing for their rights as citizens.

Many Sikh studies scholars have been actively involved in this project. W. H. McLeod, for example, has testified in North American courts on several occasions regarding disputes about the use of the turban. Indeed, on the weekend prior to the Michigan conference, he appeared in a court hearing in Calgary: the "Royal Canadian Mounted Police (RCMP) Turban Case." This case had been ongoing since 1989, and the conclusions reached had been challenged three times. The argument *against* Sikhs wearing turbans in the RCMP was that turbans were a religious symbol and that, while in uniform, such a symbol brought the loyalty of the soldier, or his neutrality, into question. McLeod's testimony indeed helped prove that the turban had traditional and religious significance for Sikhs—a significance derived from important practices in the Sikh homeland, Punjab. But it also helped Judge Barbara Reed conclude that "the wearing of the turban would operate as a demonstration and an acceptance of the present-day multicultural nature of Canada" (Singh and Barrier 1996, 8). In other words, the turban—this enduring sign from a Sikh past—and its inherent significations of belonging would not disrupt any loyalty to the modern nation-state. And, perhaps more important, if the nation-state accepted from the Sikh his turban and his loyalty, it, that is, the nation-state, would demonstrate its own greatness.

The turban dispute is not a small matter. And its success must be lauded. But it also puts Sikh studies into an extremely awkward position as far as Khalistanis are concerned, although Khalistanis would certainly celebrate the success of the "Turban Case." In this case, Sikh studies has addressed the nation-state in the nation-state's terms. Even though the nation-state valorizes multicultural diversity, it continues to demand that its citizens identify with a singular, originary place of citizenship and disavow any *determinate* relation with prior, foreign difference. Maintaining such a relation, indeed, is a sign of a social pathology, of an inability to conform to the dictates of modernity. Multiculturalism includes this difficult demand: the nation-state must accept what it considers socially pathological. Sikh studies argues that Sikhs are constituted by definitive relations with what the nation-state considers prior, foreign difference—and Sikh studies argues that these relations are valuable in themselves. From this point, by validating its difference, Sikh studies aims to *prove the humanity* of the diaspora so that it may gain access to the privileges of national citizenship and prove its loyalty to the nation.[18] But Sikh studies also produces the Sikh subject as an object of knowledge detached from the Akal Takht (i.e., it claims that the representation of the Sikh subject may emerge from the university). Ironically, however, in responding to the nation-state's demands, Sikh studies may also succeed in producing *for the nation-state* the Sikh as a *pathologized subject* that the nation- state may then cure or accept. This pathologizing is in no way the intent of Sikh studies, rather an effect of operating within the nation-state's terms.

This, I would add, is the point at which the Khalistani critique intervenes, a critique that foregrounds the violence and contradictions in the relations between the nation-state and citizens, territories, and bodies. Khalistani practice accomplishes this critique by inverting the procedures of Sikh studies — not merely by refusing significations of surrender, but, indeed, by valorizing the spectacle of the tortured body. For the most part, Sikh studies specialists have been extremely concerned with the character and quality, the provenance and transformation, of the *amritdhari* body. To repeat my citation of J. P. S. Uberoi: "We can establish a definite connection between the five symbols of Sikhism and its whole nature as a religion." The import that Sikh studies specialists lend to the image of the *amritdhari*'s total body gives priority to the structure of a *past* identity (no matter how multivalent) that is either equated with or used to evaluate the viability of the homeland and Sikh "identity" (or of a hegemonic Sikh identity) in the present. In contrast, Khalistani practices of knowledge production constitute the Sikh subject's temporality through the visualization of a present moment of danger that forms the imperative for elaborating the anteriority of a total body. They give priority to the present, while for the most part Sikh studies professionals do not address the monstrous sight and site of present violence, even when discussing the "Punjab problem."[19] This violence, however, has been the condition of possibility for Sikh studies since 1984. According to the Khalistani critique, this violence, represented by the image of the tortured body, is disavowed in Sikh studies' production of knowledge — even though Sikh studies scholars themselves may be extremely concerned with anti-Sikh violence.

This crucial difference between the practices of Khalistanis and those of Sikh studies specialists — in constituting conflicting formations of homeland, body, and diaspora — may be demonstrated by looking at the ways in which Khalistanis interact with nation-states other than India. Consider a letter from the president of the Council of Khalistan, circulated on the Internet, in response to a letter written by President Bill Clinton (solicited for the birthday of Guru Nanak). Clinton's letter, of 14 November 1997, states:

> Warm greetings to Sikhs across America observing the birth of Guru Nanak Dev, founder of Sikhism. In our country, built by men and women of many nations and many beliefs, it is fitting that we acknowledge the contributions of leaders like Guru Nanak who brought people together around a particular faith. As we search for new ways to ensure that America truly offers opportunities for people of all races, creeds, and backgrounds, it is particularly timely that we recognize the life and teachings of Guru Nanak. His message that everyone is equal in God's eyes and that God's grace is open to all is as appropriate today as it was during his lifetime in the late 15th century. By bringing people of all backgrounds together and advocating service to humankind, Guru Nanak encouraged his followers to build lives of compassion and commitment to justice. As you gather to observe this special day, you can be proud of your many contributions to the strength of our nation and the richness of our religious heritage. Hillary joins me in extending best wishes for a memorable observance.

The president of the Council of Khalistan addresses the Sikh nation:

> Please send President Clinton a note of thanks for the letter. Please mention in that thank you letter that Sikhs in Punjab, Khalistan, do not have

much to celebrate given a 13-year genocide campaign launched against the Sikhs by the Indian Government. Ask President Clinton to voice his concern for ongoing atrocities in the Sikh homeland. . . . Lastly, make it clear to President Clinton, that over 250,000 Sikh deaths have occurred in the last 13 years, all in a brutal effort to stop our PEACEFUL freedom struggle. You can contact President Clinton by writing to: The White House, Washington, DC 20500 USA. You can also send a message via the official White House website at www.whitehouse.gov.

In short, not only does Khalistani discourse constitute the Sikh subject, its anteriority, and the homeland in terms of the priority of present violence; Khalistani discourse also constitutes the *Indian nation-state as pathological and monstrous.* For Khalistanis, every engagement with other nation-states *must* have this orientation.

Sikh studies scholars may very well disagree with my depiction of their work.[20] Yet my intention is to help pinpoint, precisely, the conflict between Sikh studies and Khalistani practices of subjectification. This conflict has itself become as mobile as the Sikh body and the Sikh homeland and has serious implications for the future of pedagogical practice concerned with the Sikh diaspora. In discussing this conflict, I have suggested formulating the problems of the Sikh homeland, and its relation to the Sikh body, in terms of the priority of the present—a move inspired by Benjamin (1978). An understanding of Sikh identity politics today demands this move. Both Sikh studies and Khalistani discourses, however, have provided me with the basis for this interrogation. Their analyses of Sikh history and of the transformations of the Sikh diaspora attest to what I have been consistently concerned to demonstrate: that the processes constituting disparate Sikh subjects are often contradictory and that the situation of Sikhs in one locality may not be equated with that of Sikhs in another. My analysis, however, takes a different route. In my view, we may productively reconsider the specificity of these contradictions and the qualities of ambivalence that infuse constructions of a Sikh subject. These are not indicative of either the proliferation of multiple Sikh "identities" or a lapse in a formerly stable and singular Sikh "identity." These contradictions and ambivalences, rather, are the generative conditions of the Sikh diaspora *as diaspora.*

conclusion

It is no longer a question of judging the past in the name of a truth that only we can possess in the present; but risking the destruction of the subject who seeks knowledge in the endless deployment of the will to knowledge.
— Michel Foucault, "Nietzsche, Genealogy, History"

This book differs in significant ways from the one that I intended to write when I first began research in 1992. The original project was titled *Maps and Localities,* and its aim was to investigate the production and consumption of Sikh maps in India and England, looking closely at the ways in which cartography has become central to Sikh political struggles and the creation of new kinds of Sikh localities. The main theoretical dilemma that I hoped to address was the challenge of transnational social formations to nation-states — a challenge illuminated through alternative productions of space. That proposal guided my research in India, England, and the United States. Indeed, I collected a sufficient amount of information to write up that project. But, in the research process, I realized that, although the theoretical problem of transnationalism remained crucial, the story of *Maps and Localities* presumed a history of violence, visual representation, and knowledge production that, in my opinion, has not been sufficiently addressed. It also presumed the diaspora itself. In order to tell the story of *Maps and Localities,* another ethnography and a different archive must first be produced. That ethnography and that archive — the one that I present in this book — are of the Sikh body and the Sikh homeland, what to many scholars seem the most self-evident aspects of Sikh life around the world. In other words, the self-evident quality of the Sikh body and the Sikh homeland, with the diaspora, and the relations to productions of temporality, are exactly what need to be reexamined, not least because today the fight for Khalistan relies on and reorganizes their measure and mobility.

Today, Khalistan is the driving force, no matter how contradictory, behind the circulation of disparate Sikh bodies and homelands. These bodies and homelands are, in my opinion, the most vital sites and sources for understanding the creation of the Sikh diaspora, and they have much longer histories than does Khalistan. My discussions in chapters 1, 2, and 4 indicate how we may interrogate these histories in terms of nineteenth-century practices of surrender and portraiture, the pre-Partition scramble to negotiate territorial adjustments for a Sikh population's position within a new South Asia, and the post-Independence movements of Sikh men to England to become "colored workers." These histories do not fit neatly together to create singular images of body and homeland but, more important, help pinpoint the beginnings of the creation of specific forms of their mobility and interconnections formative of a diaspora.

These histories were the condition of possibility for Jagjit Singh Chauhan's introduction of a Khalistani politics into the purview of world media in 1971. The significance of Jagjit Singh Chauhan's 1971 advertisement in the *New York Times,* however, must be differentiated from the advertisement that appeared in the *New York Times* in 1997. In the intervening years, and particularly in the years since 1984, the struggle for Khalistan, joining images of the body and the homeland in new ways, fundamentally transformed the character and quality of the diaspora itself. Indeed, it is during this period that we may say that the Sikh diaspora emerged *as a diaspora.* Several interrelated historical processes indicate this change. Most immediately is the production of globalized forms of knowledge production addressing a world Sikh "community" and the Khalistani representation of torture as a transnational modality of Sikh subjectification. This process of globalization, however, has been inseparable from the emergence of a set of practices that effectively positioned Punjab within a Restricted Zone and generated an equation, in Indian discourses of national integration, between the Sikh body and Punjab. These diverse processes, moreover, cannot be understood apart from the establishment of a routine of torture as a modality of Sikh subjectification in India, which has effectively transformed the processes of identification of the Sikh diaspora in relation to a corporeal image. Prior to this period, the image of the *amritdhari*'s total body remained a solitary figure. Yet practices of torture and representations of torture have generalized a new kind of identification, or, more precisely, two kinds of identification, imbricated with formations of gender and sexuality. This is an important distinction, that is, between the Indian nation-state's and Khalistani procedures of subjectification. Within practices of torture in India, a dialectical relation has been set up between the tortured body and *a profile* of the *amritdhari* body, in which the beard and turban are isolated and related to the genitals and anus in the creation of a Sikh subject. Within the transnational circulation of images of tortured bodies, a dialectical relation has been set up between the tortured body and the *amritdhari*'s total body in which the Five Ks are related to a series of wounds and piercings.

These historical processes have framed the production of knowledge of the Sikh diaspora, of anti-Sikh violence, and of conflicts over national belonging that will have enduring consequences. And they ground the vicissitudes of certainty and doubt about who is a Sikh. By asserting this, I do not intend to valorize Khalistan, which, in the view of many politicians, scholars, and journalists, is the creation of a few zealots or the figment of some misguided imagination. The accusation that I am valorizing Khalistan, if I may counter it ahead of time, relies on a troubling equation of Khalistan with terrorism. It is a very weak equation, but to respond that not all Khalistanis use violence as a militant tactic is of no use because, of course, many Khalistanis do. Yet this violent practice has not been the topic of my research. I have not hoped to do an ethnography of Khalistani militants, a project that Cynthia Mahmood (1996) and Joyce Pettigrew (1995) have conducted. In this text, a historical anthropology of the Sikh diaspora, I have attempted to demonstrate that Khalistan and Khalistanis may also be something else. Perhaps I am intending to accomplish something much more difficult than a valorization of Khalistan. Perhaps I am hoping to demonstrate that the Sikh diaspora was *not* created by any individuals and that it is because of this that Khalistan has become so powerful.

I have often been asked, If the Sikhs get their Khalistan, what will it look like? I have found myself answering this question in several different ways over the years. One response takes recourse to an old anthropological appeal to diversity: not all Sikhs are fighting for a Khalistan, and Sikhs around the world understand the meaning of Khalistan in extremely different ways; alternatively, there are several different competing Khalistani groups, each having a different vision of Khalistan configured by the different circumstances in which they live. Another response attempts to reorient the focus toward productions of temporality: trying to guess what Khalistan will look like ignores the more important fact that the violence surrounding the lives of

Sikhs, the practices of knowledge production, and the circulation of images of violence are situated in a "present" and, being situated in this way, constitute a past. In other words, this response claims, the fight for Khalistan generates a future trajectory by retroactively creating a past through present conditions.

Both these answers are important to provide, but they have only a minimal effect. The questioner is never satisfied. I am almost always countered with, OK, sure, but if they get their Khalistan, what will it look like? In other words, a deconstruction of the question, in any form, is not an answer to the question. There is yet another way in which to respond that, at the end of this book, I think may be more appropriate. In chapter 2, I argue that Khalistan may be understood as a locality that a history of colonial rule made possible to imagine, and even to measure, but impossible to institute. This paradox of Khalistan's *historical* impossibility in 1947 has formed the basis for another paradox that resides within the *logic* of the Sikh diaspora since the 1990s: exemplifying, and perhaps exaggerating, Balibar's (1991) formulation that "only imaginary communities are real" (p. 93), Khalistan today indeed exists, it has a reality, and it is produced within and between diasporic social formations and nation-states.

This, however, is not a "symptomatic" reading of Khalistan. In other words, I hasten to note, Khalistan is *not* a symptom of pathological or dysfunctional processes supposedly characteristic of the Sikh diaspora. Rather, as I have argued in chapters 2 and 3, the emergence of Khalistan between the 1930s and the 1980s was an effect of the dialectics of diaspora and nation-state, and, since the mid-1980s, Khalistan has been transformed into a *constitutive* aspect of the Sikh diaspora and a social formation around which categories of violence have come to be organized. In other words, the globalization of Khalistan is a singularly important aspect of my discussion of the constitution of the Sikh diaspora. Although Khalistan may have a genealogy that leads us to negotiations between the Akali Dal and the British in the 1930s, and although Khalistanis may trace the birth of the Sikh *qaum* to Guru Gobind Singh's creation of the Khalsa initiation in 1699, it is only recently that this extremely powerful, and globally mobile, term of identification has effectively become part of Sikh life. This is not to say that Khalistan may be understood through the universality and coherence that are attributed to it by Khalistanis. Rather, highlighting and critically exploring the tensions immanent to Khalistan indicate precisely how Khalistan has become integral to the constitution of the Sikh diaspora *as a diaspora*.

This book thus introduces a somewhat different orientation to what scholars in sociology and political science have shown are important problems of globalization — which is what I take to be an important direction for historical anthropology to develop. In the most basic sense, to these fields of inquiry I have brought a concern, familiar to anthropologists, with formations of time, space, and corporeality. I have also stressed the significance of colonialism both to these cultural formations and to the dynamics of global capitalism. Some of the most powerful interventions from sociology and political science have illuminated the tensions that inhere between (1) the location of globalization within national territories or institutions, (2) the formation of privatized interstate intermediaries, and (3) the reduction of the nation-state's authority in regulating international economic activity. Of particular interest, I think, are the critical engagements of Saskia Sassen (1991, 1997, 1998) and John Ruggie (1993) with questions of the nation-state's territoriality. As I discuss in the introduction, a basic point that we learn from these widely differing discussions is that the local and the global cannot be understood as two mutually exclusive conditions (Sassen 1998, 1). My discussion of the relations between the Sikh diaspora and the modern nation-state demonstrates a specific dialectic that inheres between the local and the global. There are two difficulties, however, that arise in this formulation.

First, how do we then identify the local? Is not Southall a local neighborhood? And is not the local (i.e., the pub) located within the neighborhood? This is not merely a problem of scale in the old geographic sense. Rather, the problematic of globalization demands a radical reevaluation of empiricist limitations on the definition of the local as an isolated, geophysical entity. What an ethnographic approach may add to understanding these problems is a detailed attention to material practices and discursive formations that position the local, however defined, in a relation to the global — and this with a perspective on the materiality of localization and globalization as it becomes part of subject formation. Such an approach complicates things, no doubt, but it shows how the local and the global have each become immanent to each other, making the distinction itself quite murky.

Second, as many scholars have asked, how do we replace the state-centrist model with a transnational relations model (Sklair 1991, 5)? Sklair argues that the nation-state should be understood as "the spatial reference point for most of the crucial transnational practices that go to make up the structures of the global system, in the sense that most transnational practices intersect in particular countries and come under the jurisdiction of particular nation-states. But it is not the only reference point" (p. 7). This is an important argument, but it draws attention away from how not all transnational processes come under the jurisdiction of nation-states and how new juridical procedures—which are not situated within nation-states—are being developed (Sassen 1998). The Internet is only one, although an extremely important, example supporting these latter points. Nevertheless, I have hoped both to supplement and to counter Sklair's answer to the statist problem. Rather than arguing that the global capitalist system "is the most important single force in the struggle to dominate political and cultural-ideological transnational practices" (Sklair 1991, 7), I have outlined other reference points for transnational practices. The diaspora, most generally, and the body and the homeland, more particularly, are my points of reference. Not only does this focus help specify how we are witnessing a reconstitution of the nation-state itself (i.e., rather than its demise in the face of global forces). It also helps specify, through practices of commodity production, circulation, and consumption, how transformations of global capital have become interrelated with the reconstitution of the modern nation-state. This transformation and this interrelation are at the root of my discussion of Glassy Junction, which follows the development of what global studies specialists might call a new *consumer culture*. But there are other reference points, not the global capitalist system, but Khalistan or Punjab—elsewheres of compromised citizens and subject formation. In the terms that I have developed in this book, these references points, that is, the homeland, are points of anteriority. Here, then, may be my basic contribution to recent work in global studies: an attention to the formations of temporality generated through conflicts over territoriality.

Historical anthropology is challenged today to begin making disparate processes of globalization and localization objects of study. In my discussions, the ethnographic detail and historical specificity are always related to more general processes constitutive of the Sikh diaspora. And this, following Comaroff and Comaroff (1997), is what I think may help specify the project of historical anthropology: to discern general principles across disparate social practices, institutional forms, material conditions, and the "realpolitik of everyday life" (pp. 410–11). Bringing together questions of the Sikh diaspora as a transnational social formation with an account of the emergence of colonialism and the nation-state, this study of the Sikh diaspora may help widen the frames of anthropology and history by suggesting new objects of study, new techniques and methods of knowledge production, and alternative means for evaluating the artifacts of violence.

This interest in general processes of subject formation, however, should not be turned upon itself, making the specificity of Sikh lives appear only as a manifestation of some abstraction. The dialectic that inheres between the particular and the abstract is important continually to pinpoint, and this is why I have attempted to specify the relations and translations between very different kinds of conflicts, situated in different localities. The social practices of particular subjects, as localized processes, are what make possible the generation of more abstract forms — abstract forms that have become very "real." This formulation radically transforms what can be understood as a "diaspora" — not just an immanently contradictory category, but a mobile category of affect and cultural practice.

Let me clarify this reformulation of the diaspora. As I have noted in the introduction, two difficulties have haunted discussions of diasporas: first, a reliance on the place-of-origin thesis and, second, a conceptualization of the diaspora as a totality. To reiterate, the place-of-origin thesis posits that globally dispersed individuals, who, regardless of birthplace, supposedly originate in the same place (i.e., share a homeland), constitute a diaspora. In simple terms, the argument is that a homeland produces a diaspora. Throughout this text, I have demonstrated how homelands undergo transformations in their cartographic distinctions and in their relations to diasporas and nation-states. But, perhaps more important, I have argued that it has been the diaspora that, through disparate processes of displacement, has constituted the place and temporality designated *homeland*.

The common argument — or presumption — that the diaspora is a totality follows from the place-of-origin thesis. The notion of totality also allows scholars to avoid analyzing the difference of particular practices of diaspora individuals as constituted, indeed, as an effect of violence and displacement. Difference is understood, or presumed, to be a manifestation of the totality itself. Hence, general discussions of the vitality of the homeland *in* the diaspora are supported by discussions of a Sikh diaspora *in* Vancouver or an Armenian diaspora *in* the United States. In these terms, the posited totality of the diaspora is offered as a grounding for many of the dilemmas that diaspora individuals experience: diaspora individuals are afflicted by a disorientation; they cannot constitute themselves fully in relation to that totality, although they perceive its force. This kind of argument has gained prominence particularly after Jameson's (1984, 1988) series of popular publications that spell out the problems of postmodern experience in terms of an apparently new spatial totality, an "international space" or a "postmodern global space." The crisis instituted by this "absent totality," which is a "coherent new type of space in its own right" (Jameson 1984, 88), is that there is "a gap between phenomenological perception and a reality that transcends all individual thinking" (Jameson 1988, 353). Concurrently, in Jameson's (1984) terms, "the subject has lost its capacity to extend its pro-tensions and re-tensions across the temporal manifold, and to organize its past and future into co-herent experience" (p. 71). Calls for a reorientation in the analysis of the *perception* of this "time-space continuum" have come from many disciplines. Most significant for studies of diasporas have been Harvey's (1989) formula-tion of "time-space compression" and Gupta and Ferguson's (1992) popular call to rethink "difference through connection" by understanding how "a community" is formed "out of the interconnected space that always already existed" (p. 8).

These conceptualizations, which suggest provocative ideas about the rela-tion of space and difference, must be considered carefully, particularly in the way in which they substitute one kind of spatiotemporal totality (the nation-state) with another (global capital) that becomes the new generative force of *perception* and within which the diaspora is supposed to derive its definitive quality as diaspora. Specifically, they begin with a posited new spatial totality that leads to a troublesome reliance on categories of anteriority—prior spaces (i.e., Jameson's passage from "market to monopoly capital," Gupta and Fer-guson's [1992, 8] "colonialism [that] represents the displacement of one form of interconnection by another") and prior subjects (i.e., Jameson's "class" or Gupta and Ferguson's [1992, 7] "cultures [that] have lost their moorings in definite places"). Ironically ignoring Lefebvre's (1984) insis-tence on subjecting to critique "space in its totality or global aspect," in "fetishizing" absolute and abstract space, these scholars shift analysis from the "production of space" to "things in space" (p. 37).[1] Concurrently, from these teleological premises detailing a movement from prior to present entities, difference is transformed into distance that, in postmodern space, is annihi-lated, compressed, or unbound.

It is important to reconsider such formulations and move beyond them. One might first point out a recuperation of cartography's principle of a spatial totality. The procedures of cartography have been based on the fantasy of an original unity or totality (the earth) that is the starting point for the production of differences (i.e., territories).² From this basis, the discipline of cartography posits a teleological movement: these differences have, or will, come to be arranged into new totalities (i.e., nation-states) that, furthermore, should constitute a community of totalities (e.g., the United Nations). The cartographic understanding of difference must be made clear. In cartography, difference is a matter of *distance* — more specifically, distance measured between equivalent units (points) that may be designated in terms of longitude and latitude. Formally, difference is a relation of part to part, units that, since manifesting equivalent aspects of the original totality (the earth), must be constituted as exchangeable. In short, the cartographic principle of space as a totality demonstrates the *productivity of measurement* as a process of subjectification and commensurability, constituting relations of difference/distance as signifiers of an original, a priori, totality.

To supplement these considerations, I may reiterate how I have engaged the diaspora-as-totality thesis. In chapter 3, I locate the image of totality within the diasporic imaginary. Here, totality has its point of reference in the image of the total body. The formation of a historically specific relation between a total body and a fragmented body, I argue, is a constitutive feature of the Khalistani subject of the Sikh diaspora, itself bound to processes of gendering and sexualization. In these terms, the very process of identifying with an *image* of totality is an alienating process that, simultaneously, produces a split within the subject and supplies it with a specific form of temporality. This is a historically specific mechanism that, moving back and forth between the nation-state and the diaspora in different ways, indicates the impossibility of a totality, absent or otherwise.

The very processes, then, that constitute the *impossibility* of the diaspora's (and the nation-state's) totality are central to the creation of relations that transform individuals into representatives and representations of totalities. That is, these are the processes that make it possible to understand the relation of the diaspora and the nation-state as mutually constitutive. Specifying a major historical precedent for understanding such a transformative relation, I began this historical anthropology of the Sikh diaspora with the problem of surrender — and it may be well to end with this problem.

The surrender of the Sikh Empire to the British on 24 March 1849 inaugurated a proliferation of surrenders in different forms and made possible one basic premise in today's formations of Khalistan: *the negation of surrender.* The colonial scene of surrender, based on the enchantment of absolute humiliation, is a historically specific transformative relation that, through violent processes of appropriation, elevates the individual into the domain of representation. It is crucial to note that I am not here supporting an apologist argument about the Sikh surrender to the British. My point, rather, is that the very proposition of a relation of surrender unleashed a plethora of colonial techniques and technologies of knowledge production and discipline that fundamentally transformed processes of Sikh subjectification.

The diffuse effects of these procedures set the conditions of possibility for what are today the Sikh diaspora and the Khalistani movement, but they also constituted more general problems for colonialism. Colonial cartography provides an example. Prior to 1849, cartography in Punjab was formed around military strategy, facilitating the East India Company's battles against the Sikh Empire. After the company annexed Punjab, cartography took on a different significance: while becoming integral to the governance of the new territory and the production of an ideal image of a totalized British India, it also helped create visual and statistical knowledge of a Sikh "people" (i.e., the past great foe that would become the loyal, colonial subject). In simple terms, cartographic productions of the former Sikh Empire both re-created that empire in a new form and provided the conditions for the production of a definitive Sikh "place of origin," or "homeland," itself encompassed within a *colonial* empire. The creation of this specific relation of a Sikh people to a Sikh place took on an extreme importance in the years around Indian Independence. As I discussed in chapter 2, between 1935 and 1947, prominent Sikh politicians and militants drew on the image of Sikhs *before* colonial rule (as inhabiting a sovereign territory of their own) to construct an argument legitimizing their demand for a separate Sikh homeland that might be equivalent to the Muslim League's demand for Pakistan. Likewise, the early demand for a Khalistan (or a Sikhistan) drew heavily on almost one hundred years of colonial cartographic products in order to delineate the proposed territory of Khalistan and give details of its population's locally delimited habitations and lifestyles. In short, the identification of any Sikh subject with a particular place cannot be separated from the fixing of Punjab as a territory and as an object of cartographic knowledge. This could not have happened without the formation of a relation of surrender.

Recall now Sinha's words on which I commented in chapter 5: "God gave the Sikhs their land, a rich and fertile land blessed with much sun and irrigation, the 'land of five rivers,' the Punjab. . . . Maharaja Ranjit Singh gave the Sikhs their state, later handed in trust, first to the British then to the Hindu Raj — but *the Sikhs never surrendered their ultimate sovereignty* to any power other than their own. Today, after forty years abuse of their trust, the Sikhs are ready to create again their independent, sovereign state." In negating the surrender of Sikhs to the British and the Indian nation-state, Khalistanis are of course reaffirming the importance of a single surrender: the surrender to the guru enacted in the Khalsa initiation. This surrender locates the anteriority of the Khalistani Sikh subject, but it also locates the desire of the Sikh *qaum* in search of a state. Yet, I would venture, the Khalistani imperative to elaborate this Sikh surrender can be understood only within the series of historically specific relations constituted through the historical transformations of empire and the modern nation-state. Within these agonistic relations, the Khalistani Sikh subject is reconstituted, and it is torn: between disparate forms of desire, temporality, territoriality, and visibility. The surrender, now understood as a modality of repetition—a repetition that does not return as the same—offers an image of ambivalence, locating the effects of violence and its perpetuation.

The proliferation of both surrender and the negation of surrender indicates one way in which to organize an understanding of the historically specific contradictions and ambivalences that I have related in the story of the Sikh diaspora. I must reiterate: the analysis of such tensions within the diaspora is not intended as a deconstruction of the boundaries of a Sikh "identity." It is, rather, to understand more precisely the very nature of those boundaries and the effects of the inscription (violent or otherwise) of those boundaries on bodies and homelands. The temporal movement of the Khalistani *desh-kaal* has become a definitive movement in social and material practices, no matter how indeterminate; the *amritdhari* body, however defined, has become a very powerful site and source of identification; and the Sikh diaspora, with all its contradictions and ambivalences, finds its life with the body and the homeland. These contradictions and ambivalences generate the very values and delimitations by which many Sikhs choose to live and die today. And they are the diaspora's promise and threat.

If I have succeeded, in some way, in reorienting the study of the Sikh diaspora by turning over the self-evidential quality of the Sikh homeland and the Sikh body, then I have accomplished more than I could have hoped. However, I do not hope to have in any way succeeded in stripping the homeland and the body of their powerful reality. The significance of the homeland and the body within processes constituting the Sikh diaspora is something that I have wished to investigate and specify but *not draw into question*. My respect for the Sikh diaspora, unfortunately, is met with the limits of my own techniques of research and writing. If anything, writing this story of the Sikh diaspora has taught me — as the cliché says — that there is yet much more to learn. Situated within a highly politicized context, this text thus offers its limitations much more easily than it may offer anything else. Nevertheless, if they serve to illuminate the limits of knowledge production of the Sikh diaspora, such limitations may themselves be productive.

notes

Introduction: Promise and Threat

1 The emergence of the Sikh religion is traced to the birth and life of Guru Nanak (1469–1539); his revelation included a critique of Islam and Hinduism, and he developed a distinct spiritual and social philosophy. Guru Nanak, the first of ten living gurus, was followed by Guru Angad (r. 1539–52), Guru Amardas (r. 1552–74), Guru Ramdas (r. 1574–81), Guru Arjan (r. 1581–1606), Guru Hargobind (r. 1606–44), Guru Har Rai (r. 1644–61), Guru Har Krishan (r. 1661–64), Guru Tegh Bahadur (r. 1664–75), and Guru Gobind Singh (r. 1675–1708). The Sikh religion reveres a book of spiritual teachings called Guru Granth Sahib, and worship takes place in a locality called a *gurdwara*. In 1699, Guru Gobind Singh inaugurated an orthodox religious order called the Khalsa, which many Sikhs regard as the "pure" form of Sikh practice. Members of the Khalsa undergo an initiation ceremony in which they "take *amrit*" (sacred nectar) and are, thereafter, referred to as *amritdhari*. It is believed by Khalsa Sikhs that, before his death, Guru Gobind Singh claimed that the line of living gurus would cease with him and that henceforward the authority of the guru would pass to the corporate community (*guru panth*) and the Guru Granth Sahib (McLeod 1984, 2). Although at different points in this book I do discuss different aspects of Sikh religious life, the Sikh religion is *not* my object of study, and I am not trained as a specialist in religious studies. There are, however, several excellent contributions to the study of the Sikh religion, to which I recommend the interested reader (see McLeod 1968, 1976, 1984, 1989; Harbans Singh [1983] 1985; Nikky Singh 1993; Uberoi 1996). Extensive bibliographies can be found in O'Connell et al. (1990) and Hawley and Mann (1993).

2 There are two other aspects distinguishing the formation of the Sikh diaspora that are not discussed in this book. The first is perhaps most poignantly portrayed in Sikh historiographies and hagiographies that depict the very foundation of the Sikh community as defined by continual displacement. Particularly between the late fifteenth century and 1708, the ten Gurus of Sikhism are said to have lived nomadic lives, traveling from Mecca to China and all over South Asia. In the early years, as these narratives describe, this nomadism was integral to the teaching style of Guru

Nanak, the first Sikh Guru, who, before settling in the town of Kartarpur, went on several *udasis* (preaching odysseys). The stories of these *udasis* have become extremely popular with Sikhs around the world, and they are recorded in what are called *janam-sakhis* (birth stories) written between the seventeenth century and the early twentieth (McLeod 1968, 1984; Harbans Singh [1983] 1985). Increasingly, in the later years, the mobility of the Sikh Gurus and their disciples, who often lived in temporary camps all over the northwest of South Asia, was a result of their persecution by the Mughal rulers. Today, well over a hundred Sikh places of worship, known as *itihasak gurdwaras* (historical *gurdwaras*), memorialize the places where the Gurus are said to have either resided or paused during their travels. These have become important places of pilgrimage and are also the objects of exhaustive studies, which include detailed maps and pictures of each site (Grewal 1995; Gurmukh Singh 1995; Hari Singh 1994; Patwant Singh 1992). The second aspect distinguishing the story of the Sikh diaspora concerns the violent displacement of Sikhs away from West Punjab in the years surrounding the Partition of Indian and Pakistan. In this case, many Sikhs living not only in Indian Punjab but also in Rajasthan, Gujurat, Maharashtra, Uttar Pradesh, Bihar, and the Delhi area trace their "ancestral villages" to what is now Pakistani Punjab.

3 For an early instance of the shifting usage of the terms *sect* and *nation* in colonial discourse on the Sikhs, see John Malcolm's ([1809] 1812) "Sketch of the Sikhs."

4 For important discussions, although with a different emphasis, of the terms *panth* and *qaum,* see Dusenbery (1995), McLeod (1978), Mahmood (1996), and Oberoi (1994).

5 Dusenbery (1995), responding to Leonard (1989) and McLeod (1989c), provides an eloquent exploration of these debates. Attempting historically to distinguish a "Sikh diaspora" from a "Punjabi diaspora," Leonard and McLeod have argued that the term *Sikh* is inappropriate for discussions of late nineteenth- and early twentieth-century formations.

6 Although several human rights organizations have contributed to this inquiry, very few Sikh studies scholars have made violence and pain in the formation of the Sikh diaspora an object of study. The works of Cynthia Mahmood (1996) and Joyce Pettigrew (1995) are exceptions, and this book in many ways supplements and expands the line of investigation that they have opened up. Inspiration for this inquiry also comes from Valentine Daniel (1996), although his very important work is not explicitly engaged in these pages.

7 For relevant diaspora studies texts, see, e.g., Clifford (1994), Connor (1986), Gilroy (1987, 1993), King and Melvin (1998), Levine (1983), Okamura (1998), Safran (1991), Sheffer (1986), Skinner (1982), and Verdicchio (1997). The interested reader should note that Clifford (1994) contains an extensive bibliography.

8 By making the distinction *as a diaspora,* I mean to differentiate these studies from their predecessors that constituted their object of study as *overseas Indians.* What follows is a summary reading of several texts on the South Asian diaspora. See, e.g.,

Ballard (1994), Barrier and Dusenbery (1989), Barrier and Juergensmeyer (1979), Baumann (1996), Brah (1992, 1996), Clarke et al. (1990), Ghosh (1989), Harris (1982), Jackson and Nesbitt (1993), Hawley and Mann (1993), Karamcheti (1992), Rushdie (1991), Shankar and Srikanth (1998), and van der Veer (1995). I refer more specifically to this growing literature throughout the book. See also the detailed discussions in Axel (1996a, 1996b).

9   It is important to note that, despite the redefinition of the object of study, much of diaspora studies has reappropriated the categories of analysis that guided studies of Jewish and African diasporas. Thus, the tropes of slavery and persecution (variously articulated), in conjunction with problems of the ghetto, the stranger, and the marginal man and retheorizations of acculturation and assimilation, remain central to diaspora studies. For critical discussions, see Scott (1991) and Kirshenblatt-Gimblett (1994) (the latter also suggests an important point of critique of Clifford's [1994] provocative essay). In the volume *Nation and Migration,* van der Veer (1995, 8–9) explicitly models his analysis of the South Asian diaspora on the Jewish diaspora.

10 Consider Tololyan's (1991) proclamation in the inaugural issue of the journal *Diaspora.*

11 I do not here mean to ignore the proliferation of minority studies programs (i.e., African American studies or Asian American studies). These programs, I would argue, more often may be understood in terms of either an area studies approach or a cultural studies approach — or some amalgam of the two.

12 For an extended analysis of the problems into which diaspora studies runs in theorizing the "place of origin," see Axel (1996b).

13 One important aspect of the indenture system is often left out of diaspora studies analyses. Specifically, it imposed extreme debt on the laborers so that, by the end of the five-year term of indenture, most laborers from the subcontinent could not possibly choose to return to their birthplaces. They were forced to stay in the colonies in order to try to pay off their debts (see Gangulee [1946] 1947; Gillion 1962; Kondapi 1951; Waiz 1927).

14 The contributors to a recent collected volume (van der Veer 1995) provide examples. Aisha Khan (1995) explains Indo-Trinidadian Muslims: "Uttar Pradesh, Oudh, and Bihar, from which most Indians came to Trinidad, were regions where religious heterogeneity flourished. Hinduism and Islam were mutually influencing . . . and Sunni and Shia forms of Islam coexisted" (p. 126). Steva Vertovec (1995) likewise argues: "Gujarat is well known in the subcontinent for the number, complexity, and distinctiveness of caste and subcaste groups, and the same can be said for Gujarati caste phenomena in Britain. . . . Caste identities among Gujaratis [in Britain] have continued to be of considerable importance" (p. 144). And Parminder Bhachu (1995) states that dowry is a "cultural idiom that has existed for centuries and survived two migrations" (p. 236). If the goal of identifying these cultural and religious phenomena is not to demonstrate how the diaspora embodies

cultural or religious time, these forms of explanation do not make sense. Otherwise, the essays in this volume cannot clarify how practices and beliefs of people hundreds of years ago can configure those of people today (i.e., they do not offer a theory of historical mediation).

15   Consider the work of the first British anthropologists of "overseas Indians" to go to the field after World War II: i.e., Benedict (1961), Kuper (1960), Mayer (1961), and Morris (1968). For the significance of Evans-Pritchard to Dumont, see Dumont (1975, 1980). For one genealogy of Dumont's theorizations in area studies, see Appadurai (1986). That Evans-Pritchard's object of study in Africa was produced by the British colonial administration is an important matter and has been well established (see Asad 1973; Cohn 1977; Clifford 1988).

16   My gratitude to Terry Turner, who introduced me to the work of Evans-Pritchard and who first heard this critique in the winter of 1993.

17   Clearly, this is one point that Dumont ([1966] 1980) picks up and elaborates at great length: "To say that there has been no change *of* the society is roughly to say that there has been no revolution or overall reform: a form of organization does not change, it is replaced by another; a structure is present or absent, *it does not change*" (p. 219). See also Dumont (1975), which attributes to Evans-Pritchard the discovery of structure as an abstraction.

18   Consider de Certeau's (1984) remarks about the "law of the proper" and the "stability of place" (p. 117): place is "a determination through objects that are ultimately reducible to the *being-there* of something dead, the law of 'place'" (p. 118). One might note that this complicated route to the theorization of place as originary and constitutive has serious implications for the basic organizing principle of diaspora studies — "displacement."

19   In addition to these, several British — H. S. Morris (Uganda, 1952–55), Burton Benedict (Mauritius, 1955–57), and Hilda Kuper (South Africa, 1953–57) — and American — Morton Klass (Trinidad, 1957–58), Barton Schwartz (Fiji, 1961–62), and Philip Singer (Guiana, 1960) — social scientists went to the field.

20   These characteristics have a relevant history of critique that I will not discuss here. One genealogy of this debate concerns the long debate over India as a "region" or an "area" (see Cohn 1957; Crane 1967; Fox 1977; Dumont 1957, 1964a, 1964b; Appadurai 1986b, 1988).

21   I have not been able to come up with a use of *overseas Indians* prior to 1907, but I do not find it necessary to conclude that the term was not used commonly or in records before. It is important to note that the term became an "official" one in 1914, when the Department of Indians Overseas was created (it became the Department of Commonwealth Relations in 1944) (Kondapi 1951, 453).

22   For example, Neame's *The Asiatic Danger in the Colonies* (1907), Chapple's *Fiji — Its Problems and Resources* (1921), and Macmillan's *Warning From the West Indies* (1936). These texts formed contentious discourses, and they often produced conflicting arguments that nevertheless challenged the authority of the colonial state.

23 Among the various organizations involved were the Committee for the Comparative Study of New Nations at the University of Chicago, the Centers for International Affairs at Harvard and Princeton, the Center for International Studies at MIT, the Institute of International Studies at Berkeley, the Ford and Rockefeller Foundations, the CIA, UNESCO, USAID, and the World Bank.

24 Consider the work of Klass (1961), Niehoff and Niehoff (1960), and Schwartz (1967), anthropologists trained in the United States, in conjunction with that of the British anthropologists noted above.

25 For example, the Soulbury Constitution of 1947, the controller-general of emigration in New Delhi, and the Trusteeship Council of the United Nations (Kondapi 1951, 492–501).

26 I might add to these propositions the significance of theorists who claim that the nation-state is in a moment of crisis or possibly coming to an end (see Appadurai 1996a; Gilroy 1987; Hall 1990; Sklair 1991; "La fin du national" 1986).

27 My gratitude to Bernard Cohn and Arjun Appadurai, and to my colleagues in their "The Twentieth Century" seminar (spring 1994), for helping me develop this argument in Axel (1994). Thanks also to Bernard Cohn for directing me to the relation between the work of Benedict and that of Mead (1953) and, in this particular discussion, to the relation between studies of overseas Indians and overseas Chinese.

28 The character of Benedict's work as a study of a displaced community (despite its claims to be a study of Japan), a point of mediation for Boasian theory and methodology, and a nexus for the production of government policy, is extremely important.

29 Consider the acknowledgments in the beginning of the book: "This Manual is based on the researches inaugurated . . . under a grant from the Human Resources Division, Office of Naval Research, and according to the terms of the contract, reproduction in whole or in part is permitted for any purposes of the U.S. Government" (Mead 1953, preface).

30 But it must be kept in mind that these specialists were working closely with scholars investigating such related categories as *overseas Chinese,* which represented quite a different value (see Fried 1958). One might note that the study of race relations in Britain has a similarly definitive character in a genealogy of the deployment of Evans-Pritchard's theories of "segmentary societies" (as noted above) and Furnival's (1944) and M. G. Smith's (1965) theories of "plural societies." The precise form of conjunction of these genealogies necessitates further research.

31 For early theories of *total flow,* see Harary (1969) and Nystuen and Dacey ([1961] 1965). These works have attained a historical importance in geography and transport economics that cannot be understated; indeed, they provide the basic principles for a series of procedures that have powerful effects on the production of national economies and discourses of national identity.

32 For a much more detailed discussion of historical anthropology, see my introduction to and the various essays collected in Axel (in press a) and also Adams (1981),

Davis (1981), Dirks (1987, 1992), Faubion (1993), Ginzburg (1981, 1989), Kelly and Kaplan (1990), Krech (1991), Munn (1992), Pels (1997), and Taussig (1989).

33 My gratitude to Carol Greenhouse, who has urged me to explicate these ethnographic issues. Some of the phrasing in these sentences I owe to her.

34 Lévi-Strauss ([1950] 1987) spelled out this distinction early on: "Sociological observation . . . *extricates itself* by dint of the subject's capacity for indefinite self-objectification, that is to say (without ever quite abolishing itself as subject) for projecting outside itself ever-diminishing fractions of itself. Theoretically, at least, this fragmentation is limitless, except for the persistent implication of the existence of the two extremes as the condition of its possibility. The prominent place of ethnography in the sciences of man . . . as inspirer of a new humanism, derives from the fact that it offers this unlimited process of objectification of the subject" (p. 32). Perhaps Daniel's (1996) words are more relevant to this text: "Granted, theory, any theory, is a way of understanding reality and not a collection of observations about reality. To the extent that it enhances one's understanding of the real, it literally 'stands under' observations and gives form to these observations. But violence is such a reality that a theory which purports to inform it with significance must not merely 'stand under' but conspicuously 'stand apart' from it as a gesture of open admission to its *inadequacy* to measure up to its task. I do not mean to valorize violence hereby, but to foreground it so as to make the more general point regarding theory: that it is often forgotten that even ordinary life is not transparent to theory. Violence just brings this point home" (emphasis added, p. 6). He comments farther on: "Often forgotten are (a) that ethnographic objects are, by definition, theorized objects, and (b) that insofar as theory and object can be separated from each other by an abstract mental activity called 'prescinding', we must also remember that the two are dialectically, if not dialogically, codeterminant" (12).

35 For other work involved in this kind of inquiry, see Brah (1992), Chow (1993), Geertz (1986), Harding and Meyers (1994), McClintock, Mufti, and Shohat (1997), Parmar (1982), "La fin du national" (1986), Ruggie (1993), Skinner (1982), Tololyan (1991), Wilson and Dissanayake (1996), and Yaeger (1996). Another trajectory of research has been based in sociology, political science, and international relations. Most of these discussions, however, have little significance for the analysis that I offer here (see Haas et al. [1992], a special issue of *International Organization* that calls for the production of a new "epistemic community" that would be a "knowledge-based group" with the purpose of gaining and retaining influence on global policy-making processes). More helpful are the works of Sassen (1991, 1997), Sklair (1991), and Smith (1994). Their differences notwithstanding, the important arguments that they propose attempt to reassess the significance of nation-states in terms of transformations of capitalism. To these studies can be added the work of Rouse (1995) and Verdery (1994), which considers the dialectical relation of nations and transnational formations. Other work to consider, with respect to this dialectic, is that of the French scholars whose essays are collected in

"La fin du national" (1986) (these suggest another trajectory of transnational studies that has still not been engaged in English-language debates).

36   See also the discussions of space and time in Lefebvre (1991) and Postone (1993).

37   The area studies industry that produces the diaspora is very much akin to what Marx (1978a) calls *the transport industry,* in which the commodity sold and valorized "is the actual change of place itself" (p. 135) (see chaps. 4 and 5).

38   As we shall see in the following chapters, my research on Sikh life in particular localities of India, England, and the United States has generated an insight that responds to the former difficulties of diaspora studies: despite the generality of the Sikh diaspora, the very specific and localized contradictions basing the transformation of individuals into representations or representatives makes it *impossible* to understand the diaspora as a totality that, manifested in different forms, is supposedly embodied by the particular diaspora individuals. This much may also be said for the nation-state as well: the impossibility of the diaspora's totality reflects the impossibility of the nation-state's totality.

39   The different chapters of this book will elaborate my approach to fetishism as an aspect of subject formation (see also Apter and Pietz 1993; Bhabha 1994; Feldman 1991, 1997; Ferenczi 1995; Forrester 1990; Foster 1996; Gilman 1993; Haraway 1991; Laplanche and Pontalis 1973; Mulvey 1989, 1992; Pietz 1985, 1987, 1988; Postone 1993; Rose 1986; Taussig 1980, 1993).

40   The different theories of subject formation presented by Lacan and Foucault, it is clear, cannot be collapsed one into the other, and I do not intend to do so in my analyses in this book. The distinction between the two theories, with their contradictions and overlap, has been dealt with at length by Butler (1993, 1997b) and is not discussed in this text.

41   I hope it is clear that the masculinization of different Sikh subjects is not a consequence merely of men predominating or maintaining prominent positions within Sikh life. In chaps. 1 and 3 particularly, I offer a reading of gender and sexuality as performative (Butler 1990, 1993). Readers should be warned ahead of time, however, that this is not strictly speaking a "gender book" but considers only the importance of gender and sexuality within specific historical circumstances concerned with the formation of the Sikh diaspora. The Sikh case takes on a certain distinctiveness through the fetishization of the image of the *amritdhari* man. As I discuss in chap. 3, my focus on this valorization illuminates the historical processes that have been integral to the objectification of women as "silent and invisible." Nevertheless, although the formation of what Nikky Singh calls the Woman as Subject is an extremely important topic, it is not the concern of this book. For such discussions of women, I direct the reader to the important contributions of Nikky Singh (1993), Jakobsh (1996), Mahmood (1996, in press), and McLeod (1996).

42   I am not, however, arguing for a functionalist analysis of bodies and their relations to collectivities (Douglas 1966; Durkheim 1915; Mauss [1935] 1973; van Gennep 1965): e.g., that the Sikh body signifies Sikh society and Sikh society signifies the

Sikh body, in a reciprocal relation. Such is not a sufficient explanation of the diasporic production of the Sikh body and the Sikh homeland. The Sikh body does not merely signify or embody a cosmology of Sikh society or the Sikh homeland. Within the contexts of the Indian nation-state, the British nation-state, and the U.S. nation-state, the Sikh is also a national citizen, and the Sikh body may be constituted performatively and pedagogically as a signifier of simultaneously disparate forms of belonging, subjectivity, and affect (Bhabha 1994; Butler 1993). This simple proposition is complicated further by the histories of violence that constitute the Sikh body and fundamentally transform how to talk about that body, bringing in the necessity of understanding how productions of the body and the subject are infused with indeterminacy and uncertainty. My approach thus may be seen as supplementing the work of Appadurai (1998), Feldman (1991), and Malkki (1995).

1 : The Maharaja's Glorious Body

1 This discourse on Sikh identity emerged through over fifty years of colonial interactions (see Anonymous 1847; Burns [1834] 1973; Cunningham 1849; Garrett and Chopra 1911, 1970; Lawrence 1846; Malcolm [1809] 1812; McGregor 1846; Merivale 1840; Osborne 1840; Pearse [1848] 1970; Prinsep 1970; Steinbach [1846] 1976; Taylor 1846, 1848; Thornton 1846; Vigne 1840; Wilkins [1781] 1784).

2 This and other battles were narrated in several journals and books of the time (see, e.g., Cole 1850; Crowquill 1850; Gough and Innes 1970).

3 *Distinctive* is the term invariably used in discourses about the Sikh body.

4 Not only the *Rahit Maryada* but also many other *rahits* have been the topic of considerable debate and historicist procedures of investigation, searching either to prove or to disprove the putative *continuity* of definite aspects of a Sikh "identity." These procedures, it must be made clear, do not deny the continuity of a general Sikhism that they claim to represent, just the manner of continuity. Harjot Oberoi (1993) provides one example: "While the Sikh tradition sees the rahit as having evolved from the writings of the Sikh gurus, with additions made by Guru Gobind Singh to its corpus in 1699, recent historical research points in a radically different direction. The bulk of the extant versions of the rahit all appear to date from the nineteenth century, not from the late seventeenth or early eighteenth century as tradition would have us believe. . . . The complexity of the Sikh rahit is further compounded by the fact that there are, according to one account, eighteen works that qualify as principle texts expounding the rahit. . . . While they all share certain normative premises, they are by no means a uniform body of literature establishing what may amount to a standard code of behavior. In addition, there is the question of *how representative of the Sikh panth these works are*" (emphasis added; pp. 270–71). I return to the problem of this proposed continuity in chap. 5.

5 In the eighteenth and nineteenth centuries, *sardar* was a term signifying both smaller and larger "Sikh" rulers or landowners. Today it is used generally by Punjabi, Hindi, and Urdu speakers, to refer to any Sikh man or to an *amritdhari* Sikh.

6 One of the most challenging articulations of a colonial critique has been the 1985 publication *Lions of the Punjab* by Richard Fox. This marks perhaps the only attempt to incorporate Said's (1978) insights into an analysis of Sikh identity. Very much following Said, Fox defines his object of study in terms of a critique of the broad notion of *British sensibilities* that configured the putative production of a category of identity called *Singh:* a notion that included "biological imagery," "colonial orientations and policies," "culturally given beliefs," and bureaucratic practices (pp. 1–5). In Fox's perspective, "the British" used the contents of this space to establish "the ultimate form of Orientalism: they justified the biological determinism validating and constituting their colonial domination and having its roots in mid-nineteenth century European thought as really originating in the cultural beliefs of the Indians themselves. . . . The Raj forced indigenous society to evolve according to British beliefs. At the very moment they thought they were helping the Singhs maintain their specific traditions, the British were forcing those traditions to adapt to British beliefs about them" (p. 4).

There are some points of difficulty within Fox's analysis, most of which Sikh studies scholars indicate by reiterating the common critique of Said — e.g., the problem of a monolithic colonialist discourse, the lack of agency attributed to the oppressed "other." There are a few limitations, however, that are particular to Fox's analysis that I should mention here. Fox has placed much of the power of his analysis on conclusions arrived at from studies of recruitment strategies — organized around the notion of distinct "martial races" — that the British deployed in producing Sikh regiments. Since the British crystallized these practices in the late 1800s and early 1900s (an accomplishment articulated by Capt. R. W. Falcon in his 1896 *Handbook on Sikhs for Regimental Officers*), he has given closest attention to this period in his discussion. The isolation of this period, however, leads to an erroneous postulation that the decisive moment in the production of a Sikh identity occurred in the 1920s after the successful deployment of an "essentializing" discourse of Sikh identity as a martial race.

7 The literature on performativity in both linguistics and feminist theory is vast. The important texts in linguistics are Austin (1975), Benveniste (1971), and Derrida (1988). In addition to Butler's (1990, 1993, 1997a, 1997b) work, the reader should consult the varying discussions in Diamond (1996), Felman (1983), Garber (1992), Lancaster (1997), Modleski (1991), and Weston (1993). For excellent treatments of the position of performance theory within feminist anthropological practices of knowledge production, see Morris (1995) and Schein (1999).

8 These portraits, and particularly the Winterhalter portrait, were reproduced in texts of collected letters and correspondence in the nineteenth century as well (see, e.g., Baird 1911; Login 1890, 1970).

9 Clearly, this is not to suggest that there was a single, monolithic colonial project.

10 Mildred Archer (1979) has written: "This story of the storming of the Serngapatam and the death of Tipu [now] entered British folk history. Tipu's throne, arms and

armour, manuscripts and jewels as well as the famous Man-Tiber-Organ were taken under the normal laws of prize and sent home by the Governor-General" (p. 435). The similarity of the confiscation of Tipu Sultan's properties and that of Duleep Singh's is striking, as is the amount of attention paid to the former in orientalist art (paintings of Tipu continued to be composed into the mid-1800s) (see also Breckenridge 1989; Mitter 1977; Nochlin 1989; Pearson 1980; Pelles 1963; Verrier 1979).

11   The Lane chromolithograph was also exhibited at the Royal Academy of Arts in 1855 (Graves 1906, 377).

12   "Baron Marochetti also sculpted the white marble statues of both Prince Albert and Queen Victoria for the Royal Mausoleum at Frogmore in Windsor Breat Park, where Prince Albert was buried. Queen Victoria insisted on having her effigy prepared at the same time as that of her late husband lest there be a discrepancy in their ages as they lay together awaiting the Resurrection" (Aijazuddin 1979, 80).

For a picture of the sculpture of the maharaja, which is now in Lahore Museum, see Gur Rattan Pal Singh (1980, 121). Eleven years later, the artist Koberwein was paid eighty-four pounds to produce a copy of the Winterhalter portrait on canvas, which Victoria then gave to the sitter (Millar 1992, 318).

13   Consider also Lady Login's comments (1970, 122, 126): "Of all those present on that memorable occasion, I believe that I am the sole survivor."

14   Duleep had cut his hair and, interestingly, presented the long tress to Lady Login in 1851 (Alexander and Anand 1980, 31).

15   This disinterest in religion is echoed in many nineteenth-century Punjabi discourses. Consider Tandon's (1968, 10–11) statement: "After all, we and the Sikhs stemmed from the same stock; most Hindus had Sikh relations, customs, and they were always members of our brotherhoods." Reflecting on Tandon's statement, Oberoi (1990) adds: "It would have been far more accurate if he had made it clear that the question of religious identity was of *no great importance,* that the more enduring themes in the construction of personal identity in the Punjab had to do with the bonds of kinship and territoriality" (p. 141).

16   Dalhousie took pride in the creation of this, what he considered the maharaja's "best characteristic": it was he who gave Duleep his first Bible in April 1854 before his departure for England. Sending the Bible, Dalhousie wrote Duleep: "Since that day, when the course of public events placed you a little boy in my hands, I have regarded you in some sort as my son. I therefore ask you, before we part, to accept from me the volume which I should offer to my own child, as the best of all gifts, since in it alone is to be found the secret of real happiness either in this world or in that which is to come. I bid you farewell, my dear Maharajah, and beg you to believe me always. With sincere regard, Your Highness's faithful friend, Dalhousie" (Ganda Singh 1977, 65). Dalhousie also inscribed on the inside cover of the Bible the following: "To His Highness Maharajah Duleep Singh. This Holy Book, in which he has been led by God's grace to find an inheritance richer by far than all earthly kingdoms, is

presented, with sincere respect and regard, by his faithful friend Dalhousie. April 5, 1854." Duleep Singh later considered the irony of this inscription: "It is impossible to believe that his Lordship wished to exult over the boy whom he had deprived of his kingdom, but the inscription is curious as evidence of how little Lord Dalhousie in his best moods was capable of entering into the feelings of others" (Duleep Singh 1884, 82).

17 For later colonial military texts, see Barstow (1928), Bingley ([1918] 1970), Macmunn (1920), and Malcolm ([1891] 1971). For other colonial historiographic texts, see Macauliffe ([1909] 1978), Parry (1921), Thorburn ([1883] 1970), and Trevaskis (1928).

18 Osborne (1840) relates the tale of Ranjit's acceptance of the gifts: "Contrary to the usual native custom, Runjeet condescended to examine them very minutely, and appeared to count every pearl and jewel before he gave them into the hands of his treasurer" (p. 78). For Duleep's "retrieval" of jewels from the treasury, see Alexander and Anand (1980, 18).

It is very likely that it was not Duleep who retrieved the portrait from the treasury but his guardian, John Login. It was certainly Login who found the ring with Victoria's portrait on it. As Lady Login (1970) recounts: "My husband himself took the listing of the jewel department. . . . The way in which jewels of the highest value were stowed away was extraordinary. On one occasion Login found some valuable rings, including one with a beautiful portrait of Queen Victoria, huddled in a bag, and suggested that it would be well to tie a label to each with an account of their history and value, attaching it by a string" (p. 75).

19 It is significant to note that, in 1861, Duleep Singh was one of the first to be presented with the Order of the Star of India. His official title was Knight Grand Cross of the Order (see Login 1890, 467–68). Indeed, his perspective on the Star was very different from the nizam's. We can see him wearing his medal, *along with* the other Victoria portrait, in the 1875 portrait by Capt. Goldingham (see Aijazuddin 1979, 33).

20 They also published a translation of Major Even Bell's *The Annexation of the Punjab and the Maharaja Duleep Singh* (1882), a text that castigated the colonial state's policies in Punjab.

21 Ranajit Guha (1989) has written of this form of colonialist historiography: "Its function was to erect that past as a pedestal on which the triumphs and glories of the colonizers and their instrument, the colonial state, could be displayed to best advantage. Indian history, assimilated thereby to the history of Great Britain, would henceforth be used as a comprehensive measure of difference between the peoples of these two countries . . . all adding up to an irreconcilable difference between colonizer and colonized" (pp. 211–12). With these reflections, we might understand more clearly the stated theme of the exhibition: "East is east and west is west."

22 My gratitude to the archivists of the National Portrait Gallery, who allowed me to see the files for these negotiations.

23 My gratitude to Darshan Singh Tatla for conversations about the centenary festival and for introducing me to the members of the NTID and the publishers involved in producing and distributing these portraits.

2 : The Restricted Zone

1 Throughout, I use the term *nationalist* to refer to the domain of the nation-state, in this case India, and not as an adjective describing Khalistanis.

2 Parliamentary Archives, New Delhi, Larris Press Clipping Section, call no. 294-553-1, 12 March 1992.

3 The argument that I am developing here differs significantly from most scholarly treatments of the conflict between the Indian nation-state and the Sikhs. These discussions, for the most part, locate the beginnings of conflict during the 1970s, as a result of the contradictions of the "Green Revolution" in Punjab, the proliferation of discontent among Sikh agriculturalists, and the failure of the Indian government to fulfill its promises made at the time of the formation of the Punjabi Suba in 1966 (of which more below). Joyce Pettigrew (1995), who has produced the most important work on the Khalistani movement within India, reiterates and supplements this type of analysis. She comments: "It was during the 1970s that the bonds of the Sikhs with the state began to loosen" (p. 7). She adds an analysis of the violent events that took place in 1984 (which I discuss in the following chapter), stating that these developments led to practices of Sikh resistance: "The considerable violence to which ordinary civilians were to be subjected in the years following stems from these events when the state treated the Sikhs as a collective entity *for the first time* in post-independence India as well as attacking their institutions" (p. 8). Although I am in complete agreement with Pettigrew's stress on 1984 as a moment of transformation, I do hope to refine the terms of her analysis. This refinement concerns both the logic and the historicity of her claim that 1984 marks a period when Sikhs were constituted as a "collective entity *for the first time* in post-independence India." I have highlighted the processes of nineteenth-century surrender as a repetitive modality of subject formation that, although never complete, constituted the Sikhs as a "collective entity." This chapter considers the way in which the processes of Sikh surrender and subjectification were regenerated within the new context of Indian nation-state formation from Independence on. State violence, including the mass arrest of Sikh protestors in the 1950s and 1960s and one invasion of the Golden Temple in 1955, forms one common denominator of these processes.

4 I am indebted to an early essay by Harjot Oberoi (1987) for introducing me to the basic issues explored in this chapter. It will become clear, however, that both my genealogy of Khalistan and my theoretical intervention are significantly different. Rather than dismissing the imbrication of territoriality with processes of Sikh subjectification as false consciousness (which Oberoi's argument amounts to) or attempting to prove how Khalistan and Punjab are not "natural," my intent here, as elsewhere, is to engage the very real nature of those very entities critically.

5 For a transcription of the meeting, see Mansergh (1977, 138–41).

6 The following is a summary from Basu (1995, 65–71), *The Report on the Working of the Ministry of States* (March 1949), *The Report on the States Reorganization Commission* (1955), and the *White Paper on Indian States* (1948). See also Menon (1956), Patel (1949), and Sardar V. Patel Smarak Bhavan (1975).

7 Such a celebratory moment may be considered premature considering (not a minor example) Kashmir and considering that, because of the very tenets of the Constitution, the integration and reorganization of territories could possibly continue, and indeed has continued, without pause (e.g., the subsequent formation of Arunachal Pradesh, Gujarat, Goa, Haryana, Himachal Pradesh, Manipur, Meghalaya, Mizoram, Nagaland, and Tripura) (Basu 1995, 55).

8 This set of demands constituted the basis for what is known as the Anandpur Sahib Resolution of 1973, which became an official statement of the demands of the Shiromani Akali Dal. The resolution, and its history of many transformations, is an important, although often controversial, aspect of most analyses of Sikh history. It is not, however, the object of analysis here (cf. Gopal Singh 1994; Khushwant Singh [1989] 1991).

9 My gratitude to Khushwant Singh for explaining Khalistani currency, stamps, and passports. Khushwant Singh had been one of several people who received these *souvenirs,* as he calls them. Khushwant Singh, however, has been very explicitly anti-Khalistan. In fact, Chauhan has attempted to sue Khushwant Singh for his anti-Khalistan proclamations, which included remarks against Chauhan. Khushwant Singh does not try to hide his opinion of Chauhan, as is evident from the following: "Chauhan had a chequered career, starting off as a member of the CPI–aligned Students federation, then becoming a member of the Congress and, later, once again a communist. . . . He migrated to England, shaved off his beard and for a while worked as a railway guard. He returned to the Punjab (with his beard fully grown), fought and won the 1967 elections and became Deputy Speaker" ([1989] 1991, 310).

10 My gratitude to Gurhalpal Singh, one of the editors of the *International Journal of Punjab Studies,* for allowing me to retell this story.

11 My gratitude to the surveyor general of India, and to different officials in the office of the Survey in Dehra Dun, for clarifying the significance of these cartographic matters.

12 Quotes in the following passages come from two government documents: *Instruction for Publication of Maps* (1987) and *Constitution Amendment in India* (1994).

13 In reflecting on the problem of frontiers and juridical control over citizens, Vico ([1744] 1991) provides an apt portrayal of the originary "fable" that positions violence within the constitution of territory at the margins: "The Latin grammarians erroneously derived *territorium* from the terror of the fasces [a bundle of rods bound up with the blade of an axe projecting in the middle] used by the lictors to disperse crowds and make way for the Roman magistrates. . . . Instead the word originated in

the fact that the boundaries of the cultivated fields, within which the civil powers later arose, were guarded by Vesta with bloody rites" (p. 274). I elaborate Vico's notion of historicity and fable elsewhere (Axel, in press b). In the following chapter, I relate violent processes of territorial delimitation and marginality to the production of the *amritdhari* body and the reconstitution of the Sikh *desh-kaal.*

14   "Panjab Police told to step up surveillance" (*Hindu,* 16 March 1996). Joyce Pettigrew (1995) has provided a superb discussion of the constitution of the border. One example is quite stark: "There are 553 km of land and reverine tract between Indian and Pakistani Punjab. As from February 1993, all of this has been fenced and provided with floodlights, with observation posts every 500 yards" (p. 106).

15   This phrasing is based on a popular Hindi song from the film *Mera Naam Joker.*

16   Thanks to the archivists of the Reserve Bank of India, New Delhi, and of the Coin and Stamp Collection of the British Museum, London, for this material.

17   This very quick genealogy summarizes, and unfortunately simplifies, the complexity of narratives contained in the NIC proceedings (1960, 1967, 1981, 1984, 1986, 1990, 1993); Lok Sabha Debates (#2494, 7/8/85; #251, 5/11/86; #462, 25/11/91; #1401, 3/3/94); Rajya Sabha Debates (#320, 6/11/86; #2497, 29/8/90; #498, 4/9/91); LARRIS, Press Clipping Section, *National Integration* (1993–1995).

18   For elaborations on this process within very different contexts, see Axel (1998), Berlant (1993), Bhabha (1994), and Lefort ([1978] 1986).

19   This is an important distinction. In this historical case, I am arguing that there is something very specific about the formation of the nation-state and its regulatory procedures. Fantasy designates this difference (and provides the basis for a critique), a difference that is distinct from the way in which Khalistan is positioned within diasporic life. When analyzing, in the following chapter, what may seem like similar processes for the formation of the Sikh diaspora, I flag this distinction by developing the term *diasporic imaginary* as an analytic category. To put this crudely, the diaspora is not a new kind of nation-state or a nation-state in nascent form. The same kinds of techniques of analysis and critique may not be indiscriminately applied to each.

20   For example, speaking as the leader of the Jana Sangh Group in Parliament in 1961, A. B. Vajpayee (India's present-day prime minister) argued that the origin of the modern Indian nation-state derives from an immeasurable past that grants India a pregiven authority as an exclusive Hindu state: "India is an ancient nation. Its emancipation from the foreign yoke in 1947 marked just the commencement of a new chapter in its history" (Vajpayee 1961). It may be noted, ironically, that during his brief tenure as prime minister, in May 1996, Vajpayee went to the Golden Temple in Amritsar, where he said: "It is time to forget the past and look forward" (*Asian Age,* 27 May 1996). Gyan Prakash (1999) argues cogently that, in creating an Indian nationalism prior to 1947, Gandhi and Nehru, their differences notwithstanding, maintained a similar understanding of the origins of the nation. This is an important point because the Gandhian/Nehruvian fantasy of India's origin, successively taken

up by right-wing Hindu parties, could not be understood as the basis of the nation-state *after* 1947, particularly in constitutional law.

21 Considering my discussion of the Patel Scheme, it may be important to note that another aspect that the fantasy of the nation reflects is a certain form of forgetting, not of difference, but of the negotiation of the nation-state as a spatial totality.

22 Whether India is a federal, quasi federal, or unitary system has been a matter of much debate (cf. Basu 1995).

23 In 1993, in an article prompted by continuing debates about "communal violence" and national integration, Justice S. Mohan, judge of the Indian Supreme Court, reiterated this formulation of desire in terms of national integration, "which re-quires abolition of the hereditary social structure." He said: "The object is to create a sense of oneness as belonging to one nation, speaking one voice. Unity in diversity is the crying need of the home. . . . All communities must be drawn into the national mainstream. . . . This idea of one nation must penetrate into nook and corner. . . . A national character arises from the yearning of men to be united in a bondage of oneness" (*Hindustan Times,* 3 April 1993).

24 I hope to demonstrate here that a critical engagement with cartography is not a matter of judging degrees of failure or concealment in representing cultural diversity or of dismissing the way in which maps "capture the world in miniature" (Duncan and Ley 1993, 2). This latter kind of analysis, concerned with the varying degrees of inaccuracy of visual representation as an elision or violation of (presumably origi-nal) difference, continues to be popular in a variety of fields, including anthropol-ogy, history, cultural geography, and cartography (see, e.g., Black 1997; Blunt and Rose 1994; Cormack 1994; Coronil 1994; Crow 1996; Edney 1997; Gregory 1994; Harley 1988a and b, 1989, 1992a and b; Harvey 1989; Keates 1973; Marin 1984; Monmonier 1993; Orlove 1993a and b; Richards 1992; Robinson and Petchenik 1976; Robinson and Sale 1953; Rundstrom 1993; Soja 1989; Wood 1992).

25 For analyses of the way in which *before the law* indicates an anteriority, the constitu-tion of an ontological integrity of the subject as temporally prior, see Butler (1990, 35–78) and Derrida (1987, 139–48).

26 The questioning subject also takes on some of the qualities that are ascribed to *terrorism* and *the terrorist.* According to the Terrorist-Affected Areas (Special Courts) Ordinance of July 1984, a terrorist is "a person who indulges in wanton killing of persons *or* in violence *or* in the disruption of services or means of communications essential to the community or in damaging property with a view to: . . . endangering the sovereignty or integrity of India" (emphasis added; quoted in Major 1987, 53). The ordinance thus was phrased "so as to include 'just about anyone.' It is not hard to see how people who might more properly be labelled 'revolutionaries,' 'commu-nalists,' or even 'strikers' could be categorized as 'terrorists' under this definition" (Major 1987, 53).

27 This is a problem that Freud ([1932] 1950), Weber ([1919] 1978), Benjamin (1978), and Arendt (1969) articulate early on. Following these writers, Taussig's

(1993) reflections on the problem are relevant: "There is something frightening, I think, merely in saying this conjunction of reason and violence exists, not only because it makes violence scary, as if imbued with the greatest legitimating force there can be, reason itself, and not only because it makes reason scary by indicating how it's snuggled deep into the armpit of terror, but because we so desperately need to cling to reason — as instituted — as the bulwark against the terrifying anomic and chaos pressing in on all sides" (p. 222).

3 : *The Tortured Body*

1   I argue this against scholars who currently claim that we live in a "post-traumatic century" (Felman 1995) or a "catastrophic age" in which "trauma itself may provide the very link between cultures" (Caruth 1995, 11). Lauren Berlant (1997) has argued, I think correctly, that this discourse of trauma as unifying culture resonates too closely with problematic forms of "national sentimentality." The literature on trauma and wounding varies widely on this issue. For differing approaches, see also Brown (1995), Gordon (1997), Herman ([1992] 1997), Seltzer (1993, 1995, 1997), Strozier and Flynn (1996), Sturken (1997), and Yaeger (1997).

2   Joyce Pettigrew's (1995) work on the Khalistani movement within India between 1984 and 1992 deserves special notice. She details the struggles between the Indian nation-state and Khalistanis within Punjab and provides a unique discussion of the formation of, and the conflicts between, different Punjab-based Khalistani groups in a way that I cannot adequately treat here. She also considers questions of torture quite powerfully. On this topic, my analyses in this chapter may be taken as a supplement to both her work and that of Cynthia Mahmood (1996). See also Tatla (1999) for a related inquiry.

3   The United Nations Convention against Torture and Other Cruel, Inhuman and Degrading Treatment or Punishment was adopted by the UN General Assembly in 1984. The convention details "legislative, judicial, administrative and other measures" that each country must take to eradicate torture. It specifies the need for criminal legislation to ensure that torture is an offense, speedy and impartial investigation of each allegation of torture, prosecution of those found responsible, and full redress for the victim.

4   Human rights organizations have developed a standard narrative form to be used in the investigation of torture. This narrative moves from a general overview of the violations within a country through recommendations for the improvement of conditions and an alert to both the nation-state under inspection and the world community or the United Nations. Following this narrative are usually transcriptions of survivor testimonies that typify the allegation of transgressions. Together, these different narratives generate a picture of the torture scenario from the rounding up of victims through their release or disappearance. I mention these aspects of human rights reports in order to distinguish the aim of my own discussion, which is to critically describe and engage the dialectics of diaspora and nation-state. Toward this

aim, the narratives of human rights reports are certainly relevant, but I do not follow their model, nor do I reproduce the information that they provide. For the reader interested in the human rights narratives on these issues, I provide citations throughout the text.

5   In a recent report on human rights abuses in Punjab, Kumar, Muktsar, and Singh (1999) explain this formation of doubt in slightly different terms: "We must acknowledge another serious difficulty here: the target audience we have in mind — normal middle class Indians — do not routinely experience illegal detention, custodial torture and arbitrary executions. So they tend to be sceptical of extreme statements that berate the State institutions to be calculatedly inhuman, specially when they come from habitually anti-establishment characters. We must also admit that the meta-narrative of Punjab problem has been so successfully 'contextualized' that it generally conjures up a picture of cynical forces, bent on violence and disruption, which the security forces somehow managed to contain" (p. 11).

6   The consequences of excluding Punjab from adherence to national and international human rights law is discussed in Asia Watch (1991), Human Rights Watch/Physicians for Human Rights (1994), and Kumar, Muktsar, and Singh (1999).

7   Other relevant legislative acts that suspend safeguards against arbitrary arrest and incommunicado detention, and that also reverse the presumption of innocence, are the Armed Forces (Punjab and Chandigarh) Special Powers Act of 1983, the National Security (Amendment) Act of 1984, the Terrorist Affected Areas (Special Courts) Act of 1984, and the Terrorist and Disruptive Activities (Prevention) Act of 1987.

8   This narrative demonstrates a crucial ambiguity within these procedures of identification. The officer does not say *amritdhari* but rather "Sikh men . . . who have long beards and wear turbans." In the introduction, I discuss the distinctions between several categories of Sikh identity, including *sahajdhari*. The *sahajdhari* Sikh may indeed have a long beard and turban, and, as many informants have indicated to me, it is often impossible to distinguish a bearded and turbaned *sahajdhari* from an *amritdhari* (unless, as one man told me, you go and ask him). The implication is clear: targeting men with beards and turbans has facilitated the violation of individuals who, within nationalist discourse, are not even supposed to be representatives of a movement for Khalistan. This slippage is made even more complex by the actuality that many Khalistanis forgo the turban, cut their hair, and shave their beards in order to mobilize without being suspected. Clearly, I cannot address all the nuances of this situation in the present discussion.

9   This is not to say that Sikh women are not tortured in Punjab. The present discussion, however, centers on the torture of *amritdhari* men, who are by far the primary objects of these violations. There are several documented cases of women who, identified by police as relatives of militants, have been apprehended and tortured. This is an extremely relevant issue, one that I am intending to address in future work. Two key elements in the knowledge production of tortured Sikh women will

be the status of the apprehended women as "relatives" of militants (i.e., not themselves identified as militants) and the use of heterosexualized forms of address and rape during torture.

10 Kumar, Muktsar, and Singh (1999) describe the widespread justification for these practices: "From the very beginning of my researches in Punjab, I have been meeting important officers of the government, politicians, journalists and other members of the intelligentsia who eloquently argued that the 'excesses' were a small price to pay for upholding the territorial integrity of India. These views, mouthed so glibly and so casually, were filling us with dark forebodings, for we felt that a country's institutions, particularly in a democratic set-up, cannot for long remain unaffected by such negative collective perceptions as the brandmarking of minority groups as enemies and the orchestrated clamour for their repression" (p. 8).

11 This is not a critique of Foucault but suggestive of the historical specificity of his argument.

12 The standardized use of electric shocks applied to the genitals, beating the genitals, inserting chili powder in the rectum, and "anal abuse" have been extensively documented by human rights groups (Amnesty International 1992; Asia Watch 1991; Citizens for Democracy 1986; Human Rights Watch/Physicians for Human Rights 1994; Kumar, Muktsar, and Singh 1999; Mahmood 1996).

13 In many ways, this corresponds to Butler's (1993) argument: "'Sex' not only functions as a norm, but is part of a regulatory practice that produces the bodies it governs, that is, whose regulatory force is made clear as a kind of productive power, the power to produce — demarcate, circulate, differentiate — the bodies it controls. Thus, 'sex' is a regulatory ideal whose materialization is compelled, and this materialization takes place . . . through certain highly regulated practices" (p. 1).

14 Foucault's (1978) words are appropriate here (note, also, how his phrase "defence of society" resonates with the words of Indira Gandhi on national integration examined in the previous chapter): "Thus a formidable right to punish is established, since the offender becomes the common enemy. Indeed, he is worse than an enemy, for it is from within society that he delivers his blows — he is nothing less than a traitor, a 'monster.' How could society not have an absolute right over him? How could it not demand, quite simply, his elimination? . . . The right to punish has been shifted from the vengeance of the sovereign to the defence of society" (p. 90).

15 As I will demonstrate, Mahmood's comment includes a formulation that necessitates further investigation. Particularly, I will suggest that these photographs do indeed "mask" something.

16 Udham Singh was the assassin of General O'Dwyer (infamous for the Jallianwallaw Bagh massacre in 1919). For further discussion of the historical significance of the *shahid,* see Fenech (1996).

17 Mark Juergensmeyer (1988) also makes a passing reference to this kind of art: "The stories of the Sikhs' historical past are bloody all the same. In fact, these stories have taken on a canonical character within Sikhism, and they capture the imagination

more vividly than the devotional and theological sentiments of the scriptures themselves. The calendar art so prominent in most Sikh homes portrays a mystical Guru
Nanak, of course, but alongside him there are pictures of Sikh military heroes and
scenes from great battles. Bloody images also leap from brightly-coloured oil paintings in the Sikh museum housed in the Golden Temple. There are as many depictions of martyrs in their wretched final moments as of victors radiant in conquest"
(p. 74).

18　It is important to accentuate this conflict between Khalistani and Akali positions because scholars often conflate the two. Two prominent examples are that of Oberoi
(1993) and Das (1995), for whom Khalistani and Akali positions seem to be equivalent and both equally fundamentalist (cf. Oberoi) or both equally militant, hypocrit-
ical, and demonizing/feminizing of the Hindu (cf. Das). Oberoi and Das conflate
these discourses and their forms of differentiation in order to make a functionalist
argument about how Sikh "identity" *needs* an "Other" (i.e., an entity outside itself)
against which to create a Sikh. My interest, however, is not with the way in which
Khalistani or Akali discourses apparently "require the Other to sharpen their self-
identity and appropriate a higher moral ground relative to their adversaries" (Oberoi
1993, 273; cf. Das 1995, 134–35). More nuanced discussions of the relations between
Akali and various Khalistani discourses may be found in Juergensmeyer (1988),
Major (1987), and Pettigrew (1987, 1995).

19　This, however, is not an adequate critique of Žižek, for which I direct the reader to
Butler (1993).

20　Douglas Gray (1963), who has given an extensive treatment of these images, comments on their popularity: "The cult reached the zenith of its popularity during the
late Middle Ages. Henry Sasso is said to have drunk five times during each meal in
honour of the Five Wounds; an English king, Henry VI (1422–1461) 'ordered his
chaplain to place before him at table a picture representing the Wounds' upon which
he gazed as he ate. . . . Wealthy laymen frequently left money for the continual offering of votive masses and for bequests to the poor in honour of the Five
Wounds" (p. 87).

21　I borrow the term *virtual complex* from Lacan (1977a, 1; [1975] 1991a, 76, 140; see
also Rose 1986), but, as I discuss below, this is not to imply that the structure of the
Lacanian Imaginary corresponds exactly to the formation of the Sikh subject.

22　The classic portraits may also have been incorporated into a discourse of martyrdom
(i.e., Maharaja Duleep Singh is considered by many Khalistanis to be a martyr to the
Sikh cause).

23　For important instances in the development of the notion of the Imaginary outside
psychoanalytic practice, see Bhabha (1994), Copjec (1994), Metz (1982), Rose
(1986), and Žižek (1989).

24　In *The Ego and the Id* ([1923] 1960), Freud clearly set the precedent for Lacan's later
analysis: "A person's own body, and above all its surface, is a place from which both
external and internal perceptions may spring. . . . The ego is first and foremost a

bodily ego; it is not merely a surface entity, but is itself the projection of a surface" (pp. 19–20). For an analysis of Lacan's appropriation of Freud's notion of the bodily ego, see Butler (1993, 57–67).

25 Benjamin (1978) anticipates this relation of society, image, and temporality: "In the dream in which, before the eyes of each epoch, that which is to follow appears in images, the latter appears wedded to elements from prehistory, that is, of a classless society. Intimations of this, deposited in the unconscious of the collective, mingle with the new to produce the utopia that has left its traces in thousands of configurations of life, from permanent buildings to fleeting fashions" (p. 148).

26 This discourse has been reiterated insistently since at least 1959. One example: "The arrest of this dangerously fast galloping disintegration is a matter of the greatest national importance, cutting across party politics" (Aiyer 1961).

4 : Glassy Junction

1 Thanks to Marian Storkey, principal research officer, London Research Centre, for these statistical figures.

2 Scotland Yard's Anti-Terrorist Branch had been cut by 20 percent as a result of the IRA ceasefire. Fifty detectives of the Anti-Terrorist Branch's one hundred officers were put on the Sikh case while also investigating a major credit card fraud (*Guardian*, 21 August 1995).

3 Dipankar De Sarkar had been covering the British Sikhs for at least two years prior to Purewal's murder (see, e.g., Sarkar 1993).

4 Paragraph 2(2) of Schedule 3 of the 1971 Immigration Act states: "Where notice has been given to a person in accordance with regulations under Section 18 of this act of a decision to make a deportation order against him, and he is neither detained in pursuance of the sentence or order of a court nor for the time being released on bail by a court having power so to release him, he may be detained under the authority of the Secretary of State pending the making of the deportation order" (Amnesty International: EUR 45/01/96).

5 The disjunction between the discourses of the national media and those of Scotland Yard are clear in this reconstruction of the murder scene. In January 1995, Detective Superintendent Hardingham mentioned that the culprit would have been covered in blood. The coroner's court report, published in December 1995, stated likewise that the death was caused by a shot fired at close range (i.e., not from a sniper positioned on top of Glassy Junction). I make note of this, not to correct media representations, but to demonstrate how the British Sikh subject is constituted through different strategies of representation that take place between Scotland Yard and the national media.

6 This was the Great Western Railway, which apparently "was more than a London and Bristol Railway. It did in fact terminate at Bristol, but other companies were to carry its traffic on to the West and to Wales, while steamers, such as Brunel's *Great Western,* continued the line across the Atlantic." The Great Western Railway was the

second mainline railway to open a London terminus: on "the resolution [being made] to divert the G.W. to its own terminus at Paddington in August of 1836," "a terminal site was chosen near the basin and reservoirs of the Paddington Canal. (The Paddington Branch of the Grand Junction Canal had been opened from Bulls Bridge Junction, near Southall, to Paddington in 1801)" (Course 1962, 170, 171).

7 "Based around the Great Western Railway, about five miles west along the Uxbridge Road from Shepherds Bush, [Southall] grew up during the latter decades of the nineteenth century. The older part of the burough . . . is centered on the railway station" (Institute of Race Relations and Southall Rights 1982, 6).

8 The character of the ownership of this branch must be specified: "The Great Western & Brentford Company was incorporated on 14 August 1855, leased to the GWR in 1859 and vested in it on 1 January 1872" (White 1963, 117). This was an important moment in the history of the proliferation of railway companies in Britain, the consolidation of the railway monopolies (i.e., the Great Western), the amalgamation or "grouping" of railway companies into "the four great companies" (cf. the Railway Act of 1921), and the eventual nationalization of railways, which restructured the railway system into six regions (London Midland, Western, Eastern, Southern, Northeastern, and Scottish) under the singular directorate of British Railways (Transport Act of 1947) (see Carter 1959; Course 1962; Davies and Grant 1983; Ellis 1959; Nock 1967; White 1963).

9 A history of cartographic practice and railway engineering would supplement this observation in terms of the formation of the national landscape. For example, a series of excavations, cuttings, embankings, and levelings were necessary to transform the built-up area near the basin and reservoirs of the Paddington Canal into a "virtually level" ground for the Permanent Way (Course 1962, 171; see also Schivelbusch 1986, 16–32).

10 For a detailed analysis of the conjuncture of capital and the nation-state in the production of categories of immigration and gender, see Pratibha Parmar (1982).

11 As such, Southall has been constituted in relation to histories of the production of other places in England: Coventry, Blackburn, Bradford, Brentford, Handsworth, Hounslow, Leeds, Leicester, Sandwell, Slough, Smethwick (Birmingham), and Wolverhampton (see Aurora 1967; Ballard 1994; Barrier and Dusenbery 1989; Chandan 1986; Clarke et al. 1990; Griffith et al. 1960; Helweg 1979, 1993; Hiro 1991; Institute of Race Relations and Southall Rights 1982; Jackson and Nesbitt 1993; James 1974; Ram 1986; Singh and Barrier 1996; Tatla 1993).

12 This would be the main Sikh *gurdwara* in Southall for forty years. A new *gurdwara*, estimated to be worth £10 million, will replace this temple in the year 2000. The construction of this temple will radically change Southall's landscape. It will be about a thousand feet tall with four domes, a prayer hall for up to two thousand worshipers, an underground car park for two hundred cars, committee rooms, conference rooms, a library, and facilities for local radio stations to broadcast. Thanks to Narinder Mankoo for this information.

13 The following is a summary of John's (1969) discussion.

14 Marx (1978b) describes this distinction: "Circulation time and production time are mutually exclusive. During its circulation time, capital does not function as productive capital, and therefore produces neither commodities nor surplus-value. . . . If the various parts of capital pass through the circuit in succession, so that the circuit of the total capital value is successively accomplished in the circuit of its various portions, then it is clear that the longer its aliquot parts remain in the circulation sphere, the smaller must be the part that functions at any time in the production sphere. The expansion and contraction of the circulation time hence acts as a negative limit on the contraction or expansion of the production time" (p. 203).

15 It is necessary to note the irony of the British government's decision that the presence of colored people was the motivating problem for race riots, thus transforming the victims of violence into the guilty perpetrators. On the changing notion of "presence" prior to the 1990s, see Gilroy (1987).

16 Following Marx, Thomas Keenan (1993) has argued that "the commodity structure is the ideal of justice as fairness, as balance, symmetry, reciprocity, between humans as well as things. 'Human rights' means that, before the law of exchange, humans meet, like things, as equal, free, responsible . . . as abstract" (p. 172).

17 The trope of prostitution and heteronormative pathology is common to almost all the reports produced at this time, a topic that I cannot fully discuss here.

18 The list goes on: Balham, Fulham, Lewisham, Stoke Newington, Woolwich, Ellesworth Port, Hull, Nottingham, Preston, Reading, Sheffield, Wolverhampton, Bradford, Halifax, Huddersfield, Leeds, Blackpool, Leicester, Luton, and Slough.

19 *The Times,* 12 November 1987, 1E; 13 November 1987, 2E; 14 November 1987, 2A; 15 November 1987, 2H; and 18 November 1987, 13D. Darshan Singh Tatla (1992) has written about this incident as well, retelling the narrative that many Sikhs in England told at the time: namely, that Guru Darsham Das was believed to be a spy planted by the Indian government.

20 I would like to express my thanks to the *Big City* crew and to the producer who, also, provided me with a videotape of the Glassy Junction episode.

21 The *Big City* director and crew had initially intended the presenter to drive the horse and buggy alone. However, she was not used to horses and could not direct the horse. This unexpected circumstance led to the director grabbing the closest local to help out. It also, one might hazard, reenacted a nostalgic desire for the colonial context.

22 This part of the Glassy Junction episode was, by far, the most important, according to the director. The camera crew spent three hours working out the shots in the kitchen of the chefs cooking kabobs and other foods.

23 I procured a copy of the Ealing Council report "Community Solutions" through this Internet site, and I have also corresponded with the site's director, whose help I gratefully acknowledge.

24   Lauren Berlant (1997, 176) has termed this double formation of threat and legit-
     imacy *hygienic governmentality*. Her discussion, however, is based on a contemporary
     U.S. politics of intimacy that is concerned with very different constructions of differ-
     ence (i.e., the adult poor, the nonwhite, the unmarried, the nonheterosexual, and
     the nonreproductive). Nevertheless, inspired by a reading of Benjamin, her critique
     may be pertinent for underscoring how "the ruling bloc solicits mass support for
     such 'governing': by using abjected populations as exemplary of all obstacles to
     national life; by wielding images and narratives of a threatened 'good life' that a
     putative 'we' have known; by promising relief from the struggles of the present
     through a felicitous image of a national future" (p. 175).

5 : The Homeland

1   In other contexts, the story of Khalistan often begins with the gift of the land of
    Punjab from God (see below).
2   Chauhan's words were as follows: "An independent Sikh state in the Punjab is the
    only guarantee for peace in the sub-continent. . . . An independent Sikh state will act
    as a buffer between India and Pakistan. It will be a restraining influence on the two
    countries."
3   This had been the explicit purpose of the Michigan conference as well as of prior
    conferences in Sikh studies (see Juergensmeyer and Barrier 1979; Barrier and Du-
    senberry 1989; Hawley and Mann 1993).
4   For discussions of Sikhs "abroad" in North America, see Barrier and Dusenberry
    (1989), Hawley and Mann (1993), Johnston (1990), LaBrack (1988, 1989), Leon-
    ard (1992), and Tatla (1991, 1999).
5   One may also consider the different localities from which categories of Indian immi-
    grants came to the United States: as I mentioned previously, these include India,
    Kenya, Uganda, Tanzania, Zambia, Mauritius, Pakistan, Singapore, Burma, and
    Malaysia. These histories of movement must be related to and distinguished from
    the movements during the nineteenth and twentieth centuries that configured the
    British system of indenture. Different colonies became destinations at different
    times. For example, consider the beginnings of indenture associated with the follow-
    ing colonies: 1833 in Malaya, 1834 in Mauritius, 1838 in British Guiana, 1841 in
    Australia, 1844 in the West Indies, 1858 in St. Lucia, 1860 in Natal, 1895 in Kenya
    and Uganda, and 1896 in Madagascar (Gangulee [1946] 1947; Kondapi 1951). For
    a discussion of the contradictory process characterizing the U.S. attempts to trans-
    form migrants into citizens, and for a critique of the notion *community* as a spatial
    category, see Rouse (1991).
6   This mission is slightly different from what I have described as the facilitation and
    documentation of conversion because it aims to revitalize rather than modernize
    tradition. This formulation must not be understood as encompassing all other as-
    pects of the debate around multiculturalism. For example, the notion of the home-

land as it has been built around Asian Americans must be distinguished from the creation of other hyphenated Americans, particularly African Americans (see Appadurai 1996a; Shankar and Srikanth 1998).

7 These professors are based at the University of Santa Clara, California State University at Fresno, the State University of New York at Buffalo, and Dalhousie University.

8 To pursue the de Certeauian loop of knowledge production even further, one might consider the reverberations of these allegations in India. The narrative of the protesters tells how "written reports of two expert committees, which included heads of Departments of Religion of Punjab University, Chandigarh, and the Punjab University of Patiala, and the Principals of two colleges of Sikh religion . . . recommended action, both at Akal Takhat and under the Law."

9 Cynthia Mahmood (1996) and Harjot Oberoi (1995) have also commented on this conflict. For a critique of Pashaura Singh (based on the illegal procurement of his Ph.D. thesis, which was then circulated around the globe to various Sikh scholars), see Giani (1994), which also includes critical, if ad hominem, discussions of McLeod (e.g., "an ex-missionary from the Punjab Missionary organisation") and the project of Sikh studies in North America.

10 Helweg (1996) and O'Connell (1996) have written very frankly about the effects of these conflicts on Oberoi and Pashaura Singh: "The last three years have been an extremely difficult period for Pashaura Singh (and his family, who were adjusting to a new home in a new country) at a point in his career when the typical new professor is expected to concentrate upon developing his first set of university courses and revising his thesis for publication. Pashaura Singh not only had these normal professional and domestic demands to meet, but confronted the extra demands of encouraging Sikh donor support for building up the still incomplete endowment while facing a time-consuming and exhausting campaign of harassment. . . . The intensive campaign against Pashaura Singh for a while deflected attention from Oberoi, but with the publication of the latter's first book, the tone and tempo of Oberoi-baiting has shot upwards. As usual, Sikh newspapers are in the forefront publishing denunciatory 'reviews' of the book and providing coverage of 'conferences' staged so to call for Oberoi's removal. . . . Unfortunately, persistent carping at the operation of the UBC chair and its occupant has tended to dampen student enthusiasm for the Sikh and Punjabi courses and related activities and to diminish Canadian Sikh appreciation of what is in fact the most outstanding accomplishment of North American Sikhs yet in securing a base for Sikh studies" (O'Connell 1996, 279, 282).

11 Ghosh's (1989) discussion is different in many ways from that of Karamcheti, who speaks only about the diaspora experience. Ghosh talks more about "the curious nature of India's cultural relationship with her diaspora." By *curious nature,* Ghosh means that "the links between India and her diaspora are lived within the imagination" (pp. 74, 76).

12 As I discuss in the preceding chapter, this formulation of a diaspora community as policing itself reiterates the nation-state's alarmist discourse regarding wars in exile.

13   Clearly I do not refer here to a simple notion of the present as it is framed in classical philosophy by an underexplained relation to notions of presence, consciousness, context, communication, representation, and Being. My concept of the diasporic imaginary constitutes the present at the intersection of what Benjamin (1968), conjuring Freud ([1920] 1989a), called *memoire involuntaire* (160–62) — that is, an interruptive past — and a persistently deferred future, or a "'time of the now' which is shot through with chips of Messianic time" (263). This troubling of the present, displaced by a specific anteriority and futurity, resonates not only with the Lacanian distinctions I introduced in chapter 3, but also with Derrida's (1982) very important elaborations of the notions of *différance* and the performative.

14   There have been several discussions, however, of the "Punjab crisis" and *Khalistan* (see, e.g., Juergensmeyer 1988; Major 1987; Jeffrey 1987; Oberoi 1987, 1993). Two scholars, however, whose work may not easily be considered under the rubric *Sikh studies,* have produced extremely important studies of violence and the struggle for Khalistan (see Mahmood 1996; Pettigrew 1987, 1995).

15   My own contribution to the volume, "Notes on Space, Cartography, and Gender" (Axel 1996a), represents an early attempt to formulate a critique of these very approaches within Sikh studies.

16   For a discussion of this kind of incorporation of "prior" entities within the domain of capitalism, see Marx (1978a, 136). Simmel has suggested as much, in a somewhat different tenor, in his monumental *The Philosophy of Money* ([1907] 1991). Writing on "integration," Simmel suggests: "Such, for example, is the immortality of a king, which is independent of the accidents of his personality, his particular acts, or the changing fortunes of his society; the well nigh indestructible coin with his portrait upon it is a symbol and a demonstration of this fact. . . . For even though the reification of the social whole [under capitalism], which is a prerequisite of money, need not necessarily take a monarchical form, it is in fact monarchy that has strongly favoured the intervention of a central power in the economic functioning of the group" (pp. 186–87). On the continuity of the structures of monarchy, see also Foucault (1978, 88). Although similar to Marin's understanding of the redoubling of the monarchical presence, one may note the differences here from Foucault's (1977, 188–89) well-known discussions of monarchy.

17   Although she does make violence her object of study, Joyce Pettigrew nevertheless constitutes the Sikh subject in terms that are very similar to Oberoi's. Commenting on "the unprecedented loneliness of the present Sikh position internationally," Pettigrew (1995) reflects on the story of Khalistani militancy: "This was the story of the tragedy of modern progressive values being corrupted, betrayed, if not destroyed, by pre-modern forms of allegiance and mentality" (p. 189).

18   One might consider a genealogy of this project in relation to that history that Frantz Fanon (1967) has discussed whereby, "by calling on humanity," blacks have struggled to "win the admission . . . that the black is equal to the white" (p. 30). Later, Henry Louis Gates (1985) picks up this formulation: "While the Enlightenment is

characterized by its foundation on man's ability to reason, it simultaneously used the absence and presence of reason to delimit and circumscribe the very humanity of the cultures and people of color which Europeans had been 'discovering' since the Renaissance" (p. 8).

19 Although not explicitly stated, this avoidance pertains to an analytic model for which violence is understood to be a separable aspect of a movement rather than a process that is *constitutive of knowledge* of that movement. Harjot Oberoi's (1993) words, providing a rare statement within Sikh studies, demonstrate the way in which Sikh studies discourses separate violence from the processes of knowing. In this case, violence is understood as a "tactic" that is separable from "motives and objectives": "I have avoided the subject of violence, not because it is irrelevant to a study of Sikh fundamentalists but *simply* because I want to focus on *the motives and objectives* of the movement rather than its (and its opponents') *tactics*" (emphasis added; p. 280).

20 W. H. McLeod (1998, 1999) has offered his own powerful and insightful critique of Sikh studies. In particular, he has covered many of the issues I introduce in this chapter, including the use of the term "fundamentalism" and the demonizing of Oberoi, Pashaura Singh, and himself. I am very much in agreement with his conclusions—although I cannot engage them here—and hope that the analyses in this chapter may be taken as a supplement.

Conclusion

1 This shift is ironic because Jameson, Harvey, and Gupta and Ferguson claim to be following Lefebvre's lead. For a critical discussion of Jameson, see Bhabha (1994).

2 One might note Gupta and Ferguson's (1992) basic misconception of cartographic procedures: "The representation of the world as a collection of 'countries,' as in most world maps, sees it as an inherently fragmented space" (p. 8).

bibliography

Abraham, Nicolas, and Maria Torok. 1994. *The Shell and the Kernel*. Chicago: University of Chicago Press.

Adams, John W. 1981. "Consensus, Community, and Exorcism." *Journal of Interdisciplinary History* 12, no. 2 (autumn): 253–65.

Adhikari, G. 1945. *Sikh Homeland*. Bombay: People's Publishing House.

Agarwal, M. M. 1996. *Indian Railway Track*. New Delhi: Prabha.

Agnihotri, Rama Kant. 1987. *Crisis of Identity: The Sikhs in England*. New Delhi: Bahri.

Aijazuddin, F. S. 1977. *Pahari Paintings and Sikh Portraits in the Lahore Museum*. Karachi: Oxford University Press.

———. 1979. *Sikh Portraits by European Artists*. London: Oxford University Press.

Aiyer, C. P., ed. 1961. *Disintegration and How to Avert It*. Bombay: Bharatiya Vidya Bhavan.

Aiyer, K. A. Neelakandha. 1938. *Indian Problems in Malaya: A Brief Survey in Relation to Emigration*. Kuala Lumpur: "The Indian" Office.

Akbar, M. J. 1996. *India: The Siege within, Challenges to a Nation's Unity*. New Delhi: UBSP.

Alexander, Michael, and S. Anand. 1980. *Queen Victoria's Maharajah*. New York: Taplinger.

Ali, Imran. 1988. *The Punjab under Imperialism, 1885–1947*. Princeton, N.J.: Princeton University Press.

Althusser, Louis. [1969] 1997. *For Marx*. New York: Verso.

Amnesty International. 1996. "News Release: United Kingdom." AI Index: EUR 45/01/96.

Anderson, Benedict. 1991. *Imagined Communities: Reflections on the Origins and Spread of Nationalism*. London: Verso.

Anonymous. 1847. "The History of the Sikhs." *Dublin University Magazine* 29:546–58.

Appadurai, Arjun. 1986a. *The Social Life of Things*. Cambridge: Cambridge University Press.

———. 1986b. "Theory in Anthropology: Center and Periphery." *Comparative Studies in Society and History* 28, no. 2:356–61.

——. 1988. "Putting Hierarchy in Its Place." *Cultural Anthropology* 3, no. 1 (February): 37–50.

——. 1990. "Disjuncture and Difference in the Global Cultural Economy." *Public Culture* 2, no. 2 (spring): 1–24.

——. 1996a. *Modernity at Large: Cultural Dimensions of Globalization.* Minneapolis: University of Minnesota Press.

——. 1996b. "Sovereignty without Territoriality: Notes for a Postnational Geography." In *The Geography of Identity,* ed. Patricia Yaeger. Ann Arbor: University of Michigan Press.

——. 1998. "Dead Certainty: Ethnic Violence in the Era of Globalization." Eighth Punitham Tiruchelvam Memorial Lecture, delivered 31 January 1998, at SLFI, Colombo.

Apter, Emily, and William Pietz, eds. 1993. *Fetishism as Cultural Discourse.* Ithaca, N.Y.: Cornell University Press.

Archer, Mildred. 1979. *India and British Portraiture, 1770–1825.* London: Sotheby Parke Bernet.

Archer, W. G. 1966. *Paintings of the Sikhs.* London: H.M. Stationery Office.

Arendt, Hannah. 1969. *On Violence.* New York: Harcourt Brace.

Arensberg, Conrade M. 1961. "Preface." In *East Indians in Trinidad,* ed. Morton Klaas. New York: Columbia University Press.

Aryan, K. C. 1977. *Punjab Painting.* Patiala: Punjab University.

Asad, Talal. 1993. *Genealogies of Religion: Discipline and Reasons of Power in Christianity and Islam.* Baltimore: Johns Hopkins University Press.

Asad, Talal, ed. 1973. *Anthropology and the Colonial Encounter.* Atlantic Highlands, N.J.: Humanities Press.

Asia Watch. 1991. *Punjab in Crisis: Human Rights in India.* New York: Human Rights Watch.

Aurora, G. S. 1967. *The New Frontiersmen: A Sociological Study of Indian Immigrants in the United Kingdom.* Bombay: Popular Prakashan.

Austin, J. L. 1975. *How to Do Things with Words.* Cambridge, Mass.: Harvard University Press.

Axel, Brian Keith. 1996a. "Notes on Space, Cartography, and Gender." In *The Transmission of Sikh Heritage in the Diaspora,* ed. Pashaura Singh and N. Gerald Barrier. New Delhi: Manohar.

——. 1996b. "Time and Threat: Questioning the Production of the Diaspora as an Object of Study." *History and Anthropology* 9, no. 2:415–43.

——. 1998. "Disembodiment and the Total Body: A Response to Enwezor on Contemporary South African Representation." *Third Text,* no. 43 (summer): 3–16.

——, ed. In press a. *From the Margins: Historical Anthropology and Its Futures.*

——. In press b. "Who Fabled: Joyce and Vico on History." *New Vico Studies.*

Baird, J. G. A. 1911. *Private Letters of Marquess of Dalhousie.* London: William Blackwood and Sons.

Bakhtin, M. M. 1986. *Speech Genres and Other Essays.* Austin: University of Texas Press.

Balibar, Etienne. 1991. "The Nation Form: History and Ideology." In *Race, Nation, Class: Ambiguous Identities,* ed. Etienne Balibar and Immanuel Wallerstein. London: Verso.

Ballard, Roger. 1989. "Differentiation and Disjunction amongst the Sikhs in Britain." In *The Sikh Diaspora: Migration and Experience beyond Punjab,* ed. G. Barrier and V. Dusenberry. Columbia, Mo.: South Asia.

——. 1994. *Desh Pardesh: The South Asian Presence in Britain.* London: Hurst.

Ballard, R., and C. Ballard. 1977. "The Sikhs: The Development of a South Asian Settlement in Britain." In *Between Two Cultures: Migrants and Minorities in Britain,* ed. J. L. Watson. Oxford: Blackwell.

Banton, Michael. 1959. *White and Coloured.* London: Jonathan Cape.

Barrier, Gerald. 1969. *The Punjab in Nineteenth Century Tracts.* East Lansing: Michigan State University, Asia Studies Center.

——. 1970. *The Sikhs and Their Literature.* Delhi: Manohar.

——. 1974. *Banned: Controversial Literature and Political Control in British India, 1907–1947.* Columbia: University of Missouri Press.

——. 1979. "The Role of Ideology and Institution in Modern Sikhism." In *Sikh Studies,* ed. N. G. Barrier and Mark Juergensmeyer. Berkeley: Graduate Theological Union.

——. 1986. *India and America.* Delhi: Manohar Press.

——. 1989. "Sikh Emigrants and Their Homeland: The Transmission of Information, Resources and Values in the Early Twentieth Century." In *The Sikh Diaspora: Migration and the Experience Beyond Punjab,* ed. N. G. Barrier and Verne A. Dusenbery. Delhi: Chanakya Publications.

——. 1993. "Sikh Studies and the Study of History." In *Studying the Sikhs: Issues for North America,* ed. John Stratton Halwey and Gurinder Singh Mann. New York: Columbia University Press.

Barrier, Gerald, and Verne Dusenbery, eds. 1989. *The Sikh Diaspora: Migration and Experience beyond Punjab.* Columbia, Mo.: South Asia.

Barrier, Gerald N., and Mark Juergensmeyer. 1979. *Sikh Studies: Comparative Perspectives on a Changing Tradition.* Berkeley: Graduate Theological Union.

Barstow, Major A. E. 1928. *The Sikhs: An Ethnology, 1928.* Delhi: B.R.

Basch, Linda, Nina Glick Schiller, and Cristina Szanton Blanc. 1994. *Nations Unbound: Transnational Projects, Postcolonial Predicaments and Deterritorialized Nation-States.* Amsterdam: Gordon and Breach.

Basu, Durga Das. 1985. *Constitutional Aspects of Sikh Separatism.* New Delhi: Prentice-Hall.

——. 1995. *Introduction to the Constitution of India.* Delhi: Prentice-Hall.

Baudrillard, Jean. 1983. *Simulations.* New York: Semiotext(e), Inc.

Baumann, Gerd. 1996. *Contesting Culture: Discourses of Identity in Multi-Ethnic London.* Cambridge: Cambridge University Press.

Bayly, C. A. 1990. *The Raj: India and the British, 1600–1947.* London: National Portrait Gallery.

Beckwith, Sarah. 1992. *Christ's Body: Identity, Culture, and Society in Late Medieval Writings.* London: Routledge.

Beetham, David. 1970. *Transport and Turbans: A Comparative Study in Local Politics*. London: Oxford University Press.

Bell, Major Evans. 1882. *The Annexation of the Punjaub and the Maharajah Duleep Singh*. London: Trubner.

Benedict, Burton. 1961. *Indians in a Plural Society: A Report on Mauritius*. London: H.M. Stationery Office.

Benedict, Ruth, 1946. *The Chrysanthemum and the Sword: Patterns of Japanese Culture*. Boston: Houghton Mifflin.

——. [1934] 1989. *Patterns of Culture*. Boston: Houghton Mifflin.

Benjamin, Walter. 1968. *Illuminations: Essays and Reflections*. New York: Schocken.

——. 1978. *Reflections: Essays, Aphorisms, Autobiographical Writings*. New York: Schocken.

Benson, Arthur Christopher, and Viscount Esher, eds. 1907. *The Letters of Queen Victoria, Volume II*. London: John Murray.

Benveniste, Emile. 1971. *Problems in General Linguistics*. Coral Gables, Fla.: University of Miami Press.

Berger, John. 1972. *Ways of Seeing*. Harmondsworth: Penguin.

Berlant, Lauren. 1991. *The Anatomy of National Fantasy: Hawthorne, Utopia, and Everyday Life*. Chicago: University of Chicago Press.

——. 1993. "National Brands/National Body: Imitation of Life." In *The Phantom Public Sphere,* ed. Bruce Robbins. Minneapolis: University of Minnesota Press.

——. 1997. *The Queen of America Goes to Washington City: Essays on Sex and Citizenship*. Durham, N.C.: Duke University Press.

Bhabha, Homi K., ed. 1990. *Nation and Narration*. London: Routledge.

——. 1992. "Postcolonial Authority and Postmodern Guilt." In *Cultural Studies,* ed. Lawrence Grossberg, Cary Nelson, and Paula Treichler. New York: Routledge.

——. 1994. *The Location of Culture*. New York: Routledge.

——. 1997. "Editor's Introduction: Minority Maneuvers and Unsettled Negotiations." *Critical Inquiry* 23 (spring): 431–59.

——. 1998. "On the Irremovable Strangeness of Being Different." *PMLA* (January): 34–39.

Bhachu, Parminder. 1985. *Twice Migrants: East African Sikh Settlers in Britain*. New York: Tavistock.

——. 1989. "The East African Sikh Diaspora: The British Case." In *The Sikh Diaspora: Migration and the Experience Beyond Punjab,* ed. N. G. Barrier and Verne A. Dusenbery. Delhi: Chanakya Publications.

Bhattacharya, Vivek R. 1985. *Towards National Unity and Integration*. Delhi: Metropolitan.

Bingley, A. H. [1918] 1970. *Sikhs: A Handbook for Indian Army*. Patiala: Shashi.

Black, Jeremy. 1997. *Maps and History: Constructing Images of the Past*. New Haven, Conn.: Yale University Press.

Blackett-Ord, Carol. 1987. "Winterhalter in England." *Apollo: The International Magazine of the Arts* (November): 312–17.

Blunt, Alison, and Gillian Rose, eds. 1994. *Writing Women and Space: Colonial and Postcolonial Geographies.* New York: Guilford.

Boas, Franz. [1911] 1938. *The Mind of Primitive Man.* Westport, Conn.: Greenwood.

———. 1940. "The Limitations of the Comparative Method of Anthropology." In *Race, Language, and Culture.* New York: Macmillan.

Bonavia, Michael R. 1971. *The Organization of British Railways.* London: Ian Allan.

———. 1985. *Twilight of the British Rail.* London: David and Charles.

Brah, Avtar. 1992. "Difference, Diversity, and Differentiation." In *"Race," Culture, and Difference,* ed. James Donald and Ali Rattansi. London: Open University/Sage.

———. 1996. *Cartographies of Diaspora: Contesting Identities.* London: Routledge.

Brass, Paul. 1990. *The Politics of India Since Independence.* Cambridge: Cambridge University Press.

Breckenridge, Carol. 1989. "The Aesthetics and Politics of Colonial Collecting." *Comparative Studies in Society and History* 31, no. 2:195–216.

Breckenridge, Carol A., and Peter van der Veer. 1993. *Orientalism and the Postcolonial Predicament.* Philadelphia: University of Pennsylvania Press.

Brown, Wendy. 1995. *States of Inquiry: Power and Freedom in Late Modernity.* Princeton, N.J.: Princeton University Press.

Brubaker, Rogers. 1992. *Citizenship and Nationhood in France and Germany.* Cambridge, Mass.: Harvard University Press.

Burgin, Victor. 1986. "Diderot, Barthes, Vertigo." In *Formations of Fantasy,* ed. Victor Burgin et al. New York: Routledge.

———. 1992. "Perverse Space." In *Sexuality and Space,* ed. Beatriz Colomina. Princeton, N.J.: Princeton University School of Architecture.

Burns, Alexander. [1834] 1973. *Travels into Bokhara, together with a Narrative of a Voyage on the Indus.* London: Oxford University Press.

Butler, Judith. 1990. *Gender Trouble: Feminism and the Subversion of Identity.* New York: Routledge.

———. 1993. *Bodies That Matter: On the Discursive Limits of "Sex."* New York: Routledge.

———. 1997a. *Excitable Speech: A Politics of the Performative.* New York: Routledge.

———. 1997b. *The Psychic Life of Power: Theories in Subjection.* Stanford, Calif.: Stanford University Press.

Campbell, Lorne. 1990. *Renaissance Portraits: European Portrait-Painting in the Fourteenth, Fifteenth, and Sixteenth Centuries.* New Haven, Conn.: Yale University Press.

Carter, Ernest. 1959. *An Historical Geography of the Railways of the British Isles.* London: Cassell.

Caruth, Cathy, ed. 1995. *Trauma: Explorations in Memory.* Baltimore: Johns Hopkins University Press.

Caveeshar, Sardul Singh. 1950. *Sikh Politics.* Delhi: Ashoka.

Centre for Contemporary Cultural Studies, ed. 1982. *The Empire Strikes Back: Race and Racism in Seventies Britain.* London: Routledge.

Cerney, J. W., and B. Wilson. 1976. "The Effect of Orientation on the Recognition of Simple Maps." *Canadian Cartographer* 13, no. 2:132–33.

Chadda, Maya. 1997. *Ethnicity, Security, and Separatism in India.* New York: Columbia University Press.

Chaddah, Mehar Singh. 1982. *Are Sikhs a Nation?* Delhi: DSGMC.

Chakrabarty, Rishi Ranjan. 1986. *Duleep Singh: The Maharaja of Punjab and the Raj.* Birmingham: D. S. Samra.

Chandan, Amarjit. 1986. *Indians in Britain.* New Delhi: Sterling.

Chapple, W. A. 1921. *Fiji — Its Problems and Resources.* London: Whitcombe and Tombs.

Chatterjee, Partha. 1986. *Nationalist Thought and the Colonial World: A Derivative Discourse?* London: Zed.

———. 1993. *The Nation and Its Fragments: Colonial and Postcolonial Histories.* Princeton, N.J.: Princeton University Press.

Chow, Rey. 1993. *Writing Diaspora: Tactics of Intervention in Contemporary Cultural Studies.* Bloomington: Indiana University Press.

Citizens for Democracy. 1986. *Report to the Nation: Operation of Punjab.* Bombay: Citizens for Democracy.

Clarke, Colin, Ceri Peach, and Steven Vertovec. 1990. *South Asians Overseas: Migration and Ethnicity.* Cambridge: Cambridge University Press.

Clifford, James. 1988. *The Predicament of Culture: Twentieth-Century Ethnography, Literature, and Art.* London: Harvard University Press.

———. 1994. "Diasporas." In "Further Inflections: Toward Ethnographies of the Future," ed. Susan Harding and Fred Meyers. Special issue of *Cultural Anthropology* 9, no. 3:302–38.

Cohen, Stephen P. 1971. *The Indian Army: Its Contribution to the Development of a Nation.* Berkeley: University of California Press.

Cohn, Bernard S. 1957. "India as a Racial, Linguistic, and Cultural Area." In *Introducing India in Liberal Education,* ed. Milton Singer. Chicago: University of Chicago Press.

———. 1967. "Regions Subjective and Objective: Their Relation to the Study of Modern Indian History and Society." In *Regions and Regionalism in South Asian Studies: An Exploratory Study* (Monograph and Occasional Papers Series, no. 5), ed. Robert Crane. Durham, N.C.: Duke University.

———. 1977. "African Models and Indian Histories." In *Realm and Region in Traditional India,* Monograph and Occasional Paper Series, Number 14, ed. Richard Fox. Durham: Duke University Press.

———. 1987. *An Anthropologist among the Historians and Other Essays.* Delhi: Oxford University Press.

———. 1996. *Colonialism and Its Forms of Knowledge: The British in India.* Princeton, N.J.: Princeton University Press.

Cole, John Jones. 1850. "A Sketch of the Siege of Mooltan." *Bentley's Miscellany* 28:449–60.

Colingwood, R. G. [1946] 1956. *The Idea of History.* London: Oxford University Press.

Colomina, Beatriz, ed. 1992. *Sexuality and Space*. Princeton, N.J.: Princeton University School of Architecture.

Comaroff, Jean. 1997. "The Portrait of an Unknown South African: Identity in a Global Age." In "The Divided Self: Identity and Globalization." Special issue of *Macalester International* 4 (spring).

Comaroff, Jean, and John L. Comaroff. 1991. *Of Revelation and Revolution: Christianity, Colonialism, and Consciousness in South Africa*. Vol. 1. Chicago: University of Chicago Press.

———. 1992. *Ethnography and the Historical Imagination*. Boulder, Colo.: Westview.

———. 1997. *Of Revelation and Revolution: The Dialectics of Modernity on a South African Frontier*. Vol. 2. Chicago: University of Chicago Press.

Connor, Walker. 1986. "The Impact of Homelands upon Diasporas." In *Modern Diasporas in International Politics*. New York: St. Martin's.

Constitution Amendment in India. 1994. Edited by R. C. Bhardwaj. Delhi: Lok Sabha Secretariat.

Copjec, Joan. 1994. *Read My Desire: Lacan Against the Historicists*. Cambridge: MIT Press.

Cormack, Leslie B. 1994. "The Fashioning of an Empire: Geography and the State in Elizabethan England." In *Geography and Empire,* ed. Neil Smith and Anne Godlewska. Oxford: Blackwell.

Coronil, Fernando. 1997. *The Magical State: Nature, Money, and Modernity in Venezuela*. Chicago: University of Chicago Press.

Course, Edwin. 1962. *London Railways*. London: B.T. Batsford.

Crane, Robert, ed. 1967. *Religions and Regionalism in South Asian Studies: An Exploratory Study*. Monograph and Occasional Papers Series, no. 5. Durham, N.C.: Duke University.

Crow, Dennis, ed. 1996. *Geography and Identity*. Washington, D.C.: Maissoneuve.

Crowquill, Alfred. 1850. "Our Pen and Ink Gallery: Major Herbert Edwardes." *Bentley's Miscellany* 27:449–60.

"The Cry for Khalistan." 1992. *Times of India,* 15 March.

Cunningham, Joseph Davy. 1849. *A History of the Sikhs, from the Origin of the Nation to the Battle of Sutlej*. London: John Murray.

Daniel, E. Valentine. 1996. *Charred Lullabies: Chapters in an Anthropology of Violence*. Princeton: Princeton University Press.

Das, Veena. 1995. *Critical Events: An Anthropological Perspective on Contemporary India*. Delhi: Oxford India.

———. 1997. "Language and Body: Transaction in the Construction of Pain." In *Social Suffering,* ed. Arthur Kleinman, Veena Das, and Margaret Lock. Berkeley: University of California Press.

Davies, R., and M. D. Grant. 1983. *London and Its Railways*. London: David and Charles.

Davis, Nathalie Z. 1981. "The Possibilities of the Past." *Journal of Interdisciplinary History* 12, no. 2 (autumn): 267–75.

de Bary, W. Theodore. 1958. *Sources of Indian Tradition.* Vol. 2. New York: Columbia University Press.

de Certeau, Michel. 1984. *The Practice of Everyday Life.* Berkeley and Los Angeles: University of California Press.

————. 1988. *The Writing of History.* New York: Columbia University Press.

Derrida, Jacques. 1987. "Devant la loi." In *Kafka and the Contemporary Critical Performance,* ed. Alan Udoff. Bloomington: Indiana University Press.

————. 1988. *Limited, Inc.* Evanston, Ill.: Northwestern University Press.

————. 1982. *Margins of Philosophy.* Chicago: University of Chicago Press.

Desmond, Ray. 1982a. *The India Museum, 1801–1879.* London: H.M. Stationery Office.

————. 1982b. *Victorian India in Focus: A Selection of Early Photographs from the Collection in the India Office Library and Records.* London: H.M. Stationery Office.

Dewitt, J. 1969. *Indian Workers Associations in Britain.* London: Oxford University Press.

Diamond, Elin, ed. 1996. *Performance and Cultural Politics.* London: Routledge.

Dicey, A. V. 1927. *Introduction to the Study of the Law of the Constitution.* London: Macmillan.

Dirks, Nicholas B., ed. 1992. *Colonialism and Culture.* Ann Arbor: University of Michigan Press.

————. 1987. *The Hollow Crown: Ethnohistory of an Indian Kingdom.* Cambridge: Cambridge University Press.

Donald, James, and Ali Rattansi, eds. 1992. *"Race," Culture, and Difference.* London: Open University / Sage.

Douglas, Mary. 1966. *Purity and Danger: An Analysis of Concepts of Purity and Taboo.* London: Routledge and Kegan Paul.

Dumezil, Georges. 1970. *The Destiny of the Warrior.* Chicago: University of Chicago Press.

Dummett, Michael, ed. 1980. *Southall: 23 April 1979, The Report of the Unofficial Committee of Enquiry.* Nottingham: National Council for Civil Liberties.

Dumont, Louis. 1957. "For a Sociology of India." *Contributions to Indian Sociology* 1 (April): 1–41.

————. 1964a. "Nationalism and Communalism." *Contributions to Indian Sociology* 7:30–70.

————. 1964b. "Note on Territory." *Contributions to Indian Sociology* 7:71–76.

————. 1975. "Preface by Louis Dumount to the French Edition of *The Nuer.*" In *Studies in Social Anthropology.* Oxford: Clarendon.

————. [1966] 1980. *Homo Hierarchicus: The Caste System and Its Implications.* Chicago: University of Chicago Press.

Duncan, James, and David Ley, eds. 1993. *Place/Culture/Representation.* London: Routledge.

Durkheim, Emile. 1915. *The Elementary Forms of Religious Life.* London: Free Press.

Dusenbery, Verne A. 1988. "Punjabi Sikhs and Gora Sikhs: Conflicting Assertions of Sikh Identity in North America." In *Sikh History and Religion in the Twentieth Century,* ed. Joseph O'Connell, Milton Israel, and Willard G. Oxtoby. Toronto: University of Toronto, Centre for South Asian Studies.

———. 1990. "The Sikh Person, the Khalsa Panth, and Western Sikh Converts." In *Religious Movements and Social Identity,* ed. Bardwell Smith. Delhi: Chanakya.

———. 1995. "A Sikh Diaspora? Contested Identities and Constructed Realities." In *Nation and Migration: The Politics of Space in the South Asian Diaspora,* ed. Peter van der Veer. Philadelphia: University of Pennsylvania Press.

East, Gordon W. 1965. *The Geography Behind History.* New York: W. W. Norton.

Eden, Emily. 1866. *Up the Country.* London: Curzon.

Ellis, Hamilton. 1959. *British Railway History, 1877–1947.* London: Allen and Unwin.

Elsmie, G. R. 1908. *Thirty-Five Years in the Punjaub, 1858–1893.* Edinburgh.

Espiritu, Yen Le. 1992. "Census Classification: The Politics of Ethnic Enumeration." In *Asian American Panethnicity: Bridging Institutions and Identities.* Philadelphia: Temple University Press.

Evans, Dylan. 1996. *An Introductory Dictionary of Lacanian Psychoanalysis.* London: Routledge.

Evans-Pritchard, E. E. 1939. "Nuer Time Reckoning." *Africa* 12, no. 2 (April).

———. 1940. *The Nuer: A Description of the Modes of Livelihood and Political Institutions of a Nilotic People.* Oxford: Oxford University Press.

———. 1951a. *Essays in Social Anthropology.* Glencoe, Ill.: Free Press.

———. 1951b. *Kinship and Marriage among the Nuer.* Oxford: Clarendon.

———. 1956. *Nuer Religion.* Oxford: Oxford University Press.

———. 1963. *Essays in Social Anthropology.* Glencoe, Ill.: Free Press.

Fabian, Johannes. 1983. *Time and the Other: How Anthropology Makes Its Object.* New York: Columbia University Press.

Falcon, R. W. 1896. *Handbook on the Sikhs for the Use of Regimental Officers.* Allahabad: n.p.

Fanon, Frantz. 1967. *Black Skin, White Masks.* New York: Grove.

Farwell, Byron. 1989. *Armies of the Raj: From the Mutiny to Independence, 1858–1947.* New York: Norton.

Faubion, James D. 1993. "History in Anthropology." *Annual Review of Anthropology* 22:35–54.

Feldman, Allen. 1991. *Formations of Violence: The Narrative of the Body and Political Terror in Northern Ireland.* Chicago: University of Chicago Press.

———. 1997. "Violence and Vision: The Prosthetics and Aesthetics of Terror." *Public Culture* 10, no. 1 (fall): 24–60.

Felman, Shoshana. 1983. *The Literary Speech Act: Don Juan with J. L. Austin, or Seduction in Two Languages.* Ithaca, N.Y.: Cornell University Press.

———. 1995. "Education and Crisis; or, The Vicissitudes of Teaching." In *Trauma: Explorations in Memory,* ed. Cathy Caruth. Baltimore: Johns Hopkins University Press.

Fenech, Louis E. 1992. "The Game of Love: Martyrdom, the Singh Sabha, and the Akalis." Paper presented at the South Studies Conference, Madison, Wis.

——. 1996. "The Taunt in Popular Sikh Martyrologies." In *The Transmission of Sikh Heritage in the Diaspora*, ed. Pashaura Singh and N. Gerald Barrier. New Delhi: Manohar.

Ferenczi, Sandor. 1955. *The Final Contributions to the Problems and Methods of Psychoanalysis.* New York: Basic.

Fernandez, James W. 1982. *Bwiti: An Ethnography of Religious Imagination in Africa.* Princeton, N.J.: Princeton University Press.

Forrester, John. 1990. *The Seductions of Psychoanalysis: Freud, Lacan, and Derrida.* Cambridge: Cambridge University Press.

Foster, Hal. 1996. *The Return of the Real: Avante-Garde at the End of the Century.* Cambridge, Mass.: MIT Press.

Foucault, Michel. 1977. *Discipline and Punish: The Birth of the Prison.* New York: Vintage.

——. 1978. *The History of Sexuality: An Introduction.* Vol. 1. New York: Vintage.

——. 1980. *Power/Knowledge: Selected Interviews and Other Writings, 1972–1977.* New York: Pantheon.

——. 1988. *Language, Counter-Memory, Practice: Selected Essays and Interviews.* Ed. Donald F. Bouchard. Ithaca: Cornell University Press.

Fox, Richard. 1977. *Realm and Region in Traditional India.* Monograph and Occasional Papers Series, no. 14. Durham, N.C.: Duke University.

——. 1985. *Lions of the Punjab: Culture in the Making.* Berkeley and Los Angeles: University of California Press.

Fox, Robin. 1967. *Kinship and Marriage: An Anthropological Approach.* Harmondsworth: Penguin.

Freud, Sigmund. 1946. "Observations on 'Wild' Psycho-Analysis." In *The Collected Papers,* vol. 2. London: Hogarth.

——. 1959. *Inhibitions, Symptoms, and Anxiety.* New York: Norton.

——. [1923] 1960. *The Ego and the Id.* New York: W. W. Norton.

——. 1963. "Transference." In *The Standard Edition of the Complete Psychological Works of Sigmund Freud,* vol. 15, ed. James Strachey. London: Hogarth.

——. 1976. *The Interpretation of Dreams.* New York: Penguin.

——. [1928] 1977. "Fetishism." In *On Sexuality: Three Essays on the Theory of Sexuality and Other Works.* New York: Penguin.

——. [1920] 1989a. *Beyond the Pleasure Principle.* New York: Norton.

——. 1989b. *Totem and Taboo.* New York: Norton.

——. [1922] 1991. *Group Psychology and the Analysis of the Ego.* New York: Norton.

Fried, Morton H. 1958. *Colloquium on Overseas Chinese.* New York: Institute of Pacific Relations.

Furnival, J. S. 1944. *Netherlands India: A Study of Plural Economy.* Cambridge: Cambridge University Press.

Gallop, Jane. 1985. *Reading Lacan.* Ithaca, N.Y.: Cornell University Press.

Gangulee, N. [1946] 1947. *Indians in the Empire Overseas: A Survey.* London: New India.

Garber, Marjorie. 1992. *Vested Interests: Cross-Dressing and Cultural Anxiety*. New York: Routledge.

Garrett, H. L. O., and G. L. Chopra, trans. and eds. 1911. *The Punjab a Hundred Years Ago, as Described by V. Jacquomant (1831) and A. Soltykoff (1842)*. Monograph no. 18. Patiala: Punjab Government Record Office, Punjab Languages Department.

———. 1970. *Events at the Court of Ranjit Singh (1810–1817)*. Monograph no. 17. Reprint, Patiala: Punjab Government Record Office Publications, Punjab Languages Department.

Gates, Henry Louis, Jr. 1985. *"Race," Writing, and Difference*. Chicago: University of Chicago Press.

Geertz, Clifford. 1986. "The Uses of Diversity." *Michigan Quarterly Review* 25:105–23.

Gelner, Ernest. 1983. *Nations and Nationalism*. Ithaca, N.Y.: Cornell University Press.

Ghosh, Amitav. 1989. "The Diaspora in Indian Culture." *Public Culture* 2, no. 1 (fall): 73–78.

Giani, Bachittar Singh, ed. 1994. *Planned Attack on Aad Sri Guru Granth Sahib: Academics or Blasphemy*. Chandigarh: International Centre of Sikh Studies.

Gibson, Margaret A. *Accommodation without Assimilation: Sikh Immigrants in an American High School*. Ithaca: Cornell University Press.

Gillion, K. L. 1962. *Fiji's Indian Migrants: A History to the End of Indenture in 1920*. Melbourne: Oxford University Press.

Gilman, Sander. 1993. *Freud, Race, and Gender*. Princeton, N.J.: Princeton University Press.

Gilroy, Paul. 1987. *There Ain't No Black in the Union Jack*. London: Routledge.

———. 1992. "Cultural Studies and Ethnic Absolutism." In *Cultural Studies*, ed. Lawrence Grossberg, New York: Routledge.

———. 1993. *The Black Atlantic: Modernity and Double Consciousness*. Cambridge, Mass.: Harvard University Press.

Ginzburg, Carlo. 1981. "A Comment." *Journal of Interdisciplinary History* 12, no. 2 (autumn): 277–78.

———. 1989. *Clues, Myths, and the Historical Method*. Baltimore: Johns Hopkins University Press.

Girouard, Mark. 1984. *Victorian Pubs*. New Haven, Conn.: Yale University Press.

Glick Schiller, Nina, Linda Basch, and Cristina Szanton Blank, eds. 1992. *Towards a Transnational Perspective on Migration: Race, Class, Ethnicity and Nationalism Reconsidered*. New York: New York Academy of Sciences.

Gordon, Avery F. 1997. *Ghostly Matters: Haunting and the Sociological Imagination*. Minneapolis: University of Minnesota Press.

Gordon, East W. 1965. *The Geography behind History*. New York: Norton.

Gough, Charles, and Arthur D. Innes. 1970. *The Sikhs and the Sikh Wars: The Rise, Conquest, and Annexation of the Punjab State*. Reprint, Patiala: Punjab Languages Department.

Graves, Algernon. 1906. *The Royal Academy of Arts: A Complete Dictionary of Contributors and Their Works from Its Foundation in 1769 to 1904.* London: Henry Graves.

Gray, Douglas. 1963. "The Five Wounds of Our Lord." *Notes and Queries* 108: 50–168.

Gregory, Derek. 1994. *Geographical Imaginations.* Cambridge: Blackwell.

Grewal, D. S. 1995. *Guru Nanak's Travel to Himalayan and East Asian Region: A New Light.* Delhi: National Book Shop.

Grewal, J. S. 1990. *The New Cambridge History of India: The Sikhs of the Punjab.* Cambridge: Cambridge University Press.

Griffin, Lepel. 1865. *The Panjab Chiefs: Historical and Biographical Notices of the Principal Families in Lahore.* Lahore: McGarthy.

Griffith, J. A. G. 1960. *Coloured Immigrants in Britain.* Oxford: Oxford University Press.

Guha, Ranajit. 1989. "Dominance without Hegemony and Its Historiography." In *Subaltern Studies VI: Writings on South Asian History and Society,* ed. Ranajit Guha. Oxford: Oxford University Press.

Guha, Ranajit, and Gayatri C. Spivak, eds. 1988. *Selected Subaltern Studies.* Oxford: Oxford University Press.

Gupta, Akhil, and James Ferguson. 1992. "Beyond 'Culture': Space, Identity, and the Politics of Difference." *Cultural Anthropology* 7, no. 1:6–23.

Hall, Kathleen. 1993. "Becoming British Sikhs: The Politics of Identity and Difference in Post-Colonial England." Ph.D. diss., University of Chicago.

Hall, Stuart. 1981. "The Whites of Their Eyes: Racist Ideologies and the Media." In *Silver Linings: Some Strategies for the Eighties,* ed. George Bridges and Rosalind Brunt. London: Lawrence and Wishart.

———. 1988. "The Toad in the Garden: Thatcherism among the Theorists." In *Marxism and the Interpretation of Culture,* ed. Cary Nelson and Lawrence Grossberg. Urbana: University of Illinois Press.

———. 1989a. "Ethnicity: Identity and Difference." *Radical America* 23, no. 4:9–20. Reprinted in *Stuart Hall: Critical Dialogues in Cultural Studies,* ed. David Morley and Kuan-Hsing Chen. London: Routledge, 1996.

———. 1989b. "New Ethnicities." *Black Film, British Cinema: ICA Documents* 7:27–31.

———. 1990. *The Hard Road to Renewal: Thatcherism and the Crisis of the Left.* London: Verso.

———. 1996. "Introduction: Who Needs 'Identity'?" In *Questions of Cultural Identity,* ed. Stuart Hall and Paul du Gay. London: Sage.

———. 1997. "The Local and the Global: Globalization and Ethnicity." In *Culture, Globalization, and the World-System: Contemporary Conditions for the Representation of Identity,* ed. Anthony D. King. Minneapolis: University of Minnesota Press.

Hall, Stuart, and Daniel Held. 1990. "Citizens and Citizenship." In *New Times: The Changing Face of Politics in the 1990s,* ed. Stuart Hall and Martin Jaques. New York: Verso.

Hall, Stuart, and Tony Jefferson. 1976. *Resistance through Rituals: Youth Subcultures in Post-War Britain.* London: Hutchison.

Hannerz, Ulf. 1992. *Cultural Complexity: Studies in the Social Organization of Meaning.* New York: Columbia University Press.

———. 1996. *Transnational Connections: Culture, People, Places.* London: Routledge.

Harary, Frank. 1969. *Graph Theory.* Reading, Mass.: Addison-Wesley.

Haraway, Donna J. 1991. *Simians, Cyborgs, and Women: The Reinvention of Nature.* New York: Routledge.

Harding, Susan, and Fred Meyers, eds. 1994. "Further Inflections: Toward Ethnographies of the Future." Special issue of *Cultural Anthropology,* vol. 9, no. 3.

Harley, J. B. 1988a. "Maps, Knowledge, and Power." In *Iconography and Landscape.* Cambridge: Cambridge University Press.

———. 1988b. "Silences and Secrecy: The Hidden Agenda of Cartography in Early Modern Europe." *Imago Mundi* 40:57–76.

———. 1989. "Deconstructing the Map." *Cartographica* 26, no. 2:1–20.

———. 1992a. "Art, Science, and Power in Sixteenth-Century Dutch Cartography." *Cartographica* 29, no. 2:10–19.

———. 1992b. "Rereading the Maps of the Columbian Encounter." *Annals of the Association of American Geographers,* no. 3:522–35.

Harris, Joseph E., ed. 1982. *Global Dimensions of the African Diaspora.* Washington, D.C.: Howard University Press.

Harrison, Selig S. 1961. *India and the United States.* New York: Macmillan.

Harvey, David. 1989. *The Condition of Postmodernity.* Oxford: Blackwell.

Hawley, John Stratton, and Gurinder Singh Mann, eds. 1993. *Studying the Sikhs: Issues for North America.* Albany: State University of New York Press.

Heathcote, T. A. 1974. *The Indian Army: The Garrison of British Imperial India, 1822–1922.* New York: Hippocrene.

Helgerson, Richard. 1992. *Forms of Nationhood: The Elizabethan Writing of England.* Chicago: University of Chicago Press.

Helweg, Arthur. 1979. *The Sikhs in England.* Delhi: Oxford University Press.

———. 1993. "The Sikh Diaspora and Sikh Studies." In *Studying the Sikhs: Issues for North America,* ed. John Stratton Hawley and Gurinder Singh. Albany: State University of New York Press.

———. 1996. "Academic Scholarship and Sikhism: Conflict or Legitimization." In *The Transmission of Sikh Heritage in the Diaspora,* ed. P. Singh and N. G. Barrier. Delhi: Manohar.

Herman, Judith. [1992] 1997. *Trauma and Recovery: The Aftermath of Violence—from Domestic Abuse to Political Terror.* New York: Basic.

Hiro, Dilip. 1991. *Black British, White British: A History of Race Relations in Britain.* London: Grafton Books.

Hobsbawm, Eric J. 1990. *Nations and Nationalism since 1780: Programme, Myth, Reality.* Cambridge: Cambridge University Press.

Hobsbawm, Eric, and Terence Ranger, eds. 1983. *The Invention of Tradition.* Cambridge: Cambridge University Press.

Hooson, David. 1994. *Geography and National Identity*. Oxford: Blackwell.

Huberband, Shimon. 1987. *Kiddush Hashem: Jewish Religious and Cultural Life in Poland During the Holocaust*. New York: Yeshiva University Press.

Human Rights Watch/Physicians for Human Rights (HRW/PHR). 1994. *Dead Silence: The Legacy of Abuses in Punjab*. New York: Human Rights Watch.

Inded, Ron. 1990. *Imagining India*. Oxford: Blackwell.

———. In press. "America Teaches the World Order." In *Intellectuals and Political Life,* ed. Judith Farquhar, Leon Fink, and Steven Leonard. Ithaca, N.Y.: Cornell University Press.

Indian Council of World Affairs. 1957. *Defense and Security in the Indian Ocean Area*. New Delhi: Sapru House.

Institute of Race Relations. 1958. *Colour in Britain*. London. Pamphlet.

Institute of Race Relations and Southall Rights. 1982. *Southall: The Birth of a Black Community*. London: Campaign against Racism and Fascism.

Instruction for Publication of Maps by Central/State Government Departments/Offices and Private Publishers. 1987. Delhi: Government of India.

Jackson, Michael. 1976. *The English Pub*. New York: Harper and Row.

Jackson, Robert, and Eleanor Nesbitt. 1993. *Hindu Children in Britain*. London: Trentham Books.

Jain, Sharda. 1995. *Politics of Terrorism in India: The Case of Punjab*. Delhi: Deep and Deep.

Jakobsh, Doris R. 1996. "Gender Issues in Sikh Studies: Hermeneutics of Affirmation or Hermeneutics of Suspicion?" In *The Transmission of Sikh Heritage in the Diaspora,* ed. Pashaura Singh and N. Gerald Barrier. Delhi: Manohar.

James, Alan G. 1974. *Sikh Children in Britain*. London: Oxford University Press.

James, Leslie. 1983. *A Chronology of the Construction of Britain's Railways, 1778–1855*. London: Ian Allan.

Jameson, Fredric. 1984. "The Cultural Logic of Capital." *New Left Review* 146:53–92.

———. 1988. "Cognitive Mapping." In *Marxism and the Interpretation of Culture,* ed. Cary Nelson and Lawrence Grossberg. Urbana: University of Illinois Press.

———. 1991. *Postmodernism; or, The Cultural Logic of Late Capitalism*. Durham, N.C.: Duke University Press.

Jay, Martin. 1988. "Scopic Regimes of Modernity." In *Vision and Visuality,* ed. Hal Foster. Seattle: Bay.

Jeffrey, Robin. 1987. "Grappling with History: Sikh Politicians and the Past." *Pacific Affairs* 60, no. 1 (spring): 59–72.

Johnston, Hugh. 1990. "Patterns of Sikh Migration to Canada, 1900–1960." In *Sikh History and Religion in the Twentieth Century,* ed. Joseph O'Connell, Milton Israel, and Willard Oxtoby. Toronto: University of Toronto Press.

Juergensmeyer, Mark. 1979. "The Ghadar Syndrome: Immigrant Sikhs and Nationalist Pride." In *Sikh Studies: Comparative Perspectives on a Changing Tradition,* ed. Mark Juergensmeyer and N. Gerald Barrier. Berkeley: Graduate Theological Union.

——. 1988. "The Logic of Religious Violence: The Case of the Punjab." *Contributions to Indian Sociology* 22, no. 1:65–88.

Juergensmeyer, Mark, and N. Gerald Barrier. 1979. *Sikh Studies: Comparative Perspectives on a Changing Tradition.* Berkeley: Graduate Theological Union.

Jullian, Phillippe. 1977. *The Orientalists: European Painters of Eastern Scenes.* Oxford: Phaidon.

Kale, Madhavi. 1995. "Projecting Identities: Empire and Indentured Labor Migration from India to Trinidad and British Guiana, 1836–1885." In *Nation and Migration: The Politics of Space in the South Asian Diaspora,* ed. Peter van der Veer. Philadelphia: University of Pennsylvania Press.

Kantorowicz, Ernst H. 1957. *The Kings' Two Bodies: A Study in Political Theology.* Princeton, N.J.: Princeton University Press.

Kaplan, Ann E., and George Levine. 1997. *The Politics of Research.* New Brunswick, N.J.: Rutgers University Press.

Kapur, Prithipal Singh. 1995. *Maharaja Duleep Singh: The Last Sovereign Ruler of Punjab.* Amritsar: SGPC.

Kapur, Rajiv A. [1986] 1987. *Sikh Separatism: The Politics of Faith.* New Delhi: Vikas.

Karamcheti, Indira. 1992. "The Shrinking Himalayas." *Diaspora* 2, no. 2:261–76.

Kaur, Rajinder. 1992. *Sikh Identity and National Integration.* New Delhi: Intellectual.

Kaye, J. W. 1846. "The War on the Sutlej." *North British Review* 5:246–80.

——. 1849. "The Fall of the Sikh Empire." *North British Review* 11:618–61.

Keates, John S. 1973. *Cartographic Design and Production.* New York: Longman Scientific and Technical.

Keenan, Thomas. 1993. "The Point is to (Ex)Change It: Reading *Capital,* Rhetorically." In *Fetishism as Cultural Discourse,* ed. Emily Apter and William Pietz. Ithaca: Cornell University Press.

Kelly, John D. 1991. *A Politics of Virtue: Hinduism, Sexuality, and Countercolonial Discourse in Fiji.* Chicago: University of Chicago Press.

Kelly, John D., and Martha Kaplan. 1990. "History, Structure, and Ritual." *Annual Review of Anthropology* 19:119–50.

Khan, Ziauddin. 1983. *National Integration in India: Issues and Dimensions.* Delhi: Associated Publishing.

King, Anthony D., ed. 1997. *Culture, Globalization, and the World-System: Contemporary Conditions for the Representation of Identity.* Minneapolis: University of Minnesota Press.

King, Charles, and Neil J. Melvin. 1998. *Nations Abroad: Diaspora Politics and International Relations in the Former Soviet Union.* Boulder, Colo.: Westview.

Kirshenblatt-Gimblett, Barbara. 1994. "Spaces of Dispersal." In "Further Inflections: Toward Ethnographies of the Future," ed. Susan Harding and Fred Meyers. Special Issue of *Cultural Anthropology* 9, no. 3:339–44.

Klass, Morton. 1961. *East Indians in Trinidad: A Study of Cultural Persistence.* New York: Columbia University Press.

Kondapi, C. 1951. *Indians Overseas, 1838–1949*. New Delhi: Indian Council of World Affairs/Oxford University Press.

Krech, Shepard, III. 1991. "The State of Ethnohistory." *Annual Review of Anthropology* 20:345–75.

Krishnamurti, Y. G. 1939. *Indian States and the Federal Plan*. Bombay: Ratansey Parker.

Kumar, Ram Narayan, Amrik S. Muktsar, and H. Singh. 1999. *Enforced Disappearances, Arbitrary Executions, and Secret Cremations: Victim Testimony and India's Human Rights Obligations: Interim Report*. Delhi: Committee for Coordination on Disappearances in Punjab.

Kuper, Hilda. 1960. *Indian People in Natal*. Natal: Natal University Press.

——. 1972. "The Language of Sites in the Politics of Space." *American Anthroplogist* 74, no. 3:411–25.

LaBrack, Bruce W. 1988. *The Sikhs of Northern California, 1904–1986*. New York: American Migration Series.

——. 1989. "The New Patrons." In *The Sikh Diaspora: Migration and Experience beyond Punjab*, ed. Gerald Barrier and Verne Dusenberry. Columbia, Mo.: South Asia.

Lacan, Jacques. 1977a. *Ecrits: A Selection*. London: Routledge.

——. 1977b. *The Four Fundamental Concepts of Psycho-Analysis*. London: Penguin.

——. 1982. "Intervention on the Transference." In *Feminine Sexuality*, ed. Juliet Mitchell and Jacqueline Rose. New York: Pantheon.

——. [1975] 1991a. *The Seminar of Jacques Lacan, Book I: Freud's Papers on Technique, 1953–1954*. New York: Norton.

——. [1978] 1991b. *The Seminar of Jacques Lacan, Book II: The Ego in Freud's Theory and in the Technique of Psychoanalysis, 1954–1955*. New York: Norton.

"La fin du national." 1986. Special issue of *Peuples Mediterraneens*, nos. 35–36 (April–September).

Lancaster, Roger. 1997. "Guto's Performance: Notes on the Transvestism of Everyday Life." In *The Gender/Sexuality Reader*, ed. Roger Lancaster and M. di Leonardo. New York: Routledge.

Laplanche, Jean, and Jean-Bertran Pontalis. 1973. *The Language of Psychoanalysis*. New York: Norton.

——. [1964] 1986. "Fantasy and the Origins of Sexuality." In *Formations of Fantasy*, ed. Victor Burgin, James Donald, and Cora Caplan. New York: Routledge.

Lavie, Smadar, and Ted Swedenburg, eds. 1996. *Displacement, Diaspora, and Geographies of Identity*. Durham, N.C.: Duke University Press.

Lawrence, H. M. L. 1846. *Adventures of an Officer in the Punjaub*. London: Henrey Colburn.

Leach, Edmund Ronald. 1954. *Political Systems of Highland Burma: A Study of Kachin Social Structure*. London: Bell.

Lee, Sharon M. 1993. "Racial Classifications in the US Census, 1890–1990." *Ethnic and Racial Studies* 16, no. 1:75–94.

Lefebvre, Henri. 1991. *The Production of Space*. Oxford: Blackwell.

Lefort, Claude. [1978] 1986. *The Political Forms of Modern Society: Bureaucracy, Democracy, Totalitarianism.* Cambridge, Mass.: MIT Press.

Leonard, Karen. 1989. "Pioneer Voices from California: Reflections on Race, Religion, and Ethnicity." In *The Sikh Diaspora: Migration and the Experience beyond Punjab,* ed. J. Barrier and V. Dusenbery. Columbia, Mo.: South Asian.

———. 1992. *Making Ethnic Choices: California's Punjabi Mexican Americans.* Philadelphia: Temple University Press.

Levinas, Emmanuel. [1947] 1987. *Time and the Other.* Pittsburgh: Duquesne University Press.

Levine, Etan. 1983. *Diaspora: Exile and the Jewish Condition.* New York: Jason Aronson.

Lévi-Strauss, Claude. 1963. *Structural Anthropology.* New York: Basic.

———. 1976. *Structural Anthropology.* Vol. 2. Chicago: University of Chicago Press.

———. [1950] 1987. *Introduction to the Work of Marcel Mauss.* London: Routledge.

Liben, L. S., and R. Downs. 1989. "Understanding Maps as Symbols: The Development of Map Concepts in Children." In *Advances in Child Development and Behavior,* vol. 22, ed. San Diego: Academic.

Lincoln, Bruce. 1991. *Death, War, and Sacrifice: Studies in Ideology and Practice.* Chicago: University of Chicago Press.

Lister, Raymond. 1984. *Prints and Printmaking: A Dictionary and Handbook of the Art in Nineteenth-Century Britain.* New York: Methuen.

Livingstone, David N. 1992. *The Geographical Tradition.* Oxford: Blackwell.

———. 1994. "Climate's Moral Economy: Science, Race, and Place in Post-Darwinian British and American Geography." In *Geography and Empire,* ed. Neil Smith and Anne Godlewska. Oxford: Blackwell.

Login, Lady. 1890. *Sir John Login and Duleep Singh.* Patiala: Languages Department Punjab.

———. 1970. *Lady Login's Recollections: Court Life and Camp Life, 1820–1904.* Reprint, Patiala: Languages Department Punjab.

Lord, John. 1971. *The Maharajahs.* New York: Random House.

Macauliffe, Max Arthur. [1909] 1978. *The Sikh Religion: Its Gurus, Sacred Writings, and Authors.* 2d ed. New Delhi: S. Chand.

Macmillan, W. M. 1936. *Warning from the West Indies.* Middlesex: Penguin.

Macmunn, Sir George. 1920. *The Martial Races of India.* Quetta: Gosha-e-Adab.

Maharaja Duleep Singh Centenary Festival. 1993. Wolverhampton: NTID. Official program pamphlet of the Maharaja Duleep Singh Centenary Festival.

Maharaja Duleep Singh Centenary Trust, 1893–1993. 1993. Wolverhampton Nanaksar Thath Isher Darbar. Pamphlet distributed at the Maharaja Duleep Singh Centenary Festival.

Mahmood, Cynthia Keppley. 1996. *Fighting for Faith and Nation: Dialogues with Sikh Militants.* Philadelphia: University of Pennsylvania Press.

———. 2000. *The Guru's Gift: Exploring Gender Equality with North American Sikh Women.* Mayfield.

Maitland, Frederic William. 1936. *Selected Essays*. Ed. H. Hazeltine, G. Lapsley, and P. H. Winfield. Cambridge: Cambridge University Press.

Malcolm, Lieutenant Colonel. [1809] 1812. *Sketch of the Sikhs: A Singular Nation Who Inhabit the Provinces of the Punjab Situated between the Rivers Jumna and Indus*. London: John Murray.

Malcolm, Thomas. [1891] 1971. *Barracks and Battlefields in India; or, The Experiences of a Soldier of the Tenth Foot (North Lincoln) in the Sikh Wars and Sepoy Mutiny*. Patiala: Shashi.

Malinowski, Bronislaw. 1930. "Kinship." *Man* 30:19–29.

——. 1948. *Magic, Science, and Religion and Other Essays*. Boston: Beacon.

——. [1922] 1984. *Argonauts of the Western Pacific*. Prospect Heights, Ill.: Waveland.

Malkki, Lisa H. 1995. *Purity and Exile: Violence, Memory, and National Cosmology among Hutu Refugees in Tanzania*. Chicago: University of Chicago Press.

Mangat, J. S. 1969. *A History of the Asians in East Africa 1886 to 1945*. Oxford: Oxford University Press.

Mann, J. S., Surinder S. Singh, and G. S. Gill. 1995. *Invasion of Religious Boundaries: A Critique of Harjot Oberoi's Work*. Vancouver: Canadian Sikh Study and Teaching Society.

Mann, Gurinder Singh. 1993. "Sikh Studies and the Sikh Educational Heritage." In *Studying the Sikhs: Issues for North America*, ed. John Stratton Hawley and Gurinder Singh Mann. New York: Columbia University Press.

Mansergh, Nicholas, ed. 1970. *The Transfer of Power, 1942–1947*. Vol. 1, *The Cripps Mission, January–April 1942*. London: H.M. Stationery Office.

——. 1971. *The Transfer of Power, 1942–1947*. Vol. 2, *"Quit India," 30 April–21 September 1942*. London: H.M. Stationery Office.

——. 1977. *The Transfer of Power, 1942–1947*. Vol. 7, *The Cabinet Mission, 23 March–29 June 1946*. London: H.M. Stationery Office.

Marin, Louis. 1984. *Utopics: The Semiological Play of Textual Spaces*. Atlantic Highlands, N.J.: Humanities Press International.

——. 1989. *Food for Thought*. Baltimore: Johns Hopkins University Press.

Marriott, McKim. 1976. "Hindu Transactions: Diversity without Dualism." In *Transaction and Meaning: Directions in the Anthropology of Exchange and Symbolic Behavior*, ed. Bruce Kapferer. Philadelphia: Institute for the Study of Human Issues.

——. 1990. "Constructing an Indian Ethnosociology." In *India through Hindu Categories*. Newbury Park, Calif.: Sage.

Marriott, McKim, and Ronald Inden. 1974. "Caste Systems." *Encyclopaedia Britannica*, 15th ed., 3:982–91.

——. 1977. "Toward an Ethnosociology of South Asian Caste Systems." In *The New Wind: Changing Identities in South Asia*, ed. Kenneth David. The Hague: Mouton.

Marx, Karl. 1976. *Capital: A Critique of Political Economy*. Vol. 1. London: Penguin.

——. 1978a. *Capital: A Critique of Political Economy*. Vol. 2. London: Penguin.

——. 1978b. "On the Jewish Question." In *The Marx-Engels Reader*, ed. Robert C. Tucker. New York: Norton.

Massey, Doreen. 1984. *Spatial Divisions of Labor: Social Structures and the Geography of Production*. New York: Methuen.

———. 1993. "Power-Geometry and a Progressive Sense of Place." In *Mapping the Futures: Local Cultures, Global Change*, ed. Jon Bird, Barry Curtis, Tim Putnam, George Robertson, and Lisa Tinker. London: Routledge.

Mauss, Marcel. [1935] 1973. "Techniques of the Body." *Economy and Society* 2, no. 1:70–85.

Mayer, Adrian C. 1961. *Peasants in the Pacific: A Study of Fiji Indian Rural Society*. Berkeley: University of California Press.

McClintock, Anne, Aamir Mufti, and Ella Shohat. 1997. *Dangerous Liaisons: Gender, Nation, and Postcoloniality*. Minneapolis: University of Minnesota Press.

McDonald, Terence J. 1996. *The Historic Turn in the Social Sciences*. Ann Arbor: University of Michigan Press.

McGill, Angus. 1969. *Pub: A Celebration*. London: Longmans.

McGregor, W. L. 1846. *The History of the Sikhs*. London: James Maden.

McLeod, W. H. 1968. *Guru Nanak and the Sikh Religion*. Delhi: Oxford University Press.

———. 1976. *The Evolution of the Sikh Community: Five Essays*. Oxford: Clarendon Press.

———. 1978. "On the Word *Panth*: A Problem of Terminology and Definition." *Contributions to Indian Sociology* 12, no. 2:287–95.

———. 1984. *Textual Sources for the Study of Sikhism*. Manchester: Manchester University Press.

———. 1986. *Punjabis in New Zealand: A History of Punjabi Migration, 1890–1940*. Amritsar: Guru Nanak Dev University.

———. 1989a. *The Sikhs: History, Religion, and Society*. New York: Columbia University Press.

———. 1989b. *Who Is a Sikh? The Problem of Sikh Identity*. Oxford: Clarendon.

———. 1989c. "The First Forty Years of Migration: Problems and Some Possible Solutions." In *The Sikh Diaspora: Migration and the Experience Beyond Punjab*, eds. N. G. Barrier and Verne A. Dusenbery. Delhi: Chanakya Publications.

———. 1992. *Popular Sikh Art*. Delhi: Oxford University Press.

———. 1996. "Gender and the Sikh Panth." In *The Transmission of Sikh Heritage in the Diaspora*, eds. Pashaura Singh and N. Gerald Barrier. Delhi: Manohar.

———. 1998. "Sikh Fundamentalism." *Journal of the American Oriental Society* 118, no. 1 (January–March): 15–27.

———. 1999. "Discord in the Sikh Panth." *Journal of the American Oriental Society* 119, no. 3 (July–September): 381–89.

Mead, Margaret, ed. 1953. *The Study of Culture at a Distance*. Chicago: University of Chicago Press.

Melendy, H. Brett. 1977. *Asians in America: Filipinos, Koreans, and East Indians*. Boston: Twayne.

Mercer, Kobena. 1994. *Welcome to the Jungle*. New York: Routledge.

Merivale, Herman. 1840. "Court and Camp of Ranjeet Singh." *Edinburgh Review* 71: 263–75.

Metz, Christian. 1982. *The Imaginary Signifier: Psychoanalysis.* Bloomington: Indiana University Press.

Millar, Oliver. 1992. *The Victorian Pictures in the Collection of Her Majesty the Queen.* 2 vols. Cambridge: Cambridge University Press.

Misra, R. P. 1969. *Fundamentals of Cartography.* Prasaranga: University of Mysore.

Mitchell, W. J. T. 1986. *Iconology: Image, Text, Ideology.* Chicago: University of Chicago Press.

Mitter, Partha. 1977. *Much Maligned Monsters: A History of European Reactions to Indian Art.* Chicago: University of Chicago Press.

Modleski, Tania. 1991. *Feminism without Women: Culture and Criticism in a "Postfeminist" Age.* New York: Routledge.

Monmonier, Mark S. 1982. *Computer-Assisted Cartography: Principles and Prospects.* Englewood Cliffs, N.J.: Prentice-Hall.

———. 1993. *Mapping It Out: Expository Cartography for the Humanities and Social Sciences.* Chicago: University of Chicago Press.

Moore, Stephen. 1996. *God's Gym: Divine Male Bodies of the Bible.* New York: Routledge.

Morris, H. S. 1968. *The Indians in Uganda: A Study of Caste and Sect in a Plural Society.* Chicago: University of Chicago Press.

Morris, Rosalind C. 1995. "All Made Up: Performance Theory and the New Anthropology of Sex and Gender." *Annual Review of Anthropology* 24:567–92.

Moyer, R. 1978. "Psychophysical Functions for Perceived and Remembered Size." *Science* 200:330–32.

Mulgrew, Ian. 1988. *The Sikhs and International Terrorism.* Toronto: Key Porter.

Muller, J. C., ed. 1991. *Advances in Cartography.* New York: Elsevier Applied Science.

Mulvey, Laura. 1989. *Visual and Other Pleasures.* Bloomington: Indiana University Press.

———. 1992. "Pandora: Topographies of the Mask and Curiosity." In *Sexuality and Space,* ed. Beatriz Colomina. Princeton, N.J.: Princeton Architectural Press.

Munn, Nancy D. 1992. "The Cultural Anthropology of Time: A Critical Essay." *Annual Review of Anthropology* 21:93–123.

National Portrait Gallery. 1957. *British Historical Portraits.* Cambridge: Cambridge University Press.

Nayar, Baldev Raj. 1966. *Minority Politics in the Punjab.* Princeton, N.J.: Princeton University Press.

Nayyar, Deepak. 1994. *Migration, Remittances, and Capital Flows: The Indian Experience.* Delhi: Oxford University Press.

Neame, L. E. 1907. *The Asiatic Danger in the Colonies.* New York: George Routledge and Sons.

Niehoff, Arthur, and Juanita Niehoff. 1960. *East Indians in the West Indies.* Milwaukee: Milwaukee Public Museum.

Nochlin, Linda. 1989. *The Politics of Vision: Essays on Nineteenth Century Art and Society.* New York: Harper and Row.

Nock, O. S. 1967. *History of the Great Western Railway.* Vol. 3, *1923–1947.* London: Ian Allan.

Nystuen, John D., and Michael F. Dacey. [1961] 1968. "A Graph Interpretation of Nodal Regions." In *Spatial Analysis: A Reader in Statistical Geography,* ed. Brian Berry and Duane Marble. Englewood Cliffs, N.J.: Prentice-Hall.

Oberoi, Harjot S. 1987. "From Punjab to 'Khalistan': Territoriality and Metacommentary." *Pacific Affairs* 60, no. 1 (spring): 26–41.

——. 1990. "From Ritual to Counter-Ritual: Rethinking the Hindu-Sikh Question, 1884–1915." In *Sikh History and Religion in the Twentieth Century,* ed. Joseph O'Connell, Milton Israel, and Willard Oxtoby. Toronto: University of Toronto Press.

——. 1993. "Sikh Fundamentalism: Translating History into Theory." In *Fundamentalisms and the State,* ed. Martin E. Marty and R. Scott Appleby. Chicago: University of Chicago Press.

——. 1994. *The Construction of Religious Boundaries: Culture, Identity, and Diversity in the Sikh Tradition.* Oxford: Oxford University Press.

——. 1995. "Mapping Indic Fundamentalisms through Nationalism and Modernity." In *Fundamentalisms Comprehended,* ed. Martin E. Marty and R. Scott Appleby. Chicago: University of Chicago Press.

Oberoi, Narinder. 1964. "Sikh Women in Southall." *Race* 4, no. 1 (July): 34–40.

Ockman, Carol. 1988. "Prince of Portraitists." *Art in America* (November).

O'Connell, Joseph T. 1996. "The Fate of Sikh Studies in North America." In *The Transmission of Sikh Heritage in the Diaspora,* eds. Pashaura Singh and N. Gerald Barrier. Delhi: Manohar.

Okamura, Jonathan Y. 1998. *Imagining the Filipino American Diaspora: Transnational Relations, Identities, and Communities.* New York: Garland.

Orlove, Benjamin. 1993a. "The Ethnography of Maps: The Cultural and Social Contexts of Cartographic Representation in Peru." *Cartographica* (Special Monograph 44, "Introducing Cultural and Social Cartography") (spring): 29–46.

——. 1993b. "Putting Race in Its Place: Order in Colonial and Postcolonial Peruvian Geography." *Social Research* 60, no. 2 (summer): 301–36.

Ormond, Richard, and Carol Blackett-Ord, eds. 1987. *Franz Xaver Winterhalter and the Courts of Europe, 1830–70.* London: National Portrait Gallery.

Osborne, W. F. 1840. *The Court and Camp of Ranjeet Singh.* London.

O'Sullivan, Patrick. 1980. *Transport Policy: Geographic, Economic, and Planning Aspects.* London: Batsford Academic and Educational.

Parkin, Robert. 1997. *Kinship: An Introduction to the Basic Concepts.* Oxford: Blackwell.

Parmar, Pratibha. 1982. "Gender, Race, and Class: Asian Women in Resistance." In *The Empire Strikes Back: Race and Racism in Seventies Britain,* ed. Centre for Contemporary Cultural Studies. London: Routledge.

Parry, R. E. 1921. *The Sikhs of Punjab.* London: Drane's.

Patel, Sardar. 1949. *On Indian Problems.* Government of India, Publications Division.

Pearse, Hugh. [1848] 1970. *Memories of Alexander Gardner (Colonel of Artillery in the Service of Maharaja Ranjit Singh).* Patiala: Punjab Languages Department.

Pearson, Nicholas M. 1980. *The State and the Visual Arts: State Intervention in the Visual Arts since 1760.* London: Macmillan.

Pelles, Geraldine. 1963. *Art, Artists, and Society: Origins of a Modern Dilemma: Painting in England and France, 1750–1850.* Englewood Cliffs, N.J.: Prentice-Hall.

Pels, Peter. 1997. "The Anthropology of Colonialism: Culture, History, and the Emergence of Western Governmentality." *Annual Review of Anthropology* 26:163–83.

Pettigrew, Joyce. 1987. "In Search of the Kingdom of Lahore." *Pacific Affairs* 60, no. 1 (spring): 1–25.

———. 1995. *The Sikhs of Punjab: Unheard Voices of State and Guerilla Violence.* London: Zed.

Pietz, William. 1985. "The Problem of the Fetish." *Res* 9 (spring): 12–13.

———. 1987. "The Problem of the Fetish: 2, The Origin of the Fetish." *Res* 13 (spring): 23–45.

———. 1988. "The Problem of the Fetish: 3a, Bosman's Guinea and the Enlightenment Theory of Fetishism." *Res* 16 (autumn): 105–23.

Postone, Moishe. 1993. *Time, Labor, and Social Domination: A Reinterpretation of Marx's Critical Theory.* Cambridge: Cambridge University Press.

Prakash, Gyan. 1990. "A Different Modernity: Colonialism, Nationalism, and the Idea of India."

Presidential Address of the Sikh National Convention Held at Jallianwala Bagh, Amritsar, on 17th December, 1950. 1950. Pamphlet. Delhi: Ashoka Press.

Prince Duleep Singh: Last King of Khalsa Raj (Khalistan). 1993. Pamphlet distributed at the Maharaja Duleep Singh centenary festival, n.p.

Prinsep, Henry T. 1970. *Origin of the Sikh Power and Political Life of Maharaja Ranjit Singh with an Account of Religion, Laws, and Customs of the Sikhs.* Reprint, Patiala: Punjab Languages Department.

Puri, Harish K. 1983. *Ghadar Movement: Ideology, Organisation, and Strategy.* Amritsar: Guru Nanak Dev University Press.

Radcliffe-Brown, A. R. 1952. *Structure and Function in Primitive Society.* New York: Free Press.

Rajkumar, N. V. 1951. *Indians outside India.* New Delhi: All India Congress Committee.

Ram, Sodhi. 1989. *Indian Immigrants in Great Britain.* New Delhi: Inter-India.

Ramdin, Ron. 1987. *The Making of the Black Working Class in Britain.* Aldershot: Gower.

Reid, Bob. 1992. *The Permanent Way.* London: University of London Press.

Ribeiro, Aileen. 1987. "Fashion in the Work of Winterhalter." In *Franz Xaver Winterhalter and the Courts of Europe, 1830–70,* ed. Richard Ormond and Carol Blackett-Ord. London: National Portrait Gallery.

Richards, Thomas. 1992. "Archive and Utopia." *Representations* 37 (winter): 104–35.

Rivers, W. H. R. 1910. "The Genealogical Method of Anthropological Inquiry." *Sociological Review* 3, no. 1 (January): 1–12.

Riviere, Joan. [1929] 1986. "Womanliness as a Masquerade." In *Formations of Fantasy,* ed. Victor Burgin. New York: Routledge.

Robertson, Roland. 1992. *Globalization: Social Theory and Global Culture.* London: Sage.

Robinson, Arthur H. 1952. *The Look of Maps: An Examination of Cartographic Design.* Madison: University of Wisconsin Press.

Robinson, Arthur H., and Barbara B. Petchenik. 1976. *The Nature of Maps: Essays toward Understanding Maps and Mapping.* Chicago: University of Chicago Press.

Robinson, Arthur H., and Randall D. Sale. 1953. *Elements of Cartography.* New York: John Wiley and Sons.

Rose, Gillian. 1997. "Spatialities of 'Community,' Power, and Change: The Imagined Geographies of Community Arts Projects." *Cultural Studies* 11, no. 1:1–16.

Rose, Jacqueline, 1986. *Sexuality in the Field of Vision.* London: Verso.

———. 1996. *States of Fantasy.* Oxford: Clarendon.

Rosen, George. 1967. *Democracy and Economic Change in India.* Berkeley: University of California Press.

Rouse, Roger. 1991. "Mexican Migration and the Social Space of Postmodernism." *Diaspora* 2 (spring): 8–23.

———. 1995. "Thinking through Transnationalism: Notes on the Cultural Politics of Class Relations in the Contemporary United States." *Public Culture* 7:353–402.

Ruggie, John Gerard. 1993. "Territoriality and Beyond: Problematizing Modernity in International Relations." *International Organization* 47, no. 1:139–74.

Rundstrom, Robert A., ed. 1993. *Introducing Cultural and Social Cartography* (a Special Edition of *Cartographica*). Monograph 44. Toronto: University of Toronto Press.

Rushdie, Salman. 1991. *Imaginary Homelands.* New York: Viking.

Safran, William. 1991. "Diasporas in Modern Societies: Myths of Homeland and Return." *Diaspora* 1, no. 1:83–99.

Saggi, P. D. 1968. *We Shall Unite: A Plea for National Integration, Unity Builds the Nation, People Build Unity.* New Delhi: Indian Publications Trading Corp.

Sahlins, Marshall D. 1976. *Culture and Practical Reason.* Chicago: University of Chicago Press.

———. 1981. *Historical Metaphors and Mythical Realities: Structure in the Early History of the Sandwich Islands Kingdom.* Ann Arbor: University of Michigan Press.

———. 1985. *Islands of History.* Chicago: University of Chicago Press.

Said, Edward W. 1979. *Orientalism.* New York: Vintage.

Sarkar, Dipankar De. 1993. "Remembering a King: British Sikhs Attempt to Revive a Legend." *India Today,* 30 April.

———. 1995. "At Pains with Home Sikhness." *Telegraph,* 5 April.

Sassen, Saskia. 1991. *The Global City: New York, London, Tokyo.* Princeton, N.J.: Princeton University Press.

———. 1997. "Identity in the Global City: Economic and Cultural Encasements." In *The Geography of Identity,* ed. Patricia Yaeger. Ann Arbor: University of Michigan Press.

———. 1998. "Cracked Casings: Notes towards an Analytics for Studying Transnational Processes." Paper presented to the Global Studies Workshop, University of Chicago, October.

Scarry, Elaine. 1985. *The Body in Pain: The Making and Unmaking of the World.* New York: Oxford University Press.

Schein, Louisa. 1999. "Performing Modernity." *Cultural Anthropology* 14, no. 3:361–95.

Schivelbusch, Wolfgang. 1978. "Railroad Space and Railroad Time." *New German Critique* 14 (spring): 31–40.

Schwartz, Barton W. 1967. *Caste in Overseas Indian Communities.* San Francisco: Chandler.

Schwartzberg, J. E. 1992. *Historical Atlas of South Asia.* London: Oxford University Press.

Scott, David. 1991. "That Event, This Memory: Notes on the Anthropology of African Diasporas in the New World." *Diaspora* 1, no. 3:261–84.

Seltzer, Mark. 1993. "Serial Killers: 1." *Differences* 5, no. 1 (spring): 92–128.

———. 1995. "Serial Killers: 2, The Pathological Public Sphere." *Critical Inquiry* 22 (autumn): 122–49.

———. 1997. "Wound Culture: Trauma in the Pathological Public Sphere." *October* 80 (spring): 3–26.

Shankar, Lavina Dhingra. 1998. "The Limits of (South Asian) Names and Labels: Postcolonial or Asian American." In *A Part, yet Apart: South Asians in Asian America,* ed. Lavina Dhingra Shankar and R. Srikanth. Philadelphia: Temple University Press.

Shankar, Lavina Dhingra, and Rajini Srikanth, eds. 1998. *A Part, yet Apart: South Asians in Asian America.* Philadelphia: Temple University Press.

Sharma, P. K. 1995. *The Story of Punjab: Yesterday and Today.* Vol. 2. Delhi: Deep and Deep.

Sharma, Sudesh. 1968. *Union Territory Administration in India.* Patiala: Chandi.

Sheffer, Gabriel. 1986. *Modern Diasporas in International Politics.* London: Croom Helm.

Sihra, Kirpal Singh. 1985. *Sikhdom.* South Harrow: Sikh Commonwealth.

Simmel, Georg. [1907] 1991. *The Philosophy of Money.* London: Routledge.

Simmons, Jack. 1978. *The Railway in England and Wales, 1830–1914.* Leicester: Leicester University Press.

Singer, Milton, ed. 1957. *Introducing India in Liberal Education.* Chicago: University of Chicago Press.

Singh, Bhagat Laksham. 1965. *Autobiography.* Calcutta: Sikh Cultural Center.

Singh, Bhai Nahar, and Kirpal Singh. 1985. *History of Koh-i-Noor, Darya-i-Noor, and Taimur's Ruby.* New Delhi: Atlantic.

Singh, Burbachan, and Gyani Lal Singh. 1946. *The Idea of the Sikh State.* Lahore: Lahore Book Shop.

Singh, Chetan. 1991. *Region and Empire: Punjab in the Seventeenth Century.* Delhi: Oxford University Press.

Singh, D. S. 1995. *Guru Nanak's Travel to Himalayan and East Asian Region: A New Light.* Delhi: National Book Shop.

Singh, Darshan. 1987. *The Sikh Art and Architecture.* Chandigarh: Punjab University.

Singh, Duleep. 1884. *The Maharajah Duleep Singh and the Government: A Narrative,* n.p.

Singh, Ganda. 1965. *A Select Bibliography of the Sikhs and Sikhism.* Amritsar: Tej.

——. 1977. *Maharaja Duleep Singh Correspondence.* Patiala: Punjab University.

Singh, Gopal. 1994. *Politics of Sikh Homeland.* Delhi: Ajanta.

Singh, Gur Rattan Pal. 1980. *Illustrated History of the Sikhs.* Chandigarh: Akal.

Singh, Gurdial. 1968. "Sardar Thakur Singh Sindhanwalia: The Prime Minister of Maharaja Dalip Singh's Emigré Government at Pondicherry." *Panjab Past and Present 2,* pt. 2, no. 4 (October):

Singh, Gurmit, ed. 1989. *History of Sikh Struggles.* Vol. 1, *1946–1966.* Delhi: Atlantic.

Singh, Gurmukh. 1995. *Historical Sikh Shrines.* Amritsar: Singh Bros.

Singh, Gursharan. 1991. *History of PEPSU: Patiala and East Punjab States Union, 1948–1956.* Delhi: Konark.

Singh, Harbans. [1983] 1985. *The Heritage of the Sikhs.* New Delhi: Manahor.

Singh, Hari. 1994. *Sikh Heritage (Gurdwaras and Memorials) in Pakistan.* Delhi: Asian Publication Services.

Singh, I. J. 1994. *Sikhs and Sikhism: A View with a Bias.* Delhi: Manohar.

Singh, Iqbal. 1986. *Punjab under Siege: A Critical Analysis.* New York: Allen, McMillan and Enderson.

Singh, Khushwant. [1989] 1991. *A History of the Sikhs.* Vol. 2, *1839–1988.* New Delhi: Oxford University Press.

——. 1992. *My Bleeding Punjab.* New Delhi: UBSP.

Singh, Kirpal, ed. 1991. *Partition of Punjab — 1947.* Delhi: National Bookshop.

Singh, Nikky-Guninder Kaur. 1993. *The Feminine Principle in the Sikh Vision of the Transcendent.* Cambridge: Cambridge University Press.

Singh, Pashaura, and N. Gerald Barrier, eds. 1996. *The Transmission of Sikh Heritage in the Diaspora.* New Delhi: Manohar.

Singh, Patwant. 1992. *Gurdwaras: In India and around the World.* New Delhi: Himalayan.

Singh, S. 1994. *Illustrated Martyrdom Tradition.* Amritsar: Golden Offset Press.

Singh, Sadhu Swarup. 1946. *The Sikhs Demand Their Homeland.* Lahore: Lahore Book Shop.

Singh, Satinder. 1982. *Khalistan: An Academic Analysis.* New Delhi: Amarprakashan.

Skinner, E. P. 1982. "The Dialectic between Diasporas and Homelands." In *Global Dimensions of the African Diaspora,* ed. Joseph E. Harris. Washington, D.C.: Howard University Press.

Skinner, William G. 1958. *Leadership and Power in the Chinese Community of Thailand.* Ithaca, N.Y.: Cornell University Press.

Sklair, Leslie. 1991. *Sociology of the Global System.* Baltimore: Johns Hopkins University Press.

Smith, Anthony D. 1991. *National Identity.* London: Penguin.

Smith, M. G. 1965. *The Plural Society in the British West Indies.* Berkeley: University of California Press.

Smith, Michael Peter. 1994. "Can You Imagine: Transnational Migration and the Globalization of Grassroots Politics." *Social Text* 39 (summer): 15–34.

Smith, Neil, and Anne Godlewska, eds. 1994. *Geography and Empire.* Oxford: Blackwell.

Soja, Edward W. 1989. *Postmodern Geographies: The Reassertion of Space in Critical Social Theory.* London: Verso.

Southall Black Sisters. 1989. *Against the Grain: A Celebration of Survival and Struggle.* Southall: Southall Black Sisters.

——. 1993. *Domestic Violence and Asian Women: A Collection of Reports and Briefings.* Southall: Southall Black Sisters.

Spiering, M. 1992. *Englishness: Foreigners and Images of National Identity in Postwar Literature.* Amsterdam: Rodopi.

Spivak, Gayatri. 1986. "Some Concept Metaphors of Political Economy in Derrida's Texts." *Leftwright/Intervention* 20:88–97.

——. 1993. *Outside in the Teaching Machine.* New York: Routledge.

Srivastava, R. P. 1983. *Punjab Painting: Study in Art and Culture.* New Delhi: Abhinav.

Steinbach, H. [1846] 1976. *The Punjaub.* Karachi: Oxford University Press.

Strozier, Charles B., and Michael Flynn, eds. 1996. *Trauma and Self.* London: Rowman and Littlefield.

Sturken, Marita. 1997. *Tangled Memories: The Vietnam War, the AIDS Epidemic, and the Politics of Remembering.* Berkeley and Los Angeles: University of California Press.

Subramanian, Nirupama. 1993. "Sikh Schools: Catching 'Em Young — Worried Parents Find a Way to Preserve Ethnic Values." *India Today,* 30 April.

Taaffe, Edward J., and Howard L. 1973. *Geography of Transportation.* Englewood Cliffs, N.J.: Prentice-Hall.

Tambiah, Stanley J. 1996. *Leveling Crowds: Ethnonationalist Conflicts and Collective Violence in South Asia.* Berkeley and Los Angeles: University of California Press.

Tandon, Prakash. 1968. *Punjabi Century.* Berkeley: University of California Press.

Tatla, Darshan Singh. 1991. *Sikhs in America: An Annotated Bibliography.* London: Greenwood.

——. 1992. "Nurturing the Faithful: The Role of the Sant among Britain's Sikhs." *Religion* 22:349–74.

——. 1993. "Punjab Crisis and Sikh Mobilisation in Britain." In *Religion and Ethnicity: Minorities and Social Change in the Metropolis,* ed. R. Barot. Kampen: Kok Pharos.

——. 1999. *The Sikh Diaspora: The Search for Statehood.* Seattle: University of Washington Press.

Taussig, Michael. 1980. *The Devil and Commodity Fetishism in South America.* Chapel Hill: University of North Carolina Press.

——. 1989. "History as Commodity: In Some Recent American (Anthropological) Literature." *Critique of Anthropology* 11, no. 1 (spring): 7–23.

——. 1993. "Maleficium: State Fetishism." In *Fetishism as Cultural Discourse,* ed. Emily Apter and William Pietz. Ithaca, N.Y.: Cornell University Press.

Taylor, Fraser. 1983. *Graphic Communication and Design in Contemporary Cartography.* New York: John Wiley and Sons.

Taylor, Dr. W. C. 1846. "The Seat of War: The Sikhs and the Punjab." *Bentley's Miscellany* 19:358–69.

——. 1848. "Lord Hardinge and the Recent Victories of India." *Bentley's Miscellany* 23:1–8.

Thandi, Shinder. 1996. "The Punjabi Diaspora in the UK and the Punjab Crisis." In *The Transmission of Sikh Heritage in the Diaspora,* ed. Pashaura Singh and N. Gerald Barrier. New Delhi: Manohar.

Thapar, K. S. 1977. "From the Russian Archives Papers Relating to Maharaja Dalip Singh." *Journal of Sikh Studies* 4, no. 1 (February):

Thorburn, S. S. [1883] 1970. *The Punjab in Peace and War.* Patiala: Punjab Languages Department.

Thornton, Thomas. 1846. *History of the Punjab, and of the Rise, Progress, and Present Condition of the Sect and Nation of the Sikhs.* London: Wm. H. Allen.

Tinker, Hugh. 1974. *A New System of Slavery: The Export of Indian Labour Overseas, 1830–1920.* London: Oxford University Press.

——. 1976. *Separate and Unequal: India and the Indians in the British Commonwealth, 1920–1950.* London: C. Hurst.

Tololyan, Khachig. 1991. "The Nation-State and Its Others: In Lieu of a Preface." *Diaspora* 1, no. 1 (spring): 3–7.

Trevaskis, Hugh K. 1928. *The Land of the Five Rivers: An Economic History of the Punjab from the Earliest Times to the Year of Grace 1890.* Oxford: Oxford University Press.

Tully, Mark, and Satish Jacob. 1985. *Amritsar: Mrs. Gandhi's Last Battle.* London: Jonathan Cape.

Uberoi, J. P. S. 1996. *Religion, Civil Society, and the State: A Study of Sikhism.* Delhi: Oxford University Press.

Unofficial Committee of Enquiry. 1980. *Southall, 23 April 1979: The Report of the Unofficial Committee of Enquiry.* London: National Council for Civil Liberties.

Vajpayee, Sh. A. B. 1961. "National Integration." Note submitted at the National Integration Conference, New Delhi, 28–30 September.

van der Veer, Peter, ed. 1995. *Nation and Migration: The Politics of Space in the South Asian Diaspora.* Philadelphia: University of Pennsylvania Press.

van Gennep, Arnold. 1965. *Rites of Passage.* London: Kegan Paul.

Verdery, Katherine. 1994. "Beyond the Nation in Eastern Europe." *Social Text* 38 (spring): 1–20.

Verdicchio, Pasquale. 1997. *Bound by Distance: Rethinking Nationalism through the Italian Diaspora.* Teaneck, N.J.: Fairleigh Dickinson University Press.

Verrier, Michelle. 1979. *The Orientalists' All Colour Paperback.* New York: Rizzoli.

Vico, Giambattista. [1744] 1991. *The New Science of Giambattista Vico*. Ithaca, N.Y.: Cornell University Press.

Vigne, G. T. 1840. *A Personal Narrative of a Visit to Ghazni, Cabul, and Afghanistan and a Residence at the Court of Dost Mohammad with Notices of Ranjit Singh, Khiva, and Russian Expedition*. London: Whittaker.

Vyas, Mohan K. 1993. *National Integration and the Law: Burning Issues and Challenges*. Delhi: Deep and Deep.

Waiz, B. A. 1927. *Indians Abroad*. Bombay: Imperial Citizenship Association.

Weber, Max. [1919] 1978. *Max Weber: Selections in Translation*, ed. W. G. Runciman. Cambridge: Cambridge University Press.

Weston, Kath. 1993. "Do Clothes Make the Woman? Gender, Performance Theory, and Lesbian Erotics." *Genders* 17:1–21.

White, H. P. 1963. *A Regional History of the Railways of Great Britain: Greater London*. London: Phoenix.

Wilkins, Charles. [1781] 1784. "Observations on the Seeks and Their College." *Asiatic Researches* 1:245–49.

Wilson, Rob, and Wimal Dissanayake. 1996. *Global/Local: Cultural Production and the Transnational Imaginary*. Durham, N.C.: Duke University Press.

Wolf, Eric R. 1982. *Europe and the People without History*. Berkeley and Los Angeles: University of California Press.

Women against Fundamentalism. 1991. *Journal No. 2 July 91*.

———. 1994. *Journal No. 5 1994 Vol. 1*.

Wright, Peter L. 1968. *The Coloured Worker in British Industry*. London: Oxford University Press.

Yaeger, Patricia, ed. 1996. *The Geography of Identity*. Ann Arbor: University of Michigan Press.

———. 1997. "Consuming Trauma; or, The Pleasures of Merely Circulating." *Journal X* 1, no. 2 (spring): 225–51.

Žižek, Slavoj. 1989. *The Sublime Object of Ideology*. New York: Verso.

———. 1997. *The Plague of Fantasies*. New York: Verso.

index

Brian Keith Axel is an Academy Scholars Fellow at the
Weatherhead Center for International and Area Studies
at Harvard University.

Library of Congress Cataloging-in-Publication Data
Axel, Brian Keith.
The nation's tortured body : violence, representation, and the
formation of a Sikh diaspora / Brian Keith Axel.
p.   cm.
Includes bibliographical references and index.
ISBN 0–8223–2607–8 (cloth : alk. paper).
ISBN 0–8223–2615–9 (pbk. : alk. paper)
1. Sikh diaspora.   2. Sikhs — Foreign countries.   3. Punjab
(India) — Emigration and immigration.   4. Punjab
(India) — History — Autonomy and independence
movements.   I. Title.
DS432.S5 A94 2000
954'.5'00882946 — dc21   00-029399